The Aviation Consumer

Used Aircraft Guide

Richard B. Weeghman, Editor

Volume I

Belvoir Publications, Inc.

ISBN: 0-9613139-9-4

To order copies of Used Aircraft Guides not included in this collection, contact the Back Issues Department, The Aviation Consumer, 75 Holly Hill Road, Box 2626, Greenwich, Conn. 06836-2626, (203) 661-6111.

Contents

VOLUME I

Introduction

Coming full circle once again, by popular demand we introduce our latest collection of Used Aircraft Guides — this time in a matched set of two volumes arranged alphabetically by make and model. As with the previous editions, they offer what we think is an intriguing blend of cool analytical appraisals and intimate user reports.

The former are designed not as run-of-the-mill pilot reports, but are based upon research into the record established by each aircraft in key matters such as performance, handling, comfort, safety and maintenance. We also track significant modifications designed to correct sometimes modest, not infrequently dismal flaws left by the manufacturer. And we provide names and addresses of the owner organizations that have become so important as clearing houses of information and support, specialized service and sometimes hard-to-find parts.

On top of that, to show what has been happening to the aircraft as a form of equity, we've plotted their resale value over the past decade in chart form.

Along with the feedback we solicit from owners and operators on a regular basis, our sources of information include National Transportation Safety Board and FAA accident data and Service Difficulty Reports, plus manufacturers' service information.

Naturally, much valuable first-hand information on all these aircraft comes straight from the hearts of pilots who fly them, maintain them, dote on them, curse them and pay the bills for them. They're included in these volumes in generous doses as "Owner Comments."

The articles making up these editions were originally published in the regular mid-month issues of *The Aviation Consumer*. (Special credit to editors Dave Noland and Mark Lacagnina.) They include a number of new additions to earlier volumes, and have been broadly updated as permitted by time and resources. But prices, names and addresses, often change with alacrity.

Needless to say, the articles are written in the *Aviation Consumer's* pull-no-punches style with the intent of informing our readers of both the good, and sometimes nasty, characteristics of one of the most weighty investments—in a fiscal, emotional and safety sense—they're ever likely to make. If sometimes our findings, gathered from a broad spectrum of evidence, conflict with the personal perspective (and natural infatuation) of owners with their aircraft, we offer one suggestion to smooth ruffled feathers. The information in these volumes represents critical knowledge often unavailable from any other source. We respect our readers' ability and judgment to make their own final decision with that information as background.

Dick Weeghman, Editor

Aerospatiale Trinidad TB-20

If you're looking for a good-performing family airplane with French panache and the head-turning appeal of a rare, exotic machine, consider the Aerospatiale Trinidad. It's essentially a Comanche 250 redesigned for the eighties, with curvy lines, nice handling and very low maintenance requirements. But performance is no better than a Comanche's, and you'll have to look very hard to find one.

Genealogy

The Trinidad is part of a family of light airplanes introduced by French aerospace giant Aerospatiale, which constantly reminds us that it is the manufacturer of the Concorde and Airbus. The Tobago, Tampico and Trinidad all share the same basic airframe, differing only in engine size and landing gear. The top of the line (big engine, retractable gear) is the Trinidad, which made its first appearance on these shores in 1984. At last count about 140 aircraft were flying in this country (including a handful of turbocharged models).

There have been no major changes to the Trinidad so far, but some refining has occurred. The 1985 model got easier-to read instruments (the original model had weird vertical-scale dials that were very hard to decipher), plus a redesigned tailcone that smoothed airflow over the elevator and reduced an annoying vibration in the control wheel.

The 1986 model got a gross weight boost of 127 pounds (from 2,956 lbs. to 3,083)—and it's all there as useful load. The weight increase is allowed because of a new, faster-acting flap motor. The new flap motor allows Trinidad pilots to load in another passenger. (The mod is retrofittable to older models at a cost of about $3,000.) The 1986 model also got a thinner seat cushion, which provided an extra inch of badly-needed headroom, but also put the pilot's butt an inch closer to the wing spar, a possibly spine-crushing situation in a vertical-impact crash. The '86 also got a redesigned overhead console with improved vents, sun visors and radio speakers.

Distinguishing characteristics are the forward-placed vertical tail, constant-chord wing and stabilator, and windows that curve into the roof.

The 1987 Trinidads have a new fuel system that includes a selector relocated from the instrument panel to the center console, and a new fuel pump. Door locks have also been upgraded on the '87 model.

Resale Market

Any pilot who goes shopping for a used Trinidad will be treading new ground; there is very little resale market for the airplane. According to Chris Duplay of Aerospatiale, no more than a dozen used Trinidads have changed hands in the last two years. "The original owners seem to like them a lot," he says. However, dealer demo and training/rental aircraft

Powerplant is the reliable 260-hp Lycoming. Maintenance costs are described as light.

sometimes come on the market. A recent issue of *Trade-A-Plane* listed just two Trinidads for sale by owners, with another couple of dealer ads for demo airplanes. With privately owned Trinidads so rare on the used-plane market, it makes sense to call a dealer. See the list of dealers in the Maintenance section.

Because the oldest model is a 1984, prices are high. Lowest "bluebook" retail price for any model Trinidad is $97,500, although actual selling prices are 10-20 percent less. (A recent ad in *Trade-A-Plane* asked $92,000 for a mid-time well-equipped 1985 model.)

The Trinidad's resale value seems to be pretty good. Using bluebook retail figures, a 1984 model has held 79 percent of its original value. A representative sample of other single-engine retractables ranged from 60 percent (F33A Bonanza) to 80 percent (Cessna 210), with the average about 74 percent. So the 1984 Trinidad is near the top in resale value.

Performance

Using the same basic engine as a Comanche 250—the old reliable 250-hp Lycoming IO-540 (the dash number is -C4D5D)—the Trinidad delivers roughly Comanche 250 performance. Book cruise speed at 75 percent power is a respectable, if not dazzling, 164 knots. An *Aviation Consumer* fly-off of a 1984 Trinidad and a 1978 Mooney 201 resulted in a dead heat at about 160 knots. It's a bit disappointing that this supposedly state-of-the-art design is no faster than antiques like the Comanche 250 and P35 Bonanza that use the same power. The Mooney, in fact, was able to match its speed on just 200 hp, and two or three gph less fuel consumption.

This may be partly due to a lack of attention to aerodynamic details, particularly on the Trinidad's underside. It's festooned with rivets and lumps and bumps. The flap tracks have no fairings. The wheel wells have no doors. With Mooney-style attention to detail, the Trinidad could probably go 200 mph.

The Trinidad climbs strongly. Book rate at sea level is 1,260 fpm at the 2,943 gross weight, and presumably a bit less at the higher weight. "It still climbs well at 13,000 feet," reports one owner. Our own tests showed an average rate of 1,125 fpm between 4,000 and 8,000 feet at moderate weight—about 125 fpm better than a Mooney under the same conditions. High-altitude performance, of course, is better with the Turbo model.

Runway performance shows a split personality; takeoff numbers are among the best in the class, while landing performance is among the worst.

Payload/Range

The Trinidad shines in this department, particularly the later models with the higher gross weight. Typical useful loads for IFR aircraft run around 1,200 pounds. (Later models with the flap motor mod would have 1,300-plus.) Subtract 516 pounds to account for the hefty 86-gallon fuel capacity, and we're left with nearly 700 pounds for the cabin—enough to carry four full-sized adults. The Trinidad is one of those rare full-seats-plus-full-fuel airplanes, and it does the trick while carrying a huge fuel supply. The gross-weight increase in later models is almost superfluous.

A full tank of fuel should be good for at least five hours at the 14-gph fuel flow that results from setting 75 percent power and a lean mixture. At 65 percent power, the lean fuel flow drops to 12 gph and endurance is six-plus hours. Range approaches 1,000 miles at the more modest power settings.

Essentially, the Trinidad will take as a many people as you can fit in it for about as long as anyone would reasonably want to spend in a small plane.

Engine

The 250-hp Lycoming is a detuned, derated six-cylinder powerplant with plenty of reserve power. The same basic engine has turned in a good record of reliability in the Comanche, Rockwell 114 and Cherokee Six. TBO is 2,000 hours, and it's very likely the engine will make it that far. Overhaul cost is about $11,000, however—about a grand more than it costs to do a carbureted 250 in a Comanche.

The turbo model has an automatic wastegate—no cheapie fixed gate like in the Turbo Arrow, Seneca and Mooney 231—but overhaul cost jumps to $15,000, and TBO drops to 1,800 hours. Overhaul cost per hour is 55 percent higher for the turbo model.

Creature Comforts

The Trinidad has a monstrously wide cabin. It's listed at 50 inches, which puts every American single-engine airplane, including the born-to-be-wide Rockwells, to shame. The Mooney cabin, by comparison, is a measly 42 inches wide. But somehow the Trinidad doesn't feel all that wide when you sit in it. For one thing, there's a big center console that impinges on hiproom and gives pilot and copilot a containerized feeling.

Pilots rave about cabin comfort, except for a shortage of headroom for tall fliers.

And headroom is simply inadequate, particularly in the 1984-1985 versions that have the thicker seat cushions. Six-footers will just barely clear the roof. Fat people don't buy Mooneys, and tall people don't buy Trinidads.

The seats themselves are superb—leather or fabric-upholstered and firmly supportive. One owner says he flies six-hour legs and feels completely comfortable when he lands. Overall comfort is a plus mentioned by every Trinidad owner we heard from.

Aerospatiale bills the airplane as a five-seater, but three adults would be very uncomfortable sitting in back. Call it a comfortable four-placer. The Trinidad has oddball gull-wing doors in the manner of the old Mercedes 300SL. Although the doors look cool, they don't provide astonishing ease of entry. The Trinidad is about like any other low-winger to climb in and out of: a bit awkward.

*Gull-wing doors allow
entry on both sides
of the cabin.*

The cockpit deserves a mention. Most owners praise the ergonomics of the panel layout and cite the reduced IFR workload. The way the Trinidad panel is modularized into three sections, and its pastel-colored plastic covering give it a sort of space-cartoon look, something like what one might find in the Jetsons' family saucer.

Handling Qualities

For all its exotic appearance and heritage, the Trinidad has fairly standard control response. Pitch forces are moderately heavy, like other aircraft in this class, with reasonable—but not outstanding—stability. During approach to landing, some attention is required to hold airspeed accurately. The Trinidad is not a trim-it-and-forget-it airplane.

Electric trim on the 1984-1985 models is inordinately slow—dangerously so in case of a go-around, in our opinion. Most pilots simply use the manual trim wheel. That's okay, except during a go-around, when large nose-up pitch forces require energetic retrimming—at the same time you're supposed to be raising the landing gear and flaps. Hope you have a copilot or three hands.

The ailerons are fairly heavy and stiff, but if you put enough muscle into it, very fast roll rates are possible. This is a good compromise between sports-car handling and IFR stability; you can rack it around pretty good if you like, but it stays put on the gauges. Long-term spiral stability isn't so great, however; the Trinidad will diverge fairly quickly from a 30-degree bank. Use a wing-leveler for IFR.

The Trinidad is definitely a rudder airplane. Coordinated flying in a Trinidad is no snap, and rudder forces are heavy. But the rudder trim is powerful, and a good thing, too, since you'll be using it a lot.

Stall traits are benign in the extreme. In landing configuration, the Trinidad is virtually stall-proof. With the wheel held back to the stop, the plane will merely buffet and nod, breaking gently and recovering by itself. With power off, rate of descent is a modest 1,000 fpm in this nodding semi-stall mode, and the plane can be steered with the ailerons alone. Clean, it's possible to get a slight break. Normal approach speed is 75-80 knots.

One drawback is the low airspeed limits. Max flap extension speed is a paltry 100 knots in the 1984-1985 models, and slightly higher on the later versions with the new flap system. Never-exceed speed is also a low 189 knots—a speed that can be exceeded in only a few seconds of spiral divergence. The yellow arc begins at only 151 knots, just above where the needle sits in normal cruise.

Safety

With only 140 or more Trinidads flying, the statistical base is really too small to calculate an accident rate. We're aware of just one Trinidad accident, a fatal crash on approach to Van Nuys airport in California last year, apparently triggered by wake turbulence.

However, we see a couple of potential safety problems with the aircraft. First is the poor go-around characteristics. Flap retraction and a power increase combine to give a severe nose-up reaction, and the electric trim is too slow to counteract it. Second is the lack of a "both" position on the fuel selector. The Trinidad's left-right system, like that of many aircraft, is susceptible to mismanagement by an inattentive pilot. Third, the owner's manual is a mess. Besides containing only very skimpy information, it is so badly translated from the French that much of it is indecipherable. (Anyone care to hazard a guess as to what this means: "The uplift of fuel tanks equipped with a gauge (on spar) is carried out when fuel level is flush with the filling port." Or how about this item on the landing checklist: "By default, take VI 70 kt." Flying the Trinidad by the book can be very confusing.

Maintenance

The Trinidad was designed to be easy to work on, and it seems to have achieved this goal admirably. Central Skyport in Columbus claims it recently annualed two Trinidads for $350 or less. That's less than half what a typical single-engine retractable costs. Skyport says inspection time for a Trinidad runs about 10 hours, compared to 22 hours for a Bonanza or 210.

Owners confirm annual costs below $500, although one reports he had to pay $1,500 for his last inspection. Another mentioned $725. But overall, owners report maintenance costs much lower than a typical big retractable single.

The Trinidad's secret is twofold. First, the plane was designed to be built simply. The airframe has only about 800 parts, vs. 2,000-plus for a Cessna Skylane RG. That means fewer pieces to inspect, and to go wrong. Second, the Trinidad is festooned with inspection plates, so the mechanic doesn't spend half his time opening the airplane. The instrument panel swings out for easy access in three sections.

Airworthiness Directives

We're aware of two ADs against the Trinidad airframe. One calls for reworking the battery case to prevent acid leaking, the other calls for inspection of rivets in the stabilator actuator every 100 hours, or replacement of the rivets with bolts. There's also a service bulletin requiring beefup of the wheel well area.

Malfunction and defect reports are sketchy, and show no particular pattern. Reports mentioned problems with a worn starter drive shaft, cracked muffler, a twisted fuel line that starved the engine, a jammed nose gear, and a weak fuel filter bowl drain valve spring. In addition, one mechanic pointed out that the foam soundproofing on the hot side of the firewall could absorb oil. He said his own test showed that the foam ignited easily. Some firewall.

Cost/Performance/Specifications

Model	Year Built	Average Retail Price	Cruise Speed (kts)	Useful Load (lbs)	Fuel Std/Opt (gals)	Engine	TBO (hrs)	Overhaul Cost
TB-20	1984	$97,500	164	1,212	86	250-hp Lyc. IO-540-C4D5D	2,000	$11,000
TB-20	1985	$115,000	164	1,212	86	250-hp Lyc. IO-540-C4D5D	2,000	$11,000
TB-20	1986	$158,000	164	1,212	86	250-hp Lyc. IO-540-C4D5D	2,000	$11,000
TB-21TC	1986	$177,000	187	1,288	86	250-hp Lyc. TIO-540-AB1AD	2,000	$15,000
TB-20	1987	$170,000	164	1,212	86	250-hp Lyc. IO-540-C4D5D	2,000	$11,000
TB-21TC	1987	$185,000	187	1,288	86	250-hp Lyc. TIO-540-AB1AD	2,000	$15,000

Talks with Trinidad mechanics reveal three recurring problems that aren't covered by ADs. A batch of 42 bad windshields suffered severe cracking and crazing problems. Virtually all of these have been replaced by now, however, so they should not be a factor on any used Trinidad considered for purchase. The other persistent problem is the reliability of the combination fuel quantity/oil pressure/oil temp/CHT gauge. "You may go through two or three of 'em before you find a good one," reports one mechanic. A third problem is corrosion in the door locks, which sometimes makes it hard to insert the key.

We'd strongly advise against taking a Trinidad to a mechanic unfamiliar with the type. The three most experienced Trinidad service centers are Three Wings in Bridgeport, Conn., (203) 375-5795; Central Skyport in Columbus, Ohio (614) 237-6578 and American Air Center in Livermore, Calif., (415) 447-1801. Aerospatiale is now setting up more service centers in Orange County and Van Nuys, Calif.; Erie, Pa.; Tampa, Fla. and Minnesota. For more info, call Aerospatiale's American office at (214) 641-3601.

Trinidad Resale Value

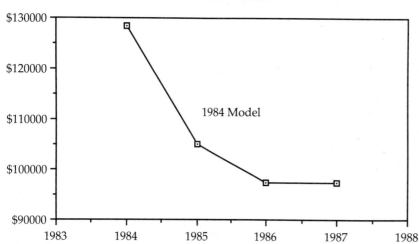

1984 Model

Factory Support

Aerospatiale got itself a bad reputation for factory support with the old Rallye series. Parts availability was lousy, and downtimes stretched into the months—and then the company shut down its American parts operation. But Aerospatiale claims it's a whole new ballgame with the Trinidad. It has appointed Van Dusen as the distributor for Trinidad parts, and says that all parts are carried in inventory, with no factory back orders to France. "You could build a complete Trinidad from the parts Van Dusen carries," insisted one Trinidad dealer. We'll see. So far, Trinidad owners report prompt shipment of parts—which is more than you can say for Cessna or Piper these days.

Owner Comments

I bought a 1985 Trinidad new in August of '85. At the time, I had just sold my Piper Lance and wanted to get into something a little smaller, since my three kids had grown up and left home, and I didn't need the six seats anymore. At first, my mind was set on the Mooney, but I flew three of them at the Oshkosh show, and everything just felt shrunk up too much. The panel was in my chest, and I felt crammed in next to the copilot. So I went over to the Trinidad booth, flew one, and fell in love with it right away. It had lots of room, and a nice feel. I paid $103,000 with full IFR King.

I've flown it a couple of hundred hours, and it's been a fantastic airplane. I normally cruise at 8,000-10,000 feet, and flight-plan 160 knots. I lean it back to about 12 gph. It has very good range—I have flown Anaheim to Chicago in 10 hours with one stop. Six-hour legs are no problem, and the great thing is that you feel good when you land. The seats are superb. In the Lance, I would be flat worn out after a long trip, and the seats were about one-tenth as comfortable as the Trinidad's. The Lance would do about 155 knots on 16 gph, so the range was not nearly as good.

The Trinidad also climbs better than the Lance, which would poop out completely at about 13,000 feet. The Trinidad has plenty of climb left at 13,000. I've had controllers ask me whether my plane was turbocharged. I've had almost no maintenance. The annuals cost under $500, which is about a third what the Lance used to cost me. I've had two maintenance problems. One was a crazed windshield, which the dealer, Central Skyport in Columbus, Ohio, replaced for free. They even picked up and delivered the plane at no charge. I also had a problem with the nose gear. I didn't get a green light even after six or seven cycles, although people on the ground said it appeared to be down. Luckily, I had a lot of baggage in the rear and two passengers, so I had the front-seat passenger move to the rear for the landing, and killed the engine as we touched down. It stopped with the dangling nosewheel off the ground, so no damage was done. It turned out a couple of lock nuts hadn't been tightened on two adjusting bolts, which had backed out and prevented the gear from locking down.

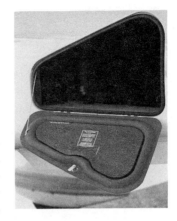

The small, triangular baggage door, just ahead of the N-numbers, makes loading difficult, often requiring a back-seat passenger to help.

The Trinidad is a little heavy on the controls—heavier than the Lance. But it holds its own in turbulence and is easy to fly IFR. I've had only one disappointment, and that was with Aerospatiale, not the airplane. When I bought it, I was told that a 150-pound gross weight increase was coming, and that it would apply retroactively to my plane. A year later, I got a letter saying that the weight increase was available for the nominal fee of about $4,000. Nobody had ever told me I'd have to pay for it. I wrote a bunch of letters, and they eventually offered to split the cost with me, but I feel that Aerospatiale backed down from what they had told me. As far as I'm concerned, their word is no good.

But the airplane itself has just been fantastic.

Chuck Loomis
Chicago, Ill.

I have owned a 1984 Trinidad for one year. During that time I've flown numerous cross-country trips and logged about 220 hours. Overall, I'm very satisfied with the Trinidad. It's very comfortable, both for pilot and passengers. It has the best panel layout and control quadrant I've seen on any single-engine airplane. It handles turbulence well and is stable in all axes.

Performance is very satisfactory. I fly out of an airport at an elevation of 6,300 feet, and the performance is more than adequate, even in the summer. I flight-plan 150 knots, which seems to be the true airspeed at 65 percent power. Fuel flow is about 12.7 gph.

My maintenance problems have been primarily in the avionics and autopilot. The only recurring airframe maintenance has been the brake pads. Parts availability has not been a problem. Hourly maintenance cost so far has been $8.50. The annual inspection cost $1,500.

The Trinidad has a few negatives. The first is the low gear and flap extension speeds. It makes the Trinidad a hard airplane to slow down, or to descend more than 500 fpm without shock-cooling the engine. The second is the relatively heavy input required for the ailerons. You have the feeling that the autopilot is still engaged. But the airplane is quick on the roll if you're willing to push real hard. The ailerons do become lighter at low speeds, however. The third drawback is the size and shape of the baggage door. It makes loading the plane difficult. It helps to have someone in the back seat to assist in loading..

Would I buy another Trinidad? Most definitely, yes.

Roger A. Webb
Santa Fe, N.M.

I put about 200 hours a year on a 1985 Trinidad. I moved up from a Cessna 182, which had been my first airplane. I was looking for something faster, and the FBO where I kept the Skylane was a Trinidad dealer. Its appearance caught my eye, and one thing led to another. The plane I bought had a Stormscope and three-axis autopilot. Price was about $140,000.

It's a versatile airplane. My useful load as it sits is over 1,200 pounds, enough for full fuel and four adults, as long as they aren't too big—certainly three people and baggage. My rear end won't last as long as the fuel. I get about 165 knots up to 7,000 feet; above that it drops off a bit. I'm conservative on the leaning, because it's always seemed to me that an extra gallon of gas every hour is cheaper than a major overhaul. At 75 degrees rich of peak, I burn about 13.5 to 14 gph.

The instrument panel's strong point is ease of access for maintenance.

The Trinidad is much more comfortable than the Skylane. The seats are excellent. It's like the difference between an expensive sports car with Recaro seats and a family sedan. The panel layout is good and reduces the IFR workload. It's very stable on instruments, once you get it trimmed. It likes to fly straight and level, and is very stable on approaches.

Maintenance has been real good. My 100-hour inspections have ranged from a low of $450 to a high of $850. There have been only a few minor squawks, other than a crazed windshield, which was replaced by the factory at no cost. The mechanics tell me it's very easy to work on. My only real complaint is headroom for tall people. I'm about six feet one, with most of my height in my legs, so it's no problem for me, but several tall friends have had to really crank the seatback down to keep from rubbing the ceiling.

Overall, it's a fine airplane that I would recommend to anyone. The only single-engine retractable I'd consider against it is an F33A Bonanza, which cost about $50,000 more than the Trinidad when I bought it.

Stewart Watson
Roanoke Rapids, N.C.

Beech
77 Skipper

The Beech Skipper was barely out of the starting blocks when the Great Aviation Depression set in. Beechcraft built only 312 of these two-place trainers, starting in 1979, and it abruptly halted production in 1981. The majority of Skippers are now in private hands, though a few still find duty on flight school lines and at Beech Aero Centers across the country. How has the airplane fared, and what can a prospective owner expect from this two-placer? *Aviation Consumer* takes a look.

History

As a competitor with the Cessna 152, the Skipper actually stood a chance at creating a similar market niche for Beech. Though the design never reached maturation, the Model 77 (its numeric designation) represented a good training airplane. Despite its pleasant flying qualities (and barring a dramatic upswing in the training market), the Skipper has taken its spot on the endangered species list of general aviation, to dwindle through the years from the forces of attrition.

We first flew the Skipper in 1979, reporting on it in our January 1, 1980 issue. At that time we were mostly interested in comparing this newcomer with the Cessna 152 (the all-time training leader) and the Piper Tomahawk (another new design). Startlingly similar in outward appearance to the Tomahawk, the Skipper flew quite differently. It also represented a "major commitment" by Beechcraft to the bottom end of their product line.

Beech started up Beech Aero Centers (more on these later), producing Jeppesen-Sanderson-style textbooks and course materials for flight training. It looked as though Beech was really getting its act together to compete with Cessna Pilot Centers, all the while furthering the brand-loyalty theory of future aircraft sales, their real motive. Then the bottom dropped out.

Light-aircraft deliveries entered the graveyard spiral from which they still have not recovered, and the Skipper was an early casualty. While the Beech Aero Center concept worked at some FBOs, only a few survive to this day. However,

The little two-placer has a nice combination of good looks, pleasant handling and a roomy cockpit.

The skid can be smashed up into the tail by an over-zealous pilot.

Beech still publishes a newsletter for Aero Centers, and active clubs have regular fly-ins around the country. We found just such an Aero Center at Hammonton Aviation in Hammonton, N. J.

Takes a Licking and Keeps On Ticking

We even found old serial number 39, the same Skipper we flew back in 1979, on their line. We were very interested to see how it had held up, after nearly 2,000 hours of training and rental time had been put on the tachometer.

Well, the engine had already been overhauled once, after a student taxied into a ditch and caught the prop, causing sudden stoppage. And the tail skid had once been rammed up into the empennage after over-rotation on a soft-field takeoff. This required moderate repair, and the new lines of rivets sit in evidence. Other than that, the airframe had held up pretty well. Oh, there are places where fairings or inspection panels look a little ratty, but this is akin to the cracked plastic fairings one finds on Cessna landing gear and struts. Incidentally, the second Skipper on the line also hit its tail skid, but it didn't take as long to fix. As George Arslanian of Hammonton Aviation said, "We got pretty good at doing tail skid repairs, the second time around."

The tail on the Skipper is reasonably powerful, aerodynamically. But the cause of dinging the skid isn't the T-tail configuration, as many might surmise. No, Beech did its homework with the tail aerodynamics on the Skipper. It delivers good control feel and response right down to taxi speeds, unlike the Tomahawk (and other Pipers with T-tails), which demonstrates an on-again-off-again behavior around rotation speed.

The Skipper's elevator control forces are light, but not so much so that overcontrol is a problem. Cessna 152s bang their tails on the ground from time to time, too, requiring sheet-metal repairs in the area of the tie-down ring. Minor accidents just come with the territory, when airplanes are relegated to the training environs.

Handling Qualities

Our evaluation pilot in 1979 characterized the Skipper "a delight to fly." Today we really can't argue with that appraisal. And our more recent flight was on a hot and gusty day with a strong crosswind—conditions that put not inconsiderable demands on the Model 77. Control forces in the airplane are well harmonized. Control response makes it easy for a student pilot to perceive the effects of his inputs. The Skipper is an "honest" airplane in that it is easy to see what the airplane is doing, versus what the pilot is doing.

Adverse yaw, for instance, is rather pronounced in the Skipper. There is no question about the rudder pressure and movement that the pilot has to employ to coordinate with aileron. However, there is a lack of good directional cues over the engine cowling, so instructors in Skippers have to guide their students' eyes to point out yaw. Pitch attitude is difficult for the beginning student to discern, as well, thanks to the sloping nose as viewed from the pilot's seat (kind of like a Porsche). But no trainer is perfect.

The ailerons on the Skipper are pleasantly light, and the roll rate is perhaps even a bit too high. (But after all, Wolfgang Langeweische does say in *Stick and Rudde*, that aileron design is the most difficult control for airplane builders to work out.)

The odd thing about the Skipper's ailerons is that they rather rapidly lose effectiveness as the stall is approached—much more than other trainers. If the pilot continues into a full stall in the airplane, it is very easy to allow some yaw-induced roll to develop. Attempting to pick up the falling wing with aileron yields little result. As soon as the stall is broken, however, the ailerons are ample to right the little ship again.

To Spin or Not?

Adverse aileron at the stall is what will spin a Skipper, however. In fact, it won't spin *without* aggravated aileron at the entry. With no aileron input, you will get a steep spiral, which must be recognized for what it is and recovered from before overstressing the airplane. This leads to the classic dilemma about the use of ailerons in stalls. Should an airplane bite you when you use adverse aileron? Or should the ailerons keep flying right through the stall? Should trainers be spin-resistant, or spin-capable?

It's only our opinion, but we like a wing that gives up flying more definitively, without need for opposite aileron to induce a spin (if indeed a spin is what you wanted in the first place). The bottom line is that the Skipper is different than the Tomahawk or Cessna 152 in this regard. It is actually more like some of the pre-World War II trainers. So instructors in Skippers ought to be sure to discuss stalls and spins in depth with their students.

As a two-seat airplane for the private pilot, the Skipper is very easy to trim. It holds trim speed tenaciously, in fact, regardless of power and flap extension. As a trainer, though, it might have been better to require the student to cope with trim a bit more. Skipper CFIs will have to be careful to make sure their students learn proper trimming. Elevator forces are light enough to allow pilots to just about ignore trim in the landing pattern—a bad habit. Incidentally, the trim indicator is an inaccurate and difficult-to-see affair below the throttle quadrant, so maybe it's good there isn't much need for it—except to make sure it is properly set for takeoff.

Landings and takeoffs in the Skipper are quite easy, even in a gusty crosswind. The airplane has sufficient controllability to do what you want it to do, despite its feeling kite-like (one pilot called it skittery), a trait it shares with the Cessna 152. It is rudder-limited in crosswind authority— more so than a lot of airplanes. The nose is easy to hold off at flare, and there is no tendency toward PIO. The elevator, as we said, is powerful, even at slow speeds.

Performance

The Skipper is no homesick angel, that's for sure. Despite the fact that it is equipped with a Sensenich propeller that develops well over 2500 rpm, the airplane takes forever to climb. And we flew it from a strip basically at sea

Skipper interior is wide and roomy. Professional-looking panel is head-and-shoulders above competitive two-placers.

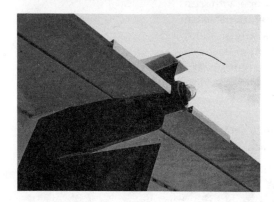

The external power plug has been moved from the nose cowl, where it was too close to the propeller. Control cables run down an enclosed channel underneath the airplane to keep the floor flat inside and make inspections easier. Odd-looking metal wedges and an anti-servo tab moderated light pitch forces on the T-tail.

level. We also had only one-third fuel on board. On one touch-and-go we didn't get organized and off again until nearly the end of the paved runway at Hammonton. We rose to about 50 feet and flew nearly level with the trees for another couple thousand feet. Consciously removing any sideslip remaining from our crosswind takeoff, we got the airplane to climb.

We'd like to fly the Skipper some more, but our impressions in the pattern, and on extended climbs, is that the Skipper is unusually sensitive to sideslip. We did lean the mixture to best power and got well over a hundred rpm more. (Referring to a Lycoming service bulletin about the O-235 engine led to the conclusion that the carburetor is definitely over-rich, and probably should be overhauled.) One thing is for sure—Beech's book figure for rate of climb is exaggerated at 720 feet per minute. The best climbing trainer around is the Cessna 152, with its advanced-design gull-wing propeller. Operating a Skipper from a high-density-altitude strip with obstacles is something to be considered with caution.

Load Carrying

The load-carrying ability of the Skipper falls right in line with other two-place trainers. Full fuel (29 gallons) and two normal-sized adults puts you at gross weight, or even a tad over. The gross weight is 1,675 pounds, and our test plane had an empty weight of 1,177 pounds, owing to a dual-navcom full-IFR panel; thus, our useful load was just 498 pounds. The cavernous area behind the seats of the Skipper usually goes for naught, since you can't really use it unless you're solo.

The day we flew the Skipper was hot, humid and turbulent. A speed check barely got us up to 85 knots indicated, and this was at 2600 rpm. At 2,500 feet and full throttle we should have been showing upwards of 95 knots, according to the book. Our flight in 1979 came out closer to book figures, so we really couldn't get down to specifics from the later flight. From our previous flight with the Skipper and the similarly configured Piper Tomahawk we know that the Skipper is the slower. The Cessna handily beats both the T-tails.

Creature Comfort

One of the Skipper's main claims to fame is its instrument panel, a wide and substantial affair crafted of metal (there is no plastic in sight). Instruments, controls and gauges are logically and clearly laid out, except for the trim indicator we mentioned earlier, and the carb heat lever, which is located and configured like the propeller pitch control on a larger plane. The engine gauges are nicely positioned above the throttle quadrant, and normal scan includes them much more often than in a lot of presumably more "sophisticated" birds.

The other thing nice about the Skipper is its cabin width—fully five inches wider than the Cessna 152's. It may be even a bit *too* wide, in our opinion. We got the impression of being surrounded by the airplane, rather than a part of it. Of course, it takes a shoehorn to get some people into the Cessna, so that's the other end of the spectrum. Cabin noise is quite high, again indicative of an unrefined design. Sitting farther away from your cabinmate means you have to speak up that much more.

Switches and circuit breakers are the typical beefy Beechcraft variety. We overheard a Skipper student say that she felt the metal panel and the kind of no-nonsense presentation were an indication of Beechcraft airplanes overall—solid and reliable. There's no doubt about it. The Skipper may fly differently than other Beechcraft, but it carries a Beechcraft motif throughout. That's okay—the Cessna 152 doesn't exactly fly like its big brother the 210 either, but it certainly *is* a Cessna in shape and form. Thus starts the brand-loyalty scheme of things.

NASA-developed GAW wing with its curling trailing edge was supposed to deliver high tech to general aviation airfoils. It delivers lots of lift, but isn't really an improvement over the Cessna 152's wing.

Maintainability

The Skipper seems to be an easy airplane to maintain. We foresee two possible considerations, however, which could cause it to cost more than the ubiquitous Cessna 150/152 series. First, there aren't many Skippers out there. We called several Beech dealers who clearly stated that they had sold Skippers in their day, but that there weren't any around anymore—and certainly none on their flight lines. One dealer said he was a full-line Beech dealer, but when queried about the Skipper said, "Oh, no. We haven't trained or rented those for years; we use the Cessna 152."

The small number in the Skipper fleet could make finding a mechanic who even recognizes one, much less has a maintenance manual, difficult. We'd recommend a new Skipper owner take his plane to a Beech dealer or Aero Center for his first inspection. The goal in this would be to learn as much as possible about the airplane, as well as to make sure everything is up to snuff (Beech service bulletins, etc.). This tactic would certainly cost a little more the first time around, but you would then be better equipped to direct a non-Skipper A&P at a future inspection.

The other problem is a source of parts, the only such being Beechcraft, of course. Beech's parts prices have historically been higher than the rest of the industry, so we'd expect the same for the Skipper. But the Skipper is such a simple airplane that, barring major airframe damage or the need for airframe parts, contributions to the Wichita economy should be minimized.

Powerplant

The engine in the Skipper is the Lycoming O-235-L2C, the same one in the Cessna 152 and Piper Tomahawk. This engine has had its problems with spark plug

Cost/Performance/Specifications

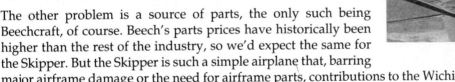

Model	Year Built	Average Retail Price	Cruise Speed (kts)	Useful Load (lbs)	Fuel Std/Opt (gals)	Engine	TBO (hrs)	Overhaul Cost
77	1979	$11,500	97	575	29	115-hp Lyc. O-235-L2C	2,000	$7,000
77	1980	$12,500	97	575	29	115-hp Lyc. O-235-L2C	2,000	$7,000
77	1981	$14,500	97	575	29	115-hp Lyc. O-235-L2C	2,000	$7,000

fouling, stuck valves and hard starting (among others), particularly in the Cessna, though its performance should be airframe-independent. Overhaul cost for the little Lycoming is listed as $7,000 in the *Aircraft Price Digest*, about $500 less than the O-320 series. Experience has showed that the O-235 can actually cost more to overhaul, since the likelihood of cylinder and/or valve problems is greater.

The most important maintenance item on the Skipper is the integrity of the exhaust system. When we first opened the door of our '79 test ship, we immediately noticed the presence of a carbon monoxide test strip, an indication that leaky exhaust can spell trouble in this airplane. There was a rash of muffler problems with early Skippers, and the cabin design lends itself to sucking in stray exhaust and promptly turning a test strip black—perhaps because of the control cable channel on the underbelly of the plane. The muffler and stack design were changed early on, and all Skippers should have the newer system, but it would make sense always to pay particular attention to the exhaust on this bird.

A minor but annoying item has to do with the fuel tank vents, located near the wing root and leading edge of each wing. It is easy to bump one of the vents (a short piece of aluminum tubing facing into the airstream), and inadvertently cause an imbalance of fuel flow from the tanks. Apparently, if the vents aren't exactly symmetrical between the left and the right, a slight pressure differential results between fuel tanks. The Skipper's fuel system has positions for both or off, so in the both position the fuel can flow preferentially from one wing. Though the flow will proceed normally with quite divergent readings on the gauges, Skipper instructors tell us it's difficult to convince a student that things are okay when one tank reads empty and the other one is still quite full.

SDRs

A search of FAA Service Difficulty Reports filed by mechanics revealed no statistically significant trends concerning the Model 77. There *were* quite a number of reports filed on the shoulder harness attach brackets, but these were back in 1981. The bracket was promptly covered by an Airworthiness Directive late in that year, correcting the problem. It was the same situation with door hinges, save for the AD. Make sure that you check the door alignment and hinges on any Skipper you're eyeing, for (as with the Tomahawk) latching the doors can be a pain. And since it is common practice to leave the doors open on the ground to improve ventilation, fumbling around with the overhead latch comes at just the wrong time—right as you're cleared onto the active runway.

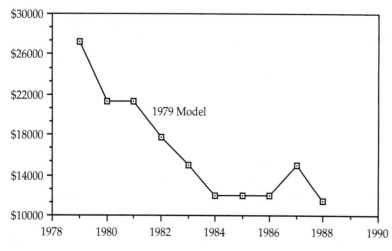

Skipper Resale Value

1979 Model

Accident History

We found four fatal accidents involving Skippers. One resulted from a student pilot taking a friend on an "unauthorized" night flight and losing control of the

The Skipper and the Tomahawk, two "modern" competitors for the throne of the Cessna 152. The Beechcraft has generally better workmanship than the Piper, and less dramatic stall behavior.

plane. He had no night experience. Another pilot had been known to skip his wheels on the surface of a lake. Nothing was found but a wheel floating in the water. The third Skipper struck trees on a VOR approach after the plane stalled due to excessive ice on the wings. And the last was a stall/spin after the engine failed because of a loose nut on an exhaust valve adjusting screw. The plane was on its test flight after top overhaul—the mechanic was in the left seat.

The other Skipper accidents were almost exclusively training-related: propeller strikes, smashed nose gears, veering off runways, landing short—that sort of thing. With the Skippers finding themselves in private hands in increasing ratio, these accidents should decline in frequency in the future.

Summing Up

We still like the Skipper, though our editor on this assignment would have to disagree with the earlier assessment that the Skipper has more retail appeal than the 152. The Skipper flies as well as the Cessna, but it's a "fifty-footer" in comparison. Sure, it looks pert, cute and friendly from a distance. But closer than 50 feet and you notice the bluntness of the cowl, the rivet heads along the whole fuselage (Beech uses such big rivets), the unsculptured sheet metal construction of the whole plane. The Cessna, on the other hand, benefits from years of evolution, so its lines are about as cleaned-up as can be cost-effectively accomplished on a two-seater.

The Skipper can be had for a little less money than a 152. The Cessnas are growing in value as flight schools snap up the good ones for their fleets. But the Beech might cost a little more to maintain in the long run, owing to its different-ness (there weren't enough made) and the unknowns of parts prices. The Skipper is noisier and slower than the 152. Its lethargic rate of climb should be of concern where it matters, but otherwise could be lived with.

The good visibility, roomy cabin and flighty controls make it fun to fly for both pilot and passenger. It would be nice to see a turnaround in general aviation include the resumption of Skipper production, but don't hold your breath.

Beech Musketeers

As the parade of aircraft cancelled for lack of interest—or overwhelming price shock—grows longer, the Beech Sundowner and Sport vie for attention as affordable, if unexciting basic transportation with wings.

In a world where performance and looks have always been boasting points, prosaic matters like cabin room and ease of access, instead, are the most often quoted selling points for these two models. "You may get there faster, in another airplane" their owners frequently concede, "but we'll arrive in greater comfort."

Alas, they won't arrive with the elegance of the rest of the Beech models, since the Sundowners and Sports were the curious legacy of a Musketeer line that sacrificed panache for utilitarianism. They used sensible construction materials like sandwich foam, and employed assembly line economies like constant-chord wings and skin bonding. Though they were designed with admirable qualities like fine, massive one-piece windshields, mile-wide landing gear and tough-enough construction to permit a utility category rating at full gross, they've rarely dazzled the beholder with good looks.

History

The Musketeers come in two basic models: the 19 and the 23. The Model 19 is powered by a 150-hp Lycoming and normally seats two. The Model 23 will seat four and most often comes with a 180-hp Lycoming. (We won't consider the retractable-gear Sierra Model 24 in this report.)

As with the Piper Cherokee, the Musketeer went through a series of engine changes before settling down. The first Musketeer in 1963 appeared with a 160-hp

A Sundowner flares for the landing, the scenario for trouble if good speed control is not used. A bungled, bounced landing can wipe out the nosegear and prop. Stiff rubber shock mounts in the landing gear contribute to the bounce problem.

Lycoming. (The first 160-hp Cherokee had led the way two years earlier.) In 1964 Beech switched engines, putting in an oddball 165-hp Continental IO-346-A. Basically an IO-520 with two cylinders lopped off, it tended to run hot in the Musketeer.

This A23 model lasted until 1968, when it was succeeded by the 180-hp B23. Meanwhile, in 1966, Beech had brought out its Model 19 Sport, a 150-hp trainer that seated two and weighed in at a gross 150 pounds less than that of the A23. In 1970, the two models became the B19 and C23, respectively.

The Sport went through some strange weight machinations as the FAA discovered that the 2,250-pound-gross B19 could not meet minimum certification standards for climb performance at that weight. So AD 73-25-4 was issued, limiting the gross weight of all B19s built up to then to 2,000 pounds. That included serial numbers MB-481 through -616. When a special Beech kit was installed, the gross could be raised back up to 2,150 pounds. All the Sports built after 1973 incorporated the mods and had gross weights of 2,150 pounds.

The B19 continued in production until 1979, when the two-place Beech Skipper made its bow (and itself experienced an ephemeral existence; production was halted in 1981). The Beech 23 Sundowner held on until 1983, when it also bit the dust.

Performance

Lackluster is perhaps a flattering description for both models. Owners talk about getting a TAS of from 91 to 100 knots in the Sport, and 100 to 117 knots in the Sundowner. These speeds are easily eclipsed by all their competitors.

The Sport has a cavernous cabin, but fill it to gross on a warm day, and expect a dismal climb rate and service ceiling.

Climb performance, especially in the Sport, can be downright dismal, especially on a hot day. Said one owner, "On a hot day at full gross count on 300-400 fpm climb *max*." Another wrote, "I have noticed at or near gross weight, my Musketeer falls off in performance in hot weather much more than the book shows." To be fair, however, several owners claimed the handbook figures claimed by Beech were quite realistic. One said he was able to climb to 9,500 feet at an average of 500 fpm with a cruise climb of 81 knots. Said another, "The speed, rate-of-climb, etc. figures published by Beechcraft are reasonable and not exaggerated."

Indeed, for the Sundowner, Beech listed the 75-percent cruise at 8,500 feet at only 136 mph, and claimed only a 792-fpm rate of climb at sea level with full throttle, loaded to gross weight.

Payload and Range

Except for earlier models of the Sport, both the 19 and 23 carry 57 gallons of usable fuel. With the Sport, that translates to a range with reserve at high cruise of about 620 nm. With the Sundowner, the figure is about 530 nm. Competitors of the Sundowner with the same 180 hp—like the Piper Cherokee, Gulfstream American Tiger and Cessna Cardinal—all carry about seven gallons less fuel. But their greater speed allows them to cover about the same distance on less fuel.

Naturally, if you load the cabins of any of these airplanes with people and baggage, to stay within the weight limits, you normally have to take off with a lot less fuel than the tanks will hold. Since the Sundowners can be expected to have an equipped useful load of about 900 pounds, that means hauling three people and a bit less than 50 pounds of baggage with full fuel. With the Sport, figure on two people and full fuel—but watch the climb.

In summary, the useful load of the Musketeers compares quite closely with the others in their class.

Cabin Comfort

Here is where all the Musketeers shine. The cabins are big and roomy, with space to spare. And all but some of the earlier models have entry doors on both sides of the cabin—a nice feature—though some owners complained of leaking doors.

Handling Qualities

Owners talk in flattering terms about Musketeer handling characteristics—*in the air*. They report smooth and responsive controls, and stability in rough air. But one owner complained of a "severe" pitchup when flaps were lowered anywhere in the white arc.

The great handling shortcoming of the Musketeers is generally acknowledged to be wicked landing habits—corroborated by accident tallies on the birds. They have a distinctly unpleasant porpoising tendency, and many a student—and even quite a few fully rated pilots—have put on a memorable display of kangaroo leaps down the runway—often ending in calamity with a collapsed nose gear and damaged prop—and therefore an engine that is a candidate for a teardown.

The trailing beam landing gear has rather stiff rubber shock absorbers instead of air-oil oleos, as on most lightplanes. And pilots ruefully note how an inadvertent three- point touchdown on this gear can result in a series of jolting crow hops down the runway before the pilot is aware of what's happening.

Musketeer owners who responded to our call for comments reported awareness of this unhappy reputation. But they figured they had mastered the idiosyncrasy and were happy with their machines. Observed one matter-of-factly: "Precise speed control is important because there is a tendency to porpoise." As with the Mooney, you carry a higher-than-needed airspeed into the flare at your own risk.

Once safely slowed down on the ground, the landing gear is praised, at least for its turning alacrity. Using just nosewheel steering alone without brakes, the Musketeers will pivot in their own wing length—great for maneuvering around the ramp, and parking.

Aerobatic Bonus

Both aircraft, incidentally, are certified for aerobatics (with only two aboard, of course) when equipped with features like quick-release doors, G-meters and inertial reel shoulder harnesses. Pilots may be reassured to know the aircraft is strong enough to handle this rating without extra strengthening measures.

Strength notwithstanding, with hard landings a fact of life for many Musketeers, it pays to check landing gear, engine mounts and wing attach fittings with special care.

Safety Record

As we mentioned earlier, Musketeer owners who commented to us for this report wrote that they were aware of the reputation of their aircraft for landing problems but were able to compensate. Unfortunately, the safety statistics suggest that a frightening number of other Musketeer pilots were not able to do so. A search of the accident records for Model 19s and 23s for 1980 through 1985 discloses by far the greatest proportion of accidents stems from botched landings—ballooning, porpoising, bouncing, loss of directional control, hard landings—you name it.

Though seldom fatal, these accidents exacted a high toll in machinery, with a sizable number of nosegears being lopped off and props (and presumably engines) damaged. On one occasion the pilot actually bashed off the nosegear but took the aircraft around, only to come around to the inevitable crunch on a final landing with only two main landing wheels.

Has the metal carnage diminished over the years? Hardly at all, as far as we could tell. For the five years overall, we estimated that about 46 percent of all Musketeer accidents involved landing mishaps. For the Model 19 Sport, 55 percent of the accidents were botched landings of one kind or another. For the Model 23 the figure was slightly lower—41 percent.

Student Calamities?

Are students perpetrating most of the damage on the landing accidents? Our tally suggests that about 64 percent of the landing problems on the Sports involved student pilots—which would seem appropriate for a trainer. And on the Sundowner, 39 percent of the landing prangs were perpetrated by students.

In a special study of accident patterns among 33 aircraft over the five-year span from 1972 through 1976, the NTSB ranked the Model 23 Sundowner worst in the hard landing category—and nearly five times as bad as both the Cherokee and Skyhawk.

In terms of overall safety rating, the Model 23 came out in the same study with a rather mediocre record—once again, not as good as aircraft like the Cherokee and Skyhawk. The Sundowner came up with a fatal accident rate of 2.5 per 100,000 flying hours, vs. 1.97 for the Cherokee PA-28 series and 1.47 for the Cessna 172. It bested the Gulfstream Traveler, however, at 2.94.

Another accident category in which the Model 23 fared poorly was overshoots. The Sundowner was third worst among the 33 compared, following only the Grumman Traveler and the Cessna 195.

Our study of accidents over the five years from 1981-1985 showed no other

Double cabin doors on all but early model Sundowners and Sports make for easy access.

particular pattern, though in three instances carburetor ice was suspected of causing engine failure accidents, and in 16 instances Musketeer pilots either exhausted their fuel totally or ran a tank dry.

Owners report door and windshield leaking in rain can cause instrument damage.

Landing Strategies

Some experienced Musketeer flight instructors we talked with said they felt the aircraft was unjustly maligned for its landing characteristics. They stressed that the key element behind most of the landing (and takeoff) problems is proper speed control. The villain in almost every instance, they said, is too much speed on final and in the flare. If the pilot tries to plant the aircraft on the runway too soon, it will bite. The greater springback reaction from the rubber shock on the nosegear (than from a conventional oleo strut) can be expected to generate a healthy bounce, and the chain of awkward events has begun, unless the pilot knows how to make a proper recovery.

One instructor said he told students to aim for an approach speed of 1.3 Vso (flaps-down stall speed), subtracting a knot or so for each hundred pounds under gross. He said that actually the wide landing gear stance on the Musketeers allowed them to handle greater crosswind components than many other aircraft. But the brakes seem more effective than normal, and an inadvertent over-strenuous stab on the rollout could lock a brake, rip a tire and cause bedlam.

One paradoxical aspect to the disadvantage of carrying too much speed, on the Sport at least, is the hazard of coming in too slow and running out of stabilator for the flare, dropping the nose for the inevitable bounce. Pilots report the aircraft is nose heavy, especially with flaps down, and a better strategy is to keep on a bit of power right through the flare.

At one Beech dealership they reported they were surprised by better landing characteristics that resulted from putting on the optional spin kit, which added strakes to the nose and stabilator along with a ventral fin to the rear fuselage. Other Musketeer instructors we talked with said they did not see any benefit from this strategy.

Maintenance

Owners who responded to our survey reported they were for the most part happy with the low maintenance demands of the Musketeers. Said one, "It is by far the best mechanical device I have owned." The reliability of the 180-hp Lycoming in the Sundowners received high marks as well. What few complaints there were centered around leaky windshields and doors, and water getting into the vacuum pump or air filter, shutting down the gyros.

Service Difficulty Reports show some evidence of gear stress from landing problems. There were a half dozen instances of gear housing cracks and breaks on the Model 23 and several cases of broken engine mounts, and severe shimmy on landing from broken nosegear components.

On the Model 19 there were 11 cases of aileron push-pull tubes and rod ends that failed. Identical reports were made out on 11 cases where fuel cells had delaminated at the top skin between the skin and ribs near the filler opening. Another 11 reports told of cracks in the right inboard side of the keel assembly under the rudder pedal support. And 19 identical reports were filed on heavy corrosion at station 68 where the firewall pad contacts the aluminum structure. Beech issued mandatory service instructions (No. 1245) calling for inspection of this area.

There were 14 cases of cracked elevator spars during inspections made according to Beech Service Instructions No. 1167. Another AD on the Musketeer stabilators (78-16-06) called for inspection of the trim tab actuator rod. Among the key ADs affecting the Musketeers is the repetitive one (73-20-07) calling for inspection of the forward wing attach frames and brackets for possible cracks. A1985 AD on these aircraft (85-05-02) ordered a fuel selector stop to be installed (along with a decal) on the fuel selector valve guard to reduce the chance of accidentally turning the fuel selector valve to the off position.

In 1988 FAA issued an AD requiring that electric fuel boost pumps in certain S uper Musketeers and Sierras be replaced with units having nylon-graphite vanes. The old carbon-graphite vanes were reported breaking and causing engine stoppages. And the NTSB said fuel caps of Musketeers over 10 years old should be pressure checked yearly because of the threat of leakage causing water contamination in the fuel and engine stoppages.

Modifications

There is a paucity of mods for the Musketeer series, except for the usual autopilot and strobe and carb ice detector accessories. There is, however, an STC for an adjustable trim tab on the left aileron, by Aero-Trim, Inc. in Bay Harbor, Fla.

Recapitulation

As the great shakeout of the 80s continues, the chief virtue of the Musketeers is their low price. They have to be considered the bargain buys of their respective classes. (Check the nearby comparison chart.) And here we are talking about the Sundowner in particular. We believe the Sport is, frankly, too doggy to consider even in these dog days.

Cost/Performance/Specifications

Model	Year Built	Average Retail Price	Cruise Speed (kts)	Useful Load (lbs)	Fuel Std/Opt (gals)	Engine	TBO (hrs)	Overhaul Cost
19	1966-67	$8,400	108	875	57	150-hp Lyc. O-320-E2C	2,000	$6,300
19A	1968-69	$9,600	108	875	57	150-hp Lyc. O-320-E2C	2,000	$6,300
B19	1970-73	$10,700	108	875	57	150-hp Lyc. O-320-E2C	2,000	$6,300
B19	1974-77	$12,000	108	875	57	150-hp Lyc. O-320-E2C	2,000	$6,300
B19	1978	$13,000	108	875	57	150-hp Lyc. O-320-E2C	2,000	$6,300
23	1963	$9,500	111	1,000	57	160-hp Lyc. O-320-D2B	2,000	$6,500
A23	1964-66	$10,800	119	1,025	57	165-hp Cont. IO-346-A	1,500	$7,800
A23	1967-68	$11,600	119	1,025	57	165-hp Cont. IO-346-A	1,500	$7,800
B23	1968-69	$12,600	119	975	57	180-hp Lyc. O-360-A2G	2,000	$7,000
C23	1970-73	$13,800	119	975	57	180-hp Lyc. O-360-A4G	2,000	$7,000
C23	1974-76	$17,500	119	975	57	180-hp Lyc. O-360-A4J	2,000	$7,000
C23	1977-79	$22,000	119	975	57	180-hp Lyc. O-360-A4K	2,000	$7,000
C23	1980-81	$30,000	119	975	57	180-hp Lyc. O-360-A4K	2,000	$7,000
C23	1982-83	$44,000	119	975	57	180-hp Lyc. O-360-A4K	2,000	$7,000

Though both aircraft are followed by a cloud of suspicion because of their horrible landing accident record, a careful checkout by a knowledgeable Musketeer instructor may remove much of the onus for aficionados of (1) low prices, (2) abundantly roomy cabins, (3) low maintenance and (4) easy two-door access. Buyers willing to sacrifice five to 10 knots of cruise speed and who-knows-how-much climb rate will find the Sundowner a surprising bargain.

Owner Comments

Maintenance costs have varied with the number of ADs and where the annual was performed. Expensive ADs have included main gear remounting and one-half valves in the cylinders. Anyone considering purchasing an older Musketeer should verify that the engine has the one-half-inch valve stems instead of the original three-eighth- inch stems.

A potentially costly AD requires removal of the wing tips to check for corrosion inside the wings. Also, a recurring AD requires checking wing attach bolts and spars annually for cracking, etc. Older Musketeers had a free swivel on the nose gear, and braking was required while taxiing. On an icy ramp, braking just doesn't cut it. The Beech nose wheel steering kit is a necessity for winter flying "up north."

Another kit, no longer available, I wish I had installed is the split nosebowl. This allows removal of the bottom engine cowling without having to pull the prop spinner and prop off first. A simple adjustment such as tightening the generator belt requires removing both the top and bottom cowlings with the nosebowl attached to the bottom cowling. The split nosebowl kit should result in much cheaper annual labor costs.

Musketeers have a greater fuel capacity than most competitors, but slower cruise speeds eliminate the potential advantage in range.

Maintenance headaches include multiple problems with the Goodyear brakes. There is a series of brake system improvements available, primarily to fix air lock problems with a shuttle valve which controls the four master cylinders. Going to a firewall-mounted master reservoir and Cleveland brakes (originally certified in 1963 but not factory installed until the early 70s) should solve all brake problems.

The early Musketeers did not utilize a battery box, but instead used a special vented 25-amp/hr battery with two small plastic tubes going through grommets in the fuselage bottom. The problem is that no battery manufacturer currently produces this size of vented manifold battery. Beech has a kit available with a new mounting bracket, battery box, large vent hoses, etc., for $600 or so. I found a used battery bracket and box with hoses in a salvage yard and had it installed in accordance with the service instruction for under $150 with a 35 amp/hr standard aircraft battery, which really helped starter cranking on cold days.

Douglas E. Mulloy
Seattle, Wash.

As for performance, our 1980 Sundowner isn't fast, but it's solid, docile, forgiving and as friendly as an old glove. We cruise at 9,500 feet at about 2250 rpm indicating 113 knots and burning 9.8 gph. Our average climb rate from sea level to altitude with a full load is about 500 fpm at a cruise climb of 81 knots. It takes us about 18 to 20 minutes to get up there.

There are no handling problems or idiosyncrasies that I know of. The plane handles turbulence very nicely, and control pressures are always very light and responsive. It's not likely that a power-on stall would come without the plane talking to the pilot for several seconds before it tipped. Stalls under slow flight or approach to landing are more subtle, but still with considerable warning, both from the buzzer and from buffeting. It's as if the plane really doesn't want to stall.

As for maintenance, since new, the plane has had only one airworthiness directive (the oil cooler). The maintenance on this plane has been very minor. It has required no major

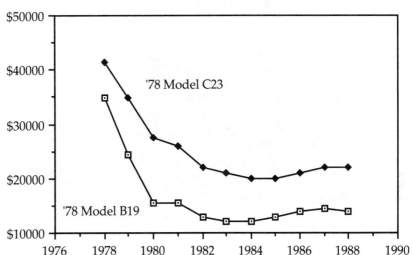

Beech Musketeer Resale Value

work at all yet, at 1,400 hours TT. The vacuum pump has been replaced, and the starter gear shaft went through a bearing.

Annual inspections have cost from $250 to $750, with me participating as much as I'm allowed. The higher-cost annual occurred when we had to fix the starter and vacuum pump. My total maintenance cost for 1985 was $1,380, with close to 100 hours flown. The two years before that the Sundowner required significantly less maintenance for the same amount of flying. My average maintenance cost since new has been very close to $9 per tach hour.

In terms of comfort, the Sundowner is very roomy and comfortable. We have taken some five-hour non-stop flights with no discomfort. The noise level seems very tolerable; we can carry on an almost normal conversation in flight. Heating, ventilation, defrost and control layout are quite adequate and well done. The seats are comfortable, and the large windows and high seating position make for very good visibility. The two doors are commonplace to us, but much appreciated when we see other folks crawling across their planes to get to the pilot's seat. Weakness: when it rains, it leaks—getting the floor carpeting wet. The paint job is of questionable quality. It has developed lots of pimples or very small bumps on the top surfaces.

Overall, the important thing to us is reliability, comfort, friendliness and troublefree operation. We are not enamored by great speed or high performance or the added maintenance that comes with retractable gear or variable pitch props. The Sundowner has probably hit our specs as close to anything we know.

Ray Bell
Los Gatos, Calif.

I have owned my 1975 Sundowner over nine and a half years, and have many good things to say about it. It is by far the best mechanical device I have owned. It has been very reliable and is consistently available whenever I need it. It is very good on maintenance. The Lycoming 180 is a very reliable workhorse and goes extremely well on 100LL. The aircraft is solid, well built and stable in rough air.

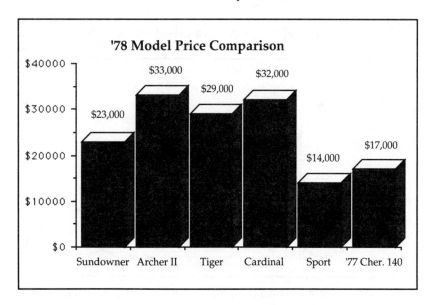

'78 Model Price Comparison

There are some drawbacks, however. The plane is now out of production, and parts are getting hard to come by; consequently, the price of an annual inspection has gone up more than a little. During the first seven years of ownership the average price of an annual ranged from $600 to $1,000. For the last two years, however, it was $1,400 and $1,800 respectively. Although I did use the Beechcraft East maintenance facility the last two years, this year I'm going back to the original, a former Aero Center dealer versed in dealing with the smaller aircraft. The established Beechcraft maintenance facilities are fine for the larger Beechcraft, but I don't recommend them for the Aero Club line.

Secondly, I did get hit with that infamous surprise of which all Sundowner owners must be aware. I keep my aircraft outside in harsh New England weather, and for nine years the plane weathered well until the seals on the instrument vacuum pump filter eventually deteriorated. All Sundowners leak around the doors and windshield and must be dried out after a heavy rain. One fine August day after one such rain, I innocently flipped on my master switch only to have an aging, tired vacuum pump proceed to dump about a cup and a half of pure rain water directly into the innards of my directional gyro and artificial horizon. It was (expensive) overhaul time for these!

Beechcraft East subsequently relocated the filter mount in accordance with a previously issued service bulletin, but why wasn't this done ahead of time? Even at the factory? My insurance company disowned me.

However, in spite of these conditions, I still love my Sundowner. I know I could not afford to replace it with any comparable still-in-production model. It is indeed unfortunate that the Aero Club line never sold very well. Often this line was shadowed by the stigma that they were slow, and expensive to buy, and the fact is that they are roomy and very comfortable. Any slowness is noticed only on paper next to the competitors' figures. The speed, rate of climb, etc. figures published by Beech are reasonable and not exaggerated. After arriving from a long cross-country, one feels comfortable and relaxed.

The Sundowner is a very good value for the money. I would suggest to those looking for a used model to first check that all service bulletins have been complied with (especially the one described above). The Beech factory often pro-rates the parts and labor for compliance, and in some cases have paid for the entire job.

Once this is done, any owner can expect to get very good enjoyment and practical transportation for his investment.

Lowell G. Powers, Jr.
Newport, R. I.

We have a '74 Sundowner. Performance is excellent. Usually flown 200 pounds under max gross, it will climb at 78 knots at 800 fpm at density altitudes over 3,000 feet. At cruise, the numbers are close to the POH. Handling is excellent—smooth and very responsive. There is a moderate pitch-up, pitch-down with power changes, and a severe pitch-up when lowering flaps at any speed in the white arc.

Maintenance has not been a problem. In 200 hours, one set of brake pads, my request; one leaky spark plug wire, replaced complete set, my request. Added oil filter and adapter. Replaced battery. Comfort is fantastic. You get out without being tired because you are not fighting the airplane. Noise level with the air vents open measured 73 dBA at 2500 rpm. Parts availability: Stock at the parts houses in the Los Angeles area or at Beech FBOs locally. Cost: Fuel consumption the last 200 hours has averaged 8.2 gph; oil consumption, one quart every seven to eight hours; annual inspection, $350. The Sundowner, I believe, is a much neglected aircraft. Flying one will make you a believer.

David Lipsky
La Mirada, Calif.

Until recently I owned a 1968 Beech Musketeer B23 with the 180-hp engine. Performance: Cruise 117 knots at 5,000 feet with 75 percent power at 10.5 gph. Handling: Cruise aileron response much like a Cherokee 140, not particularly crisp. Landing: Precise speed control is important because there is a tendency to porpoise.

Maintenance: Typical Beechcraft with good documentation and adequate accessibility. Very high quality support from Beech with continuing service letters and high-level support. The Lycoming 180-hp is obviously reliable and Beech even has the larger plugs, harness and high-altitude mags fitted. I fixed the brakes, DG, voltage regulator, and our Musketeer did evidence cylinder cracks, requiring a top overhaul at 1,100 hours. This was likely due to a previous owner flying the aircraft in unapproved aerobatics with sudden engine cooling.

Comfort: There is excellent front and rear seat room. Parts availability: Very good. Cost of operation: maintenance $1,000 (due to top overhaul), $20 hourly in gas. Average annual is $400.

In summary, this is a much maligned plane which actually is a real bargain to fly and own, if not very exciting in airwork or appearance. It is very well built and quite strong, but slightly slow and can tend to porpoise if not landed properly. It really would be an excellent first plane for a careful pilot and can be bought for next to nothing with careful shopping.

Dr. Andrew Reiland
Leominster, Mass.

Beech
Sierra 24R

Has history smiled upon the Beech Sierra after almost two decades of life in the slow lane? Perhaps, in a sly Mona Lisa way. Has it qualities that commend it over a quartet of rivals? Some, indeed; but it also has a few faults—some rather nasty.

A glance at the facts suggests that the Model 24R merits rating, once again, as a very average airplane in the 200-hp retractable class. Sort of an equal among equals. It ranks along with the Cessna Cardinal RG and Rockwell 112 as one of the least costly (to buy) used economy retractables around. The Mooney 201 way exceeds it in price. (Check the nearby graph.) Even the Piper Arrow costs a few thousand dollars more, year for year, on the average. And you have to go back another decade or more earlier to find a 225-horse Beech Debonair that costs as little. Presumably these price differences can be equated with pilot esteem, because all these airplanes cost about the same when new.

History

A 200-hp fixed-gear Model 24 called the Super III came out back in 1966. Then, the Model 24R with retractable gear came on the scene in 1970. The A24R in 1970 came without two features everyone praises on later models: a second cockpit door and a third, left-side baggage door. These features were added in 1971. With the B24R in 1973 came a new instrument panel and quadrant-style (multi) powerplant controls instead of push-pull controls. Also, the baggage door was enlarged and a Hartzell prop replaced the McCauley.

One of the aircraft's most attractive qualities is its price on the used market. It's one of the cheapest retractables in its class.

In 1977 the C24R came out with aileron gaps and nicer bearings for smoother aileron control, plus a bit of extra usable fuel, a new cabin vent system along with a two-inch longer prop giving more thrust. Finally, wheel-well fairings were added under the wing to reduce drag when the gear was retracted.

Cabin Comfort

This has always been the big selling point among owners, as with the Rockwell 112. "The superb visibility, spacious and comfortable interior and door configuration are the plane's greatest virtues," echoed one pilot. Along with right and left doors for the front seat, there is a largish door for the baggage compartment that can handle kids nicely. There is even an optional small jump seat. The rear compartment is structurally capable of holding a whopping 270 pounds—about the heaviest in this class of aircraft. But can you actually throw kids in the jump seat and stay within the Sierra's weight and balance limits? Our calculations show you probably can. We figured, in fact, that with a modestly equipped airplane, you could get two 170-pounders in the front seat, a couple of 115-pounders in the middle seats and still toss a couple of 70-pound kids in the rear while carrying better than 50 gallons of fuel.

Can you ever load a full 270 pounds in the rear compartment, realistically? Once again, our calculations say you can and still stay within the weight-and-balance envelope, though it probably wouldn't make much sense because you probably would end up with empty middle seats. One pilot said the first thing he did was throw out the jump seat to avoid temptation.

Comparing the Sierra's useful load with that of its competitors in the 200-hp retractable class, it appears the Beech comes out slightly short—on the order of 50 pounds or so for IFR-equipped birds. Figure on an IFR useful of about 925-950 pounds. If you use 925 pounds, that allows you full fuel, three 170-pound adults and 60 pounds of baggage. With four adults, count on about 25 gallons of fuel.

Performance

This is the area where pilots typically say they trade off for the large, comfortable, beamy cabin. The Sierra isn't fast. In its class, it brings up the rear in cruise speed with the equally sluggish, beamy, comfortable Rockwell 112. Owners say to count on about 135 knots/155 mph TAS with 75 percent power and 132 knots or so at 65 percent. The Piper Arrow with the same engine should go about seven knots faster; the Cardinal RG some 11 knots faster, and the Mooney 201 a crazy 20 to 30 knots faster. The addition of wheel well fairings in 1977 is reported to have reduced the drag of the main gear dangling out in the breeze, and added a few knots. The fairings smoothed the turbulent airflow. But the nose gear still dangles rather low.

With the '77 Sierras fairings were added to the main gear wheel wells to reduce drag caused by the dangling wheels. Rubber donut shock absorbers (like the Mooney's) contribute to less than feather-smooth touchdowns.

However, even the fixed-gear Gulfstream Tiger can be expected to go sailing by the Sierra at full bore with only 180 horses.

In a perverse sense, the Sierra is slower where you want it to be fast, and faster where you want it to be slow—on final approach and in the stall payout. Figure on a power-off stall speed, dirty, in the Sierra of 60 knots/69 mph. That's 11 knots higher than the Arrow, nine higher than the 112B and five higher than the supposedly "hot" Mooney 201.

Handling

Everybody agrees the Sierra is a delight in the air, but something less when landing. The ailerons are marvelously light, and the airplane is fun to maneuver in the air. Though the stall speed is relatively high for this class of aircraft, it's tough to get a stall break because of limited stabilator travel. And the stalls you can induce are mild and give good warning.

The landing gear acts as a good speed brake because, as with many other Beechcraft, the gear can be lowered at a fairly high airspeed—135 knots/155 mph, in fact—or darn close to cruise speed.

Landing Problems

Through the years, the Sierra's landing qualities have stirred the most excitement among pilots—just like the other fixed-gear Musketeers, Sundowners, etc. Collectively, they have a rotten record of botched landings and collapsed gear and bent props to their credit. The Sierra is no exception. Instructors and chauvinistic owners may rant and rave that the airplane does not deserve its poor reputation because it was perpetrated by ill-trained pilots. And that may be so, but the record is a miserable one, to say the least.

If the airspeed is not just right, the Sierra can float, and the stabilator can tend to

oscillate and contribute to over-controlling. Also, the aircraft tends to run out of nose-up pitch authority during landing (without a load in the rear), and this can result in a nosewheel-first wheelbarrow landing. Naturally, confronted with a history like this, any wary buyer should have a mechanic pay the utmost attention to the integrity of the landing gear. Also, check for evidence of gear-up landings. They happen with disturbing frequency in this aircraft.

Maintenance

Owners report they are fairly happy with upkeep of their Sierras—with a modest cost burden. Annuals reported

There are doors all over the place, for great ingress and egress. The rear compartment can take a jump seat for kids, or hold a great quantity of baggage (up to 270 pounds structurally).

to us ranged well below $1,000. There was some grumbling by owners about the high cost of Beech parts, but these days we'd be surprised if they weren't all high. At least the parts appear to be available. Also, one owner positively raved about how supportive Beech was when he needed help and information.

The Service Difficulty Reports point the finger of blame primarily on the landing gear. A study of SDRs from the beginning of 1980 to the end of November 1986 showed landing gear problems outnumbering most other mechanical problems by a factor of seven or so. (See the nearby chart.) Checking the records to see how consistent a problem this has been, we noted most of the SDRs showed up in the first two years of our study, in 1980-1981, with 10 the first year and 14 the second. From then on, the rate dropped sharply, to where an average of only 4.4 landing gear SDRs were reported each year. So presumably the problem has been diminished greatly.

Problems leading to gear collapse or failure to retract included: failure of torque shaft arm; plunger on limit switch was hanging, not letting retract arms lock; downlock spring broken; gear actuator shaft broken; downlock switch failed; nose gear yoke broken, etc.

Fuel Pump Problems

We noted seven instances of failure of the Dukes fuel pump in Sierras through the last six years. Naturally, the unpleasant result was that the engine quit. Also we noted half a dozen reports of broken or worn aileron rod ends. These sometimes resulted in ailerons failing to respond or jamming (once on takeoff).

There were only a half dozen cases reported of engine mechanical problems, and these showed no particular trend—i.e., dowel pin sheared, crankcase cracked, crankshaft broken, piston cracked, valve stretched and cylinder cracked. The

Model 24Rs appear to have had a rather mild history of Airworthiness Directive concerns. The only AD to appear in the 80s mandated a fuel selector stop and decal designed to prevent inadvertently shutting off the fuel.

Safety

Accident reports for the six years up to 1987 echo the gear problems disclosed in the SDRs. The preponderance of accidents in the Sierra stem from (1) inadvertent gear-up landings, (2) gear mechanical problems, (3) hard landings. Obviously, most are pilot-related since dummy fliers forget to put the gear down for landing or retract it after landing or before getting completely airborne on takeoff. Sometimes the gear-up crunch results from poor coordination with a flight instructor. And hard landings and groundloop/swerves (there were quite a few of the latter) can be classified either as pilot error or design-induced error, depending on your inclination. Most likely, both are to blame.

In a study we conducted in 1984 comparing accident rates of 17 single-engine retractables, the Beech Sierra showed up poorly in fatal rate—14th best out of the 17 (or fourth worst) and even worse in total accident rate—16th. These are determined by accidents per 100,000 hours. Far better, incidentally, were the Beech 33 Debonair and Cardinal RG. The Piper Arrow and Commander 112/114 also were ranked better. Our most recent figures showed only nine fatal accidents since 1980, from a variety of causes and no trends: one from weather, another from an engine problem, one from fuel mismanagement, another from a stall/mush problem and five from miscellaneous causes.

Safety Features

The Sierra has some nice features that might help in a crash. All four seats have shoulder harnesses as standard equipment, and the ability to scram in case of a problem on the ground through the three doors is a major asset. But the "horned" control wheels mostly have no padding or protection against pilot impact.

Also, in terms of fuel management, the location of the fuel gauges in a hard-to-see place at the bottom left of the control panel hardly can be considered ideal. But we counted only half a dozen cases of fuel exhaustion over the last six years and just three of fuel mismanagement. As mentioned above, an AD called for installation

Cost/Performance/Specifications

Model	Year Built	Average Retail Price	Cruise Speed (kts)	Useful Load (lbs)	Fuel Std/Opt (gals)	Engine	TBO (hrs)	Overhaul Cost
A24R	1970	$19,000	131	1,140	52	200-hp Lyc. IO-360-A1B6	1,800	$8,500
A24R	1971	$19,500	131	1,140	52	200-hp Lyc. IO-360-A1B6	1,800	$8,500
A24R	1972	$20,500	131	1,140	52	200-hp Lyc. IO-360-A1B6	1,800	$8,500
B24R	1973	$21,500	131	1,140	52	200-hp Lyc. IO-360-A1B6	1,800	$8,500
B24R	1974	$22,500	131	1,140	52	200-hp Lyc. IO-360-A1B6	1,800	$8,500
B24R	1975	$24,000	131	1,140	52	200-hp Lyc. IO-360-A1B6	1,800	$8,500
B24R	1976	$25,500	131	1,140	52	200-hp Lyc. IO-360-A1B6	1,800	$8,500
C24R	1977	$28,000	137	1,065	57	200-hp Lyc. IO-360-A1B6	1,800	$8,500
C24R	1978	$30,500	137	1,065	57	200-hp Lyc. IO-360-A1B6	1,800	$8,500
C24R	1979	$33,000	137	1,065	57	200-hp Lyc. IO-360-A1B6	1,800	$8,500
C24R	1980	$36,000	137	1,065	57	200-hp Lyc. IO-360-A1B6	1,800	$8,500
C24R	1981	$40,000	137	1,056	57	200-hp Lyc. IO-360-A1B6	1,800	$8,500
C24R	1982	$47,000	137	1,065	57	200-hp Lyc. IO-360-A1B6	1,800	$8,500

of a stop to prevent inadvertent selection of the "off" position. The fuel selector is located below the throttle quadrant where both pilots can see it.

Owner Comments

I bought my '78 Sierra in '82 (on my wife's insistence) while looking for a "neater" ship. She liked the ease of entry, comfort and roominess. If a non-pilot wife, knowing nothing about planes, agrees we ought to *buy* a plane and points to *that* retractable, I am smart enough to keep my mouth shut. We got the plane with 1,000 hours on it as a bank repo for $22 grand—hard to pass up.

Sure, for a retractable, it does only 137 knots at 75 percent power; and at 65 percent it offers a sedate 132 knots. But it does it in such a stable and predictable manner, and with remarkable visibility, including almost straight down by the wing root. The 135-knot gear-drop speed has come in very handy entering major airport areas where I keep speed up until the 45-degree entry, plop the gear and watch the speed drop to approach numbers slick as silk. Flaps at 100 knots and I'm at 75 knots on final.

Sure, it looks like a tank, but flies easily with only moderate pressures on the yoke. Added a remote-controlled aileron trim tab this year, and the resulting lateral balance made this a hands-and-foot-free straight-tracking machine.

I find the wide wheel-track a comfort in crosswind landings. And landings are easy. When I first read that 61 to 65 knots was touchdown, I understood why people had difficulty making smooth landings in this plane. They hadn't trained in the Grumman TR-2, "the rock!" Like the TR-2, it takes a bit of power to paint on. The plane is, incidentally, placarded against slips of more than 30 seconds. I avoid slips as my Lycoming tends to go into an immediate coughing spasm in three seconds.

Insurance has run between $1,400 and $1,500 each year. Over four years, annuals ranged between $60 and $375 for an average of $240. At 1,300 hours I replaced a starter ($300). Overhauled the prop for $720. Redid the interior for $950. My numbers show about a $44/hour total cost for the first 100 hours per year.

Sure, it takes longer to fly there than in other retracts. But we've traveled 850-mile clips in a one-stop day (5.5 hours plus pit stop) and have enjoyed a roomy, com-

Owners rave about air handling on the Sierras, but concede they're almost the slowest in their class. Presumably a drag cleanup of items like the dangling nosegear would help.

fortable, broad-visibility environment. My fuel burns are around 9.6-10 gph at 75 percent and 8.5-9 gph at 65 percent.

Rudy Leeman
Antioch, Calif.

I have owned my '78 Sierra for five years. I bought it from a flight school with 900 hours on it, and it is now at TBO. I added a Precise Flight vacuum backup system and had an avionics shop put a connection in the number one nav antenna line for my Terra handheld radio.

The plane has a door on the pilot's side, and has a cargo door that is unexcelled in single-engine aircraft. The superb visibility, spacious and comfortable interior and door config- uration are the plane's greatest vir- tues. The large and easily accessible cargo area allow me a great deal of flexibility in loading.

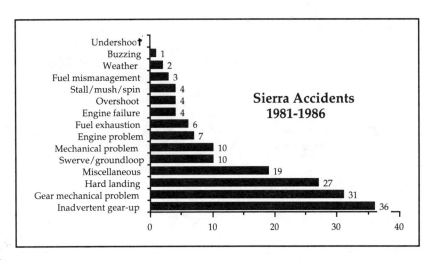

Sierra Accidents 1981-1986

Gear-up landings, gear mechanical problems, hard landings and swerve/ groundloops dominate the accident roster of the Sierra.

Although the door seals were replaced, all the doors still leak during heavy rains while tied down, and I have never accustomed myself to the smell of wet carpets. The no-nonsense flat metal instrument panel is the best overall design I have seen in a plane in this class. It makes no difference that the fuel gauges are hidden by the yoke, since they are terribly inaccurate. The plane has manual flaps and trim.

The worst aspects of the plane are the noise level and cruise speed. I know all planes are noisy, but I have never found any comfort in that fact. Ear plugs by EAR and headsets have been the solution. At 65 percent I get close to book fig- ures: 125 KTAS @ nine gph. It's an airslug. I wonder what a flap gap seal kit would do for the plane. Handling is very good and the plane makes a good IFR platform .

Maintenance, not including annuals, never runs less than $10 per hour. Annuals average around $1,500. Part of that high cost has been Beechcraft's pricing policy for parts. One piston, the door seals, landing gear actuator seals, a door window and a starter motor are some items requiring replacement since I have had the plane. If the plane were faster and the parts less expensive, I would think this Beechcraft is one of the greatest singles around. It is just too slow to stir up any excitement.

Raymond Ritter
Oakland, Calif.

I have owned a Sierra for two years and flown it for approximately 350 hours. I have had no maintenance difficulties whatsoever, outside of routine replace- ments—tires, brakes, etc. I figure on a cost of $6 per hour for annual inspection, based on 100 hours per year.

Fuel and engine gauges are in a less than optimum location at the bottom left of the panel. Note multi-style power quadrant.

I consider the Beech B24R to be a fine airplane.

Harold B. Wessels
Cypress, Calif.

I purchased a '74 Sierra in 1982 and have owned it for four years and put just over 400 hours on it.

Performance: POH is accurate for cruise. I operate at 75 percent on trips and flight plan for 135 knots and 11 gph. Endurance with full tanks is five hours at 75 percent power. The Sierra is not a particularly fast airplane, compared to the Arrow or Mooney 201, but there are other advantages.

Handling: Ground handling is very good. Visibility is terrific. In the air, the Sierra is very stable. Landing is different from most aircraft in its class. The plane is so high off the ground, and the pilot sits so upright that he is much higher when he lands than in an Arrow or 201. Also, the rubber biscuit shock absorbers will not absorb an ugly landing like an oleo. Plan on a firm arrival every time in a Sierra, and once in a while the rubber biscuits will bounce you back off the runway. I can count my real greasers on one hand in 400 hours. The Sierra is a paved-runway aircraft. I've never flown it in and out of small grass strips, but was never thrilled with the ground acceleration and climb performance.

Maintenance: The IO-360 engine is wonderful. Starts terrific, hot or cold and never misses a beat. I installed a factory reman engine and prop three months after purchase. The work was done at the Textron-Lycoming service center in Williamsport, Pa.

Incredible as it sounds, they (and I'm sure other facilities as well) will hang a $10,000 engine and $2,000 prop on your aircraft and never do a vibration analysis at running speeds. After the installation in early '83, I brought the aircraft to Summit Aviation in Delaware and found that the engine/prop assembly exceeded tolerances by four times. The vibration was so high that the people at Summit couldn't believe it. They thought the prop must have been bent. Anyway, weights were added to the spinner, and the aircraft is now incredibly smooth.

The Sierra has no AD notes of any consequence. I recently went through the nose and main gear with all new shims, bushings and biscuits and brought them up to new specs. The wear was surprising for a 1,700-hour plane, but I believe it was a result of Aero Club use and poor maintenance before I owned it. I feel the Sierra is very well built and reasonably easy to work on. Most of my maintenance headaches have been caused by cob-jobs by mechanics before I owned the plane. Comfort: This is the strongest point of the Sierra. Very roomy interior, comfortable seats, terrific visibility and more doors than you know what to do with.

The Sierra panel is very well set up and easy to use. But I don't care for the positioning of the engine gauge and fuel tank gauge. Noise is high, as in any single. The heating and ventilating system is adequate.

Parts availability and backup: Beechcraft has everything for the Sierra in stock. I've ordered lots of parts, both cosmetic and mechanical, and the factory has always had stock. As far as prices go, it's all relative. The key thing is that Beech's parts support is superb. In a number of instances my mechanic or I have had to call Beechcraft in Wichita for technical help. The people are absolutely terrific, and we've dealt with two or three different people in the last four years. They always call back when they'ved promise they will, give you as much info as you need, provide part numbers, schematics, etc. I can't say enough good about my experience with the factory.

Cost of operating works out to about $55 an hour. This includes all routing maintenance, annual, insurance, fuel, oil and T-Hangar. Reserves for engine and prop would add about $5 an hour to this figure. Normal annuals, without any major projects included, are $400.

Idiosyncrasies: Usable fuel—tanks hold 60 gallons total, but usable fuel is only 52 gallons. That is eight gallons or nearly a full hour of cruise that cannot be used. I believe this problem was straightened out in later models, but it sure is annoying to make an intermediate fuel stop when you know there are plenty of reserves sloshing around in the tanks that you can't get at.

Oil filter: There isn't one. The engine is so close to the firewall that it cannot be installed. This is ridiculous on a $38,000 airplane ('74 new cost) and a 10-grand engine. I change oil every 25 hours to compensate for the lack of the oil filter.

Landing gear: Strange is the best word I can think of. The mains fold outward and hang in what could be the cleanest part of the wing. The nosewheel pivots 90 degrees and more or less stows behind the bottom engine cowl opening. Unfortunately, the nosewheel still hangs down in the slipstream quite a bit. This must account for some of the drag on the aircraft and its slow speed.

In defense of the gear system, it is very sturdy looking (massive magnesium castings) and has the simplest emergency extension system going. Also, there is a very nice pressure switch in the pitot system that prevents retraction at low airspeed (approx. 60 mph). This prevents accidental retraction on rollout or while taxiing.

Engine cowling: The only thing that can be checked without removing the top half of the cowling is the engine oil and brake fluid. The top cowl should have been a hinged affair, like a Bonanza's.

The fifth and sixth seats are someone's idea of a joke. I threw mine out so I would never be tempted. The Sierra is a real nice four-place aircraft. Among the nice features are: two taxi lights and one landing light. You never have to worry about burning out a light bulb and landing in the dark. Quadrant style engine controls.

Huge luggage compartment and 250-pound capacity. I have a 950-pound useful load with full IFR. Landing gear lights—three green and one red transition light. No annoying door latches. All three doors open just like a car, and I've never had one come open on me. Overall, I am very happy with the Sierra.

Michael E. Capocefalo
Auburn, N.Y.

Beech T-34 Mentor

The T-34 is a Bonanza in military dress. The aircraft is legal for aerobatics. The tail is ugly but practical.

Pilots may have stopped buying new Wichita airplanes, but the demand for leftover military aircraft keeps growing. Popularly known as warbirds, these thundering nostalgia machines have attracted a devoted following among macho pilots who want noise, a sense of history and brute horsepower. But to own and fly a P-51 or the like, you've got to be both wealthy and a very sharp pilot. For most of us, a warbird is an impossible dream.

But there is such a thing as a poor-man's warbird. Earlier, we reported on the T-6, an ex-Air Force and Navy trainer available for less than $50,000. Poor man's warbird, okay, but the T-6 has handling qualities on the ground and in the air that, by general aviation standards at least, can only be described as demanding. It's not the kind of plane the typical private pilot can hop right into.

Is there a poor man's Warbird that flies like a Bonanza? You bet there is: the Beech T-34 Mentor, the Air Force/Navy trainer that replaced the T-6 in the mid-50s. The T-34, in fact, *is* a Bonanza in many respects, sharing the same wing, landing gear and fuselage parts with its V-tail stablemate. Compared to the T-6, the T-34 is more docile in the air, vastly easier to handle and see out of on the ground, cheaper to maintain, and far more frugal on fuel.

T-34s have attracted almost a cult following among their civilian pilots, who have come to prize them for their warbird appeal, aerobatic prowess, good cross-country speed, safe flying qualities and reasonable maintenance. A T-34 is not easy to find, but for the sport pilot of reasonable means, the Mentor is a tempting choice.

Genealogy

The prototype T-34, then called the Beech Model 45, made its first flight in 1948, and Beech got an FAA type certificate (in the acrobatic category) in 1950. The Air Force bought a trial batch of YT-34s for evaluation that same year, and the production model T-34A Mentor entered service with the Air Force in 1953, replacing the aging fleets of T-6s. A year later, the Navy ordered its own version, the T-34B. Numerous foreign countries also bought T-34s, and Fuji in Japan and Canadian Car & Foundry built a small number under license.

Beech production continued until 1959, at which time Beech had built a total of 1,094—423 for the Air Force, 353 for the Navy, and 318 for various foreign countries and overseas training schools.

The T-34A served for almost a decade with the Air Force, until 1961, when the Air Force switched to the T-41, a military version of the Cessna Hawk XP, for the first few hours of primary training, and then transitioned students into the T-37 jet. The Navy liked the T-34 better; it kept the -B in service until 1976, then switched to a turboprop version of the Mentor called the T-34C, currently the Navy's primary trainer. (In 1987 Beech even offered a few of these turboprops for sale to civilians, for over $1.4 million each. Not too surprisingly, there were no takers.)

There were no huge differences between the Air Force T-34A and the Navy T-34B, but the Navy did demand a few changes for the -B. Among them: a castoring nosewheel (for better maneuverability on carrier decks), a fuel selector with a "both tanks on" position (the -A had a left-right selector), a fixed seat with adjustable rudder pedals (the Air Force had it the other way round), one boost pump instead of two, and one degree more dihedral in the wings (nobody seems to recall why). In addition, the already beefy landing gear was beefed up a bit more to account for the Navy's slam-it-on style of landing.

The differences led to an interesting state of affairs over the legality of aerobatics in current civilian T-34A and -B versions. According to Charlie Nogle, president of the T-34 Assn., here's the story: the T-34A version for the Air Force was FAA-certified in the acrobatic category before the Air Force started flying it. But the T-34B was not originally FAA-certified because the Navy couldn't have cared less about the FAA. But when the T-34B was retired and some were turned over to Navy flying clubs, the Navy discovered that the planes had to be FAA-certified before the flying clubs could legally rent them out to members. So the Navy requested that Beech certify the T-34B with the FAA, as quickly and cheaply as possible. To save time, Beech recertified the aircraft in the Utility category, not Aerobatic.

As a result, if you follow the letter of the law, the T-34B today is not legal for aerobatics. But of course the -B is just as suitable for aerobatics as the -A, and everybody ignores the small print.

Incidentally, the T-34's status as an FAA-certified airplane makes insurance companies very happy. Hull and liability rates are reportedly about the same as for comparable Bonanzas.

CAP Pipeline

After their retirement from front-line duty, the T-34s scattered far and wide. Some were given to military flying clubs or to the Civil Air Patrol squadrons. Others ended up with other various government agencies like the U.S. Forest Service, which still uses them as spotter planes. Some were put in storage at Davis-Monthan AFB in Arizona. (Sadly, more than a few were simply scrapped.)

But it wasn't long before T-34s started trickling into civilian hands, usually through sales by CAP units. About 180 T-34s are currently active in the civil fleet (130 -As and 50 -Bs), with another 150 or so still in quasi-military or government hands in this country. Nearly 100 T-34Bs are currently hanging on with the Navy, either in base aero clubs or with the recruiting service, which uses them to charm prospective naval aviators. Civilian T-34 buffs wait like vultures, drooling and hoping these airplanes will eventually find their way into the civilian registry. Another 250 or so T-34s are still in service with various foreign countries, primarily in South America.

The one factor that has made the T-34 a practical civilian airplane is a very popular engine switch. The original 225-hp Continental O-470-4 or -13 engine, a military oddity that provides mediocre climb performance and for which spare parts are virtually unattainable, may be replaced with a 285-hp IO-520-B like that in the Bonanza and Baron. About 60 percent of the T-34 fleet has been converted to the 285. (More on this mod later.)

Resale Market

Apparently the number of pilots who want T-34s is somewhat larger than the 180 or so flying civilian planes, for T-34 prices have shot up dramatically in the last few years. A real showpiece T-34, with every rivet polished and a low-time 285-hp engine, can command as much as $150,000. (Our term "poor man's warbird" is relative; we mean too poor to buy a P-51.) Good solid 285-hp T-34s go in the $80,000-$100,000 range, and even a barely flyable 225-hp dog should command $40,000.

Compare those values to their civilian equivalents: a mid-50s V-tail Bonanza is generally worth only $15,000-$20,000 on today's market. Even completely updated and refurbished with a big engine, an old V-tail would bring no more than $50,000. The military warbird appeal of the T-34 triples the value of the equivalent Bonanza.

Most of that difference has come in the last few years as demand for T-34s has skyrocketed. We're told of one fellow who bought one in 1980 for about $25,000, and his friends told him he got robbed. Five years later he sold it for $85,000. That works out to an average annual return on investment of about 23 percent—a lot better than the Dow Jones index or pork belly futures."The T-34 has appreciated more than any airplane I've ever seen," according to Jeff Ethell, a warbird fanatic who took flying lessons from his dad in a T-34 when he was eight years old.

Performance

Not surprisingly, the T-34's performance is virtually the same as the equivalent Bonanza's. The 225-hp airplanes originally had a book cruise speed of 173 mph and a listed climb rate of 1,230 fpm. As was typical in those days, the numbers were pretty much a fantasy; in the real world,a 225-hp T-34 typically cruises in the 160-mph range (just like a G35), while the 285-hp jobs will top 190 mph. (One fellow who owns both a 285 T-34 and an F33A Bonanza says it's virtually a dead heat when they race side by side.)

Climb rate of the 225-hp T-34 is perhaps 800 fpm, less on a hot day when a fast, flat climb is necessary to keep the oil temperature from going off the scale. ("It's a real pooper in climb," commented one T-34 expert about the 225-hp airplane.) But the 285-hp T-34 climbs strongly, about 1,400 fpm at gross weight.

Aerobatic performance is only fair in the underpowered 225-hp airplane, and pretty good in the 285s. But in vertical maneuvers, the T-34 doesn't compare to all-out competition machines like the Pitts S-2A or Christen Eagle. Moreover, it doesn't have an inverted fuel or oil system, and can't be used for outside maneuvers. The T-34 is for fun, not competition.

Payload/Range

Fuel capacity is 50 gallons. A 225-hp T-34, burning an average of 12-13 gph, can fly three hours with a good reserve, and cover perhaps 500 miles. A 285-hp airplane with 50-gallon tanks, burning perhaps 15 gph, will have less endurance but about the same range. (STC'd tip tanks can stretch capacity to 80 gallons, but they're not legal for aerobatics, cost a bit in cruise speed and horrify the purists with their appearance.) Fuel consumption is higher during aerobatics, so endurance will be less. (Who could stand three hours of aerobatics anyway?)

Gross weight is 2,950 pounds for the -B and 2,925 for the -A version. Military empty weight was 2,170, but the typical civilian T-34 weighs about 2,250 empty. (Surprisingly, the 285-hp mod weighs *less* than the 225 by about 15 pounds.) Thus typical useful load of a T-34 is about 700 pounds. That's plenty for 50 gallons of fuel and two people.

The STC for the 285-hp engine does not allow for a gross weight increase, but a 285-hp T-34 could be safely flown many hundred pounds overweight. After all, the A36 Bonanza grosses 3,600 pounds using the same engine and landing gear, and the T-34 wing is ultra-strong. We're aware of only one T-34 in-flight breakup, which came when a couple of Navy flight instructors apparently tried to outdo each other. According to Charlie Nogle, the Navy calculated that the wing finally broke at negative 13 Gs. But such discussions of overweight flying are mostly academic; even with full fuel, two fat occupants with parachutes and the max

Visibility and ground handling of the T-34 are far superior to the T-6, another popular "poor man's warbird."

allowable baggage, all-up weight wouldn't likely exceed 3,100 pounds.

The T-34 does not have the severe aft-c.g. problems of its V-tail Bonanza clone. Two reasons: the stabilizer does a better job of stabilizing and can tolerate a more aft c.g.; and the single rear seat and 100-pound baggage limit make it hard to put much weight aft. But the Mentor pilot can't totally ignore balance. A humongous dude in the back and a 97-pound weakling in front might push the c.g. envelope.

Creature Comforts

By general aviation standards, the T-34 is spartan, but that's part of its warbird appeal. The cockpit is more compact than a T-6's, and the controls and instruments are closer at hand. "It's a lot more comfortable than a T-6," says a pilot with many hours in both. Because it was designed for a backpack parachute rather than a seatpack, the seat itself is much more comfortable. (Many civilian T-34s have been completely reupholstered.) Baggage space is not bad; there's a baggage door on the left side behind the rear seat, and one can stuff in a reasonable amount of soft luggage. (Suitcases are something else, however.) Placard limit is only 100 pounds.

The cockpit is well laid out, with no oddities like the T-6's hydraulic power switch. "It's so simple, you can fly it without a checklist," says one T-34 pilot.

First prototype T-34 (Beech called it the Model 45) flew in 1948 and was FAA-certified in 1950.

Flying Qualities

One reason for the T-34's popularity is its sweet handling. The V-tail Bonanza is known for its nice flying qualities, but the T-34 is better in almost every respect. It has none of the rudder-aileron interconnects required by today's sissy civilian FAA. The elevator is more effective and provides better pitch control—much like the straight-tail 33 Bonanzas and Debonairs. The yaw stability is much better than the V-tail's. It also has the advantage of three-axis cockpit trim.

"It's as docile as you can get," says one owner. "Easier to fly than a Bonanza. As easy to land as a Debonair. You could train somebody from zero, and they could get their license in 40 hours." Aerobatic handling is graceful, if not as ultra-quick as the competition biplanes. Roll rate is about 100-120 degrees per second, and spin recovery is quick and positive.

Engines

The Continental O-470-4 and -13 in the original T-34 are military engines not compatible with the civilian O-470s that appeared in later Bonanzas. Case, crankshaft and accessory drives are all different. ("That military O-470 is a piece of junk," commented one T-34 buff.) It's now virtually impossible to overhaul or do major repairs on a 225 engine unless you're a consummate scrounger or have engines to cannibalize. "The engine is virtually unsupportable," says Charlie Nogle. Concedes Continental's Fred Fihe, "We don't have many parts around anymore." Overhaul time of the 225-hp engine is about 1,200 hours, according to T-34 experts we queried.

The one factor that's revitalized the T-34 market and made it a practical airplane is the 285-hp engine conversion. There are two STCs, one offered by Charlie Nogle (Nogle & Black Aviation, Tuscola Airport, Tuscola, Ill. 61953, (217) 253-4342), the other by Texas T-34 maven Earl Parks (Parks Industries, Amarillo, Tex., (806) 622-0602). One T-34 buff describes Parks's place as "virtually a T-34 factory. They're perfect. Customer satisfaction is excessive." These two guys probably know more about T-34s than anybody; if one or the other can't answer a T-34 question, the answer probably doesn't exist.

The IO-520-B used in both conversions is the same engine used in thousands of late-model Bonanzas and Barons; virtually any mechanic knows how to work on one, and parts will almost certainly be available for the next few decades. Virtually the only difference between the two installation is that the Nogle engine is mounted straight, while the Parks engine is canted slightly to offset torque effect, as are the Bonanza engines.

Cost of the conversions, which include a complete firewall-forward job including prop, range from about $25,000 to $40,000, depending on the condition of the trade-in engine and whether the 285 is new, reman or just serviceable.

Both companies now also offer the 300-hp IO-550 that started showing up on Bonanzas a few of years ago. Parks pushes the 300, saying it offers more extra performance than the 15-hp difference would suggest, while Nogle soft-pedals it, saying he'll wait for a few more years of service experience on the 300 before he'll abandon the 285 entirely.

Obviously, a 285-hp T-34 is a big plus. On the marketplace, it makes about a $20,000 difference in the value of otherwise identical planes.

Safety Record

FAA data show a total of eight fatal T-34 crashes since 1980. Based on some very rough FAA hours-flown estimates, we figure a fatal accident rate of about five per 100,000 hours—a rather high rate. (Typical general aviation aircraft in this class run around two.) We counted 35 non-fatal accidents, which bring the total accident rate to about 30 per 100,000 hours—again, much higher than comparable civilian aircraft.

Among the fatal accidents, we counted three stalls or stall/spins, two weather-related crashes, two involving low-altitude aerobatics, and one aircraft that disappeared and was never found. The stall/spin crashes follow in the family tradition; the Bonanza has historically had a high rate of stall accidents, particularly the older V-tails of Mentor vintage.

Of the non-fatals, landing gear accidents predominated. About half were simple gear-up landings, the other half involved some sort of landing gear malfunctions. Rarely did they hurt anybody.

Buyer Checkpoints

Although the T-34 is basically a reliable, trouble-free airplane, as a 30-year-old machine, it has some potential for serious deterioration. T-34 experts tell us there are four major potential problems that an unsuspecting "tire-kicker" T-34 buyer might run into. Three of them involve possible corrosion—not surprising, considering the fact that virtually all T-34s have sat outside for most of their lives (at least until doting civilians took over ownership). Here's what to check for— and make sure that an experienced T-34 man, such as Charlie Nogle or Earl Parks, does the checking

• Control surfaces. The original ailerons, flaps, stabilizer, elevator, fin and rudder were magnesium. Although feather-light and strong, magnesium is simply not as durable or corrosion-resistant as aluminum, and a prudent buyer will want them all replaced. "If they're original, you're absolutely looking at replacing them," says Nogle. The ailerons, flaps, fin and stabilizer may be (and almost always are) replaced with aluminum parts, but Beech insists that the rudder and elevator be magnesium. (Hinges aren't strong enough to take the heavier aluminum ones, says Beech.) A complete replacement could cost up to $8,000.

• Wing spar and attach fitting. Intergranular corrosion has been a problem on T-34s (as well as older Bonanzas). To replace corroded parts could cost anywhere from $1,500 to $3,000, according to Nogle.

• Outer wing panel "bathtub" attach fitting. The forebear of the notorious bathtub/bolt assembly whose failure caused three King Air wing failures, the T-34 bathtub fitting is susceptible to corrosion. Replacement fittings are in short supply, and cost about $350 each. Replacement labor would be in the $600-$1,000 range.

• Landing gear system. Although the T-34 landing gear system is one of the strongest ever (it survived years of Navy student landings, and essentially the same gear is used on 6,000-pound Barons), after 30 years things can get a little raggedy. Nosegear collapses are a fairly common event in T-34s. If the gear system is worn out, a complete overhaul will run about $6,000.

Owner Group

T-34 owners are a fanatical lot who like to band together. The T-34 Association (c/o Julie Clark, 3114 Boeing Rd., Cameron Park, Calif. 95682, (415) 449-3234) has about 300 members, including about 80 percent of current T-34 owners. You'd be crazy not to join. Virtually all T-34 knowledge extant resides within the membership. If you like partying with other Mentorites, they have fly-ins. The club also sponsors an excellent formation-flying school, which is why you see so many T-34s flying around glued to each other's wingtips.

Owner Comments

I was a member of the Robins AFB, Georgia Aero Club for a number of years, and flew a T-34 that had been retired from Air Force pilot training. The club also had a 1955 F35 Bonanza, which was its contemporary (same 225-hp Continental engine), and made for an interesting comparison.

Both aircraft had the old E-225, a six-jug predecessor of the O-470. The whole cowl opened up for preflight, which was nice, but you needed a large screwdriver or a quarter to work the Dzus fasteners. Since the nosewheel retracted to the rear, the engine had a dry oil sump up on the firewall. The primer and the auxiliary fuel pumps were both electric, whereas they were both manual on the Bonanza. For some reason, only four of the six cylinders had primer ports. This was never a problem, but might be farther north. Although the plane was stressed for aerobatics, neither the engine nor the fuel system was designed for sustained inverted flight.

As far as I could tell, the wings, landing gear, engine, prop and cowl were the same on both aircraft. What was different was the tail, fuselage and cockpit. The T-34 was also a few hundred pounds heavier than the Bonanza in both empty and gross weight, and some of that went into the acro beefup. With only two seats and a tiny luggage bin under the rear seat, it was nearly impossible to load out of limits. The USAF tech manual had a prohibition about putting anything in the luggage bin for aerobatics if both seats were occupied. If you were just going cross-country, you could take a small bag or two.

A souped-up C model version with a turboprop engine remains the primary trainer for the U.S. Navy. Beech offered them for sale as civilian aircraft in 1987 on a limited basis, as shown here. But there were no takers.

The Bonanza had four tanks—two 18-gallon mains and two aux tanks that fed as one and held 15 gallons. Fuel management was a mess, with a four-position selector valve on the floor and a single gauge with two switches to select the proper tank. The T-34 was much better—two larger mains and no aux tanks, a two-position valve and two gauges. The engine had a pressure carb, and excess fuel was routed back to the left tank. You always had to use the left main for the first hour or so, to leave room for the other tank later.

It burned about 10 gph, full throttle, at 6,000 to 8,000 feet and the rpm down a few hundred from max. This gave about 160 mph in the Bonanza and 145 in the T-34. This difference was unique to our particular T-34, which didn't have nosegear doors. We never could get replacements.

Getting in was no problem, after the first stretch to the wing. The big seat was comfortable, nicely adjustable, and had a four-point belt. A sidewall storage compartment would take everything needed for a planned trip, but not a whole flight kit. If you tried to put something on the floor, it would either get lost or jam the stick. Rudder pedals could be adjusted for leg length. I'm a big guy, 6 feet 5, and I found everything within reach but not cramped. It's the nicest tandem cockpit I've been in.

Both canopies can be flown open or closed. There is, however, a stiff breeze through the rear cockpit with both canopies open. I was in rain only once, but nothing leaked. Visibility is outstanding, and so is the sunburn if you don't wear a hat.

Instrumentation was out of the Middle Ages. There were plenty of gauges, but they're scattered everywhere haphazardly. The turn needle was DC electric, the two gyros ran on 400-Hz AC from an inverter in the belly. The gyros had caging knobs for acrobatics. There was no vacuum system. It had three-axis trim, but no autopilot. All the real aircraft controls were in the front seat, with the rear controls linked through pushrods. These can wear or get loose, and therein lies the only time I've ever declared an emergency in flight. I turned on the fuel valve from the rear cockpit, but because of control rod play, the real valve in the front cockpit only turned halfway on. There was enough gas to start and taxi, but not enough for full power, and it began coughing on climbout. To make a long story short, I landed safely. Always preflight the T-34 from the front seat.

Flying the T-34 was pure delight. Any Bonanza lover would be right at home. The controls were excellent, feather-light and balanced. It did not fishtail as much as the V-tail in turbulence. Light acro (rolls, spins, whifferdills) were nice and predictable. The pressure carburetor kept it from quitting in zero-g, but you had to be sure not to stay inverted or do outside maneuvers. Landings were the same as the Bonanza, except that you were a few hundred pounds heavier and sat a foot or so higher than the usual sight picture. Spins were a bit odd—it would snap around nose low for half a turn, then turn slower with the nose almost level for the other half.

It would keep this up all day, and recover instantly. In fact, it was rather hard to teach spins in the T-34—many times it would be flying again before the student could complete the standard spin recovery procedure. I never had any problem flying the Bonanza with my left hand and the T-34 with my right. It just seemed to fit beautifully and to be a natural thing to fly.

Maintenance was a problem. We had no problem with the bits and pieces, but larger items had to be fabricated or done without. Second headache was the engine. We usually needed a jug or two between overhauls, and overhaul time was only 1,200 hours or so, I think. There were a lot of rubber hoses and vents that left a quart of oil on the belly every eight hours or so. We made the swap to Cleveland brakes, which helped that department. It seemed to eat a lot of post lights, but I never flew it much at night. Except for the antiquated avionics, it didn't seem to have any more downtime than the Bonanza. Both were well-built and sturdy.

We had a lot of discussion about whether the augmentor tube cooling contributed to short engine life. The augmentors were large annular ducts around the exhaust stacks. There were no cowl flaps, but the Bonanza with the same engine did have the flaps. I noticed maybe a 125-degree difference between full-power climbs and low-power letdowns, but in neither case did the engine temps reach extremes. With the Bonanza's cowl flaps you could keep the swing a little tighter. I believe the augmentors did help during long ground holds—you could race the engine and pump the cooling flow better. Besides, the augmentors gave a nice, throaty bellow to the exhaust sound.

In summary, I adored the airplane. My years with it were the most fun I've ever had flying, and I regret I no longer have access to one. It was a joy to fly, had good speed, and was reasonably economical for this class of airplane. It's a great utilitarian traveler if you don't have a family to haul around. If I owned one, I would sacrifice authenticity for a better panel layout and more modern systems—all DC instruments, second alternator, modern radios.

Gary Hoe
Albuquerque, N.M.

Beech 33
Debonair

Beech's Model 33, called both Debonair and Bonanza in its various versions, has emerged in the past few years as perhaps the most prestigious blue chip on the used-aircraft market. While the value of most used planes has fallen precipitously during general aviation's recent hard times, the Bonanza and Debonair have held virtually all their value. Ironically, the increasing demand for the 33 has come about mostly because of the slumping value of its V-tailed stablemate, the 35 Bonanza, due to worries about its high in-flight breakup rate. The 33, along with the larger A36 model, has become known as "the Bonanza that doesn't break up."

Used-Plane Market

The turnaround in the relative value of the V-tail and straight-tail Bonanzas has been startling. In 1979, before the V-tail's breakup record was widely known, the 35 reigned supreme. In those days, a two-year old 1977 V35B was valued at $84,000, while a 1977 F33A—identical in every way except for the tail—commanded only $77,500. By 1982, the tide had started to turn; that same 1977 V35B had dropped $15,000 to $69,000, while the F33A had lost only $10,000 and was still worth $67,500. By 1987, the V35B had declined another $5,000, to $64,000, while the F33A had *increased* in value to $73,000.

The F33A is the ultimate refinement of the 33 breed. Distinguished by the squared-off rear window, it became more sought after on the used-plane market than the classic V-tail Bonanza.

Over the entire eight-year period, the 1977 V-tail lost 24 percent of its value, while the straight-tail F33A declined just six percent. The premium price pilots used to pay for the looks and "prestige" of a V-tail now goes for the better safety of the straight-tail airplane. Whether the trend in values will change with addition of Beech's AD-mandated V-tail strengthening fix, issued in late 1987, remains to be seen.

The 33 still looks good compared to other aircraft, however. We're aware of only one late-model single or light twin that's held its resale value better than the F33A over the past five years: its big brother the A36 Bonanza. Not even the Mooney 201, a darling of the used-plane market since its introduction in 1977, can match the F33A's resale record.

Genealogy

The straight-tail 33 was an outgrowth, of course, of the original V-tail Bonanza. The V-tail was introduced back in 1947, and had the high-performance single-engine market sewed up until the late 1950s, when Piper brought out the Comanche, and Cessna introduced the 210—both at prices way below the Bonanza's.

Rather than lower the price of its cherished prestige flagship, Beech fought back against the 210 and Comanche with the model 33—an "economy" Bonanza without the distinctive V-tail and with a 225-hp engine instead of the Bonanza's then-250 hp. To avoid sullying the Bonanza's regal moniker by association with a less expensive airplane, Beech named the new economy model the Debonair. It debuted in 1960. List price of that first Model 33 was $19,995, about the same as the Comanche and a bit less than the 210. (The "real" Bonanza listed at $25,300.)

Efficiency-minded connoisseurs prefer the later 225-hp versions. Autogas is an option. This is a C33.

Beech lost little time refining the Debonair. The A33, introduced in 1961, featured a small third cabin window in the rear, and a hat shelf behind the baggage compartment. Gross weight was increased 100 pounds, from 2,900 to 3,000 pounds. In 1962, the B33 was fitted with the standard 74-gallon Bonanza fuel tanks, a big advantage over the previous four-tank system, which had less capacity (63 gallons) and required dangerously arcane fuel management procedures. (More on this in the Safety section.) The B33 also had a much-improved instrument panel, along with a fillet in the vertical fin to give it a more flowing look. Since the B33 is the oldest model with the big tanks, higher gross weight and the new panel, some owners consider the 1962-1964 models the best bargain of all the 225-hp Debonairs.

With the C33 in 1965 came a couple of cosmetic changes: a larger third window and a still sleeker dorsal fin. Gross weight was bumped up another 50 pounds to 3,050 while convenience features like rear bucket seats (no more bench), a new ram's-horn control wheel, a bigger hatshelf and an improved heater were added. The E33 and F33 (vintage 1968 and 1970) had no significant changes, except the dropping of the name "Debonair." At last, the 225-hp straight-tail airplane was officially welcomed into the "Bonanza" brotherhood.

In 1966, Beech decided to add another Debonair to the line. In addition to the 225-hp C33, it introduced the 285-hp C33A—essentially a full-fledged "big" Bonanza with a straight tail instead of a V-tail. (For psychological and marketing reasons, however, the straight-tail airplane carried a slightly lower price tag.)

To add to the nomenclature confusion, Beech also called the C33A a Debonair until 1968, when it changed the name of the 285-hp airplane to Bonanza as well. Also in 1968, it introduced a short-lived aerobatic 285-hp version called the E33C. Both the aerobat and the 225-hp airplane were phased out in 1970. By 1971, there was only one standard-body straight-tail Bonanza: the 285-hp F33A. (The stretched 36 Bonanza had been introduced in 1968, but that's another story.)

The "economy" Bonanza made a brief comeback in 1972-1973, however, with the 260-hp G33, but from 1974 on, only the F33A remained. By this time, Beech had abandoned the pretense that the V-tail was somehow more desirable, and it set the prices of the V-tail V35B and straight-tail F33A exactly the same. Throughout the 1970s, the V-tail outsold the straight-tail by about a two-to-one margin, but in 1980, shortly after the V-tail breakup controversy became public, the F33A pulled even in the sales race, and in 1981 and 1982, the F33A outsold the V35B by two-to-one. The V-tail, soundly repudiated in the marketplace, was laid to rest in 1983, while the

F33A continues in production.

Performance

The 33 series, in the Bonanza tradition, has excellent performance. The 225-hp airplanes will cruise at 170-180 mph on 11.5 to 12 gph, while the more powerful 285-hp models will top 190 mph on about 15 gph. (If the plane has been modified with the Smith Speed Conversion, an aerodynamic slick-up mod, these speeds will increase by 15-20 mph.

Rate of climb is listed at about 900 fpm for the various 225-hp models and about 1,200 fpm for the 285-hp versions. Not surprisingly, the 260-hp G33s fall in the middle, at 1,060 fpm. As with most aircraft, in the real world, these figures are rarely matched, but pilots and owners report strong climbing abilities under most conditions. The 225-hp airplanes, however, are sometimes judged wanting in high-altitude climb and high-density-altitude takeoffs.

Again, climb performance is substantially improved with the Smith Speed Conversion.

Payload-Range

Standard useful load of the 225-hp Debonairs is about 1,200 pounds, but a well-equipped IFR airplane would have about 1,000 pounds available for payload and fuel. With the 74-gallon tanks full, payload is only about 550 pounds—three average people and not much baggage. Because of the limited loading, says one Debonair pilot, "All Deb owners habitually overload their aircraft, especially those planes with the large tanks." The small-tank (50 gallons) A33 has an extra 120 pounds' payload with full fuel, but the straight 33, with its lower gross weight, is comparable to the B33 and later airplanes in full-fuel payload (with less fuel, of course).

The 285-hp Debonairs have enough extra load-carrying ability to make them four-pax-plus-luggage airplanes from the poundage standpoint. But watch the center of gravity! The entire Bonanza series is notorious for its limited c.g. envelope, and the stretched A36 model was developed primarily to solve this problem. The 33 series has a wider c.g. envelope than the otherwise-identical V-tails (the straight tail does a better job of stabilizing and therefore permits more aft loading), but the 33s are still somewhat limited. In most cases, it's simply not legally possible to put two adults in the rear seats and a bunch of bags in back.

The balance situation is complicated by the fact that all fuel is carried in front of the c.g. As fuel burns off, c.g. shifts aft. That means that for takeoff on a long flight, a Debonair must be well forward of the rear limit to account for the aft shift as fuel burns off.

Handling Qualities

The Bonanza series has always been a pilot's favorite. The handling is delightfully quick and smooth in the air, with controls well harmonized in all three axes. "My Debonair is the best-flying airplane I've ever flown," crows one typical owner.

But the other side of the "light and responsive" coin is poor stability in IFR conditions. As one Debonair owner put it, "The model 33 is not a particularly good instrument airplane. The same qualities that make it such a pleasure to fly turn it into a handful on instruments. It has almost neutral stability, and one must devote a great deal of attention to just controlling the aircraft. If any serious instrument flying is anticipated, a reliable autopilot should be a high priority."

The 33 is not particularly stable in the yaw mode, although it does not have the stomach-wrenching Dutch roll in turbulence that the V-tail has.

Landings are particularly easy in the Debonairs; most pilots agree that the Deb has an excellent combination of handling qualities and landing-gear geometry. However, a 1966 NASA "secret" report on the handling qualities of various general aviation aircraft criticized the A33 Debonair it tested for poor lateral stability in the landing configuration. NASA test pilots also criticized the A33 for awkward crosswind takeoffs because of the rudder-aileron interconnect.

The 33s, like the 35s, stall rather sharply, particularly with gear and flaps down and power on. Watch the go-arounds and base-to-final turns. However, the 33 is apparently not so violent as the 35; the NASA test pilots criticized the V-tail's stall traits in the 1966 report but found no fault with the A33's.

Fuel selector is in a less than ideal location below the pilot's left knee.

Cabin and Cockpit

Bonanzas have won fame for their roomy, airy cabins, and the 33 model is no exception. There's so much headroom that a pilot of average height looks like a midget from the outside. Forward visibility is excellent out the panoramic windshield, and, in the later models with the three large cabin windows, out the sides as well. Noise is about average for this class of aircraft—that is to say terribly noisy.

The 285-hp Debonair has been listed as a six-seater, but this was an optimistic delusion of the sales department. The optional fifth and sixth seats are tiny and claustrophobic, and are virtually impossible to use because of c.g. restrictions anyway. Unless you have four little kids to haul around, consider all the 33s to be strictly four-place airplanes.

The B33 and earlier 225-hp models have old-fashioned bench-type rear seats, but they are surprisingly roomy and not really a liability from the practical standpoint.

From the pilot's point of view, the 33 line has the traditional Bonanza ergonomic quirks. A single throw-over control wheel was standard equipment on the Debonairs, although many have been fitted with optional dual controls. The massive control bar connecting the yoke or yokes to the center control column can block the pilot's view of parts of the panel and get in the way of the engine controls.

In the older models, the mixture knob is located below the throttle instead of to the right of the prop control, as in most airplanes. And the landing gear and flap switches are reversed from their normal positions in most aircraft, a quirk that has caused many embarrassing (and expensive) gear retractions on the ground. (During the years 1974-78, in fact, inadvertent gear retractions were the leading cause of non-fatal accidents in 225-hp Debonairs.) These quirks aside, however, the post-1963 Debonairs have generally good instrument panel layouts.

The fuel selector is less than ideal, located low on the cockpit side wall by the pilot's left knee. Thus, to switch tanks, a pilot must crane his neck and reach down in a rather awkward cross-hand manner. Also, there is no "both" position on the selector, which assures that the pilot will be switching tanks at least once during a long trip. (From the safety point of view, the less tank-switching a pilot has to do, the better.)

Operating Costs

Fuel efficiency of the Debonairs is good, with fuel costs running from $25 to $30 per hour. (That's figuring gas at $2 per gallon.) Owners of 225-hp Debonairs can cut their fuel costs dramatically, however, by using auto fuel. With the proper STC paperwork (available for $112.50 from Petersen Aviation, Rte. 1, Box 18, Minden, Neb. 68959, 308-832-2200) it's entirely legal to use either lead-free or leaded regular autogas in the 225-hp airplanes, which normally burn 80-octane avgas.

Engine overhaul reserve amounts to about $6 per hour for both the 225-hp and 285-hp models. (Oddly, the smaller IO-470 costs very nearly as much to overhaul as the bigger IO-520.) Count on about $9,500 to overhaul the smaller engine and $10,250 for the bigger one; the 285-hp powerplants have 1,700-hour TBOs, compared to 1,500 hours for the 470s.

Adding it all up, assuming 200 hours per year, operating costs—excluding maintenance—should run from $40 to $50 per hour. Whether *total* operating costs end up at $50 or $100 per hour depends, of course, on the unpredictable and potentially heavy maintenance bills.

Maintenance

According to owner reports and conversation with mechanics, Debonair maintenance costs can run from pretty low to pretty outrageous—depending on hourly utilization, the owner's mechanical aptitude and blind luck. While the well-proven, solidly built airframe has stood up well over time, three potential bugaboos haunt the Debonair owner: cracking crankcases, leaking fuel bladders, and Beech's high parts prices.

Assuming nothing major goes wrong—and in many cases it doesn't—Debonair annuals are reasonable. "Annual inspections run around $400 unless additional parts and labor are required," said one owner. "To date (I've owned it three years) there have have been no surprises at annual time." The owner put his total

Cost/Performance/Specifications

Model	Year	Average Retail Price	Cruise Speed (kts)	Useful Load (lbs)	Fuel Std/Opt (gals)	Engine	TBO (hrs)	Overhaul Cost
33	1960	$25,500	156	1,170	44/63	225-hp Cont. IO-470-K	1,500	$9,500
A33	1961	$27,500	161	1,250	44/63	225-hp Cont. IO-470-K	1,500	$9,500
B33	1962-64	$31,000	161	1,170	44/74	225-hp Cont. IO-470-K	1,500	$9,500
C33	1965-67	$36,000	161	1,170	44/74	225-hp Cont. IO-470-K	1,500	$9,500
C33A	1966-67	$43,250	174	1,525	44/74	285-hp Cont. IO-520-B	1,700	$10,300
E33	1968-69	$41,000	161	1,200	44/74	225-hp Cont. IO-470-K	1,500	$9,500
E33A	1968-69	$46,000	174	1,375	44/74	285-hp Cont. IO-520-B	1,700	$10,300
E33C	1968-69	$44,000	174	1,380	44/74	285-hp Cont. IO-520-B	1,700	$10,300
F33	1970	$42,500	161	1,375	44/74	225-hp Cont. IO-470-K	1,500	$9,500
G33	1972-73	$49,000	168	1,365	44/74	250-hp Cont. IO-470-N	1,500	$10,300
F33A	1970-72	$52,500	174	1,400	44/74	285-hp Cont. IO-520-K	1,700	$10,300
F33A	1973-75	$61,500	174	1,400	44/74	285-hp Cont. IO-520-B	1,700	$10,300
F33A	1976-78	$73,000	174	1,400	44/74	285-hp Cont. IO-520-B	1,700	$10,300
F33A	1979-81	$91,000	174	1,400	44/74	285-hp Cont. IO-520-B	1,700	$10,300
F33A	1982-84	$114,000	174	1,400	44/74	285-hp Cont. IO-520-B	1,700	$10,300
F33A	1985-87	$142,000	174	1,400	44/74	285-hp Cont. IO-520-B	1,700	$10,300

maintenance cost at an extraordinarily low $2 per hour. Others disagree. "Maintenance costs are very high, if not exorbitant," writes one. "We try to keep everything working, and that costs a lot." Echoes another, "The Debonair is not a high-maintenance airplane, but it *is* expensive to maintain. This is because...anything purchased from Beech is outrageously expensive." Another owner reports maintenance costs of about $13 per hour, and this seems to be fairly typical.

The massive connecting bar is the penalty imposed by dual controls, in place of the standard throw-over wheel. It shields some panel controls.

Cracking crankcases have been a continuing problem in the 285-hp Debonairs (along with many other aircraft). The so-called "heavy" cases introduced in the mid-1970s didn't help much, and cracks continue to crop up despite all manner of design and material changes over the years. Case cracks usually aren't immediately dangerous, and small ones can be lived with until overhaul, at which time the crack can be welded up and the case heat-treated. (Cost: typically, $500-$700.) If the crack is bad enough to ground the plane (an AD sets out the guidelines), an owner faces two expensive options: overhaul the engine prematurely (about $9,000, plus the cost of case repair) or completely disassemble the engine and repair the case ($4,000 or so, mostly for assembly/disassembly labor and the extra new parts required when the engine is put back together again).

Moral for F33A shoppers: check with microscopic care for crankcase cracks.

Fuel bladders are another weak spot in the Debonairs. The Goodyear tanks in older airplanes are particularly prone to cracking; Uniroyal bladders are a better bet, experience has shown. If the bladders do develop leaks, the tab can be $2,000 or more for replacement, according to owners. The 33 and A33 with the four-tank systems have an even bigger potential for disaster.

Another Goodyear product—the brakes on early models—are also short-lived and trouble-prone. Many Debonair owners have replaced them with Cleveland brakes, which have proved superior. Look for Clevelands on any Debonair you buy, or anticipate putting them on soon.

The 225-hp models are susceptible to lead-fouling of the spark plugs if 100-octane fuel is used instead of the 80-octane the engine was designed for. (Even "low-lead" 100 has four times the lead of 80 octane.) If 80 is unavailable, get autogas certification and try unleaded auto fuel.

Beech parts prices are the demon that haunts any Debonair owner. The buyer of a new $200,000 A36 may not balk at a $2,000-plus price tag for a control wheel yoke assembly, but that amounts to nearly 10 percent of the value of a 1961 A33. That's the problem with new replacement parts—they cost the same whether the plane is old or new, cheap or expensive.

Safety

Here's the best news: the 33 series has the lowest fatal accident rate of any single-engine retractable, according to *The Aviation Consumer* statistics for the period 1972-81. The 33's fatal rate was only 1.4 per 100,000 flight hours, compared to an average of 2.3 for 16 other single-engine retractables. (The Cessna 210, for example, had a fatal rate of 2.3; the Mooney M20J 2.4. The Piper Comanche had a rather high 2.9.)

By comparison, the late-model V-tail Bonanzas (1964 and later) had a fatal rate of 1.7, and the older V-tails (1947-63) a rather terrible 3.3.

The B33, circa 1962-64, is recognizable by the small rear window. Though cabin length was modest, it still shared the broad cabin width and excellent fenestration of the Bonanza line.

Where the straight-tail 33 really shines is in-flight breakups. An *Aviation Consumer* study for the years 1977-1983 shows that the 33 (and 36) have a break-up rate just one-tenth of the V-tail's. We're aware of only three in-flight breakups of 33 series Beeches, compared to more than 200 for the V-tails.

The reasons for this big difference aren't entirely clear. The 33 has slightly better pitch stability and heavier pitch forces than the 35, and so may be less prone to pilot loss of control and overstress. The straight tail also provides slightly better lateral stability, reducing the tendency to enter a "graveyard spiral" in instrument conditions. The straight tail also gives better yaw stability, reducing Dutch roll gyrations in turbulence.

Another possibility: the straight tail is simply stronger and stays intact through all manner of high-speed dives, pullouts and turbulence that may break a V-tail. The V-tail, of course, was the focus of an AD requiring a strengthening kit in 1987 on many models, if owners wished to resume normal speeds. Earlier, the FAA required all V-tail Bonanza pilots to slow down pending research into what kind of improvements were needed to reduce the relatively high rate of in-flight airframe failures the airplane was experiencing.

Although they have an excellent overall record, the early Debonairs have a quirk or two to watch out for. Pre-1970 models had no baffles in the fuel tanks, which allowed fuel to slosh away from the fuel line pickup in slips, skids or during fast turns on the ground (such as those preceding a hurried takeoff).

Beech was aware of the fuel unporting syndrome (which affected Debonairs, Bonanzas and Barons) as far back as 1961. It issued a service letter warning that a turning-type takeoff could result in a "momentary power interruption" at "about the same time the airplane becomes airborne." The letter assured owners that "...this does not create a hazard."

But the FAA identified 16 fuel-unporting accidents by 1971 and issued an AD prohibiting takeoffs with tanks less than a quarter full. Beech installed baffles in 1971 and later models and retrofit kits for the older airplanes, but few have been retrofitted. We'd consider the fuel tank baffles a must in any Debonair considered for purchase. The early Bonanzas had a bad record of fuel mismanagement accidents, and the early 33 and A33 Debonairs have similar fuel systems, with multiple tanks that require lots of switching, an out-of-the-way fuel selector that's hard to see and a gauging system that makes it easy to read the wrong tank.

Modifications

When it comes to airframe and cosmetic mods, Debonair owners are in hog heaven. Literally dozens of mods are available to make an old Debbie look new: windows, windshields, panels, spinners, interiors, etc. Chief purveyor of Debonair cosmetic mods is Beryl D'Shannon Aviation Specialties, P.O. Box 840, Lakeville, Minn. (612) 469-4783.

The aforementioned Smith Speed Conversion includes a series of detail aerodynamic improvements that typically improve cruise speed by 15-20 mph. Smith also offers a modified cowling that is claimed to improve cooling, cut drag and allow better engine breathing for more power at high altitudes. Mike Smith Aero, Stanton County Airport, Box 430, Johnson City, Kans. (316) 492-6840.

Bonanza Society

One of the most active of the owner groups is the American Bonanza Society, P.O. Box 12888, Wichita, Kans. (316) 945-6913. The ABS publishes a monthly newsletter with technical info and how-to tips, along with the usual rah-rah stuff about members' creampuff planes. While the ABS is sometimes timid about confronting safety problems head-on (it likes to maintain good rapport with Beech), the club is still a good source of info and a good bet for any 33 owner. (Yes, the Bonanza boys do allow straight-tail owners to join their ranks.)

Owner Comments

The bigger rear window first appeared in 1965 on the C33 model. It can be easily retrofitted to older aircraft.

I have had a Model 33 for six years. I usually fly it at 60 percent power using 2300 rpm. It uses 10.8 to 11.2 gph and trues out about 135 knots. As you can see, it doesn't come up to the handbook data, but it is a sturdy, comfortable but noisy bird. Annuals run $600 to $900. The original 600 x 6 tires were replaced with 700 x 6, and their life is considerably longer, with no clearance problems. The tail does waggle like the V-tail, but by holding the rudder so it doesn't move, you can stop the waggle. (The same technique worked on the V-tail I had before the Debonair.)

Of the light aircraft I've flown, the 33 has the best visibility, and as far as I'm concerned is the safest and best-built of the lot

Newton Kerr
Olmstead, Ohio

A year and a half ago, I purchased a 1962 B33 with 1,600 hours total time and 350 hours on a chrome major. The Deb is one of the smoothest planes I've ever flown. It's a good instrument ship as long as you're wide awake, stay ahead of the airplane and maintain proficiency. Load-carrying and range (over

1,000 nm) are good as long as you realize that the c.g. moves aft as fuel burns off. My Deb has the speed-slope windshield and aileron gap seals, and I have removed the step. I climb and cruise better than book numbers, 180 mph cruise on 12 gph or less. Stall speed with everything hanging out is 50 mph indicated. I wonder what's being built this year that will match it in speed, range, comfort and safety record?

Cost of operation runs about $25 per hour for gas, a quart of oil every six hours, $1,000 a year for insurance, $400 for annuals. In 200 hours and 19 months, the only problems have been with the prop control and propeller lubrication. My only complaint is a universal one: the high cost of Beech parts.

Raymond McDonald
Ferndale, Wash.

My partner and I have owned a 1964 B33 Debonair since October 1981. It's been a pleasure to own and fly, providing us with 200 to 300 hours a year of safe, reliable transportation.

Beech Debonair Resale Value

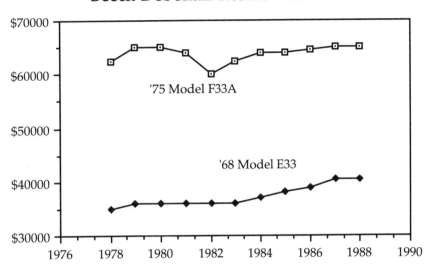

Because of the quick and smooth roll characteristics, an autopilot is recommended for serious IFR flying. The Deb can be a handful in turbulence. We can carry four passengers and baggage for as long as we're able and still have a reserve. Rear c.g. is the only thing to watch carefully, as the c.g. shifts to the rear as fuel burns off. We count on burning 12 gph while averaging 165 mph.

In 1984 we flew 318 hours with maintenance costs of $13 per hour for mechanical and only $1.00 per hour for radios. Our annual ran an additional $500, which is typical unless we let some things go until the annual. The 1968 Cherokee 180D I owned previously cost about the same amount per mile to operate. Our insurance runs $1,018 per year for $30,000 hull and $2 million liability.

As far as the IO-470-K engine goes, it has been all routine so far. We have 1,200 hours on it and expect to get TBO without a problem. We run platinum plugs to avoid the lead-fouling problems we have with 100 LL gas. We are now considering the autogas STC. Leaky exhaust gaskets have always been a problem. We recently had all the studs removed and the cylinder seats resurfaced, and that has solved the problem so far. Oil consumption is about a quart every two or three hours because of improper break-in.

Like most Beech owners, we have many mods, including one-piece windshield, Beryl side windows, Beryl rear air exhaust, Cleveland brakes, three-inch gyros, alternator and instrument post lighting.

Gary Otto
Duluth, Ga.

Three partners and I own a 1966 C33. We spent $10,000 on it in 1982 for a complete firewall-forward overhaul, including propeller.

Performance has been by the book in all phases of operation. We consistently get 158-160-knot cruise speeds at 6,000 to 8,000 feet with fuel burn of 13.5-14.0 gph. I try to lean the mixture to about 25-50 degrees on the rich side of peak EGT.

I find the Deb very enjoyable to fly, with light, harmonized controls. Longitudinal stability is adequate, whereas lateral/directional stability is somewhat weak. The cabin is as comfortable as anything in its class. The only problem I've found is that the landing gear geometry leaves a very lightly loaded nosewheel if the plane is near the aft end of the c.g. envelope. There have been times when I thought the tail would hit the ground. (It hasn't actually happened yet.)

After 19 years and 3,100 hours on my aircraft, Beech quality is apparent. Other than spark plugs, batteries, tires and brakes, we've had very few mechanical expenses. Checking the numbers for the past 300 hours of operation, the average hourly cost works out to about $41 (not including avionics or reserve for overhaul). Maintenance accounts for about $2 of this figure. Annual inspections run around $400, plus whatever parts and extra labor are required beyond the inspection.

Sturdy gear and door are testimony to traditional Beech high gear-lowering speeds.

Jerry Jordan
Leawood, Kans.

As an airline pilot with extensive general aviation background, I believe the Beech 33 is the most satisfying cross-country single-engine airplane I've ever flown. The early Debonair provides an outstanding combination of economy and performance. The Continental IO-470 engine at 65 percent power will burn 11.5 gph at 10,000 feet and give an honest 150 knots. I flight-plan one gallon of fuel for every five minutes of flight time, and can usually tell the line person how much fuel the tanks will hold to within half a gallon.

The Debonair is a real four-place airplane. My full-IFR airplane will *legally* carry four 170-pound adults, 100 pounds of luggage and 50 gallons of fuel (full tanks in my plane), enough for three hours plus a reserve. That's as long as I can stand to sit in a light airplane cabin, anyway. VFR, I plan 500-mile legs. IFR, I would like to have more fuel capacity. Factory-installed aux tanks on the early 1960-61 models are of limited value because they only added about 20 gallons but increased weight substantially. The Flight Extender tip tanks made by Beryl are a better choice.

Cabin comfort improves with each year up to about 1967. In my plane, ventilation is better than a Comanche, but not nearly as good as a 210. Visibility is excellent. Noise level is average (high).

The Model 33 is not a particularly good instrument airplane. The same qualities that make it such a pleasure to fly visually make it a handful on instruments. It has almost neutral stability, and one must devote a great deal of attention to just controlling the aircraft. If any serious instrument flying is anticipated, a reliable autopilot should be a high priority.

Beech
Bonanza 35, 36

The word "legend" is tossed around rather freely when people talk about airplanes, but the Beechcraft Bonanza probably has a better claim to legendary status than any other modern lightplane. Unfortunately, this has both good and bad connotations, because the V-tail models have been the focus of sharp controversy.

A decades-long record of calamitous inflight airframe breakups attached a strong stigma to the line that culminated in a premature halt to production in 1982. Eventually, flight and wind tunnel testing was undertaken by Beech Aircraft Corp. that showed the aircraft had insufficient tail strength. The FAA mandated a beef-up operation in 1987, and Beech launched a program to supply parts for the entire V-tail fleet at no cost to owners.

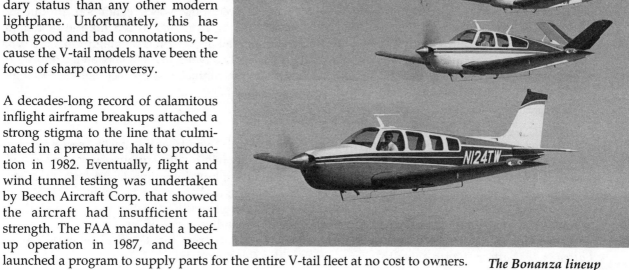

The Bonanza lineup shows the 35 in the center, with the 33 on top and the 36 at the bottom of the echelon. The 36 series was stretched 10 inches ahead of the wing, greatly reducing rear c.g. problems and the tail-waggle of the V-tail.

History

The Bonanza was the first high-performance post-war design (it was introduced in 1947). Some models have been in continuous production since then, and despite the rocky history of the line are still considered by many to be the best single-engine airplanes flying.

The Bonanza's astonishing success is the result of generally excellent performance, sleek good looks, responsive handling and a "Mercedes of the air" image. The loading limitations, high parts prices, cracking crankcases (and, of course, inflight airframe failures by the V-tail models) are not part of that image, however.

For many years, the Bonanza enjoyed a blue-chip reputation on the used-plane market. Because of high demand and huge inflationary price increases of new Bonanzas during the 1970s, it was routine for a decade-old Bonanza to be worth more than its new selling price. Owners reported paying top dollar for a used Bonanza, then selling it a few years later at a profit.

But the V-tail version of the airplane in the 1980s suffered a sharp decline in value because of the aforementioned record of inflight breakups. Before the beef-up program was begun, a V-tail was worth about 10 percent less than an equivalent straight-tail 33 Bonanza. A few years earlier the reverse was true. The generally bearish used-plane market of the mid-80s has hurt resale value of virtually all other aircraft, but the 33 series has taken over from the 35 the role as one of the best resale investments among light aircraft.

A prospective Bonanza buyer should carefully examine his motivation for buying. On a coldly rational cost-effective basis, a used Cessna 210 or Piper Comanche may often provide more airplane per dollar. But pilots seem to be more impressed by macho appeal, plush interiors and the "feel" of the airplane. In this realm the Bonanza is supreme.

Models

There is a bewildering variety of Bonanza models. There are three basic types: the Model 35, the classic V-tail form of the aircraft that was in continuous production from 1947 until 1982, with power ranging from 185 to 285 hp; the model 33, introduced in 1960 with a conventional tail and engines ranging from 225 to 285 hp; and the Model 36, a stretched six-seat conventional-tail version introduced in 1968 with a 285-hp engine. Adding to the confusion is the fact that the 33 model was called the Debonair for seven years.

Engines

The V-35B is the culmination of the line, incorporating a large series of structural changes. Production was halted in 1982 after inflight breakups cast a pall on the design.

Early Bonanzas up through the G35 in in 1956 had Continental "E" series engines. Although the powerplants are reasonably reliable, the supply of parts and knowledgeable mechanics for these engines is rapidly dwindling. Continental no longer makes remanufactured E series engines, and there are no more crankcases or crankshafts being made. Other parts are generally available, but rapidly becoming more expensive as production dwindles. Cost of an overhaul for an old Bonanza is about $11,000, a hefty fee considering that the airplane itself may be worth only $15,00 or so, even with a fresh overhaul.

Later Bonanzas have either the IO-470 or IO-520 Continental engines. Prior to 1970, both these engines were rated at 1,200 hours TBO. In 1970 the valves were improved, and TBO went up to 1,500 hours. Older engines overhauled with the better valves also have the 1,500-hour TBO. This, of course, should be a checkpoint for buyers.

Cracking Cases

Literally thousands of Bonanza owners have suffered the "Curse of the Cracking Crankcases," either directly or indirectly because of overhaul considerations. The cracking problem is not a safety issue, but an economic one because of the cost of welding repair, or replacement of the case, at about $6,000 a shot. And of course this doesn't factor in the inconvenience and downtime. In 1977 the matter came to a head with issuance by the FAA of an airworthiness directive (77-13-22), that mandated inspection of so-called light-case IO-520, TSIO-520 and GTSIO-520 engines for cracks every 100 hours. This is still in effect and includes both sandcast and Permold cases. The Permold cases have the alternator mounted in front; the sandcast in the rear.

Continental began producing heavy-case engines in 1976, and although they are not prey to the repetitive-inspection AD, they have turned out to be at least as prone to cracking as the light cases. Therefore, wise owners (or prospective buyers) should check for cracks. The heavy cases can be easily identified because they have bumps along the top spine where bolts join the halves. The light case juncture is smooth and level on top. If cracks occur, the case need not necessarily be junked or sent out for welding. It depends on the location and length of the crack. Cracks in the top portion of the case shorter than two inches can be kept in service. Stop-gap measures are stop-drilling and applying epoxy.

History in the making: Walter and Olive Ann Beech check out the early Bonanza 35 in 1947.

However, if the cracks are in critical lower areas, the cases must be replaced or repaired. Some relief is available from the engine manufacturer in the form of pro-rata coverage on cracked cases. This happily is in effect no matter what the age of the engine. So the owner can get a discount on a new (meaning remanufactured) case equal to the percentage of the TBO time remaining. Furthermore, the core penalty is disregarded on the damaged trade-in.

On the other hand, in an overhaul, light-case engines carry an extra penalty to the owner because a lot of shops will refuse to do the job without replacing the cases with heavy ones—at a big surcharge.

As if crankcase cracking weren't enough of a problem all by itself, IO- and TSIO-520 engines have been hit by a scary number of crankshaft failures. It turned out that certain cranks made between 1965 and 1977 had subsurface defects. Unfortunately, there was no way to identify the engines which received the potentially defective crankshafts. Continental issued service bulletins telling owners to have ultrasonic inspections of crankshafts in certain serial number engines at overhaul time or when teardown occurs. The engines of greatest risk are ones built before 1978. Improved cranks were introduced with engines that have a suffix "B," such as IO-520-BB and IO-520-CB.

Maintenance Problems

Two other major Bonanza maintenance checkpoints are shared with various other aircraft: the Hartzell prop AD and the leaking Goodyear rubber fuel tanks. The prop AD—which applies only to IO-520-powered Bonanzas—generally costs $1,000.

The fuel tank AD is not as expensive in most cases, since only an inspection is required. However, if a leak is discovered, replacement can be costly. There is no consistent pattern, but most Bonanzas built between 1961 and 1975 are subject to the Goodyear AD. All Bonanzas have rubber bladder tanks of some sort, and their life expectancy is six to eight years. Replacement cost can run between $1,500 and $2,500, depending on the model.

Several *Aviation Consumer* readers also mentioned vacuum-pump failures, and the Airborne pumps used in many Bonanzas have a poor record. Failure of the vacuum pump in IFR conditions, of course, can be unpleasant.

Safety

The Bonanza's overall safety record is generally good—with a couple of important exceptions. According to *Aviation Consumer* studies of NTSB and FAA statistics for the period 1972-1976, the 33 and 36 have excellent records. The 33, in fact, has one of the lowest fatal accident rates of any single-engine airplane, and the 36 is not far behind.

The V-tail 35 model is another story. Newer V-tails, including the 1964 S model and later models, all with 285-hp engines, have a reasonably good fatal accident rate, but the older models rank very poorly, with a fatal accident rate nearly twice as high as the later V-tails and nearly quadruple that of the 33 series.

The prototype Bonanza flew in 1945 with a 165-hp engine. When it went into production in 1947, power had been raised to 185 hp. The early models have a serious wing strength deficiency if not upgraded with a Beech kit.

Inflight Breakups

A major reason for the poor fatal accident rate of the older V-tails is the relatively high rate of fatal inflight airframe failures in those models. Over the years, there have been over 230 Bonanza inflight breakups, in which some 500 people have died.

Worst of the pack is the original "straight" 35. This model has insufficient wing strength because it lacks a web shear in the outer wing, unless it has been beefed up with a Beech retrofit. And very few models in the field were upgraded because of the high expense. We therefore strongly recommend buyers avoid this model. In our opinion it is one of the most dangerously understrength airplanes in the skies and ranks with the Cessna 411 as a hot potato to regard with extreme caution.

What makes the V-tail's high record of inflight breakups all the more ironic is the very low breakup rate for the straight-tail 33 and 36 models, which are essentially identical to the 35 except for the tail. The V-tail breakup rate has been approximately 24 times higher than the straight-tail's through the years.

Handling Qualities

The V-tail airplane has very light ailerons and low lateral stability—what test pilots call high spiral divergence. Once a wing drops a little, it tends to keep going. In instrument weather and turbulence, this low rolling stability can put the pilot into the "graveyard spiral" quickly.

The V-tail models are also very light on the controls in the pitch axis. This low longitudinal stability means turbulence or pilot inattention will cause larger, quicker airspeed and altitude excursions. The light controls also mean that just a moderate pull on the wheel results in a sharp pull-up and high g-forces.

The V-tail Bonanza's low longitudinal stability is exacerbated by the rather narrow center-of-gravity envelope. (Some models even have 30 pounds of lead in the nose to counter the balance problem.) With any passengers in the back seat, a V-tail Bonanza can be very close to its aft c.g. limit, and it's not uncommon for V-tails to be flown illegally beyond their aft limit.

An aft c.g. further reduces the V-tail's already low longitudinal stability, making the airplane even more sensitive in pitch and making wheel forces even lighter.

The low stability in the roll and pitch axes can team up against the pilot. A typical scenario: pilot looks down at chart while gust drops right wing. Airplane begins rolling to the right, simultaneously dropping the nose and picking up speed. Pilot looks up from chart, notes very high airspeed, and pulls back on the wheel abruptly. Airplane pulls six gs and breaks off the wings or tail.

The aircraft also has very poor Dutch roll characteristics in turbulence, manifested in the form of the famous "Bonanza waggle." One not inexpensive, but effective antidote is installation of an electronic yaw damper.

The throw-over control wheel was innovative but awkward for dual training or copiloting. Power controls and gear/ flap controls are placed unconventionally.

Cost/Performance/Specifications

Model	Year	Average Retail Price	Cruise Speed (kts)	Useful Load (lbs)	Fuel Std/Opt (gals)	Engine	TBO (hrs)	Overhaul Cost
35	1947-48	$15,000	150	1,092	39/60	185-hp Cont. E-185-1	1,500	$10,800
A35	1949	$15,500	148	1,075	39/60	185-hp Cont. E-185-1	1,500	$10,800
B35	1950	$16,000	148	1,075	39/60	196-hp Cont. E-185-8	1,500	$10,800
C/D35	1951-53	$17,000	152	1,050	39/60	205-hp Cont. E-185-11	1,500	$10,800
E35	1954	$17,800	160	953	39/60	225-hp Cont. E-225-8	1,500	$10,800
F35	1955	$18,500	160	978	39/60	225-hp Cont. E-225-8	1,500	$10,800
G35	1956	$19,500	160	1,000	39/60	225-hp Cont. E-225-8	1,500	$10,800
H35	1957	$21,800	165	1,080	39/60	240-hp Cont. O-470-G	1,700	$10,300
J35	1958	$24,000	174	1,080	39/60	250-hp Cont. IO-470-C	1,500	$10,500
K35	1959	$25,000	169	1,118	49/70	250-hp Cont. IO-470-C	1,500	$10,500
M35	1960	$26,000	169	1,118	49/70	250-hp Cont. IO-470-C	1,500	$10,500
N35	1961	$27,500	169	1,270	50/80	260-hp Cont. IO-470-N	1,500	$10,500
P35	1962-63	$29,000	169	1,270	50/80	260-hp Cont. IO-470-N	1,500	$10,500
S35	1964-65	$33,000	178	1,385	50/80	285-hp Cont. IO-520-BA	1,700	$11,500
V35	1966-67	$37,500	178	1,485	50/120	285-hp Cont. IO-520-BA	1,700	$11,500
V35TC	1966-67	$43,000	195	1,450	50/120	285-hp Cont. IO-520-BA	1,700	$11,500
V35A	1968-69	$41,000	177	1,440	44/74	285-hp Cont. IO-520-BA	1,700	$11,500
V35A-TC	1968-69	$46,000	200	1,373	50/120	285-hp Cont. TSIO-520-D	1,400	$13,500
V35B	1970-72	$48,000	172	1,313	44/74	285-hp Cont. IO-520-BA	1,700	$11,500
V35B-TC	1970	$50,500	200	1,373	50/120	285-hp Cont. IO-520-BA	1,400	$13,500
V35B	1973-75	$54,000	172	1,313	44/74	285-hp Cont. IO-520-BA	1,700	$11,500
V35B	1976-78	$66,000	172	1,313	44/74	285-hp Cont. IO-520-BA	1,700	$11,500
V35B	1979-81	$84,000	172	1,313	44/74	285-hp Cont. IO-520-BA	1,700	$11,500
V35B	1982	$96,000	172	1,313	44/74	285-hp Cont. IO-520-BA	1,700	$11,500

History of Tail Repair

Despite the V-tail's long history of inflight breakups, Beech Aircraft year after year ardently defended the aircraft' strength and flying qualities and blamed the problem on pilot incompetence. Typically, the explanation went, pilots would get caught in bad weather beyond their skill level and lose control of the aircraft. In the ensuing dive the aircraft would exceed redline limits, and in attempting to pull out, the pilot would rip off the wings and/or tail. Stay within the envelope, the message was, and all would be fine.

Strangely, however, a minuscule fraction of Beech 33s, identical to the V-tails except for the tails, were experiencing inflight airframe failures.

At any rate, after the resale value of the V-tails had plummeted alarmingly, members of the American Bonanza Society asked the FAA to check out the airplane and once and for all come up with an assessment as to whether

Starting with the N35 in 1961 larger third side windows were added, along with 74-gallon fuel cells. They still had the blunter two-piece windshields, though. This is a 200-hp P35.

the aircraft was flawed. Beech Aircraft agreed to cooperate fully in the investigation, according to then-president Linden Blue. The FAA thereupon commissioned the Department of Transportation to study the matter, and a blue-ribbon panel of engineering experts did so.

Their findings, in a nutshell, were that although the V-tail Bonanzas evidently met the certification regulations, those engineering requirements failed to encompass the idiosyncracies of the V-tail configuration. The DoT report therefore recommended further testing of the tail. Beech Aircraft, which had pledged its support, flew into a tizzy and fired a legal salvo aimed at preventing release of the report to the public. The company sued the FAA, the Dot, etc. A judge ruled Beech was out of line, however, and that the public interest overbalanced their private interest, and the report was made public.

With some alacrity, interesting considering decades of refusal to publicly retest the aircraft to corroborate its strength, Beech launched a series of wind tunnel and flight tests, with the FAA looking on. And surprise! Beech and the FAA discovered the tail didn't meet the FAA's strength requirements. It turned out there was a corner of the "legal" envelope in which the tail could be overstressed.

Slow-down Order

Result: The FAA issued a slow-down order (AD 86-21-07) to remain in effect until a fix was provided. And Beech came out with a tail-bracing kit almost identical to one offered by B&N on the aftermarket as a safety measure (so similar, in fact, that Beech purchased the rights). On some aircraft, skin doublers were added as well. Another interesting aspect to this development was that while Mike Smith, B&N and Knots 2 U all were offering similar kits to strengthen the tail, Beech Aircraft, echoed by the American Bonanza Society, was counseling Bonanza own-

The naked truth about the Bonanza structure. Though it had the structural strength to take a Utility Category rating, the aircraft's V-tail was the Achilles heel that spoiled an otherwise good safety record.

ers to steer away from them because they might insidiously transfer dangerous loads elsewhere. The Beech leading edge tail cuff goes on the C35 through V35B models, thanks to AD 87-20-02, but an extra wrap-around reinforcement goes on C35 through G35 models. As it turns out, certain V-tail models are deemed sufficiently safe to require no tail beefups. These are the original model 35, the A35 and the B35. We would caution potential buyers of these models that their record is not exactly lily-white, however. The DoT report showed that no fewer than 75 model 35s have gone down in pieces from in-flight structural failure through the years, along with 19 A35s and nine B35s.

Stall/Spin

Older Bonanzas also have logged a poor record in stall/spin accidents. According to NTSB accident statistics for the period 1965-73, the Bonanza had a fatal stall/spin accident rate of 0.68 (per 100,000 flight hours)—second only to the Beech 23 series (Sierra, Sundowner, etc.) among modern aircraft. By comparison, the Cessna 210 had a fatal stall/spin rate of only 0.24—only about a third as high. The Bonanza does have a sharp stall, often accompanied by a wing drop. There is little aerodynamic buffeting or warning of an impending stall. Some pilots have reported severe wing drops, even to the point of ending up on their backs in certain situations. We asked a former Beech engineer about the Bonanza's stall, and he said that no two Bonanzas stall alike. "Even at the factory, some of them were very straightforward in the stall, while others dropped off rather abruptly."

Fuel Mismanagement

Another major cause of design-induced accidents is fuel mismanagement. Again,

Cost/Performance/Specifications

Model	Year	Average Retail Price	Cruise Speed (kts)	Useful Load (lbs)	Fuel Std/Opt (gals)	Engine	TBO (hrs)	Overhaul Cost
36	1968-69	$53,500	168	1,620	50/80	285-hp Cont. IO-520-B	1,700	$11,500
A36	1970-72	$61,000	168	1,443	44/74	285-hp Cont. IO-520-BA	1,700	$11,500
A36	1973-75	$72,000	168	1,443	44/74	285-hp Cont. IO-520-BA	1,700	$11,500
A36	1976-78	$85,000	168	1,443	44/74	285-hp Cont. IO-520-BA	1,700	$11,500
A36	1979-81	$107,000	168	1,443	44/74	285-hp Cont. IO-520-BA	1,700	$11,500
A36	1982-84	$145,000	168	1,443	44/74	285-hp Cont. IO-520-BA	1,700	$11,500
A36	1985-87	$235,000	168	1,443	44/74	285-hp Cont. IO-520-BA	1,700	$11,500

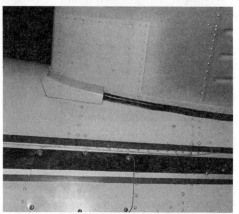

Much of the concern about the tail's structural integrity centered around an extension of the leading edge ahead of the spanwise spar (indicated by the rivet line). Starting with the C model, it was lengthened without being fastened to the fuselage. In many breakups, warpage of the leading edge suggested extra aerodynamic forces resulted, generating excess wingloads. An AD mandated installation of a Beechkit that anchored the leading edge to the fuselage as in the pictures at the right. Certain models also required an extra stiffener, as in the middle photo.

the older Bonanzas are near the top of the list in fuel mismanagement accidents. According to a 1964 CAB report on fuel mismanagement, the Bonanza ranked second worst (to the Piper Tri-Pacer) in fuel mismanagement accidents that year. An NTSB study for the years 1965-69 ranked the Bonanza as having the highest incidence of fuel starvation accidents of any light aircraft. And a study of fuel starvation accidents during 1970-72 put the Bonanza in the "higher-than-average" group along with three other aircraft.

One factor in the Bonanza's high incidence of fuel mismanagement accidents is presumably the placement of the fuel selector and the rather odd fuel pump operation in older models. The selector valve is on the floor under the pilot's left leg, which forces him to crane his neck and divert his attention from the windshield and instrument panel to change tanks. Consequently, Bonanza pilots may switch tanks by feel rather than by sight—a riskier procedure. Also, the selector detents are poorly defined in some models, and it's possible to hang up the selector between tanks, which shuts off the fuel.

Boost Pump Dilemma

If an engine does quit from fuel starvation, the Bonanza pilot faces a dilemma: turn on the boost pump or not? If he doesn't, according to a CAB study, the engine may take as long as 35 seconds to restart. If he does, he may flood the engine if the pump is left on too long. The owner's manual of one model Bonanza instructs the pilot to turn on the boost pump "momentarily" when switching from a dry tank.

The pilot must tread a narrow line between a fuel-starved engine on the one hand and a flooded-out engine on the other hand. Not a happy choice.

And then, of course, there is the notorious "fuel porting" syndrome that resulted in numerous Bonanza accidents and lawsuits against Beech. In extended slipping or skidding maneuvers or in fast turning takeoffs in pre-1970 models, fuel would slosh away from the fuel pickup if the tank was less than half full. Beech issued a service letter as far back as 1961 on the fuel unporting phenomenon. It warned that fuel unporting was a possibility after a turning takeoff, and stated that in such a case the air bubble in the fuel line would "reach the engine at about the same time the airplane becomes airborne and could cause momentary power interruption." The letter went on to say, "This does not create a hazard..." We believe a lot of people would argue with that statement.

In any case, the FAA had identified 16 accidents caused by fuel unporting by 1971, when an AD was finally issued. The AD required no modification of the fuel system, merely a yellow arc on the fuel gauge and an admonition not to take off or slip or skid excessively if the fuel quantity needle was in the arc. Beech did modify the tanks in 1970, and offered a retrofit kit for older Bonanzas, but only a handful of the retrofit kits was sold. Thousands of pre-1970 Bonanzas still have the unmodified tanks and are susceptible to fuel unporting. Buyers should check whether the baffle kit has been installed, and consider having it installed if it has not been done.

Summing up, while the straight-tail 33 and 36 models and the more recent 285-hp V-tail airplanes have good to excellent safety records, the older V-tails rank poorly. Some of these older less-than $30,000 Bonanzas might be alluring, but not for the overconfident or under qualified. More than 30 percent of the fatal accidents in older V-tails have been inflight breakups, and the stall/spin and fuel mismanagement accident rates have also been quite high. Clearly, the older Bonanzas demand the pilot's full attention and adequate skills.

Loading

Early 185- and 225-hp Bonanzas have useful loads of about 900 pounds with normal equipment, and equipped useful load has grown to about 1,200 pounds in later 285-hp models over the years as horsepower was increased. (The all-time Bonanza lifting champ is the 1968-69 straight 36 model, which had a standard useful load of 1,620 or about 1,400 with normal equipment.) Although 1,200 pounds is a fairly creditable figure, it is well short of the later Cessna 210s. Standard useful load of the 35 model took a big jump in 1961 with the N35, and took another in 1964 with the S35, paralleling horsepower increases to 260 and 285. Generally speaking, Bonanzas are not full-seats-and-full-fuel airplanes with baggage—even the 285-hp four-placers.

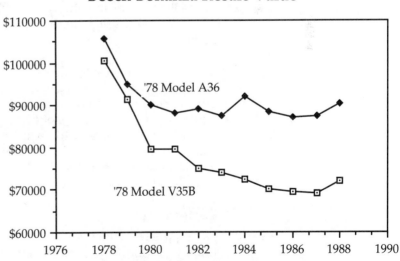

Beech Bonanza Resale Value

'78 Model A36

'78 Model V35B

However, most owners find that their loading is limited by c.g. restrictions before gross weight restrictions. The 35 models have especially narrow c.g. envelopes, and it is very easy to load them aft of the limit, even with the 30-pound lead weights that some have in the nose for ballast. In many cases, it simply isn't possible to put two adults and significant baggage in the rear of a Bonanza, no

Starting in 1984, the A36 received the bigger 300-hp engine, the Continental IO-550-B. Aside from the extra horsepower, a bonus is expected to be less crankcase cracking.

matter how much fuel is off-loaded. In fact, c.g. problems become more pronounced with less fuel because the Bonanza's leading edge fuel tanks are ahead of the c.g. As a result, c.g. moves aft as fuel is burned off. This can be quite tricky for the pilot, who may be entirely legal when he takes off, but could find himself well out of the c.g. envelope to the rear as he approaches his destination after a long flight.

One of the results of a too-far-aft c.g., of course, as mentioned before, is decreased pitch stability and lightened stick forces. Considering the Bonanza's already light pitch control forces and its tendency to build up speed quickly, an out-of-c.g. Bonanza can really take a pilot by surprise. If you plan to buy a Bonanza for four-person voyaging, be sure to do some weight-and-balance computations for each particular airframe you look at. Note also that the Beech beefup kit added extra weight to the tail, which did nothing to improve an already less-than-desirable weight-and-balance situation.

Performance

Here is where the Bonanzas shine. The first ones totally outclassed all the competition in performance, and there's still no non-turbocharged single-engine airplane in production today (except maybe the SIAI Marchetti SF 260) that will catch a good, clean V35B. All Bonanzas deliver excellent speed for their horsepower and therefore good fuel economy. Book speeds range from 148 knots for the old A and B models to 178 knots for the V35 (and a snorting 200 knots at altitude for the turbocharged V35TC). Real-world speeds may be somewhat lower than the book, but owners nevertheless report good speeds: 165 to 174 knots for the 250-, 260- and 285-hp models, and 152 to 161 knots for the Bonanzas with the 225- to 240-hp engines. Fuel consumption runs from a high of about 16 gph with the 285-hp models to 10 gph with the E-185.

Rate of climb is also energetic, with only the very oldest Bonanzas climbing less than 1,000 fpm at gross weight (by the book, at least). Bonanzas are excellent short-field aircraft, partly because of their good performance, partly because of the rugged landing gear. The beefy gear, incidentally, is virtually the same one used for the Baron, which weighs a ton more.

Creature Comforts

Again, the Bonanza is strong in this respect. The cabin is quite large, especially in terms of headroom. (In fact, most pilots look like midgets while flying Bonanzas because of the high roof and window line.) Back-seaters aren't quite as well off because of the fuselage taper, but room is still adequate. Excellent visibility from broad windows accentuates the feeling of roominess of the airplane.

Interior appointments are traditionally excellent in Bonanzas. Beech apparently believes that a man who pays five or ten times the price of a Cadillac expects to have a quality interior—a philosophy apparently shared by few other manufacturers. Interior plushness is an important part of the Bonanza mystique. The mid-windows open at the bottom in taxi to provide a welcome breeze during summer ground operations.

Rear passengers in V-tail Bonanzas can expect to be uncomfortable in turbulence, however because the aircraft fishtails excessively, usually requiring several oscillations to recover from a good jolt. Look out at the wingtip, and you can see it perform little ellipses in the sky during turbulence.

Later models received conventional dual control wheels without the massive connecting bar. Also, gear and flaps and throttle quadrant have conventional arrangement.

The 36 and A36 Bonanzas have a "club car" seating arrangement, with two pairs of rear seats facing each other, often with a fold-out table in between. With three or four people aboard, this is a wonderfully roomy compartment, but a fifth and sixth person makes things chummy. The handicap in carrying six people on an A36, however, is that there is no room at all for baggage, except perhaps behind the pilot/copilot seats and on the rear seats themselves. (And care must be taken when placing baggage behind the pilot's seat not to restrict movement of the emergency gear crank.) A small rear baggage compartment was added in 1979. Another nice feature of the 36s is a big double-door in the rear opening onto the passenger compartment. The right-side front pilot door remains, of course.

Many of the 33 and 35 models are called five- or six-seaters, but this is an optimistic delusion. A fifth or sixth seat, if installed, fits in the luggage compartment and is suitable only for small children. In most cases, c.g. and/or baggage loading considerations make it impossible to use the rear seats, even given a supply of willing children with cast-iron stomachs.

Handling

While the sensitive controls can prove a safety hazard, the other side of the coin is that the airplane feels marvelously responsive and light to the touch. Pilots normally praise the Bonanzas for their well-harmonized controls, and almost everyone agrees that the aircraft are the easiest of all to land. The A36 models are not quite so nimble on the controls, but they also, thankfully, do not share the Bonanza waggle syndrome.

Modifications

There is a welter of airframe modifications available for Bonanzas, and many owners have modified their older aircraft to the point that they're virtually indistinguishable from brand-new models. Among the more popular Bonanza mods:

• Sloped and thicker windshields, upgraded instrument panels, baggage doors, pointed spinners and a host of other interior and exterior touch-ups. Biggest of the specialists in this field is Beryl D'Shannon Aviation Specialties, Inc., in Lakeville, Minn., (800) 328-4629. Tiptanks go for $3,495 and, according to the company, greatly reduce the waggle syndrome.

• The Smith Speed Conversion is a wide-ranging aerodynamic cleanup that increases speed by 13-17 knots. Smith resets the wing incidence, installs flap gap seals and performs a myriad of other small aerodynamic cleanups. But taken all together, their effect is large. A modified cowling is also available that cuts drag, improves cooling and allows better engine breathing. The mods aren't cheap, however; the full speed treatment is $14,900. Smith Speed Conversions, Box 430, Johnson, Kans. 67855, (316) 492-6840.

A small baggage compartment behind the rear seats is a bonus only in later A36s. Before then, bags had to be dumped in the rear seats.

• Smith also developed two beefup kits to strengthen the V-tail. One, called Tail-Safe, received FAA approval in the spring of 1988 as an equivalent means of satisfying AD 87-20-02. Beech, of course, was providing its own kit free of charge to owners. Where the Beech kit consists of a cuff that anchors the leading edge of the stabilators to the fuselage skin, the Smith kit provides two larger brackets that in effect anchor most of the stabilators to the fuselage. The Smith kit costs $395 installed, and is promoted by Smith as extra security for V-tail Bonanzas.

His original famous, and not so inexpensive, stub-spar tail strengthening kit failed (by a small margin, he says) to pass the FAA test requirements. Smith went after approval of the kit to save previous buyers the trouble and loss of time in waiting for installation of the Beech kits, since there was a backlog of up to several months at some installation shops. Smith, incidentally, also installed the Beech kit for customers.

• Various autopilots have yaw dampeners that help smooth out the waggle. S-Tec Corp., Mineral Wells, Tex., (817) 325-9406 makes one. Price $1,695. These are well worth the trouble and expense.

• Numerous engine conversions are available to upgrade older Bonanzas to 240-, 250-, 260- or 285-hp engines. Also, an STC allows conversion to a 300-hp Lycoming (for $25,900, with a new prop), which has a crankcase less prone to cracking, and a 2,000-hour TBO. Continental conversions are done by Beryl D'Shannon. A 350-hp Lycoming mod by Machen, Inc., in Spokane, Wash., has been discontinued.

American Bonanza Society

The American Bonanza Society offers a good-looking technically oriented newsletter without so much of the gushy effusiveness of some other owner association newsletters. Their address: Box 12888, Wichita, Kans. 67277, (316) 945-6913.

Owner Comments

The Bonanza is excellent for cross-country flight in smooth air. In turbulence you quickly find that yaw stability leaves much to be desired. Rear-seat passengers find the well-known Bonanza tail wag to be particularly objectionable.

Weight-carrying capability of the Bonanza is good, but it is nearly impossible to load it to gross weight without exceeding the aft c.g. limit.

Club car seating in the rear is the most common configuration. Fold-out table is a nice, but astonishingly expensive touch.

The Bonanza is fun to fly. It handles nicely and offers ample performance. All of us had previous experience in high-performance singles, and had little trouble learning to fly and land the Bonanza smoothly.

Some undesirable characteristics deserve mention, though. Low-speed aileron control becomes sluggish, making for interesting encounters with gusts on short final. Stalls call for an alert pilot, since the plane tends to drop its left wing abruptly at the break. In this circumstance the pilot finds himself looking for more rudder control, as he does during landings in strong crosswinds.

Also, in transition from landing approach to go-around, the pilot finds himself straining to keep the nose down while he takes out the high degree of nose-up trim used in the approach. The bungee interconnect in the controls gets criticized from time to time, particularly after crosswind landing and other maneuvers performed using cross-controlling.

Hot starts of the fuel-injected Continental can be exasperating. When cold, it generally starts after the first few blades.

Parts are extremely expensive. The Beech dual control yoke costs $1,800. The new fuel cell costs $1,252, but by the time it was installed, we were out $1,600. We found this out after discovering that one cell leaked and could not be repaired. The cell was replaced, but the replacement also leaked and was, in turn, replaced.

After the fuel cell, the second most expensive maintenance item was the replacement of the vacuum pump. This makes the fifth vacuum pump on the plane since new, indicating a history of problems with the pressure system. We recently replaced the pressure regulator as well.

Double doors in the rear make for dramatic entries and exits, and allow grand loads of cargo with the seats removed. The pilots have their own door up front.

As with most older aircraft, performance is somewhat less than published figures after antennas, rigging and engine age impose their penalties. Our F model (225-hp) trued out at 142 knots, while our M model (250-hp) gave an honest 158 knots. Twenty-five additional horsepower gives 17 extra knots. We have often wondered whether Beech did more than just increase power. The additional power, speed and perhaps a bit of redesign also provided a firmer IFR platform.

• • •

When Beech engineers started to make plans for a civilian single-engine high-performance airplane after World War II, they asked military pilots what should be included in a civilian airplane. The answer that came back was "very light control forces." Therefore, the engineers at Beech decided that the airplane they planned would have balanced surfaces with very little force changes through the whole range of airspeed.

The first Bonanza, with a gross weight of 2,550 pounds, had a very low stall speed (40 knots) which meant it had outstanding short-field performance. Today's Bonanza, with an increase of more than 100 hp and 1,000 pounds gross weight, requires more takeoff and landing space.

The first engine on the 1968 V35A went to 1,750 hours and was showing good compression. Oil had been changed every 25 hours since new, but we got nervous about paying the core charge if the crankshaft or case went bad. The engines have needed a cylinder or two topped because of valve guide and exhaust wear, but we count on 1,600 per engine.

An S or V model Bonanza is an excellent buy because the style hasn't changed in 19 years—the performance stays the same, and they can be updated to look like new.

As in every airplane, there are areas for improvement. Of primary importance to me are the Continental crankcase AD, the Hartzell prop AD and the fuel cell AD. The engine burned or spilled an inordinate amount of oil, but the installation of a Walker Airsep has cured that.

My pet peeves are two: the price of parts is astronomical. And Beech loves to issue service letters. I have received no fewer than 10 in the year I have owned the airplane. While I admire their concern for safety, the cost of the various retrofits and inspections has amounted to a considerable sum.

Having flown both models, I feel the F33A is more stable in yaw in turbulence than the V-tail, but still displays some fishtailing.

Overall, other expenses have been reasonable. While a Bonanza is a more expensive aircraft to own in terms of initial cost and parts, it offers superior performance and a quality of construction second to none. It is a rugged, dependable machine which holds its value very well.

• • •

Takeoffs and landings require no special effort or technique. Good landings are simple to achieve. The well-known yaw is there occasionally, in certain air conditions. Riding the rudders eliminates most. The Airskeg also reduces yaw.

When modifying a Bonanza, don't expect to get all of your money back. Windows, panels, cabin interiors, wing lights and paint can be changed, but you will still be flying an older Bonanza that looks pretty with essentially the the same performance as before. If you do modify, our recommendation is to use only Beech parts. When turning a plane over to a modifier, insist on a written completion time. We had our F-35 tied up for four months on one occasion, and seven weeks on another. My number one recommendation is to save the money you would put into a major modification and trade up.

In order to more fully understand the cost, performance and specification difference between the various models, we made an analysis of true value based on weight age, speed, range, useful load and cost. The results were fascinating: In the $20,000-$30,000 bracket the K and M models were outstanding. The J model was dragged down by range limitations.

The performance of the S35 Bonanza is excellent, though not quite as advertised. Although my partner and I are used to cruising at 75 percent power on Lycoming-engined aircraft we have owned before, we have chosen to fly our Bonanza at 65 percent power for greater engine smoothness and reduced noise level. This consistently produces block-to-block speeds of 160 knots, and the altitude chosen seldom changes this.

The Bonanza handles more smoothly than any Piper or Cessna I have flown. I find no other characteristics to be unusual except for the tail-waggle in turbulence. The Bonanza is the easiest airplane to land smoothly consistently of any aircraft I have flown. This feature alone is probably reason enough to buy the airplane.

Maintenance for us has been no problem. The big maintenance problems were the two AD notes out on engine crankcase cracking and Goodyear fuel tank bladders.

The only maintenance problem which has not been resolved is the large amount of oil thrown off by the wet vacuum pump. The pump works adequately, although vacuum is always on the low side, but there is always oil along the firewall and belly of the airplane. So far, we have not been willing to bear the expense of converting to a dry-type vacuum pump. It has had no effect on the operation of the aircraft, but it is bothersome.

A flyoff between a 285-hp A36 and a Cessna 210 showed the Cessna had the edge in both climb rate and top speed. The high-winger also has a greater useful load and fuel capacity.

Beech A36TC/ B36TC Bonanzas

The Beech Bonanza has always been considered the top-of-the-line in single-engine aircraft (recent V-tail structural foibles aside), and the top of the Bonanza line for the last decade have been the A36TC and B36TC turbocharged long-fuselage straight-tail models.

The 36 turbos offer a sizeable cabin, good high-altitude cruise numbers and the security of the straight-tail design. They have held their value extremely well. But the A model had serious range shortcomings, and both aircraft tend to run hot and fall short of rated engine TBO times.

Genealogy

The history of the turbo Bonanza is a truncated one. Back in 1966, Beech brought out a turbocharged version of the standard butterfly Bonanza called the V35TC. Those were the early days of turbocharging, and apparently neither Continental nor Bonanza pilots were up to the task; the V35TC had terrible turbo reliability problems. The V35TC lasted five years, and only 132 were built.

Among the many improvements of the B36TC over the A model are longer wings, higher gross weight and greater fuel capacity.

But as turbocharging grew more popular, Beech reintroduced the idea of the turbo Bonanza in 1979. The company wisely chose to turbo the more stable straight-tailed A36 model Bonanza, and the result, powered by a 300-hp Continental TSIO-520-UB, was the A36TC. It had a sophisticated variable absolute pressure controller that automatically maintained manifold pressure during altitude and temperature changes.

The A36TC was a modest success, selling a total of 272 aircraft in three years, but pilots, with some justification, beefed about the limited fuel capacity of 74 gallons. So in 1982, Beech finally made the airplane what it should have been all along: the B36TC, with a longer wing for better high-altitude performance, and 40 gallons more fuel capacity. The two big changes improved the book range by nearly half.

Significant Improvements

The B36TC had many other improvements as well. Gross weight went up by 200 pounds to 3,850. The wing, in addition to getting the four-foot tip extension, also got a whole new carry-through structure. In effect, Beech put a Baron 58 wing on the B36TC. A new propeller and hub improved ground clearance. The B36TC had anti-siphon fuel caps, flush fuel drains, a new boost pump system that eliminated some complex fiddling required during takeoff in the A36TC, and larger fuel lines for better resistance to vapor lock. The B36TC also has a couple of weird-looking vortex generators on the wing leading edge out near the tips. The extended wing tips apparently played havoc with the airplane's spin recovery, and after trying all sorts of other things (like limiting rudder travel and increasing down elevator travel) Beech finally came up with the vortex generators, which allowed the B36TC to meet the minimum FAA spin-recovery requirements. Nobody's quite sure how they work, but they seem to do the job.

Resale Market

The A36TC and B36TC are real blue-chippers on the resale market. They were fearsomely expensive to buy new, and they're fearsomely expensive to buy used. In 1979, a new A36TC cost $137,000 and is worth $112,500 today (we're using bluebook retail figures, which tend to run a bit higher than actual selling prices). That's 82 percent after eight years. By comparison, the same numbers for a 1979 T210 are $99,000 new and $65,000 used for a 66 percent resale value. The Mooney 231's numbers are $85,000 new, $56,000 used and 66 percent.

Later model 36TCs took a huge jump in new sticker price, so percentage value retained is only a bit higher than the T210 and 231. But the fact remains that, for any given model year, you'll have to pay about double the price of a Mooney 231, which has similar performance through the middle altitudes. Obviously, people put a lot of stock in the Bonanza TC's comfort, quality and extra high-altitude capabilities—not to mention the perception of quality and status.

Performance

The 36TCs are good performers in terms of cruise speed. The 36TC can generally keep up with the likes of the Mooney 231 and Cessna T210N, but newer planes like the Mooney 252, Turbo 210R and Piper Malibu are faster. Owners report typical cruise speeds in the 180-knot range at middle altitudes.

Conventional tail is one of the blessings of the 36 line.

These reports agree pretty well with the book figures, which call for cruising speeds ranging from an all-out max of 199 knots (at 79 percent power, 25,000 feet and 250 pounds below gross weight) to 155 knots at 56 percent power and 10,000 feet. The book number for 75 percent/20,000 feet is 190 knots; at 69 percent/15,000 feet, the figure is 174 knots.

There's very little speed difference between the A and the B models. At very high altitudes, where the B's bigger wing comes into play, the B has an edge of a couple of knots.

Owners report fuel flows of 17-18 gph at cruise power. That assumes a middling power setting and a mixture rich enough to keep the valves from cooking.

Pilots praise the airplane's climb performance. They consistently report climb rates between 1,000 and 1,500 fpm, and have no trouble getting on up to 20,000 feet. Much higher than that, and the turbo wastegate is fully closed in the "bootstrap" mode, and manifold pressure begins to fall off. But cruising at the max certified ceiling of 25,000 feet is a reasonable thing to do, say TC pilots, unless the day is hot and the load heavy.

Payload/Range

The A model has a gross weight of 3,650 and a typical IFR empty weight of around 2,400 to 2,500 pounds. Typical useful load is around 1,150 pounds. With only 74 gallons (444 pounds) of fuel available, a hefty 700-800 pounds is available for the cabin even with full tanks. That's the equivalent of four people and some baggage.

The bad news, of course, is you can't fly very far on 74 gallons. Factory specs list ranges from 609 to 730 nm, depending on altitude and power setting, but these are a bit optimistic. Taking into account full-rich climbs to altitude (necessary for engine cooling), richer-than-peak cruising (also a good idea for engine longevity) and IFR reserves, you wouldn't want to fly one more than three hours. Five or six hundred nm is more like it. If you want to take advantage of the big cabin and put six adults inside, range will be limited indeed. Six 170-pounders, each carrying 20 pounds of luggage, leaves zero—yep, *absolutamente nada*—for fuel. (You could hold a nice conference on the ramp, though.) The A36TC is a six-place airplane only if two or three of the six are little kids.

The B model does a bit better. Empty weight is about 60 pounds higher, but gross weight is up by 200 pounds, for a net useful load boost of 140 pounds. If you take the bonus in fuel, the B36TC will carry three adults up to 1,000 nm, or even a bit more if you throttle way back. If you want to settle for the short range of the A36TC and only pour in 74 gallons, the B will carry one more passenger than the A.

However, even the B36TC looks bad next to a Cessna T210R in terms of payload. The big Cessna will haul 250 pounds more weight, comparably equipped, which translates into an extra passenger and a half, or an extra 40 gallons of fuel—enough to fly 500 miles farther.

Creature Comforts

Unlike the T210R, however, it's actually possible to fit six people in the cabin. (The back two seats of a 210 are suitable only for midgets.) Virtually every 36TC has the optional "club car" seating, which puts the four rear-seaters facing each other, Orient Express-style. Owners seem to like the bizjet-style separation of crew and passengers, but tall folks in the back will require some sort of intricate leg-interlock system. Weight limitations almost assure that at least a couple of the club section passengers will be kids. The big right-side cargo door is also a boon to the rear-seaters.

Cabin noise level is fairly low. "It's quieter than the S35 and the Skylane I used to own," commented one B36TC owner.

Handling

The stretched 36 model Bonanzas handle much differently than the shorter V-tail 35s and straight-tail 33s. The 36s were stretched several inches forward of the wing, which lengthened the cabin and improved the limited c.g. envelope of the short-body Bonanzas. The result is a much heavier-feeling airplane. Lateral response is also slower. "It's not as much fun to fly as the V-tails," commented one owner. "You fly it by the numbers instead of by feel." With two people up front and the rear cabin empty, the 36TCs tend to be nose-heavy on landing and takeoff.

While the heavier pitch forces may not feel as sporty, they certainly contribute to better stability and make the 36 a safer airplane to fly IFR.

Engine

All the 36TCs have the same engine: a 300-hp Continental TSIO-520-UB. TBO is 1,600 hours, but reports suggest that not many make it that far. Few 36TCs have been around long enough to go to 1,600 hours (many are flown by private individuals who put 200 hours or less a year on them), but the pattern seems to be a top overhaul somewhere in the 800-1,200 hour range. We queried one overhauler about the engine, and he replied, "It has no major problems I'm aware of, but the last major we did came at about two-thirds the TBO time. It needed a top overhaul, and the guy decided since he was spending that much money anyway, he might as well do the major."

Part of the problem may be hot running due to a lack of cowl flaps—an odd engineering choice by Beech for such a sophisticated temperature-sensitive aircraft.

Watch for Cracks

The engine is subject to the notorious cylinder-cracking AD, number 86-13-4, which calls for inspection of the cylinders for cracks every 50 hours. (The -UB

Cost/Performance/Specifications

Model	Year	Average Retail Price	Cruise Speed (kts)	Useful Load (lbs)	Fuel Std/Opt (gals)	Engine	TBO (hor)	Overhaul Cost
A36TC	1979	$112,500	199	1,388	40/74	300-hp Cont. TSIO-520-UB	1,600	$14,000
A36TC	1980	$117,500	199	1,388	40/74	300-hp Cont. TSIO-520-UB	1,600	$14,000
A36TC	1981	$125,500	199	1,388	40/74	300-hp Cont. TSIO-520-UB	1,600	$14,000
B36TC	1982	$155,000	200	1,468	102	300-hp Cont. TSIO-520-UB	1,600	$14,000
B36TC	1983	$167,000	200	1,468	102	300-hp Cont. TSIO-520-UB	1,600	$14,000
B36TC	1984	$190,000	200	1,468	102	300-hp Cont. TSIO-520-UB	1,600	$14,000
B36TC	1985	$215,000	200	1,468	102	300-hp Cont. TSIO-520-UB	1,600	$14,000
B36TC	1986	$297,000	200	1,468	102	300-hp Cont. TSIO-520-UB	1,600	$14,000

engine is not alone; virtually all 520s are subject to it.)

The engine is also prone to crankcase cracks, as are virtually all other front-alternator Continental 520 engines. Check carefully for cracks on any 36TC considered for purchase—a bad crack will cost a minimum of $5,000 to replace or repair, mostly because of the teardown costs.

The engine/boost-pump combination on the A36TC is an odd one that requires some extra fiddling by the pilot on takeoff. The A36TC book calls for a full-rich fuel flow of 32.5 to 34.0 gph on takeoff. If this is not achieved, the pilot must turn on the fuel pump to "Low" or "Auto" (the book doesn't say how you decide which one), and then lean the mixture back to the correct fuel flow. The same complex rigmarole must be continued throughout the climb in warm weather.

The B36TC book warns the pilot not to use the boost pump in the "Hi" position because of excessive fuel flow. Beech, in a masterpiece of understatement, says that this "may cause engine combustion to cease on the takeoff roll."

Safety Record

We have not computed precise accident rates for the A36TC and B36TC per se. However, the 36 series of Bonanza as a whole has an excellent safety record. For the period 1972-1981, the 36 series had the fourth-best fatality rate out of 17 single-engine retractables evaluated by *The Aviation Consumer*. Fatal accident rate was 1.5 per 100,000 flight hours. (The range of the other 16 retractables was from 0.8 to 3.3.)

A36TC engines tend to run hot and have an awkward fuel boost pump arrangement.

In total accidents, the 36 series did even better—second best. Total rate was 4.5 per 100,000 in a range of 4.6 to 15.0. FAA records show a total of 14 fatal 36TC accidents from 1980 to 1985, 12 for the A model and two for the B. Part of the reason for this discrepancy is the larger number of A models built and their longer exposure to accident risk. But even adjusting for exposure factors (figuring aircraft-years), the B model seems to have a fatal rate half that of the A. We have no explanation for this and suspect it may be a statistical aberration. (The number of B accidents is, after all, very small, which makes it statistically less significant.)

Of the 12 A36TC fatal crashes, five were weather-related. In one case, a VFR pilot wandered into IMC and lost control. In the ensuing spiral dive, the airplane broke up in flight—one of the very few instances of a straight-tail Bonanza coming apart in the air. Two fatal crashes came after engine failures, another during a landing overrun.

One gruesome accident occurred after an in-flight fire. A leaking idle mixture adjustment screw fed raw fuel onto the turbocharger, and the engine erupted in flames shortly after takeoff. The pilot, blinded by the fire, managed to get the plane on the ground and survived (barely), but the front-seat passenger burned to death.

The two rear-seat passengers escaped through the big rear door—a good argument for a rear exit if there ever was one. (This accident is described in detail in the December 1, 1984 issue of *The Aviation Consumer*.)

The two B36TC fatal accidents were both weather-related: a spiral dive into the ground by a disoriented pilot and an ILS approach that went awry.

Two's company in club-car seating, though a third would be okay. High roof line, big windows give the cabin a sense of spaciousness.

We noticed a familiar Bonanza pattern in the non-fatal accidents: inadvertent gear retractions on the ground. The 36TCs, like most other Bonanzas, have the flap lever on the left and the gear lever on the right—the reverse of the common arrangement. As a result, hundreds of pilots have inadvertently retracted the landing gear after touchdown when they meant to retract the flaps. Five A36TC pilots suffered this embarrassing fate.

There was confusion of another sort involving the flap lever; one hapless pilot, meaning to raise the flaps after takeoff, mistakenly turned on the boost pump instead. The A36TC has an unfortunate (in our opinion) boost pump arrangement that can flood the engine and stop it stone-dead. The plane crash-landed in a field. Fortunately, no one was hurt.

Service Difficulty Reports

FAA records of service problems highlight several areas to watch out for when inspecting an A36TC or B36TC for possible purchase. Here's a list of the main A36TC problems in SDR files since 1980:

• Cracked boarding steps. Beech service instruction 972 refers to this problem, but A36TCs aren't listed as having it. Check it anyway.

• Cracked oil cooler baffles (10 reports).

• Cracked crankcases (10 reports).

• Cracked cylinders (four reports).

• Cracked turbocharger inlet, part number 642668 (15 reports).

The B36TC models, with benefit of 20/20 hindsight, did not reflect these problems. However, two B model trouble spots were the fuel return line, which tended to chafe against the wastegate drain (four reports) and cracked cooling baffles at the air pressure pump inlet above the oil cooler (four cases).

Merlyn intercooler mod adds a scoop to the lower left cowl.

Airworthiness Directives

The 36TC models have only a couple of ADs that are unique to the type. One, for older A models, requires modification of the fuel drain hose. Both A and B models are subject to 84-8-4, which requires modification of the oil line check valves.

But 36TC owners don't get off easy; the airplane is subject to many of the "shotgun" ADs on engines and accessories that cover numerous aircraft types. Examples: Hartzell props, Airborne pumps, ELT batteries, air filters, Bendix mags, and cracked cylinders. The biggest potential problem is the repetitive inspections for cylinder cracks, AD 86-13-4.

Modifications

A36TC buyers should look for the 30-gallon tiptank STC offered by Beryl D'Shannon (P.O. Box 840, Lakeville, Minn. 55044; (800) 328-4629), one of the best-known purveyors of Bonanza mods. Fuel in the tip tanks must be transferred with a pump into the main tanks. Speed will probably suffer a few knots. Cost is $3,495 plus $195 for strobe lights. Installation time is estimated at two or three man-days, which should bring total cost to roughly $4,000.

Mike Smith Aero (Stanton County Airport, Johnson City, Kans. 67855 (316) 492-6840) offers the Smith Speed Conversion, a series of aerodynamic cleanups that can add 15-20 mph to top speed and increase climb rate as well. Cost is $14,900 for the whole works, but partial mods can be made at less cost.

Two companies now offer intercooler mods for the A and B models. Both mods allow power to be produced at lower manifold pressures, thereby reducing stress and heat in the engine. Considering the 36TC's reputation for running hot and failing to make TBO, we think an intercooler is a superb idea.

Merlyn Products (W. 7510 Hall Ave., Spokane, Wash. 99204; (509) 838-1141) intercooler system is $5,995 (kit only) or $6,495 installed. Weight is 21 pounds. Turboplus, Inc. (1520 26th Ave., NW, Gig Harbor, Wash. 98335; (800) 742-4202) offers a similar intercooler system for $4,995 for the kit; add some 30 hours of labor for installation. This company also sells a "jet-type" spoiler system for $3,495 for the kit, plus about 40 hours of

Beech 36TC Resale Value

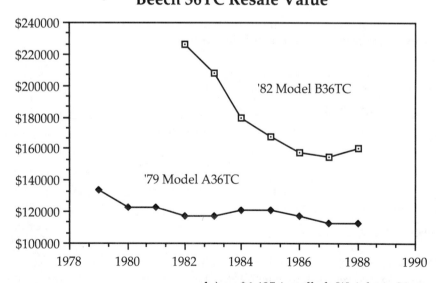

'82 Model B36TC

'79 Model A36TC

installation time. Another desirable mod to look for on a used 36TC (or to consider adding after you buy it) is a set of speed brakes for descending rapidly from high altitudes without overcooling the engine. Precise Flight (P.O. Box 7168, Bend, Ore. 97708, 800-547-2558) offers wing-mounted speed brakes at a cost of $3,695. Installation time is estimated at 48 man-hours, which should bring total cost into the $5,000 range.

For protection in case of unplanned flight into icing conditions, there is now an STC for the TKS system. This works on wing and tail leading edges by forcing an anti-ice substance out of stainless steel mesh panels. Kohlman Aviation Corp., 319 Perry St., Lawrence, KS 66044, (913) 843-4098.

Owner Comments

Common to all Bonanzas is a lift-up cowling that allows easy access for inspection. Silver battery box is conveniently located, has a short run to the engine.

I purchased my 1983 B36TC in January 1985 as a demonstrator with about 100 hours on it. Since then I have flown it another 300 hours or so. I moved up from an F33A primarily to gain more cabin room for a growing family. My wife and two young children have flown several long trips, including one coast-to-coast, with a great degree of comfort.

The plane flies well, although it tends to be a bit nose-heavy on landing with only the front seats occupied. On takeoff, the engine has a slight tendency to overboost a couple of inches, especially when cold. This amount of overboost, however, is approved for up to five minutes and has never caused a problem.

Engine cooling is good, although there are no cowl flaps. Forward speed plus extra-rich fuel mixture keeps it cool. Only once have I had to reduce climb angle for engine cooling, and that was on a 90-degree-plus day. Climb fuel flows are about 30-32 gph, but fortunately you don't have to spend that much time climbing, since the plane will get to FL 200 in about 18 minutes.

I flight plan for 160 knots at sea level, increasing two knots per 1,000 feet of altitude. Fuel burn is 17 gph at 65 percent power, which the plane will maintain up to its certified ceiling of 25,000 feet. By comparison, the F33A burned 14 gph at the same power setting. Endurance is five hours with a reasonable reserve.

As far as maintenance goes, I've had some problems, although nothing overwhelming. A turbo controller was replaced under warranty, and the plane had to be repainted, apparently due to factory quality control problems. (I battled with Beech over this.) Landing gear uplocks have to be adjusted every inspection, but that's no big deal.

Our annual/100-hour inspections run about $1,300 at Beechcraft East on Long

An improved boost pump system on the B36TC eliminated some complex fiddling during takeoff in the A36TC. Vapor lock resistance was improved by larger fuel lines.

An improved boost pump system on the B36TC eliminated some complex fiddling during takeoff in the A36TC. Vapor lock resistance was improved by larger fuel lines.

Island, N.Y. Oil is changed every 33 hours. The oil filter lives behind a maze of hoses and brackets, and I always make sure I'm not around to hear the mechanic's comments as he struggles to change it. Parts availability is excellent, with most parts available the next day by Federal Express if not in stock. Parts prices are high. (If you're not building planes, you've got to make money somehow.) Total operating costs seem to run in the $145/hour range. That includes hangar and insurance, but not engine reserves.

In short, Beech set out with the B36TC to rectify the problems they had with the A36TC, and they did their homework. There are no tricks to perform in the middle of the takeoff roll, range is excellent, and the plane is a delight to fly.

Lorne Sheren
Watchung, N. J.

I purchased a 1982 B36TC in October 1986. I am the third owner of the aircraft, which has 670 hours total time and 400 hours on a Continental factory reman "zero-time" engine. I was told the original engine failed because of loss of oil at the turbo oil feed line. I can't verify the cause of the failure, but the plane was landed safely with no airframe damage.

I have flown the plane about 100 hours and have had failures of the pressure pump and the starter vibrator. The airplane just had a $1,200 annual at PT Aero in Providence, and there were no discrepancies. I think the price is quite reasonable for such a complex aircraft.

This is my fourth straight-tail Bonanza, and I think it's the best one. My basis for this statement is speed, low noise level, excellent c.g. envelope, 102 gallons of usable fuel, built-in oxygen for all seats, better wing loading (with the extended wing, it carries ice very well, as opposed to the A36), and superb passenger comfort and loading.

My only complaint is the lack of cowl flaps and the resulting high cylinder head temperatures during long climbs. I am installing a Merlyn intercooler, and will let you know how that works out. With the extra fuel, the range is fabulous. I have made non-stop flights from St. Louis and Tampa to Providence.

Speed buildup on descents is very moderate, and when I take my eyes off the gauges, the wing does not drop and the red line isn't the first thing I see when I look back. (That should be a fix for the in-flight breakup problems suffered by the

V-tail models.) I believe the wingtip extension has a great deal to do with this improved stability, along with the extended fuselage and wing placement.

Justin Strauss
Cranston, R.I.

I bought a 1981 A36TC with 500 hours on it in 1983. I paid $125,000. It now has about 1,300 hours on it, which works out to about 200 hours a year.

I generally plan on getting about 170 knots block-to-block, usually at about 12,000 feet, although sometimes I have to go higher to get over the mountains out here. That's at 75 percent power. I lean it about 50 degrees rich of peak TIT, and this results in a fuel burn of about 17 gph. It has very good climb performance; I typically see 1,400 or 1,500 fpm after takeoff, although that's usually below gross weight. For the cruise altitudes I usually fly at, it takes less than a minute per thousand feet to get there.

I do have to watch the cylinder head temps on climbout. On a warm day, I may have to climb as fast as 130-135 knots to keep the CHT 50 degrees below the red line, which is where I like to see it.

I've had no major problems with the machine. The airframe has been pretty much maintenance-free, and the annual inspection usually runs around $1,200 to $1,300. I have had avionics problems, however. And the engine required a premature top overhaul at 1,200 hours because of low compression and excessive oil consumption. TBO is supposedly 1,600 hours, but I think it's pretty standard among A36TC owners to need a top overhaul at half or two-thirds of the TBO.

The standard tanks hold only 74 gallons usable, but I have tip tanks that give me an extra 40 gallons, so I have good range. Comfort is good, and the noise level is lower than the Skylane and the S35 Bonanza that I owned before. The V-tail was more fun to fly, though. It was lighter on the controls and more responsive. The A36TC feels like a bigger, heavier airplane, and you tend to fly it more by the numbers than by feel.

The TC is the only plane I've ever bought that hasn't depreciated. I had its value checked recently when I renewed my insurance policy, and it was the same I paid for it four years ago. If I had bought a Baron or something like that, I'd be looking at about half the value.

Robert Day
Steamboat Springs, Colo.

Wedge-shaped vortex generators on the wing leading edge were added to aid in spin recovery after the wings were extended .

We bought our 1980 A36TC about four years ago and paid $122,000. It had only about 300 hours when we bought it, and now has 850. It has been a very trouble-free airplane. Our engine has been excellent, with the compression never registering less than 74. There have never been any oil leaks. When you look in *Trade-A-Plane*, you see lots of ads with total times of 800 or 1,000 hours and 300 hours on a factory reman engine, but I don't think those people used common sense when they operated the engine. If you run it according to the fuel flows in the book, you'll burn it right up. You have to run on the lean side of peak to match the Beech fuel-flow numbers. We have recently installed a Merlyn intercooler. We haven't had a chance to run it during the summer or at real high altitudes yet, but so far we are pleased with it. If we run the same manifold pressure settings as before, we get about a four-five-knot speed increase with a very slight increase in fuel flow—maybe 0.2 or 0.3 gph more. (On a recent trip, we got 196 knots at 19,000 feet at 29 inches and 2,400 rpm.) Running the same fuel flow, we definitely go faster. Or, we have the option of running the same speed as before, but use 26 inches of mp instead of 29 and use about one gph less.

Ability to climb handily up to 20,000 feet or better affords passengers the comfort of a better ride over the weather.

Cylinder head temperatures seem to be running about the same as before. The TIT seems a little lower, but we find we're still mixture-limited by the TIT redline (1,650 degrees) at the higher power settings. The intercooler has to be removed to change the plugs or inspect the turbocharger, but it can easily be done in about five minutes. Merlyn product support seems to be good—they've made some improvements since ours was installed, and they just called to say they'd be retrofitting the improvements to our airplane for free. Overall, I'm happy with it.

In terms of performance, our airplane seems to indicate 155 knots almost all the time. At our typical cruise altitude of 11,500 or 12,500, that usually works out to 183-187 knots true. That's at 29 inches and 2400 rpm, which is about 67 percent power. We burn 18 gph, so both our speeds and fuel flows are higher than the book. Rate of climb is good, about 1,100 fpm at gross on a cool day. Recently we went to 16,500 feet in about 15 minutes. In normal weather, we can climb at 110-120 knots and keep the CHT needle at 200 degrees or below, but out in the desert, we have to increase climb speed to 120-130 knots. CHTs in cruise are no problem It's a little short on fuel, so we installed the Beryl D'Shannon tip tanks, which bring capacity up to 104 gallons. There's supposedly a 200-pound gross weight increase that goes along with the tiptank STC, but I've never seen it on paper.

We've had almost no maintenance problems. The only defect I can recall is a cracked fairing that cost about $10. There was a vapor-lock service bulletin a while ago, which required replacement of the fuel lines (with half-inch ones, like the B36TC has), fuel selector and modification of the fuel pump. The bill was something like $2,600, but Beech paid for everything. That was pretty amazing for a five-year old airplane on its second owner.

It's a very quiet airplane, much quieter than the Baron 58 I used to have. It flies nicely, very similar to the Baron. My partner used to have a V35B, and at first he thought the A36TC felt trucky by comparison. But it's much better on the dials. The V35B is like a Porsche 911, the A36TC is more like a Lincoln Town Car.

Dave Zalibra
Los Angeles, Calif.

Beech 76 Duchess

In 1974, Beech's designers—beset with the task of creating a step-up plane for the Beech Aero Centers—started laying the groundwork for a simple, yet advanced, light twin based on the Beech Sierra design. The prototype sported a T-tail, two doors (à la Musketeer), and a pair of conventional-rotating 160-hp Lycomings (which were later replaced by counterrotating 180-hp engines). Forty-four months after its inception, the Model 76 Duchess attained FAA type certification and began rolling off the Liberal, Kans. assembly lines.

No sooner had the Duchess hit the market, of course, than the light-twin arena suddenly became quite crowded, what with the Grumman Cougar's debut in 1978 and the arrival of Piper's Seminole in 1979. (Cessna's T303 Crusader—née Clipper—was to have been an entrant in the light-light-twin derby, but Cessna thought better of the move at the last minute and reconfigured the T303 as a Seneca-class medium hauler.)

Nonetheless, Beech's Aero Centers quickly placed orders for over 200 of the bonded-construction T-twins; and in the first few years of sales, Beech's lightest light twin held its own with the competition—slightly outpacing the Seminole and Turbo Seminole in combined sales.

Novel Construction

Although the Duchess's lines clearly reflect its Musketeer ancestry, the Model 76 is anything but a double-breasted Sierra in actual construction. The Sierra's outward-retracting gear design was abandoned in the Duchess, for example, along with the Mooney-style rubber shock biscuits. (The Duchess displays a pair of megalithic oleo shocks on the main gear, while the nose strut is taken *in toto* from the A36 Bonanza.) Like the Sierra, the Duchess has bonded wet wings; but unlike the other Aero Center airplanes, the Model 76's main tanks extend to the wingtips, carrying 50 gallons usable (each). Also, the Duchess's ailerons are bigger (and travel farther) than the Sierra's.

In the fuselage, extensive use was made of honeycomb-sandwich construction

High-flying T-tail pays off in both stylistic and aerodynamic ways.

techniques to produce a light, crashworthy, and at the same time vibration/noise-resistant cabin. A feature unique among twins is the Duchess's cabin door configuration (borrowed from the Sierra): there are doors and walkways for both pilot *and* copilot, plus a large baggage door on the left aft fuselage behind the wing.

T-tail Trade-offs

The Duchess's most distinctive design hallmark, however, is its T-tail. Although considered by many to be merely a stylistic (i.e., marketing) device, the T-tail actually contributes in meaningful ways to the airplane's performance. Because the horizontal surfaces are out of the propellers' slipstreams and sit far to the rear atop a *swept* tail fin, their effectiveness is enhanced; and as a result, the horizontal tail area can be reduced—with a commensurate reduction in drag—at no penalty in pitch control. (In fact, the pitch authority of the Duchess tail is so great that the original prototype experienced problems with excessively high nose angles in stalls. This problem was ameliorated, however, with the switch to heavier, 180-hp engines from the earlier 160-hp Lycomings.) As a side benefit, propwash buffet is also eliminated.

The real-world payoff of the T-tail for the Duchess can be measured in terms of pitch control in the flare (excellent), allowable c.g. range (10.9 inches total, versus 8.3 for the Sierra), and the amount of trim change needed after gear or flap deployment (little, if any). The T-tail's end-plate effect also contributes to rudder effectiveness, providing a low single-engine minimum control speed (Vmc) of 67 knots CAS, which is one knot below the airplane's clean stall speed (Vs) of 68 KCAS. (In a twin-engine plane, it is desirable from a safety/controllability standpoint to encounter the stall at an airspeed higher than Vmc.) Of course, these benefits do not come without a modest weight penalty for the added structure needed to carry the lofty horizontal stabilizer—estimated by Beech, in this case, at 15 pounds.

Bonded wet wings hold 50 gallons of fuel each. Wingtips are made of flexible plastic, to reduce "dings."

Following the Model 76's introduction, few substantive design changes were made (although myriad minor adjustments have been incorporated in later models and published as service bulletins; see below). In early 1979, improved door locks became standard, and cowl flap hinges were changed from aluminum to steel; in mid-1980, an improved engine mount was introduced; in 1981, a landing gear horn muting system (to keep the horn from sounding prematurely during high-speed power-off letdowns) was introduced. For 1982, Beech increased the number of static wicks from five to 12. Overall, the design of the Model 76 remains virtually unchanged since 1978— a testament, perhaps, to the airplane's basic soundness.

Performance

Owners praise the Duchess as a capable medium-range cross-country machine, with 75-percent power cruise speeds typically in the 160-knot/184-mph region at fuel flows of just under 10 gallons per hour per engine. To underscore the plane's obvious economy-of-operation appeal, Beech in 1982 appended a "super economy" cruise performance page to the Duchess handbook, claiming a 142-knot/163-mph speed at 14,000 feet, with props at 2100 rpm and manifold pressures at 18.0 inches (fuel consumption: 6.8 gph/engine). We doubt, frankly, that anyone would choose to operate the plane in this fashion, but the point is well taken: this *is* a bonafide economy twin. With a maximum takeoff weight of 3,900 pounds (100 pounds more than the normally aspirated Piper Seminole—25 pounds *less* than the Turbo Seminole), the Duchess turns in rather mediocre takeoff numbers; to wit, a sea level ground roll of 1,017 feet and a 50-foot obstacle clearance distance of 2,119 feet—no better than the Travel Air (Beech's original 180-hp twin) and actually quite a bit worse than the competition (Piper's Seminole gets off and over in 880 feet and 1,400 feet, respectively).

On landing, the comparisons with Brand 'P' are even more striking: the Duchess rolls a full 1,000 feet after touchdown at gross weight, versus the Seminole's 590 feet. With heavy-duty brakes, the Seminole will—according to Piper—roll a mere *383 feet* after a no-wind touchdown. One wonders whether Piper's tape measures are made in the U.S.

Rotation speed in the Duchess comes at 71 knots (81 mph), which corresponds with Beech's "intentional one engine inoperative speed" (Vsse) as well as with the two-engine best angle of climb speed (Vx). Upon attaining 85 knots (the best rate of climb speed for single- *or* all-engine operation), a full-throttle climbout yields a 1,248-fpm rate of ascent initially, decaying to 1,000 fpm at 4,000 feet.

In both looks and flying qualities, the Duchess is a quantum leap better than its single-engine progenitor, the Sierra.

The Duchess's single-engine performance specs are nothing to write home about—although, of course, the same is true for other twins in this category. On one engine, the Duchess turns in an anemic 235-fpm sea-level climb rate at gross (vs. a complexion-whitening 217 fpm for the Seminole and 180 fpm for the Turbo Seminole). The climb dwindles to 50 fpm at the service ceiling of 6,170 feet (vs. 4,100 feet for the lighter-gross-weight Seminole—again, a question of whose numbers you believe).

The usable fuel capacity of 100 gallons gives the Duchess an endurance, at 75-percent cruise, of around four hours with IFR reserves. The published range (with reserves) varies from 623 nautical/717 statute miles to upwards of 800 nautical and 900 statute, depending on whether 75-percent cruise or "super economy" power settings are used.

All in all, the Duchess's performance is on a par with—and in most cases no better than—that of the 1958 Travel Air's. Which raises the obvious question: Why would Beech go to the trouble and expense of certifying a *new* 180-hp light twin when it could just as easily have revived the Travel Air, a proven (and much-loved by some) design?

When we put this question to a Beech spokesman in 1979, he answered by saying that the Travel Air was and is a complicated design, expensive to produce (as are the Barons that derive from that same type certificate); the Duchess employed state-of-the-art materials and construction techniques, affording a lighter airframe (by about 200 pounds, compared to the Model 95); and in designing the Duchess, Beech had the opportunity to create a twin with truly superior slow-speed handling characteristics.

Counter-rotating 180-hp Lycomings yield a cruise speed of 158 knots and a range of about 700 nm with reserve.

All of which is true. In 1982, one could only lament the fact that Beech's efforts did not result in a twin with a lower price tag. The 1982 Duchess sold for a whopping $171,875 (average-equipped) —two and a half times more than a comparably equipped Travel Air sold for in 1968.

Handling and Comfort

The Duchess is nothing if not comfortable. Although the cockpit tapers noticeably just forward of the pilots' thighs, the Bonanza-like head room and 44-inch cabin width (the cabin is wider, amazingly, than that of the Baron) contribute to the feeling that one is actually flying a much larger airplane. The accommodations are strictly first-class.

Pilots transitioning to the Duchess from single-engine aircraft will appreciate the fact that the plane's panel layout (with the exception of the vertically displaced tachometers) is both logical and eyepleasing. Gear and flap switches are where they should be—gear on the left, flaps on the right—as are the power levers (mercifully, Beech abandoned the irksome center-panel "prop/throttle/mixture" grouping found on the Barons and placed these controls in the standard TPM arrangement in the Duchess).

Starting the Duchess's carbureted O-360s is easy enough if you remember to press *in* on the ignition switch while cranking, to engage the primer (a solenoid-operated system which, mysteriously, feeds fuel only to cylinders one, two and four of each engine).

On the ground, the Duchess handles a bit differently from its Piper counterpart. The slow damping action of the main gear oleos—combined with the plane's large spanwise mass distribution—gives the Duchess a curiously ponderous feel while taxiing, even setting up a Dutch-roll-like oscillation as one goes around corners. Likewise, the slightest touch of the brake pedals tends to collapse the nose oleo. These idiosyncrasies are basically harmless, however.

On takeoff, the Duchess requires a positive tug on the yoke to break ground (not too much, though, or you'll overrotate). In the air, visibility is excellent. In fact, the nose slopes away so precipitously that it is difficult, at first, to judge the plane's angle of attack.

Unlike the Aero Center singles upon which the Model 76 design is based, the Duchess has no rudder-aileron interconnect—nor is one needed. The controls are light (as twins go) and well-harmonized, inviting comparisons with such single-engine aircraft as the Bonanza and Saratoga. Stability is excellent in the pitch and roll modes; yaw is less good, with some tendency toward short-period waggle in turbulence. Overall, however, the plane is decidedly well-behaved.

Slow-Speed Traits

True to the designers' original intentions, the Duchess excels at low-speed controllability—with or without both fans turning. Pitch, roll, and yaw control remain crisp at speeds near blue-line (85 KIAS), and—thanks to the presence on the center pedestal of trim knobs for ailerons, rudder, *and* elevator—the plane trims up quickly for hands-off flight after shutting down either engine. (Handling is the same with either engine out, of course; there is no "critical" engine.)

Stalls are conventional in all respects, except that the controls remain surprisingly effective at vanishingly low airspeeds. With both engines developing power, the airplane can be flown well below 50 knots IAS, dirty, without stalling.

One of the nice aspects of the T-tail is that, since it sits high above the wing's wake, it doesn't "feel" disturbances caused by lowering/raising the gear or flaps. On deploying the landing gear (at up to 140 knots) or flaps (up to 110 knots), there is no noticeable change in pitch attitude.

An interesting quirk of the airplane is its maximum gear-*raise* speed of 113 knots, occasioned by the design of the forward-retracting nose strut. Once the gear has been lowered (as a speed brake, say), it cannot be raised again until airspeed has been allowed to bleed off to under 113 knots.

Safety

According to NTSB records, there were only six accidents involving Duchesses in the first few years after the aircraft was introduced in 1978, two of them fatal. (Interestingly, only one of the six pilots involved was over the age of 33.)

• One Duchess was destroyed (and the two persons aboard killed) on a VFR flight from Long Beach to Ramona, Calif. when the aircraft encountered zero-visibility weather and collided with the ground in a controlled descent.

• A Duchess sustained heavy damage on a training flight from Little Rock, Arkansas when the flight instructor allowed his student to land gear-up.

• Confusion in the cockpit resulted in another gear-up landing (again with substantial damage)—this time in Sioux City, Iowa—when an instructor told his student to cancel a practice single-engine go-around. The CFI landed the plane wheels-up.

• Inclement weather claimed a non-instrument-rated Duchess pilot with 20 hours in type on a flight from Wyoming to Salt Lake City. The aircraft crashed out of

Cost/Performance/Specifications

Model	Year Built	Average Retail Price	Cruise Speed (kts)	Useful Load (lbs)	Fuel Std/Opt (gals)	Engine	TBO (hrs)	Overhaul Cost
76	1978	$43,000	158	1,456	100	180-hp Lyc. O-360-A1G6D	2,000	$7,000
76	1979	$48,000	158	1,456	100	180-hp Lyc. O-360-A1G6D	2,000	$7,000
76	1980	$52,000	158	1,456	100	180-hp Lyc. O-360-A1G6D	2,000	$7,000
76	1981	$58,000	158	1,456	100	180-hp Lyc. O-360-A1G6D	2,000	$7,000
76	1982	$68,000	158	1,456	100	180-hp Lyc. O-360-A1G6D	2,000	$7,000

control at night, in icing conditions.

• A hard landing in icing conditions caused major damage to a Duchess on its nighttime arrival in South Bend, Ind. Four people escaped serious injury.

• Fuel exhaustion and fuel mismanagement were mentioned in the description of "probable cause" for a double-engine-stoppage accident. The 24-year-old pilot had departed Monmouth, N.J. for West Chicago, Ill., nonstop, against undetermined headwinds; substantial damage occurred when the plane, out of fuel, made an off-airport landing near its intended destination.

Note: Perhaps it's worth mentioning that none of the 12 persons involved in the four non-fatal accidents cited above suffered serious injuries. (Perhaps it's worth observing, too, that although weather radar is available as an option on the Duchess, anti-icing equipment of the type that might have prevented two of these accidents is not.)

A review by our sister publication *Aviation Safety* showed the Duchess to have a fatal accident rate much better (lower) than its peers in the "new" light twin class, the Gulfstream American Cougar and the Piper Seminole and, in fact, a much better rate than the general aviation fleet as a whole.

Economics of Operation

Beech in 1982 estimated the direct hourly operating cost of the Duchess at $63.79—including $37.05/hr for gasoline ($1.95/gal at 19 gph), $1.59/hr for oil, $15.57/hr for "inspection, maintenance, and propeller overhaul" (assuming shop rates of $27/hr), and an engine exchange allowance—including FWF accessories and installation labor—of $9.58/hr (total, for both engines together). One owner claimed a direct operating cost of $53.24/hr *minus* engine reserves, so it appears Beech's numbers are pretty much on target.

Twin doors make coming and going a breeze. A large third door in the rear cabin serves bags and kids.

Piper, for what it's worth, estimated a direct hourly operating cost of $60.57 for the normally aspirated Seminole, based on 17.7 gph fuel consumption (at $1.95/gal). The Turbo Seminole's higher fuel flows and greater overhaul costs brings its direct operating expense to $70.49 per hour.

Maintenance Considerations

From a reliability standpoint, the Duchess has one thing going for it that the Seminole does not: namely, the A-series Lycoming O-360 engine. Unlike the E-series O-360s installed in the Seminole, the Model 76's O-360-A1G6D engines are among Lycoming's oldest and most proven O-360 variants, utterly worthy of the 2,000-hr TBO bestowed upon them. The Seminole's O-360-E1A6D engines, on the other hand, are a more recent design with valve train components common to the O-320-H "Blue Streak" engine of Skyhawk fame.

As almost everyone knows by now, the O-320-H has had a history of severe tappet-spalling problems. (The spalling—which seems cold-weather related—is partially preventable by the use of Lycoming's special LW-16702 oil additive.) What you may *not* have known is that the O-360-E (and TO-360-E) engines on the

Seminole also have the potential for tappet-destruction problems. In fact, Lycoming requires regular use of the LW-16702 "mystery oil" as a prerequisite to warranty coverage for O-360-E engines. (The oil additive is *not* required for the Duchess.)

This is not to say, of course, that the Duchess does not have its share of maintenance problems; seven AD notes and 45 service bulletins in the first four years of operation say otherwise. For the most part, however, the Duchess's maintenance glitches are minor. Most of the ADs, for example, involve one-time inspections or fixes applicable to early-serial-number aircraft. The only important repetitive AD affecting the aircraft (other than the one targeting the plane's Southwind combustion heater) is a 1980 AD (80-19-12) requiring 50-hr checks of the engine mounts for cracks. Unfortunately, the AD names all Duchesses from S/N -1 on up, and even though an improved engine mount is available, it is not clear from the wording of the AD whether installation of the heavy-duty mount eliminates the repetitive inspection requirement.

Beech Duchess Resale Value

Space prohibits an exhaustive listing of Duchess-related Service Instructions here. Most of these bulletins involve minor product improvements or non-mandatory inspections. Some, however, are of major importance (such as S.I. 1147 pertaining to engine mount replacement; and S.I. 1166, regarding improved main gear doors). Prospective Duchess buyers would be well-advised to crosscheck aircraft logbooks against the Beech S.I. Master Index available through any Beech dealer) to see whether applicable service bulletins have been complied with.

Owner Comments

Our company operates two Duchess aircraft. They have both exceeded our expectations in all aspects. The handling characteristics are very good, although the elevator seems to be a bit light. True airspeeds vary between 155 and 160 knots at 65 percent power with a fuel flow of 19 gallons per hour.

Our direct operating cost averaged $53.24 per hour with no engine reserves. These figures were for a seven-month period during which the aircraft flew 506 hours. Their normal load is one and occasionally two passengers, and we average about 150-mile stage lengths.

Our only major unscheduled problem was one engine overhaul at 1,400 hours, due to a lifter that disintegrated. As far as the airframe is concerned, our problems have been the gear doors, which tend to develop cracks, and an engine mount inspection at 50-hour intervals. We had one cracked mount. Beech has provided a fix for the gear doors and has given us very good product support. Single-engine performance is a little better than average for this class of aircraft, and handling characteristics on one engine are very good. From a pilot's point of view, these aircraft are a delight to fly, and from an accountant's standpoint, easy to feed.

Marvin Pippen
Wharton, Tex.

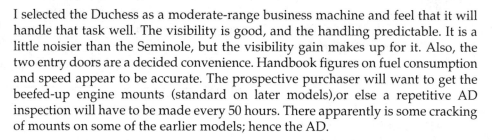

Duchess has the luxury of trim controls not only for pitch, but rudder and ailerons as well. Note carb heat knobs above mike. Engines are not fuel injected. Crossfeed control levers are at bottom.

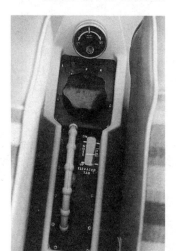

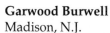

I selected the Duchess as a moderate-range business machine and feel that it will handle that task well. The visibility is good, and the handling predictable. It is a little noisier than the Seminole, but the visibility gain makes up for it. Also, the two entry doors are a decided convenience. Handbook figures on fuel consumption and speed appear to be accurate. The prospective purchaser will want to get the beefed-up engine mounts (standard on later models),or else a repetitive AD inspection will have to be made every 50 hours. There apparently is some cracking of mounts on some of the earlier models; hence the AD.

The Duchess pilot will want to take special care when securing after a flight. The rudder trim should be rolled full down and the rudder locks installed. They're hard to figure out, but do it anyway. The elevator surface droops naturally at rest and will damage the rudder if the rudder is allowed to swing in the wind.

Last, but not least: have a set of "starter engaged" indicator lights installed on the panel if the airplane doesn't already have them. As I learned, extended cranking will cause the starter relay to hang up, keeping the relay engaged. The result of all of this is that the starter will be damaged (probably destroyed) and the battery run down. The trouble is that you don't know it. A voltmeter would be handy at times like this. (The lesson here is to get familiar with the electrical system.) Incidentally, I have to give high marks for the position of the circuit breakers and engine instruments in the Duchess. All are handy and well laid out.

Garwood Burwell
Madison, N.J.

Mine is a 1980 aircraft which has proved to be fairly satisfactory. There were considerable problems with the gear actuators, which required replacement six times. They continually leaked and blew seals. Also, the passenger windows are now showing stress cracks where they are riveted. Beech was supposed to be looking into this. Handling qualities are very satisfactory, and landings and takeoffs are to the book. Speed on the average is 165 knots at 75 percent power. Fuel burn is seven gal/hr/side. The carbureted system is easy to start. The interior is very roomy and quite comfortable. There is easy access through the twin cabin doors and rear door.

The annuals run around $1,200, with about $125 per month for general maintenance. The avionics panel is small, limiting equipment choice, and the yoke doesn't accommodate sufficient space for wiring push-to-talk buttons or remote ident switches, etc. Sound in the cabin could be better, and a prop synch would be nice. Visibility is excellent and loading adequate. In summary, I would like to see more horsepower to obtain a cruise of 185 to 190 knots. Range is good, but with larger engines or turbocharging, this could be increased. In all, it is a good economical twin with fine handling characteristics—a high-quality aircraft.

Nathan Goldenthal
Peoria, Ariz.

Beech
Barons

Beech's Baron is widely regarded as the "class" item among light twins— sort of a twin-engine Bonanza—with lots of performance, superb handling and a reputation for luxury and quality.

More than 5,000 Barons have been built over the past 27 years, ranging from the basic 260-hp 55 model to the pressurized 325-hp 58P. As an investment, the standard Baron has few peers, retaining a high proportion of its original value and, in most cases, appreciating steadily after a few years.

History

The Baron was introduced in 1961 as an outgrowth of the Model 95 Travel Air series. That first Model 55 Baron had 260-hp Continental engines (up from 180-hp on the Travel Air) and a gross weight nearly 700 pounds higher than the Travel Air's. The 55 was Beech's answer to the very popular Cessna 310, which had been introduced six years earlier.

A matched pair: the E55 on top, and the B55. The main difference between the two: 50 extra horses in the E model.

The 1962 and 1963 Barons were called the A55, and offered a sixth seat as an option. The fuselage of the A55 was also 10 inches longer than the straight 55's. In 1964 it became the B55, a designation that lasted until production of the 260-hp Baron was suspended in 1983. In 1966, the gross weight of the B55 was increased from 4,880 to 5,100 pounds (actually, the higher gross weight applied to the last 11 of the 1965 models as well). With the gross weight came another nose extension to accommodate a larger front baggage compartment.

In 1966, the 260-hp B55 was joined by the 285-hp C55, which offered blistering performance (210-knot top speed) and 200 pounds more gross weight. The 1966 and 1967 big-engine Barons were the C55s, evolving to the D55 in 1968 and 1969, and finally to the E55 in 1970. Until the end of their production run in 1982, the 260-hp B55 and the 285-hp E55 remained virtually unchanged.

In 1967, the short-lived 56TC Baron was introduced. It was powered by monstrous turbocharged 380-hp Lycoming engines and a cruise speed of 247 knots was claimed. However, only 94 56TCs were sold over the next five years, and the airplane was discontinued after 1971. Apparently the lack of a large six-place cabin and pressurization doomed the airplane, and single-engine characteristics were reportedly, shall we say, challenging.

Taking up the slack from the unsuccessful 56TC in 1970 was the stretched 58 Baron, which at last provided a full six-seat interior instead of the four-plus-two arrangement of the standard-body Barons. It used the same 285-hp Continental

engines as the big-engine 55 Barons, and had virtually the same performance as its short-bodied stablemate. The 58, with its wide double-door entry and club-car seating, has continued to be a strong seller, though in 1988 it listed for about half a million dollars equipped.

In 1975, Beech introduced the pressurized 58P, with 310-hp engines. These were upgraded to 325 hp in 1979. In addition to the pressurization and bigger engines, the 58P has 100 pounds extra gross weight and a cruise speed that is 19 knots higher than the standard 58 (by the book at least). A "non-pressurized 58P" was introduced in 1976, called the 58TC. The TC has the same engines as the P model, and got the boost to 325 hp at the same time, in 1979. Production was halted in 1982, however.

Investment Value

Like the Bonanza, the Baron is a real blue-chip in resale value in most cases. For example, a 1970 B55 originally cost $13,000 less than the 1970 310, but in 1988 was worth $8,500 more. The big-engine E55 also looks good; a 1978 E55 cost $186,000 new and was worth $96,000 in 1988 (52 percent). A 1978 310 returns 44 percent, and is worth a fat $20,500 less

In addition to the pilots' door, the Baron 58P has a single left rear cabin door instead of double doors on the right side. Certified to newer standards, the instrument panel has conventional throttle quadrant, gear and flap sequence.

than the E55 on the used-plane market. The 58 series does even better; a 1978 long-body Baron 10 years later in 1988 was worth 60 percent of its original value.

The pressurized Baron 58P, however, doesn't seem to match the rest of the family in resale value. "The P-Baron has taken a real hit on the used-plane market," one big broker told us. Based on *Aircraft Bluebook Price Digest* retail figures, a 1978 P-Baron is today worth under 50 percent of its original price. For a straight 58 Baron, the figure is about 60 percent. "For the same money that a used 58P costs, you can buy a 421 that's just one year older. And the 421 is full cabin class, a hell of a lot more airplane," explained the dealer.

Another resale loser among the Barons is the ill-fated 56TC. The net value of those big engines over the years has been just about zero; a used 56TC is worth several thousand dollars less than an E55 of the same vintage, which had non-turbocharged engines of 100 fewer horsepower each. Overhaul price on the 56TC engines runs about $23,000 apiece—about twice that for the powerplants on the E55 Baron.

Performance

Here is the Baron's strong suit. The big-engine Barons are faster than any light twin except the Aerostar, and the 260-hp 55, A55, and B55 aren't too far behind. Owners report real-world cruising speeds of about 191 knots for the B55 and 195-200 knots for the E55 and 58 models. The turbocharged versions—56TC, 58TC and 58P—are of course much faster at high altitude, with max cruise speeds ranging from about 209 knots for the 310-hp 58P and TC to well over 217 knots for the monster 56TC. The 325-hp 58TC and 58P, introduced in 1979, are listed by the books as about 9-13 knots faster than their 310-hp counterparts.

Standard fuel capacity in the small-body 55 Barons is normally 112 gallons (100 gallons usable), which gives a rather marginal endurance of less than four hours, with no reserve. Many 55s have optional tanks that raise capacity to a more reasonable 142 gallons (136 usable), good for over five hours at moderate cruise power. The 285-hp airplanes burn about five gph more than the 260s, so even the 142-gallon tanks are not exactly generous. The 1973 and later E55s, however, have an optional capacity of 166 gallons, which is satisfactory for most IFR flying.

All the 58 models have standard 166-gallon fuel tanks, and most have optional tanks that raise capacity to 190 gallons. Obviously, a used Baron with long-range tanks is more desirable because of the greater flexibility for ultra-long-range flights with light passenger loads. (But extra tanks can be a mixed blessing from the maintenance standpoint. More on that later.)

Takeoff performance of the Baron is also excellent, particularly in the C, D and E55 models. Even at gross weight, an E55 needs little more than 1,000 feet to clear

Cost/Performance/Specifications

Model	Year	Average Retail Price	Cruise Speed (kts)	Useful Load (lbs)	Fuel Std/Opt (gals)	Engine	TBO (hrs)	Overhaul Cost
55	1961	$30,000	191	1,920	112	260-hp Cont. IO-470-L	1,500	$10,300
A55	1962-63	$32,500	191	1,920	112	260-hp Cont. IO-470-L	1,500	$10,300
B55	1964-66	$36,500	188	1,895	112	260-hp Cont. IO-470-L	1,500	$10,300
B55	1967-69	$43,000	188	1,895	112	260-hp Cont. IO-470-L	1,500	$10,300
B55	1970-72	$49,000	188	1,895	100/136	260-hp Cont. IO-470-L	1,500	$10,300
B55	1973-75	$60,000	188	1,895	100/136	260-hp Cont. IO-470-L	1,500	$10,300
B55	1976-78	$77,000	188	1,895	100/136	260-hp Cont. IO-470-L	1,500	$10,300
B55	1979-81	$106,000	188	1,895	100/136	260-hp Cont. IO-470-L	1,500	$10,300
B55	1982	$132,000	188	1,895	100/136	260-hp Cont. IO-470-L	1,500	$10,300
E55	1970-72	$56,000	200	2,033	100/136/166	285-hp Cont. IO-520-CB	1,700	$12,000
E55	1973-75	$69,000	200	2,033	100/136/166	285-hp Cont. IO-520-CB	1,700	$12,000
E55	1976-78	$87,000	200	2,033	100/136/166	285-hp Cont. IO-520-CB	1,700	$12,000
E55	1979-81	$126,000	200	2,033	100/136/166	285-hp Cont. IO-520-CB	1,700	$12,000
E55	1982	$164,000	200	2,033	100/136/166	285-hp Cont. IO-520-CB	1,700	$12,000
58	1970-72	$64,000	200	2,063	100/136/166	285-hp Cont. IO-520-CB	1,700	$12,000
58	1973-75	$84,000	200	2,063	100/136/166	285-hp Cont. IO-520-CB	1,700	$12,000
58	1976-78	$110,000	200	2,063	100/136/166	285-hp Cont. IO-520-CB	1,700	$12,000
58	1979-81	$155,000	200	2,063	100/136/166	285-hp Cont. IO-520-CB	1,700	$12,000
58	1982-84	$220,000	200	2,063	100/136/166	285-hp Cont. IO-520-CB	1,700	$12,000
58	1985-87	$374,000	200	2,063	100/136/166	285-hp Cont. IO-520-CB	1,700	$12,000
58P	1976-78	$120,000	214	2,115	166/190	310-hp Cont. TSIO-520-LB	1,400	$17,000
58P	1979-81	$165,000	220	2,230	166/190	325-hp Cont. TSIO-520-WB	1,600	$17,500
58P	1982-84	$280,000	220	2,230	166/190	325-hp Cont. TSIO-520-WB	1,600	$17,500
58P	1985-87	$535,000	220	2,230	166/190	325-hp Cont. TSIO-520-WB	1,600	$17,500

a 50-foot obstacle on takeoff (under standard conditions, of course). This requires some fairly extreme piloting technique that puts the airplane in the air below Vmc, however. With normal technique, takeoff distances under 2,000 feet are still possible at gross weight in the 55 Barons.

'78 Baron Resale Value

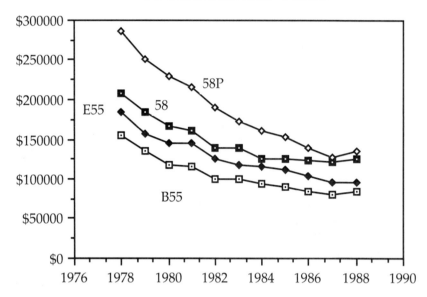

Handling

A major reason for the Baron's popularity and owner loyalty is the aircraft's superb handling qualities. The Baron is responsive and well harmonized—a delight to fly. "The Baron is a beautiful-flying aircraft, and it is just plain fun to handle the controls," is a typical owner comment. There are no handling idiosyncrasies (such as severe pitch-up with flap deployment, as in the Aztec) we're aware of. "Real aviators" like the fact that there are no downsprings or aileron-rudder interconnects in most models of the Baron.

The other side of the "responsive" coin is, of course, sensitivity in turbulent IFR conditions. The same light control forces that win oohs and ahs from pilots demand more attention in the clouds, and a good autopilot is almost a necessity in a Baron flown IFR. One owner reports, "I have had several frightening moments because of its unstable flying characteristics in turbulence."

Like the Bonanza, the Baron is famed for its easy landings (except for the 58P), with a combination of pitch response and landing gear geometry that really boosts the egos of pilots. For many pilots, the way an airplane "feels" can overcome many performance shortcomings; the Baron's handling qualities have doubtless won over hundreds of pilots who may have been on the verge of buying something else.

Accommodations

The Baron pilot sits high, wide and handsome, with a plush, roomy cockpit and a professional-looking panel thankfully devoid of the plastic found in most other airplanes. Headroom is particularly good. The 55 Barons are labeled "six-seaters," but the two rear seats are cramped afterthoughts, suitable only for kids or midgets on long flights. The 58 models have the famous "club car" seating, which puts the back four passengers face to face in the style of the Orient Express. Although lacking Orient-Express roominess, the rear compartment of the 58 is adequate by light aircraft standards, and the fifth and sixth seats at least qualify as small-sized adult repositories.

The 58 models also have a big, wide double-door entrance to the rear compartment—a very nice touch. The 55s have the standard single right-side pilot's door, which entails a certain amount of clambering for the hindmost travelers. Baggage capacity is good, with front and rear compartments that allow reasonable balancing and good capacities in most models.

Up front, a couple of items on the panel are worth noting. First, the Baron's throttle quadrant is notorious for its reverse throttle and prop positions: the prop lever is on the left, with the throttle in the middle. An airplane could not be certified that way today, but Beech kept on building them that way for some reason. Also, the gear and flap levers are reversed from their normal position in other aircraft, which could lead to the sound of crunching metal when the pilot retracts the "flaps" during rollout after landing. (The 58P is an exception. And Beech finally got around to reversing the position on other Barons with the 1984 models.) NTSB, which a couple years earlier recommended Beech change the configuration, has figures that show many accidents of this type. The single throwover yoke is also an unusual feature, one that sometimes makes multi-engine instruction a tricky business (see "Safety" section for details).

Make sure the door is latched securely to prevent an inadvertent opening.

Maintenance Checkpoints

The "Curse of the Cracking Crankcase" has depleted the bank accounts of more than a few 285-hp Baron owners. While crankcase cracks are rarely a safety-of-flight item, they can be expensive maintenance headaches. One operator of a fleet of Barons reports he spent over $70,000 in premature overhauls triggered by case cracks.

As you shop for used Barons, you may hear references to "light cases" and "heavy cases." Pre-1976 airplanes had cases which were particularly prone to cracking. Continental then introduced a beefier case which was supposed to lick the problem. It didn't. An *Aviation Consumer* survey in 1982 showed that, if anything, the "heavy" cases cracked a bit more often—and earlier in the engine's life—than the so-called "light" cases.

There have been so many permutations of IO-520-C crankcases that we can't advise one type as preferable to any other. As far as we can tell, they all are prone to crack. More important than case "heaviness" or "lightness" is heat-treating for stress relief. The crankcases are not heat-treated when they come from the factory, but some owners have their cases heat-treated during overhaul or when cracks are repaired. This apparently reduces internal stress in the metal, dramatically reducing the cracking tendency. "I've heat-treated hundreds of IO-520 cases," one repair shop told us, "and not one of them has cracked that I'm aware of."

The bottom line: carefully check the crankcases of any 285-hp Baron considered for purchase. And count it a plus if the case has been heat-treated.

B55 "economy" Baron is fast, has sturdy gear, high lowering speeds, and trim for all three axes.

Despite the epidemic cracking crankcases, the Baron's owner loyalty is striking. One hyperenthusiastic 1974 Baron 58 owner wrote us, "Over a period of five years, my Baron operated flawlessly, with very minor problems, except the usual

Lineup of 1978 Model 58 Barons includes, from top, the 58TC, a big-engined "unpressurized P model," the 58 and 58P.

crankcase crack problems occurred at about 950 hours, necessitating the replacement of both engines at considerable expense...".

The other big maintenance headache for Barons is the rubber bladder-type fuel cells. The lifetime of these cells can be as low as three or four years, and 10 years seems to be about the maximum. The tanks of any used Baron should be carefully checked for leakage, and a buyer would be wise to set aside a bladder replacement fund for the inevitable $3,500-plus wallop and accompanying downtime. Like the man in the cigar commercial says, "We're gonna get you...". Some pre-1964 Barons may still have the so-called "light" cylinders, which proved troublesome and are subject to an AD requiring 20-hour inspections.

Other Baron problems to look out for: crazing windshields, unreliable Goodyear brakes, old B-series autopilots (very difficult to get service anymore), electric cowl flaps on pre-1974 models, 100-amp (Presto-Lite or Crittendon) alternators, and Airborne high-capacity vacuum pumps used for de-ice applications.

Safety

In terms of overOwners' Groupall accidents, the Baron ranks about average among light twins. Fatal accident rate was also about in the middle of the pack. From 1972-76, the entire Baron/Travel Air series scored 2.8 and 8.3, respectively, for fatal and total accident rates (per 100,000 hours). The same group improved to 1.4 and 5.3 in 1977-82, for overall scores of 2.0 and 6.5 for the entire decade. We decided to separate the 58 and 55 models out of the group to see if there was a difference between the long-body 58s and their smaller forebears. The answer: not much. For the period 1977-82 only, the 58 had a low 1.1 fatal rate, while the 55 was a not-quite-so-low 1.4. The 58 also had a better overall accident rate, 4.5 to 6.4.

The Baron's accident rate might have been better without a bunch of stall/spin accidents. An earlier study commissioned by *Aviation Consumer* showed that for the years 1970-74, the Baron had a much higher stall/spin rate than other light twins. In fact, about a quarter of all fatal Baron accidents during that period were stall/spins. Eliminate those, and the Baron's accident rate would improve noticeably. The Baron stall/spin rate has apparently declined in recent years, however, as more attention has been focused on the subject and Beech has mailed Baron owners handbook supplements warning of the problem. That may be a big part of the Baron's improved accident rate during the last half of the decade.

A 1974 Army test report on the single-engine stall characteristics of the T-42A, the military version of the Baron, sheds some light on the subject. (The special test came after a series of fatal stall/spin accidents during Army training flights.) The Army test pilot reported that the T-42A would enter a spin within one second after a single-engine stall unless immediate anti-spin action was taken. Even if stall recovery was initiated within one-quarter second after the stall break, said the Army report, a split-S and 1,000-foot altitude loss resulted. The author of the report also criticized the T-42A operator's manual for not warning of the serious consequences of a single-engine stall, and not explaining, for example, that single-engine stall speed was up to 20 knots higher than the listed stall speed under symmetric power conditions.

Later Baron manual revisions carry blunter warnings in the safety section, however. And Beech has energetically promoted use of a Vsse "minimum safe single-engine speed" that adds a few extra knots to the point above which pilots should attempt to yank a throttle and expect safe and sane performance.

Modifications

Among the major aftermarket upgrades available for 55-series Barons is Friday International's V/G System, which uses vortex generators on the wing leading edges and the left side of the vertical stabilizer to improve the airplane's low-speed handling and stall characteristics. The company claims its system reduces stall speed in landing configuration 10 knots, Vmc by 12 knots (to 75 knots) and accelerate-stop distance by 1,070 feet (to 2,100 feet) for the big-engined models. A kit, including a new airspeed indicator with revised markings, costs $3,450 and requires about seven hours to install. Friday International Corp., 600 Franklin Drive, Friday Harbor, Wash. 98250; (800) 992-3435.

Bigger engines are available from Colemill. Factory-rebuilt 300-hp IO-520E engines and three-blade Hartzell props turn 55, A and B models into "President 600s" for $42,500. Rebuilt 300-hp IO-550Cs and four-blade Hartzells turn C, D and E models into "Foxstars" for $55,000. (Brand-new engines tack about $10,000 onto the bill.) Colemill Enterprises, P.O. Box 60627, Cornelia Fort Airpark, Nashville, Tenn. 37206; (615) 226-4256.

Mods like one-piece windshields and updated side windows are available from Beryl D'Shannon, Lakeville, Min., (800) 328-4629.

Petersen Aviation has STC'd an alcohol/water-injection system that allows Barons with IO-520 engines to run on 91-octane auto gas. (At press time, approval of the system on IO-470-powered Barons was pending.) The system costs $4,350 and takes about 35 man-hours to install. Petersen is, however, providing free installations through the end of 1988. Petersen Aviation, Route 1, Box 18, Minden, Neb. 68959, (800) 352-3232.

Another mod worthy of mention is baffled fuel tanks. Barons built before 1971 didn't have them, and a few have experienced power losses due to unporting during slips and turning takeoffs. The tanks costs $1,400, each, and take about eight hours to install. They're available from Floats and Fuel Cells, 4010 Pilot Drive, Suite No. 3, Memphis, Tenn. 38118, (800) 647-6148.

Owner's Group

Baron owners don't have an association of their own, but the Wichita-based American Bonanza Society, (316) 945-6913, counts 400 Baron owners among its 8,200 members. The ABS publishes an informative newsletter and conducts service and proficiency clinics at about a dozen locations each year.

Owner Comments

When I bought my Model 55 Baron (one of the first produced) in 1973, it was not in very good condition. I upgraded the airplane with Cleveland brakes, a new one-piece windshield, new avionics and a new interior and paint job. The Baron has been a joy to fly. It's similar to the Travel Air I owned previously but is more stable and powerful. Generally, it is very comfortable; but the cockpit is a bit noisy and crowded. There's little room for pilot supplies in the front seats. Reliability over the years has been outstanding. Operating costs are at a minimum for a twin. I recommend a 55 Baron to anyone who enjoys flying a multiengine airplane. At today's prices, it is a genuine bargain.

George C. Burnett, Sr.
La Jolla, Calif.

The B55 Baron's IO-470L engines are strong and seem to be a great match with the airframe. No turbos and no pressurization make this a low-maintenance airplane. "Beechcraft-only" parts, however, are expensive; but Beech has a strong support network, which is a big advantage. The American Bonanza Society has been a big help, too. Over the last five years, owner-assisted annual inspections of my 1978 B55 have averaged about $900, each, and have taken about 35 man-hours. The original engines went to TBO easily. The remans now have 400 hours with no problems. Among major items that had to be replaced were a windshield (covered by Beech warranty), a fuel cell ($1,800) and a Bendix radar magnetron ($1,500). The airplane has excellent speed: 186 knots on 23 gph at 65 percent power and 8,000 feet. Single-engine performance is typical of light twins. Don't do full stalls!

Jim Morris
Melbourne Beach, Fla.

I have owned a B55 Baron for seven years. I plan on 190 knots at 7,000 to 12,000 feet and a block-to-block fuel burn of 25 gph. I have the 142-gallon system, so range and endurance are excellent. I have flown all Baron models; the B seems to be an excellent airframe and engine combination. It is almost as fast, burns five gph less fuel and is much quieter than the IO-520-powered Barons. It is fun to fly and has a harmonious control feeling that is remarkable. It's very easy to land and doesn't pitch up when you use flaps. The fifth and sixth seats are good either for small people or for short trips, though the large windows don't give people back there a closed-in feeling. I would recommend the extended rear baggage bay, which was an option. Also, Cleveland brakes are a must; they were well worth the $800 it cost to put them on the plane.

I could complain about the high cost of Beech parts, but at least you can always get them. Also, the plane is well-designed and built like a Swiss watch, so you don't need airframe parts that often. For parts that are common to other makes, like engines and brakes, you can go to another supplier, such as Van Dusen. It's nice to know, though, that Beech stands ready to support the plane. I don't think I've ever owned anything that has brought me as much satisfaction as my Baron. It's extremely well designed and built—a class act.

Bill Packer
Flint, Mich.

Beech 60 Duke

Beech's Duke pressurized twin is billed as the ultimate personal airplane, and it would be hard to argue its hairy-chested appeal. The Duke is sleek, well-built and carries perhaps the most prestigious status symbol of them all—a monumental price tag. A new one during the last year of production in 1982 cost nearly $600,000, and you'll have to get a pretty ratty old one if you want to spend less than $100,000. For this kind of money, you absolutely must know the ins and outs of the used Duke market, for some models have had some serious problems that, if uncorrected, could cause astronomical maintenance costs.

History

The Duke was first introduced in 1968 and was then known as the model 60. Since then the airplane underwent steady refinement, but no major changes in configuration. The A60 model was introduced in 1971, and had a modest increase in gross weight, up 50 pounds from 6,725 to 6,775 (useful load actually went down a bit, however) and modest decreases in performance because of the extra weight. (According to the book figures, short-field performance of the straight 60 is much better than the A60, but Duke owners tell us the early figures were very optimistic, and that the A60 is only slightly poorer in takeoff and landing performance than its predecessor.)

The B60 was introduced in 1974, and featured a slightly larger cabin, more fuel capacity, with small degradations in speed and useful load; otherwise there have been no major configuration changes since then.

Engines on all Dukes are 380-hp Lycoming TIO-541s. Early models of this engine were troublesome nightmares with 1,200-hour TBOs, but the engine has been improved over the years with various modifications; TBO is now 1,600 hours, and we've talked to several Duke owners who have gone well past that figure. We'll go into detail about the various engine modifications and what to look for later in the article.

Performance

The Duke is a movin' machine, but it does slurp up the petroleum. Owners report a maximum cruise speed of about 220 knots (250 mph) at 68-70 percent power at 24,000 feet. This is a bit better than other pressurized twins, with the exception of the fleet Aerostar 601P, which can fly 10-15 knots faster on about 25 percent less fuel. The Duke's fuel flow at 220 knots is about 40 gph. Fuel consumption can be reduced to about 30 gph at 55 percent power, but speed drops down to 185 knots or so—and you might as well be flying a 310. One owner tells us he flightplans at 195 to 200 knots with 65 percent power, burning 40 gph, however.

For a pressurized aircraft designed to cruise above 20,000 feet, climb performance is critical, and the Duke again makes a good showing in this department. One corporate operator reports about 28 minutes to 24,000 feet—at full gross and on a warm day. Other owners confirm that the airplane climbs well at high altitudes, reportedly 700 to 1,000 fpm depending on weight. Climb performance of the Duke is generally considered superior to any other owner-flown pressurized twin—except, again, for the pressurized Aerostar.

Front baggage compartment can hold 500 pounds structurally. Chances of loading too far aft are reduced since there is no rear baggage compartment.

With a standard fuel capacity of 142 gallons, range is rather limited, but virtually all Dukes have optional long-range fuel tanks with capacities ranging from 202 to 232 gallons, depending on the model. With optional tanks full, a four-hour trip can be made with IFR reserves at a good cruising speed. That translates into a full-fuel maximum range of about 900 nm; at reduced power, range may be stretched well over 1,000 nm. This is about average for this class of aircraft.

The Duke is definitely not a STOL airplane, however; most operators consider a 3,000-foot runway the absolute minimum. Motorcycle daredevil Evel Knievel

once ordered the pilot of his Duke to land on a drag strip. He didn't make it, and the plane ended up with its nose poked through the truck trailer that Knievel uses as a mobile dressing room. Owners also report the initial climb after takeoff is rather poor. "It doesn't really seem to start climbing well until it's got 500 feet under it," one corporate pilot told us.

According to the book, single-engine performance is about average for this class of airplane—that is to say barely adequate under ideal conditions. Single-engine ceiling is 15,100 feet.

Weight and Loading

Here's where the Duke shines. Useful load of late-model Dukes generally runs better than 2,000 pounds, even when loaded with equipment. Earlier model Dukes weigh several hundred pounds less empty and tend to have less equipment; some straight 60 and A60 models have useful loads approaching 2,300 pounds. These numbers are markedly superior to anything else in the Duke's class, and the equal of even the cabin-class Cessna 421. Since the Duke has only six seats to fill (the 421 has seven), there's plenty left for baggage and fuel.

Unfortunately, the Duke's healthy appetite for fuel cuts into payload somewhat; other small pressurized twins will use a couple hundred fewer pounds of fuel over a long trip. Nevertheless, the Duke is still a full-fuel-plus-two-to-four people airplane. One corporate operator reports he routinely flies six people and 136 gallons of fuel (enough for a three-hour, 600-mile trip) in a lavishly equipped Duke. However, another private owner is at gross with full optional fuel, two people and 100 pounds of baggage.

Muscular 380-hp engines give the aircraft enviable speeds, but at the cost of high fuel consumption. Count on a hefty $46,000 tab to overhaul two.

Unlike some other Beech airplanes, the Duke is not sensitive to balance. "You can hardly get it out of c.g.," reports one owner. The plane has ample baggage capacity since the huge nose compartment holds 500 pounds. There is no rear compartment. "I wore out three calculators running payload-range numbers on all the pressurized twins, and the Duke came out on top for the operation we have," claims a Duke pilot.

Passenger Comfort

For an aircraft that is often used as a corporate aircraft to haul around executives, passenger comfort is an important, if not critical, factor. One company pilot, in fact, reports that his company chose the Duke partly because the company president was rather elderly and feeble, and didn't like to negotiate the airstair doors of other pressurized airplanes. Frankly, though, it's difficult to imagine he found the single retractable step of the Duke much of an improvement.

Although users rate the Duke high in overall passenger comfort, it must be noted the airplane has a typical Beech cabin, tapering at the rear like the Barons and Bonanzas. This means that two men would find things cramped sitting together in the rearmost seats. The B60 model introduced in 1974 did offer a bit more lateral cabin room by reworking the side panels and ducting, and recent models are supposed to have gained a couple of inches in apparent aisle space thanks simply to reengineered seats.

The Duke has a cabin pressure differential of 4.7, which is higher than any other six-place pressurized piston aircraft. It allows a cabin altitude of 10,000 feet at maximum cruising altitude of 24,000 feet.

Flight Characteristics

Pilots praise the Duke's manners in the air. It is a rock-solid instrument platform (as one might expect from the heaviest of all the six-passenger airplanes). Pitch changes with flap and gear extension are minimal and pilots tell us the Duke trims up well and holds its airspeed—all big plusses for instrument flying. "It flies beautifully in the 19,000-20,000-foot range and gives you a nice, secure feeling," comments one owner.

Looked at in another way, however, stability translates as heaviness on the controls. The airplane indeed demands rather ponderous inputs on ailerons and elevators, and at least one owner said he'd like to see a bit more alacrity and responsiveness in the bird. We'd frankly rate it about on a par with likes of a Cessna 340, however.

Cockpit Engineering

Praise be, that on the Duke, Beech has placed the power controls in the standard order, along with the gear and flap levers. (In the Barons, they are all "reversed," except in the 58P.) The flap system is beautifully simple; the lever has three positions: up, approach and land—with little lights for transition, APH and LDG. And there are even two separate control wheels as standard (not throwover).

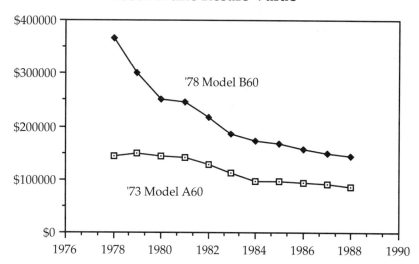

Beech Duke Resale Value

Cowl flap operation is electric. Glance out the window to see if they are extended or not. The gear whirs down in a zippy four seconds flat and can be lowered for drag at the typically phenomenal Beech airspeed of 175 knots. Visibility out the front of the Duke is what we'd call barely adequate, and to see over the glareshield, an average-height pilot who pulls the seat forward (and up, automatically) may find his head nestled against the headliner.

Incidentally, thanks to the narrow opening to the front cockpit, getting to and from the pilot seats takes a bit of elasticity. Once snugly seated, however, the Duke pilot can be assured of a beautifully smooth, quiet ride rarely matched in a piston twin.

Safety Record

The Duke doesn't have a bad fatal accident record, but NTSB statistics show a surprising number of gear collapse accidents, which usually don't hurt anybody but can be painfully expensive.

Of the 500 or so Dukes built, seven had been involved in fatal crashes at the time of our study in 1978. Three of these were IFR approach accidents caused by pilot error. A fourth occurred when the airplane accumulated ice and was unable to maintain altitude over the Utah mountains. Three of the fatal crashes were not weather-related. In one Duke accident, which killed noted air race and sport pilot Leroy Penhall, a propeller overspeeded. Penhall was unable to maintain control of the airplane while attempting to return to the airport. Investigators believe Penhall failed to exercise the props before takeoff (it was a very cold day) and congealed oil caused the overspeed. Two other fatal Duke crashes were a result of mid-air structural breakups—one likely caused by severe turbulence, the other under unknown circumstances.

There have been no reported Duke accidents due to fuel unporting, which has caused several Baron and Bonanza crashes. (The three airplanes share a similar wing and main fuel tank.)

Among NTSB's listing of non-fatal Duke accidents, landing gear collapses and inadvertent gear retractions led the way. At least two gear retractions on rollout were laid to Beech's inconsistence in the placement of gear and flap levers of its different-model twins. In one case, a pilot who'd been flying Queen Airs inadvertently hit the Duke gear lever instead of the flaps during rollout. The positions of the levers in the Duke, it turns out, are the reverse of their locations in the Queen Air.

The substantial number of gear collapse accidents is no doubt a reflection of the Duke's heaviness (nearly 7,000 pounds) and high touchdown speeds. Also, the plane has a tendency to wheelbarrow during braking, which can result in blown tires and/or collapsed gear. Anyone shopping for a used Duke should snoop carefully through the logbooks for evidence of any landing gear damage.

Operating Costs

Any pressurized twin-engine airplane costs a small fortune to maintain, of course, but the Duke seems to stand out even in this posh company. Beechcrafts, of course, are considered the Cadillacs of the industry, and the owner pays accordingly. Two Duke owners we queried for this report used virtually the same phrase when they described the high charges they've been socked with for parts and maintenance: "Anytime you take a Duke to get fixed, man, they see you coming a mile away." (See the "Other Service Problems" section for specific examples of some of the extraordinarily high repair costs incurred by Duke owners.)

Massive instrument panel holds everything, including the kitchen sink. Visibility out the front is not the greatest.

An owner gave this sampling of the cost of parts for his Duke: battery $1,000, generator $2,800, tires $90, $240 for a small cowl flap motor, new engines installed were $35,000. He reported maintenance costs of $72 per hour. Another owner reported a grand total operating cost (including depreciation) of $166/hr based on 300 hrs/yr, and $127/yr based on 500 hrs/yr. One Duke owner who found he couldn't afford the airplane's upkeep reports, "We almost cried when we had to give it up for something more economical." It seems typical of Duke owners that they wince when paying the bills, but still feel deep affection and fierce loyalty for the airplane. Many wouldn't fly anything else.

Engine Troubles

Pre-1976 Dukes had some major engine problems, and any buyer of a used Duke should make it his number one priority to determine if the engines have had the fixes for those problems. At $46,000 a pair for overhaul, the 380-hp Lycoming TIO-541s can be expensive nightmares if something goes wrong. The engine problems of the Dukes fall into three main categories:

• Turbochargers. Model 60, A60 and the 1974 B60 models had cast-iron turbo housings, and they had a tendency to crack from the heat. (A turbocharger failure in a pressurized airplane, don't forget, can be critical, since partial or total cabin depressurization will result.) In 1974, stainless steel blowers were fitted, and the cracking problems stopped. Almost all cast-iron turbo housings have been replaced with the stainless steel ones by now, but a few of the old ones remain. Be absolutely positive you're not getting one of them, or at least get a price reduction to cover the cost of replacement.

• Crankcases. Continental isn't the only company to have crankcase cracking problems. Dukes up through 1977 had a high incidence of cracks. The problem was solved when Lycoming beefed up the cases, effective with engine serial number 781.

Rear cabin is long on elegance, short on shoulder room for rear-seat passengers. There's no rear compartment to store valises, etc.

• Cylinders and pistons. TBO of the TIO-541 was only 1,200 hours until 1974, mostly because of cylinder problems. Engines built or overhauled with improved pistons and cylinders since then have a TBO of 1,600 hours. The original problem (cracking around the exhaust ports) was exacerbated by less-than-perfect pilot technique during letdown. If power was reduced too much, the engines cooled too quickly, resulting in cylinder distress. Dukes built in 1976 and later (engine serial number 804 and up) have the completely "up-to-date" engines with 1,600-hour TBO, and owners report getting 1,800 and even 2,000 hours out of them.

Other Service Problems

In keeping with its big-ticket image, the Duke was equipped with a jet-style nickel cadmium (ni-cad) battery. This has proven to be a persistent and expensive nuisance for Duke owners. The battery is improperly cooled, and a slight misadjustment of the voltage regulator can ruin it. Average life of a Duke battery is two years or less. Now this doesn't seem so bad, except for the fact that a new battery costs $2,080! Current production Dukes now have lead-acid batteries; and Beech used to offer lead-acid conversion kits for older Dukes, but no longer does. Summing up, look for a Duke with a lead-acid system.

Mixture control cables also have a troublesome history. Again, this doesn't sound like a big deal, but the bill for replacing them both is several thousand dollars. Be sure to determine whether this modification has been performed.

Turbocharger controllers are also notoriously unreliable, and it's a good idea to check for manifold pressure drift during the demonstration ride. One large used-plane dealer told us that only three or four of the last 25 Dukes he'd flown had properly working controllers.

Which Model?

During the first six or seven years of its life, the Duke had a rather poor reliability record, and proved very expensive to maintain. But starting with the 1976 models, Beech seems to have gotten most of the problems under control, and later Dukes, we feel, are no more expensive to maintain than other high-horsepower piston twins like the Cessna 421.

Therefore, a buyer shopping for a Duke who can't afford the $100,000 to $200,000 for a late model should use extreme caution when shopping for a straight 60 or A60 model in the $70,000-$86,000 range. It's a Catch-22 situation—if you can't afford to consider a late-model airplane, you're less likely to be able to afford the high maintenance of the older models. The solution to the dilemma: careful study of the airplane. If all service bulletins have been complied with, and the engines have been updated to the latest standards, and the airplane has been flown competently by a professional pilot, there's no reason an older Duke can't be reasonable to maintain. But beware of the marginal older airplane that's had less than top-flight service and lots of different owners. If you buy a Duke and get a lemon, the taste will be sour indeed.

If you're looking for raw performance, the Aerostar 601P is a better bet, but for style the Duke is still pretty much unsurpassed among light airplanes. There are fewer than 600 Dukes flying, and this exclusivity adds to the airplane's appeal for many people. It also means a rather unstable used market. "The Duke market goes up and down," one big used-plane dealer told us. "For a few months there'll be a glut of them for sale, but all of a sudden the supply dries up and you can't find one anywhere." This fact makes it even more important to shop around in various parts of the country.

Owner Comments

For looks, handling, and comfort, rate the Duke tops. But for that kind of horsepower (760) one would hope that you could slip through the sky a little faster and carry another 100 or 200 pounds. Our Baron had as much full-fuel useful load.

Our Duke was a high maintenance aircraft. Most parts and labor were higher than on a smaller or less sophisticated airplane. It gave you the feeling that they saw you and your Duke coming.

A nicad battery was $1,000, generator $2,800, tires $90, $240 for a small cowl flap motor, special brake pads $100 a set; new engines installed were $35,000. The annuals were about $1,000. Parts usually had to come from a district Beechcraft

Cost/Performance/Specifications

Model	Year Built	Average Retail Price	Cruise Speed (kts)	Useful Load (lbs)	Fuel Std/Opt (gals)	Engine	TBO (hrs)	Overhaul Cost each
60	1968-69	$58,500	236	2,625	142/204	380-hp Lyc. TIO-541	1,600	$23,000
A60	1970-71	$71,500	237	2,625	142/204	380-hp Lyc. TIO-541	1,600	$23,000
A60	1972-73	$82,500	237	2,625	142/204	380-hp Lyc. TIO-541	1,600	$23,000
B60	1974-75	$103,000	233	2,436	142/232	380-hp Lyc. TIO-541	1,600	$23,000
B60	1976-77	$130,000	233	2,436	142/232	380-hp Lyc. TIO-541	1,600	$23,000
B60	1978-79	$151,000	233	2,436	142/232	380-hp Lyc. TIO-541	1,600	$23,000
B60	1980-81	$197,000	233	2,394	142/232	380-hp Lyc. TIO-541	1,600	$23,000
B60	1982	$245,000	233	2,394	142/232	380-hp Lyc. TIO-541	1,600	$23,000

center or from the factory. It was a "mean machine" but proved expensive. We almost cried when we had to give up pressurization for something more economical.

• • •

I cannot say enough good things regarding the performance, handling, maintenance and comfort of the Duke. It will take on weather as well as sunshine. I have had no problem with parts availability. (However, I happen to be hangared next door to a Beechcraft dealer, and we have an excellent supply line to Wichita.)

It is an expensive monster, but I don't feel that the Duke has any equal in the twins available today. The Lycoming engines are extremely reliable, as is the entire airplane.

• • •

For my money, it is the best owner-flown twin available, and we have been very pleased with it. The Duke is an honest airplane and an excellent instrument platform. The Lycoming TIO-541 engine has to be the easiest starting engine, hot or cold, I have ever flow with. Our first engines had 1,200-hour TBOs, but we ran them 1,385 hours. The new engines have 1,600-hour TBOs, and we expect 1,800 hours before we touch them. Our first set of engines had a tendency to leak oil, but the new ones run bone dry.

Landing gear has to stand up to aircraft weights of nearly three and a half tons. Gear collapses are in the top group of non-fatal accidents.

In the past, people had some trouble with the earlier engines but I attribute this as much to rapid throttle jockeying by inexperienced second-owner pilots as to anything else. So far as I am concerned, anyone who purchases a Duke and does not go through the Beech Duke school is making a great mistake.

The Duke, we find, burns about 43 gallons per hour on a less than three-hour flight; 40 gallons per hour on a flight of over three hours. Our speed is about three mph less than the book shows, but ours has every available option, including King Gold Crown and the heavy H-14 autopilot. The load carrying capacity is four people, plus luggage, plus full-fuel (202 gallons).

The negative features of the airplane include the fact it is certainly not a short-field aircraft; our minimum field length is 3,000 feet. The Models 60 and A60 had shorter exhaust stacks, which tend to cause corrosion on the flaps. At engine change time, we installed the new B60 type pipes, which eliminated the problem.

Perhaps the best way to describe our feelings is to say that our next new airplane will be a Duke.

• • •

The Duke is a fast aircraft, but the published specifications are overstated. My airplane runs consistently about 10 knots less than book performance. Unlike with other airplanes I've owned, the performance specifications are figured on 600 pounds less than certified gross. The Duke handles very well, slows up for landing easier than comparable aircraft because of the high gear and flap speed, and in my opinion, it is easier to land than a 300 series Cessna. It is a quiet airplane and very comfortable, although the pilot and co-pilot need some practice to get in and out of their seats easily.

As far as maintenance is concerned, I have not owned the airplane long enough to be able to assess what my costs are going to be on the long haul. My plane is currently going through an annual, and the left flap has to be replaced as a result of corrosion from the exhaust stack, which I understand has been a problem in several other Dukes.

Several of the earlier Dukes do not have a prop synchronizer and the props will simply not stay in synch no matter how hard you try. A prop synch is a must for this airplane, and I had to have one retrofitted. I had a lot of problems with the heater when I first bought the airplane but I feel that most of these were a function of the maintenance of the prior owners.

The Duke has been criticized as being a fuel hog. My Duke burns between 40 and 42 gallons per hour in cruise at approximately 68 percent power and 67 to 70 gallons per hour in climbout. I have installed a Fueltron in my Duke to monitor the fuel more closely. In summary, I am satisfied with my Duke and look forward to flying it many more hours.

• • •

I purchased a 1973 Duke; selling price was $165,000. It was equipped with King avionics, RCA 47 radar, air conditioning, all deicing equipment, club seating and other standard items. Total time was 68 hours on both the airframe and engines. I have been extremely pleased with its performance and flight characteristics. Average annual inspections are about $2,500. It is a little difficult to get into pilot and co-pilot seats, but once there, things are very comfortable. Workmanship is of the highest quality. It flies and feels like a solid, safe aircraft.

The doorway to macho heaven. It's a tight squeeze into the pilot's compartment, but once there, you won't want to leave.

There are roomier aircraft available, but none as sporty looking. The 400 Series Cessnas are big, but either underpowered or powered with the 520 geared engine, making them hard to maintain. I do not see anything on the market that comes close to the Duke's looks, power and handling characteristics. It is the Mercedes-Benz of the light twin market.

Bellanca Viking

How fast can a Viking fly? Cruise speeds up to 174 knots are claimed for late models. Dacron - covered fuselage and mahogany wing present a rivetless surface.

Riding on the wooden wings of yesteryear, the Bellanca Viking is an airplane Howard Hughes would have approved of. The spruce-and-mahogany wings, the Dacron-coated fuselage, dangling wheels and quaintly bestrutted empennage, combine to give the Viking a charm all its own.

As with most "distinctive" aircraft, the Bellanca Viking has its own loyal cadre of boosters and supplicants, who literally praise it to the skies as "the best all-around high-performance single." Owners mention easy handling, simple systems, and cruise speeds in the 160-175-knot ballpark as reasons for continued ownership; and routine maintenance seems to require no special connections with the International Monetary Fund. Owners consistently report annuals below $1,000, although some said parts—while easy to get—were "high." (Non-routine maintenance is another matter: Several operators cited wing repair bills that were, in their words, "sufficient to cause heart attack" and "impressive.") But then you could say the same about repairs to Cessna and Beech bladder tanks. (The Bellanca, incidentally, has steel fuel tanks.)

Mahogany & Sitka

When Viking owners talk of their planes' family "tree," they're not just speaking figuratively. The Bellanca mahogany-covered Sitka spruce wing dates to before World War Two; and the latest of the Super Viking wings off the 1988 assembly line differs little from the original. The same glass-smooth, curvacious wing that marked the Cruisaire (the Viking's forerunner) as a "hot ship" in the Forties still draws praise from owners today as "the most perfect wing of any modern light aircraft." Nary a rivet-head protrudes to ruin the airfoil's perfect contour.

Unfortunately, other portions of the Bellanca are not so slick aerodynamically. The bottoms of the wings sprout drag-producing wheel bumps; the horizontal stabilizer has struts (a la Curtiss Robin). But with wheel fairings the factory claims their burly-engined bird can motor along at a healthy 176 knots at 75 percent power. And that puts the Viking in the Bonanza, C-210 class.

But there are other reasons for buying an "old-fashioned" airplane like the Bellanca.

Its methods of construction demand a high level of craftsmanship, and in this area, Bellancas excel: Owners report unusually fastidious workmanship throughout the aircraft, especially inside the typically well-appointed cabin. The fit-and-finish is far above industry standards for this size aircraft.

Different Models

How do the various year models differ? For the most part, they don't, until 1979. Since the first Viking's appearance in 1967 (which marked the end of the triple-tailed, 260-hp Cruisaires), subsequent models have differed externally only in paint scheme, until '79. A variety of powerplants can be found under the hood, however. The original staple engine was the 300-hp Continental IO-520-D (TBO 1,700 hours), which could be supplanted (at customer request) by a 290-hp Lycoming IO-540-B (TBO 1,200 hours, normally aspirated) or IO-540-G (TBO 1,400 hours, turbocharged). Post-1970 models sported either the 300-hp Continental IO-520-K or the 300-hp Lycoming IO-540-K (TBO 2,000 hours), which—for $8,000 extra— could be fitted with dual Rajay turbochargers. Most Vikings have the Continental engine.

Bellancas currently coming off the production line in Alexandria, Minn. have the 300-hp Continental IO-520-K powerplant.

Yes, the line is still in production, if at an extremely modest pace. Bellanca went bankrupt in 1982, and Champion bought the high-wing line of Citabrias, Scouts and Decathlons and took them to Houston Tex. Production of Bellancas was resumed in Minnesota under new ownership in late 1983, and by mid 1988 some 13 aircraft had been built, all of them Model 17-30As. The company tries to complete one every six weeks. Base price in '88: $99,500, not counting avionics or autopilot.

Performance and Handling

"Performance," according to one owner, "is adequate but not outstanding." However, the owner of a Super Turbo model said it trues out at 186 knots at 12,000 feet. One operator reported 170 knots at 10,000 feet; another said he flight-plans 140 knots, based on 60-percent power and block-to-block fuel burns of 15 gallons per hour. Apparently, there is considerable variation among individual airplanes, due to rigging and vagaries of construction over the years. Late models claim a 75 percent cruise of 176 knots, as we mentioned before.

Owners of some of the earlier models seemed less than enthusiastic about the airplane's short legs: Standard fuel tankage on aircraft built up to 1978 is a mere 60 gallons (three hours plus reserves), all in the wings. The 15-gallon fuselage aux tank is a common option; but even with 75 gallons, it's difficult to fly a 700-nm trip without stopping for gas. Later models, however, received the benefit of another eight gallons of fuel.

Strutting its stuff, the horizontal tail is slender, and of wood construction.

Pleasant Handling

On the plus side, owners offer nothing but euphoric praise for the Viking's handling, one (typical) owner describing it as "an absolute joy to fly." Ailerons are light and creamy-smooth; rudders heavy but responsive; pitch forces, moderate to challenging, depending on c.g. location. In other words, controls are not well harmonized. But flaps do not betray any rude behavior, nor does gear deployment (at the manageably high speed of 124 knots). Gobs of drag and a 3,000-lb.-plus gross weight combine to give very steep descents for the unwary, however.

Useful loads for well-equipped Vikings (which most are) run around 900 pounds—a bit less than you'd expect for a 300-hp low-wing retractable (and far short of the Cessna 210's 1,500 pounds). Given the poor payload, it's perhaps a blessing that the airplane was not given larger fuel tanks, or a more capacious interior.

Speaking of interiors, owners are generally complimentary of seats, fabrics, etc. (which is good, since it diverts passengers' attention from the lack of shoulder and leg room), but the noise level is almost universally regarded as too high—no doubt a consequence of the large engine and fabric-skinned fuselage construction. "The airplane has got to have the highest noise level of any modern production aircraft," one owner observed, adding: "Headset, ear plugs, and intercom should be go/no-go items." Super soundproofing of post-'79 models is reported to have made cabin sound levels quite competitive with other aircraft, however.

If stealth is a consideration, one owner reports that the Viking exhibits an extraordinarily poor primary radar return—no doubt the result of mahogany's elusive X-band signature. The fuselage, however, is welded tubular steel, with a Dacron fabric covering.

Systems

Sitka spruce spars and wooden ribs are sheathed in mahogany and dipped in preservative. Annual inspections are made for dry rot.

Like many older designs, the Viking betrays a number of idiosyncrasies which a new pilot would do well to study. The absence of cowl flaps on most early models is a plus point, at least in terms of pilot workload (although it may compromise cylinder and accessory life). The prop, throttle, and mixture controls are all vernier types—with the prop knob directly above the mixture knob—which may cause some vertigo for all but Bonanza pilots.

Then there's the fuel system. On some early models, there were two fuel selectors with eight possible combinations of selector settings; later models have just one selector (between the front seats, at knee level) with four positions, of which one can be used in level flight only. Fuel quantity is read on vertical-readout gauges which owners say are highly non-linear—i.e., accurate only in the "full" and "empty" extremes. The three-position boost pump rocker switch is also a source of confusion, as reflected in pilot's statements in accident reports. Many pilots are not aware that the Viking's boost pump is so powerful that it can flood the engine, preventing easy restart. What's more, pump usage varies according to the type of engine installed. Obviously, it behooves the pilot to get a thorough checkout, and study the handbook.

Until May 1968, Vikings had an unusual combination flap-and-gear actuation system that worked off the engine-driven hydraulic system and was located between the pilots' seats. In 1968, electric flaps were substituted for hydraulic, and control levers mounted on the front lower panel, in conventional arrangement (gear left, flaps right).

Panel layout is good, with flight instruments where they should be, nav heads in midpanel, radios in a stack on the right, and autopilot-cum-miscellany to the far right, above the flap switch and circuit breakers. Reclining seats are optional.

Gear Guard

A pneumatic switch in the landing gear circuit forms the basis of something called "Auto-Axion," which automatically lowers the landing gear at an airspeed of 83 knots (which is about what you'll indicate in cruise going over the Rockies). To our knowledge, it has caused owners no grief, and may actually be preventing gear-up accidents: in a three-year period, we could find in NTSB files only four gear-up landings involving Bellancas—two of which were pilot-induced, not mechanical.

The fuel drain knob is under the cowling, but it drains only the tank you've selected, so count on lots of walking between cabin and cowl to get all points drained. One owner reported that his alternator belt always slips in heavy rain.

Although miscellaneous airframe parts are expensive, and repair costs for replacement of the Viking's "lifetime fabric" or wings can rival the Polish national debt, routine upkeep is said by owners to be quite reasonable. Extensive annuals can run upwards of $2,500, but the average inspection seems to come in about the same as the tab for a Bonanza, 210, etc.

Several important repetitive Airworthiness Directives apply to the Bellanca Viking. The most important (and notorious) of these is AD 76-08-04, the 1976 directive on wood rot. Under the terms of this AD, the Viking wing must be inspected for moisture content in accordance with Part I of Bellanca Service Letter 82A at each annual inspection. Since not all shops are familiar with Bellancas, it pays to seek out expert counsel for this type of work. Owners recommend Tom Witmer at Cap Aviation in Reading, Pa.; Miller Flying Service in Plainview, Tex., and Dave Poole at Dennis Martin Aircraft at Ft. Lauderdale Executive Airport. (Miller is also a good source of Viking info, in general, and a longtime dealer.)

Wing Moisture Check

The wing moisture check should be a starting point for any pre-purchase inspection. Don't take the word of the previous owner nor a logbook entry; actually have a qualified shop check the wings prior to delivery. Special tools are required for this; it requires more than "an eyeball and a screwdriver" (as one man states)—unless, of course, you open the inspection covers and find, as one owner did, "mushrooms growing in right wing."

Other important ADs are 76-23-03 on exhaust failure (an inspection is required each 100 hours); 77-22-02 on nose landing gear engine mount sections; and 75-20-06 on vertical side fuselage tube cracking in the tail section (repetitive inspection each 100 hours until Service Kit SK1234789-0004 is installed). Additional ADs may apply to individual accessories installed on various airplanes (certain magnetos, Lycoming oil pump impellers, etc.); make sure to have an A&P do a complete AD listing for the particular plane you intend to buy.

In 1983, the Viking line went back into production, with first deliveries to Miller Flying Service. This, of course, had a positive effect not only on parts availability, but aircraft resale value as well. The new manufacturer is Bellanca, Inc., P.O. Box 964, Alexandria, Minn. 56308 (phone 612- 762-1501). Their dealers: Miller Flying Service, P.O. Box 190, Plainview, Tex. 79072 (phone 806-293-4121) and Bill Walker & Assoc., McKinnon Airport, St. Simon's Island, Ga. 31522 (phone 912-638-3191).

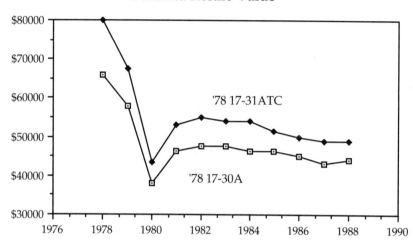

Bellanca Resale Value

'78 17-31ATC

'78 17-30A

The factory, of course, is supporting the line and can repair the wooden wings and outfit the aircraft with new interiors.

Safety

The Bellanca Viking was one of several aircraft spotlighted as having a particularly poor safety record in the National Transportation Safety Board's 1979 study of accident rates by aircraft type. (Other poor-showing airplanes included the Grumman AA-1 series and the Cessna Skymaster.) Shortly after the NTSB released its report, Bellanca Aircraft Corp. sent a cheer-up letter to aviation editors, defending the Viking's safety record.

As it turns out, the Safety Board did lump Viking data together with Cruisaire (i.e., early-Bellanca) data to arrive at its findings. And this did produce a skewed result, at least for non-fatal accidents—the Cruisaire series (mostly taildraggers) had many more non-fatal accidents than the Viking, on an apples-to-apples exposure basis. However, the *fatal* accident rate for the Viking and Cruisaire is the same: 4.5 fatal accidents per 100,000 flight hours)— about twice the rate of the Mooney M20 series (2.4 per 100,000 hours), and quite a bit worse than the Beech Bonanza (at 2.6). In a nutshell, the Viking does not compare well with its peers for safety.

The Viking's non-fatal accidents seem to be lumpable into three categories: a broad category subsuming all the more-or-less "expected" bad-luck events that befall all planes more or less equally (hard landings, crankshaft failure, water in the fuel, and so on) . . .engine failure for undetermined reasons. . .and fuel mismanagement. In a review of data covering the years 1979 through 1981, we found that out of 37 total Viking accidents, 32 were non-fatal; and of those, six involved unexplained powerplant failure, while 10 involved fuel mismanagement, and the rest fell into the grab-bag category. It's clear that fuel mismanagement and engine problems loom large in the Viking's accident picture.

Breakup Record

In the fatal-accident category, we found that about half of the accidents were attributable to VFR pilots who blundered into IFR weather. More ominously, looking at the 56 fatal Viking accidents that occurred through 1981, we find that *one out of eight* fatal Viking crashes involved in-flight airframe failure. On an equal-exposure basis, this makes the Viking's in-flight breakup rate not much different from that of the Beech Bonanza. (Remember that there are only about 1,000 Vikings on the civil registry, compared to 10,000 Bonanzas; and the Viking's flying history starts in 1967, whereas the Bonanza's starts in 1947. Thus there is greater statistical significance to the Bonanza's breakup data.)

The Viking is a strong airplane. But contrary to the bold rhetoric of the factory a few years ago (when Bellanca claimed that there had *never* been an in-flight structural failure of a Viking), there *have* been breakups—eight fatals, in fact, at the time of our last check. Most have been weather-related. But it is interesting to note that of the eight fatal Viking breakups on record, six happened in 1969-70 model airplanes. (There has been only one breakup of any Bellanca made after 1970, to our knowledge.) This strongly suggests structural problems in a small batch of airplanes. Former Bellanca factory personnel say, however, that there were absolutely no changes in materials or methods of construction in the Viking line over the period in question.

In sum, it appears that the Bellanca Viking—while not gifted with a particularly superb safety record—need not be a particularly hazardous plane to own if pilots will simply avoid aerobatics, invest in good maintenance (particularly of the wing and fabric), take time to understand the fuel system (including in-flight restart techniques), and stay clear of thunderstorms and/or weather for which the pilot is not prepared.

Owner Comments

The Viking is at least as well designed and as well built as any single on the market today. My opinion is that it is better crafted and far better detailed, both inside and out, than any other single. I think it is quieter, more stable in instrument conditions, provides a more structurally safe airframe and offers a much more plush and pleasant passenger environment than any other single.

I am referring to the latest Viking improvements since 1979, when the aircraft was cleaned up. A post-1979 Viking will cruise and max out neck and neck with an F-33, 210 or 201.

Morris E. Bellis, M.D.
Norton, Va.

Vikings have an automatic gear-extension system with no frills. Gear drops when the airspeed falls below 83 knots, except at full throttle.

I have owned three Bellanca Vikings since 1973 and have found them to be an exceptional value and one of the last vestiges of craftsmanship in American manufacturing. In particular, the last two new Bellancas were very well built. Everything was working and tight when I picked the airplanes up from Miller Flying Service in Plainview, Tex. The interior and exterior finishes are particularly nice. The crush velour with leather (or vinyl, I'm not sure which) has held up well. The Imron paint has stayed new-looking with very little attention. No unscheduled maintenance was required in the first 200 hours on either airplane. My direct operating cost including gas, oil, maintenance, insurance and hangar have run about $40 per hour. In 1,500 hours of flight time spanning seven years, other than routine maintenance, I have required replacement of a propeller governor, an overvoltage relay, and a nose gear strut seal. The aircraft is an absolute joy to fly. The handling is very responsive. It is especially nice in the banked maneuvers such as steep turns and chandelles. With very little effort one can imagine he is at the controls of a WWII fighter instead of a good, stable cross-country airplane.

Viking handling is marked by very light ailerons, but heavy pitch forces.

In any large, powerful aircraft, proper attention to speed management is important, and this aircraft is no exception. Speed and power must be controlled on approach in order to prevent excessive sink rates. Power off, C-150-type landings require considerable pilot technique, but power-on landings are very easily done. The aircraft is especially good in a crosswind. The low wing, large flaps, and wide gear make it very stable at touchdown. The cross-country profile is good. I generally plan 500-nautical-mile legs in 3.25 hours and have a 100-mile reserve. My airplane will carry two couples, overnight baggage and four hours of fuel and be well within its weight limit. The airplane is very stable in instrument conditions and has no tendency to fall off into a spiral. The panel layout is good and the radio options are quite varied. I have a two-axis autopilot but seldom use it because the airplane is so stable.

In general, I am quite pleased with my Bellanca. I was delighted to hear that the aircraft is back in production. I plan to buy another one if the present one ever wears out.

Bill Bass, Jr. M.D.

I purchased my 1975 17-30A Continental Super Viking in June 1976, as a dealer's demo with about 200 hours on it. I have put about 1,000 hours on it since then. My use is 100 percent business, traveling from Ohio to Montana and south as far as Missouri and Kansas. The plane has done all that was asked of it and some that wasn't, such as carrying a whale of a load of ice into South Bend, Ind. one cold winter day.

It is a good solid airplane, steady instrument platform, and reasonably fast. I flight plan 140 knots. Fuel consumption leaned at 22/23 is 12.5 gph. Try as I may, block to block, it works out to 15 gph. Handling is superb; it is very responsive but will hold a course, hands-off without use of autopilot, with tinkering. Trim changes on gear/flap extension/retraction are noticeable but easily controlled with the electric trim button on the yoke. I have managed significant wind shear and crosswind situations that even caused tower personnel at a large (DTW) airport to comment on doing a better job than the large commercial jets. The Viking responds to being flown like a light twin—carry a little power right down to the flare. I don't take my plane into unapproved fields—the fiberglass main wheel doors don't take kindly to abuse. Full-flap slips are permitted and you can really get down in a hurry but need power to stop the sink. Overall, it does a fine job, but I would caution against low-time or occasional-use pilots trying anything unusual. This is a heavy, powerful, high-performance airplane that takes time and experience to get the most out of.

The cabin is tight for four, but so well done that you really don't notice. Workmanship is just what you would expect from an almost custom hand built plane; i.e., it is terrific!

Maintenance between annuals is minimal if plane is properly cared for. I change the oil every 25 hours, Philips X/C 20W-50W, capacity is 12 qts.; however I run one new quart through it and add 11 qts. since the 12th quart always seemed to end up on the belly anyway. Between changes I'll add two qts. and be a quart low (10 qts.) when the next change comes up. I've replaced one vacuum pump (about 700 hrs.) and one exhaust valve. Compression is 70 to 75 over 80.

The most recurrent problem I've had is with the gear not retracting due to low strut pressure, and freezing up of the auto switch on the right main. One to two hundred dollars a year covers between-annual maintenance, and annuals have ranged from $350 to $1,300 not including a recent repainting—$3,000. Average is about $750-$800. Finding a maintenance facility familiar with the Viking can be a problem. I solved this by taking my plane back to Alexandria, Minn. where it was built, and I have Weber's Aero Repairs do the work. They are Viking Specialists— quick, thorough, reasonable, and trustworthy. Never a problem with parts.

Needless to say I am very pleased with the plane, and since Continental raised the TBO from 1,500 to 1,700 hours, I feel it is better to keep it than to sell and then try to replace it. I understand they are starting to build them again which should help the resale value. In the meantime, I think a properly maintained, well kept Viking is the best buy on the market.

Cost/Performance/Specifications

Model	Year Built	Average Retail Price	Cruise Speed (kts)	Useful Load (lbs)	Fuel Std/Opt (gals)	Engine	TBO (hrs)	Overhaul Cost
17-30	1967-70	$19,500	163	1,300	58/92	300-hp Cont. IO-520-D	1,700	$10,300
17-30A	1971-73	$24,000	163	1,125	60/75	300-hp Cont. IO-520-K	1,700	$10,300
17-30A	1973-75	$28,000	163	1,125	60/75	300-hp Cont. IO-520-K	1,700	$10,300
17-30A	1976-78	$40,000	163	1,125	60/75	300-hp Cont. IO-520-K	1,700	$10,300
17-30A	1979-80	$52,000	174	1,125	68-83	300-hp Cont. IO-520-K	1,700	$10,300
17-30A	1984-86	$95,000	163	1,125	60/75	300-hp Cont. IO-520-K	1,700	$10,300
17-30A	1987	$115,000	163	1,125	60/75	300-hp Cont. IO-520-K	1,700	$10,300
17-31A	1971-73	$23,000	165	1,078	68/83	300-hp Lyc. IO-540-K1E5	2,000	$12,800
17-31A	1974-76	$28,000	165	1,078	68/83	300-hp Lyc. IO-540-K1E5	2,000	$12,800
17-31A	1977-78	$38,000	165	1,078	68/83	300-hp Lyc. IO-540-K1E5	2,000	$12,800
17-31ATC	1970-72	$26,000	187	953	68/83	300-hp Lyc. IO-540-K1E5	2,000	$12,800
17-31ATC	1973-75	$30,000	187	953	68/83	300-hp Lyc. IO-540-K1E5	2,000	$12,800
17-31ATC	1976-78	$44,000	187	953	68/83	300-hp Lyc. IO-540-K1E5	2,000	$12,800
17-31ATC	1979	$54,000	187	953	68/83	300-hp Lyc. IO-540-K1E5	2,000	$12,800

As a final note, I'd like to comment on the expense of insurance. I carry high limits, both hull and liability. I recently had some correspondence with my agent and I think you might be interested in a quote from his letter. "One last comment is that your aircraft is a very difficult aircraft to insure and most insurance carriers are no longer insuring this type of aircraft. I would expect the insurance rates to periodically increase because of the difficulty of obtaining insurance on this type of aircraft. Most carriers are not enthused with wood wings and fabric fuselages, and that is why it is difficult to take care of." A pox on insurance companies!

Incidentally, I've never had a problem with my wood and fabric despite having flown through some large-size hail on at least one occasion. Try that in one of the "conventional" aluminum cans and see what happens.

Dean I. Grauer, Jr.
Allen Park, Mich.

My latest Bellanca is a 1976 Super Viking. I have owned this plane for four years and have never had any difficulty. The annuals are done by Miller Flying Service, and the cost runs from a low of $590 to a high of just around $700. I did Microlon the engine when I first got it at a little over 300 hours. It now has approximately 1,000. There have been no problems in starting the Lycoming engine. I true out at about 186 knots at 12,000 feet. If there is anything to complain about concerning the Bellanca, in my opinion it would be the room on the inside. I am 5'9" and weigh approximately 210 pounds and make a number of trips cross-country.

I am probably prejudiced, but I sincerely believe this to be the best-flying and best-handling of any plane this size.

Ellis B. Qualls
Show Low, Ariz.

An unusual feature is a rear fuselage aux tank holding 15 gallons, or about an hour's cruise flight.

I have owned my 1970 Super Viking since May 1973, and it continues to be a delight. It is fast enough and comfortable enough to arrive well relaxed after 10 hours in the air. Its Lycoming IO-540 is exceptionally smooth and quiet after 1,694 hours since new, and compression and oil consumption are still high and low, respectively.

The wings and spars have remained dry and with the proper moisture content. I have wing and stabilizer and canopy covers, which have definitely helped the moisture problem and also kept cabin and radios working like new. I resanded and repainted the entire aircraft in 1980 with Imron polyurethane by Tom Green and Turner Field in Ambler, Pa. They did an outstanding job. Also can recommend Tom Witmer at Cap Aviation, Reading, Pa. for all types of Bellanca repairs. Parts are available but high. Just ordered pair of flap cables with fittings—$87. Cost of annual inspections averages $350 to $500 each.

Maintenance cost including amortization of the propeller and new paint but not including avionics or engine overhaul is approximately $12 per hour. So the airplane is really economical compared to many, and so easy and fun to fly that I am more than satisfied.

Charles C. Edwards
Chatham, N.J.

Boeing Stearman

For pilots who consider the modern lightplane yawn-provoking, there is a robust, swaggering alternative guaranteed to blast away boredom and represent a spanking-good investment in fun, sport and aeronautical assets. Searchers who reach beyond the more humdrum realm of the Luscombes, Navions and J-3 Cubs will stumble upon a treasure lode of classics known as the Boeing Stearman Model 75s.

The great charm of these lusty biplane warriors is that they were built like the classic brick biffy and cranked out in vast armadas. And the parts that aren't still legion can be made by a competent mechanic with a small outlay in fuss and bother. Even the old radial engines have been guaranteed a kind of immortality since the same basic type (220-hp Continental) used in many Stearmans was built in great numbers as powerplants for military tanks. And this has left a serendipitous legacy of still-unused engine cylinders.

Combine these practical considerations with the aircraft's intrinsic panache and machismo, and the appeal is obvious.

History

About 8,500 Boeing Stearman Model 75s were built over a nine-year span from 1936 to 1945 as military trainers. The FAA reports it still had 2,237 of the aircraft on the books at last count. For the Army, the airplanes were designated PT (primary trainer) -13s, -17s and 18s. The Navy designated them N2S. The nickname for both services was the Kaydet. The Royal Canadian Air Force received 300 winterized PT-17s labeled PT-27s.

Sunday afternoon amid the daisies at Kobelt Field. Ancient, but ageless, this airframe had over 3,000 hours on it.

The PT-17s, and the Navy counterpart, the N2S-1, -3 and -4, all with the 220-hp Continental engine, were built in the greatest numbers—about 6,000 during the 1940s. About half as many PT-13s (and Navy N2S-5s) were built with the 225-hp Lycoming radial for which parts now seem to be in very short supply. The third powerplant supplied for the aircraft was the 225-hp Jacobs, with about 150 PT-18s built carrying this engine.

Presaging the future role for some Stearmans in civilian life, a batch of PT-17Bs was actually built for the military as mosquito control dusters.
After the war, hundreds of Stearmans were dumped on the market as surplus, available for a song—$200 to $500, some say, in crates. Many of these were snapped up and converted to cropdusting, often with 300-hp or 450-hp engines and a hopper installed in place of the front cockpit.

Buying Tips

According to Tom Lowe, president of the Stearman Restorers Assn., an average flyable Stearman in reasonable condition can be found these days for from $25,000 to $28,000. A battered one with a high-time engine might go for around $20,000. And one that has been recently restored might be available for $30,000 to $40,000. Owners of prime freshly rebuilt models at the top are asking $40,000 and up.

For the *creme de la creme* in custom conversions, Mid Continent Aircraft Corp. in Hayti, Mo., will totally reconstruct one to like-new condition for $69,000 to $145,000, depending on the powerplant (220 hp up to 450 hp) and options.

As for ex-cropdusters, some Stearman aficionados say they've found examples in good condition with extra corrosion protection, but most Stearman critics believe a lot of extra travail and money will probably be needed to bring a tired, old workhorse duster around to top condition because of the hard use and chemical corrosion. Also, the wings may have been clipped.

Before the needle, there was the ball. . .and precious little else. No vacuum pump worries, however.

Word is also that front cockpit hardware is in short supply as restorers seek to convert dusters to the standard tandem cockpit configuration. Furthermore, extra fuselage structural work has to be done to finish the conversion.

The 220-hp Continental powerplant is probably the preferred one, mainly because parts are more readily available than for the 220-hp Lycoming or the 225-hp Jacobs. The nine-cylinder Lycoming may be a bit smoother in operation than the seven-cylinder Continental, but some pilots feel the Continental has "more guts" and a better throttle response. Also, they characterize the Lycoming as a bit greasier and oilier, and the "shaky Jake" Jacobs as the worst in this respect.

The McCauley propeller might deter some buyers, since there is an Airworthiness Directive that requires removal for inspection and magnafluxing every 100 hours. A Hamilton-Standard metal prop does not have this limitation. Then again, some of the birds have wooden props.
Potential buyers might also keep an eye out for the tailwheel configuration. Originally, the Navy Stearmans had a tailwheel that (1) would swivel freely or (2) lock for takeoff and landing, while the Army models were steerable with the

rudder pedals. Obviously, the Army system is more manageable, and lots of Navy models have been converted.

The brake system is a source of constant debate among Stearman owners. Most have long since converted to automotive master cylinders for better durability, though other diehards maintain that the original ones were just fine if you knew how to maintain them. One expert, Lary Kampel, says Cleveland brakes are the best of all, with new-type linings. At any rate, Stearman pilots say you want good brakes since you'll need all the help you can get for proper ground handling with the tailwheel configuration, especially with a nonsteerable tailwheel.

Handling and Performance

Pilots label the Boeing Stearman as a pretty honest, straightforward aircraft that was, after all, designed as a trainer. It will do all the basic aerobatic maneuvers—loops, spins, hammerheads, snap rolls. The engine is not designed for continuous inverted operation, however, and it will quit if you hold it upside down for long.

With a 220-hp Continental ticking away, this Stearman climbs at 70, lands at 70 and cruises at 95.

Also, aerobatic devotees should be aware that it's no Pitts Special—the controls are heavy—heavier than a T-6's, and a protracted spate of aerobatics will leave you arm-weary. The original models had only one set of ailerons, on the lower wings. Some fancy aerobatic mods add another pair of ailerons on the top wings for more maneuverability.

Stearman cognoscenti say you shouldn't worry too much about the wings or tail coming off if the aircraft is in proper condition, since it is supposed to be able to take about 12 Gs positive and seven to nine negative. "Built like a truck" is the favorite description by owners. No speed demon, though, the 220-hp Stearman will climb out at about 70 mph, cruise at about 95 mph behind a nice slow-ticking 1900 rpm max, burning about 12 gph, and come down final at about 70 mph.

A newcomer will be struck by the airplane's general docility. It's like a big kite. It doesn't have or need flaps. "It glides like a brick," said one owner in the time-honored expression. Pull the power off on final, and she'll come down sharply. In a stall, she'll buffet nicely and drop off on a wing.
The toughest maneuver in the Stearman's repertoire is probably a gusty crosswind landing. Cockpit visibility of the runway on the flare is nearly nonexistent, and the pilot has to use a sixth sense and great powers of peripheral vision. And he's got to have dancing feet.

The landing gear stick out like a pair of giant tree trunks, and they're about as unyielding when you hit the ground if you haven't eased it on—there's very little give to the oleos; the monster tires probably provide as much cushion as a hard

Truss-like tubular fuselage is the core on which everything is hung, as this page from the aircraft manual shows.

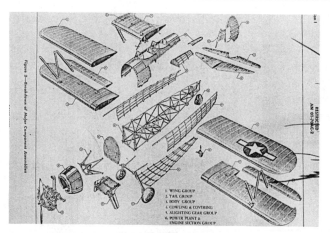

landing will allow. But the tailwheel has the luxury of its own oleo, for what that's worth.

Instrumentation will range from crude original to elaborate custom fittings. Most of the original aircraft came without electrical systems—that meant starting by the old-fashioned inertial crank, or by propping. The high prop intimidates some for hand propping, however. But some models have been updated with batteries and electric starters and navigation lights.

Systems on the airplane are rock-bottom basic. The fuel gauge consists of a graduated plastic tube with a float marker about six inches long dangling from the bottom surface of the upper wing, in the breeze, right in front of the pilot's nose. The fuel tank is located in the center section right above the fuselage. You can switch it on or off—period.

Other system controls are a throttle, mixture and mag switch. The pitch trim control is a simple swiveling knob on the left side of the cockpit—a joy to use, and an object lesson to modern aircraft designers. Naturally, this airplane has a control stick, not a wheel.

Get Parts and Maintenance

Cork-in-a-tube fuel gauge dangles below the single wing tank. Round mirror aids in inter-cockpit communications.

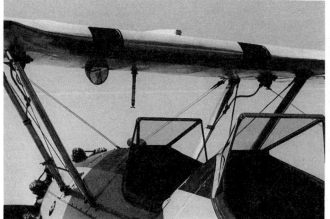

Dusters & Sprayers Supply in Chickasha, Okla. (405-224-1201), is the big name in Stearman parts. President Bob Chambers says they can supply just about any Stearman part needed, and those they don't have they can make under PMA authority in their machine shop. Chambers claims to have about 3,000 customers in this country as well as in Mexico and Argentina, where they apparently still use the aircraft as trainers.

Dusters & Sprayers even has parts for the Lycoming, Continental and Jacobs engines, and makes all the hardware for the front cockpits except the seats, according to Chambers.

Scroungers can also get help locating parts from members of the Stearman Restorers Assn. (more about that later) and from *Trade-A-Plane*. One of the Stearman gurus, Chris Stoltzfus in Coatesville, Pa., has a good selection of parts, too (215-384-1145).

Although there are quite a few capable mechanics around the country who can work on the aircraft with no great problem due to its straightforward design and construction, the older hands with experience in wood and fabric are preferred, naturally. And a few are known as Stearman specialists. Among them are Larry Kampel of Kampel Enterprises in Wellsville, Pa.; and Tom Cawley of Cawley's Aviation Service at Kobelt Airport in Wallkill, N.Y. For engine overhaul, Gulf Coast Dusting in Houston, Tex., is one of the better known shops (713-991-3520).

Owners say the Stearmans are quite reasonable to maintain. Big front fuselage panels open on hinges and are held up by metal hooks for beautiful access to accessories and the master brake cylinder.

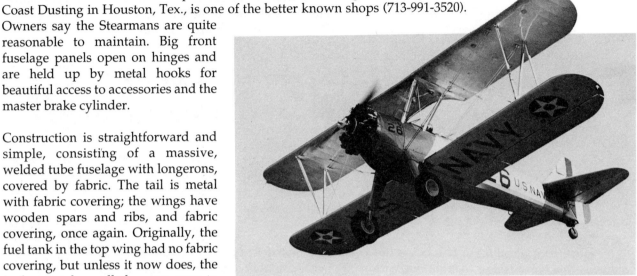

Construction is straightforward and simple, consisting of a massive, welded tube fuselage with longerons, covered by fabric. The tail is metal with fabric covering; the wings have wooden spars and ribs, and fabric covering, once again. Originally, the fuel tank in the top wing had no fabric covering, but unless it now does, the tank must be pulled every year to allow an inspection of the center section, to meet the requirements of an AD.

Handling is honest and straightforward. It will do all the basic aerobatic maneuvers, but controls are heavy.

And talk about nice touches, the flying wires that fasten to the horizontal stabilizer go through little plastic viewports, allowing easy walk-around inspection for security—another object lesson for modern designers. Since the wing ribs are wooden, great care must be taken to ensure against rotting from moisture, especially along the aileron bay. An AD calls for drilling drain holes to prevent moisture accumulation.

A Boeing service bulletin (available from the Stearman Restorers Assn.) outlines the modifications necessary for conversion from the original military to civilian status. By now, most of these have presumably been complied with, but buyers should confirm. The service bulletin requires items like: no spin strips on the upper wing only, replace the aluminum firewall with a stainless steel one, installation of a battery cutoff switch and CAA-approved position lights on ships with electrical systems, etc.

Modifications

Most of the Supplemental Type Certificates on the aircraft are aimed at converting to ag configuration, but a bunch allow use of Seconite or fiberglass covering. And one even installs metal wing ribs with the wooden spars—by Vincent Aeronautical, Covington, La.

Books and Manuals

A nice history of the entire Stearman line comes in the *Stearman Guidebook,* by Mitch Mayborn and Peter M. Bowers, published by Flying Enterprise Publications in Dallas, Tex. Air Service Caravan Co. in New Bedford, Mass. (617-992-1655), can provide Stearman pilot manuals along with maintenance and parts handbooks.

Organizations to Join

As we've already mentioned, the Stearman Restorers Assn. is the one. They publish a nice-looking newsletter and can provide everything from moral support to a clearing house for parts and services. President of the Association is Thomas E. Lowe, 823 Kingston Lane, Crystal Lake, Ill. 60014 (815-459-6873). They hold an annual fly-in at Galesburg, Ill., the week after Labor Day.

No matter how good it looks from the outside, check for 40-year-old wood behind the compression members in the wings.

Owner Comments

I first soloed a Stearman in 1948 as a new private pilot. The checkout consisted of three or four landings and seemed easy at the time, but I had flown nothing but tailwheel planes prior to this. I flew the Stearman only a few hours but concluded that if I could ever afford one I would buy one. I bought one with a 300 Lycoming and constant-speed prop in 1967 and am still flying it. The airplane has been very serviceable. It is a fine trainer both for landings and takeoffs and for aerobatics. These skills, well developed and practiced in a Stearman, transfer to adept handling of much more modern and sophisticated airplanes.

Much has been written and said about Stearmans being hard to land. They are not, but need to be kept straight, and even a strong crosswind on a paved runway can be handled with the control available. The aircraft is heavy on the controls, and one needs considerable muscle to do aerobatics. Maneuvers develop relatively slowly and must be properly flown through for good execution. This doesn't make it easy but is a training virtue. I have flown some indifferently maintained stock Stearmans and also some highly modified working dusters, and they have all flown and handled fine, which says a lot for the underlying strength and design, which are superior to most planes of that vintage.

Fuel consumption on the 300 is about 11.5 gph cross-country and 14 for aerobatics, and roughly one quart of oil per hour. Stearmans seem to be almost universally greeted with affection, but in the last year or so more than one line boy has said, "Gee mister, what kind of airplane is that?"

• • •

I've got a pristine PT-27, which was the only Boeing Stearman produced with an electrical system and starter as standard. No other biplane has such delightfully smooth control feel. The input is through torque tubes and bell cranks, so the slack and binding of the ordinary cable setup is absent.

The Stearman is very roomy and solid. Its cowlings are like armor plate and look as if they belong on a DC-4. The tubular framework is truly massive. All this gives you a secure feeling, but with its standard engines, the 225 Lycoming and the 220 Continental, it is unimpressive in climb rate and cruise speed. I'm never in a hurry when I fly my Stearman, so it doesn't bother me. If you want speed or sustained performance in vertical maneuvers, the P&W 450 would be the answer.

Certainly this is the safest biplane around. Besides being overbuilt, it has the most predictable low-speed handling characteristics. The stall is a long time in coming, with all kinds of signals; and with its huge wings you generally can fly out of any problems by releasing back pressure.

Once you get used to the limited forward visibility, the landings are a cinch, though you've got to stay tuned to the rudder on the rollout, particularly in a crosswind since the gear legs are so close together. It is crucially important to keep airflow over that rudder as long as possible. For this reason newcomers to the Stearman should probably avoid days when the wind is shifting around rapidly. A nice steady 10 knots within 30 degrees of the nose is fine. Always use grass runways when available.

Parts for some old airplanes are impossible to find. You need a tool and die maker for a close friend. The Stearman is a notable exception. Apparently during the war spares were produced in amazing quantities. Any part you want is available right away from outfits like Dusters & Sprayers.

All these old airplanes have wooden wings. A lot of supposedly "rebuilt" Stearmans have 40-year-old wood behind compression members and other out-of-the-way spots. The only way to be sure is to insist on brand-new wings built up from scratch. We dismantled an airplane completely a few years ago after a crackup. It had a beautiful cover and finish. The wood you could see with the cover off was excellent, but in the inaccessible spots behind permanent fittings dry rot and corrosion were severe.

I've got close to $40,000 in my Stearman. If a man didn't have at least thirty to spend on a completely remanufactured airplane, he'd be better off with a good clip-wing Cub or T-craft.

• • •

Cost/Performance/Specifications

Model	Year	Gross Weight (lbs)	Fuel (gals)	Engine	TBO (hrs)	Overhaul Cost
PT-13	1936-41	2,950	46-	225-hp Lyc.	650	$6,000
N2S-5	1943-45			R-680-B4B, -E		with 2 engines*
PT-17	1940-45	2,950	46-	220-hp Cont.	1,000	$3,950
PT-27				W-670-6A, N		with exch
N2S-1, 3, 4						$4,450 outright
PT-18	1940-41	2,950	46-	225-hp Jacobs $TC6 R-755-7	1,000	
Modifications			3,200-3,520	300-hp Lyc. R680-E3, -A, -B	1,500	$6,200 with 2 engines*
				450-hp P&W R-985-AN-1, 3	1,400	

*Overhauler demands two engines, one for parts.

Cessna 150/152

Cessna 150

Cessna 150s abound like lemmings to provide a truly mass market in fairly "modern" configuration aircraft at prices that range from modest to dirt cheap. Although most began life as trainers, they can provide fairly inexpensive personal transportation and good sport flying for any whose financial and performance aspirations are not too high.

The 150 line is an all-metal, tricycle-gear derivation of the venerable Cessna 120 and 140 tailwheel models. It first showed up in 1959, and in the years to follow it established itself as the world's premier trainer, multiplied in staggering numbers and continued right up to today (as the 152) in what has become a dynasty of no small proportions. The line has undergone a bewildering number of modifications and "improvements" over the years, but the basic qualities have remained immutable:

Durability

The aircraft are built to take it. Otherwise they never could survive the incessant pounding and manhandling of bumbling students, the rigor of bone-rattling beginners' landings, the buffeting of stalls, the wrenching of practice spins and the dynamic and thermal wear and tear on the engine of simulated emergency landings, slow flight and touch-and- goes. The Cessna 150 has few secrets. It has few elements and components that haven't been tested and tried to a fare-thee-well.

The classic 150 trainer: old-fashioned but tough and really never eclipsed on the market. Later models like this one (1973) had tubular landing gear struts to smooth ground operations.

Capacity

The 150s, especially the post-1965 models, have a baggage space of monumental proportions, but all have a cockpit of straightjacket dimensions. Cessna engineers through the years have bowed the doors out, lowered the floor pans, pared away the center pedestal and even lowered the seats in an attempt to provide more millimeters of cabin room. But they still haven't made the cabin structure basically any wider. Hence, any two adults of more than medieval stature who fly together in a Cessna 150 are destined to develop a close relationship for the duration of the flight.

Speed

When the original, bulky-fuselaged 150 showed up on the aviation scene in 1959 powered by a peanut-sized 100-hp Continental O-200, it would cruise at 121 mph at 75 percent power. The latest model, after a raft of changes like redesigned cabin, swept tail, modified wheel fairings, better streamlined cowling and bigger engine—today cruises at 123 mph at the same power setting. Visibility: Nothing to brag about.

Aerobatics

The Cessna 150 Aerobat would seem to have the makings of an ideal aerobatic trainer, since it allows students to transition right into an airplane they feel comfortable with. There's a nicely illustrated instructional manual and a well-planned curriculum to whet a student's appetite. Experienced aerobatic pilots give it good marks in such maneuvers as spins and aileron rolls. But it has serious shortcomings when it comes to anything much more sophisticated.

Big rear cabin in rare cases had an optional child's seat. The rear compartment will take up to 120 pounds of baggage or kids.

Since it has a control wheel rather than a stick, for example, while doing point rolls, the "other rider" can expect to be pummeled by the pilot's elbows as he whips the wheel back and forth in the cramped cockpit. The Aerobat also is not designed for negative maneuvers, and this not only excludes a whole repertoire, but means the engine will not operate upside down for any length of time. Instructors also report that one marginal characteristic of the airplane is its tendency to get moving too fast when coming down from an inverted position, as in a split-S or perhaps even on top of a roll. Also, the prop pitch seems set so "fine" that it's too easy to overspeed the engine in descending maneuvers.

But the airplane probably suffices at least to give students a taste of something other than straight-and- level, as an appetite-whetter to advance to better aerobatic aircraft, or to allow him to get out of awkward situations he may never have encountered before.

Handling

Forgiving and always recoverable, but sharp-edged enough to demand the precision that lots of instructors prefer. The bird has a dandy set of "para-lift" flaps which will allow awesome approach angles, but until a diminution of full flap angles from 40 to 30 degrees was made on the 152, the bird was known as an anvil in a balked-landing go-around with full flaps. In general, though, the 150 is a delightful airplane to fly.

Powerplant

The introduction of 100 LL initially gave the Continental O-200 powerplant in the Cessna 150 a dose of lead-fouling problems, but users have learned to live with low-lead fuel by increased care to leaning, changing sparkplugs and oil more often, and by use of TCP additive. Deterioration of valve seat heads has been reduced by substitution of new ones made of a different material. The Cessna 152 comes with a 110-hp Lycoming O-325 engine that copes with low-lead fuel more gracefully. Reports of unexplained reduction of static rpm or uneven operation in this engine led to a Lycoming service letter listing several possible causes. One of these was possible excessive wear or looseness on the ball end of the push rods, and shortening of the rods.

Flexibility

There is a patroller version with long-range fuel tanks and a Plexiglas door, and a seaplane version that never quite caught on because of what old salts regard as too long a takeoff run with floats.

Comparative qualities

Stacked up alongside the newer but also out-of-production two-place trainers like the Beech Skipper and Piper Tomahawk, the Cessna 152 shows up surprisingly well in nearly every performance category. Only in styling and visibility is the basic old Cessna airframe eclipsed by the newer birds—which doesn't say much for "modern" lightplane technology.

The first Cessna 150s had poor visibility to the rear, thanks to the full- enclosed cabin, were placarded against spins and had a not unattractive, stubby, vertical tail. They had manual flaps that were a delight to operate, with a lever between the seats. Baggage space, though, was quite limited. The airplane also had a disquieting idiosyncrasy which would manifest itself at odd times, as after a flight, when the pilot had just taxied up to the fuel pump and shut down the engine. The airplane might then slowly and majestically raise its nose up to the sky and squat—*clank*—on its tail.

But in the 1961 model 150, this trait was corrected by relocating the main landing gear struts two inches aft on the cabin. Also, rearward visibility was improved a mite by the enlargement of the two little aft windows by about 15 percent. In 1964 the most dramatic change in the history of the line was instituted: the fuselage was chopped down behind the wing and a neat, little wraparound window placed in the rear. This was the birth of "omni vision." At the same time, a generous-sized baggage space was opened up under the little rear greenhouse window.

Growth Trends

Perhaps to accommodate the extra baggage, the 150 received its first jump in gross weight, 100 pounds, from 1,500 pounds up to 1,600 pounds. The C-152's gross went up another 70 pounds to 1,670. In 1966 Cessna felt impelled to cut the price of the 150 by a stunning 10 percent from $7,825 to $6,995. Adding a bit of flair (though negligible aerodynamic improvement) Cessna went to the modish swept vertical tail on the 150.

In addition, 50 percent more baggage space was added as they moved the cabin wall aft by one bay. On top of that, the electric stall warning horn was given the boot in favor of the wailing, sighing symphony of a pneumatic reed stall warning which could not be disconnected by the failure of an electrical circuit. In another rather radical change the same year, Cessna did away with the quick, sure manual flaps and introduced the very modern and very languid electric flaps.

The 1967 models marked the first attempt to give cramped 150 pilots a bit more elbow room—by bowing out the doors slightly for an alleged three-inch increase in cabin diameter. Also, the floorboard just aft of the rudder pedals was lowered slightly. Other little touches: the seven-inch nosewheel strut extension was shortened to four inches and an alternator replaced the traditional generator for better power output at lower rpms.

This was also the year the seaplane version was introduced—a delightful- handling machine that failed to make it in the big time, ostensibly because it took just too long to become unstuck and away on takeoff in the lake country where every cattail length of water run had to count. In the 1968 model, Cessna provided yet another smidgen of knee room by paring a couple of inches off the width of the center console separating the pilot and copilot knees. A revised flap system was offered to allow "hands-off" flap retraction.

More Upgrades

The 1970 model gained one aesthetic distinction: cambered wingtips. A year later in 1971 the 150 inherited the nice tubular landing gear struts of the Cardinal, for smoother touchdown and taxi, along with a 16 percent wider tack width. To quiet the drumming of the prop air against the cowling and windshield slightly, the propeller was extended out front a bit. Also, the landing light was moved from the wing (where it never seemed to illuminate the correct portion of the runway) to the nose inlet.

The 1975 models were marked by newly styled speed fairings and cowling that generated an alleged five-mph higher cruise speed. In addition, both fin and rudder area were increased to provide more rudder power in cross- wind landings.

Aerobatic models demand several hundred to several thousand dollars more than commuters on the market. Use of control wheels rather than sticks is a disadvantage.

The year 1976 saw the introduction of vertically adjustable pilot seats, and 1977 was the year of a pre-select flap control (again like the Cardinal's) along with a new vernier mixture to replace the traditional push-pull plunger.The 1978 Cessna 152 introduced the new 110-hp Lycoming engine, a (troublesome) 28-volt electrical system, a one-piece cowling and redesigned fuel tanks that reduced the unusable fuel to 1.5 gallons. Flap extension was limited to 30 degrees to give better performance during a balked landing. And the new Lycoming engine gave an extra 200 hours of TBO over the Continental—for 2,000 hours.

Cessna 152

Sleek and shiny, with good manners aloft, and designed to digest 100LL with ease, the Cessna 152 was to have been Cessna's ultimate improvement on the ultimate trainer—the venerable 150. But alas, a panoply of mechanical gremlins, plus high parts prices and high acquisition cost (not to mention one of the worst recessions ever to hit the U.S. aviation industry) sent new-152 sales into a screaming spiral dive just three years after the model's 1978 introduction.

The used market, as a result, now draws from a reservoir of late-vintage Cessna 152s. Though not so many years ago many were available at fire-sale prices, things have changed. With no new production trainers coming off the line, the value of the used birds has taken a dramatic upturn. Whether a used 152 represents a true bargain is another question. For the owner willing to live with 100-knot cruise speeds, frequent bouts with lead fouling, and relatively expensive (for a trainer) annual inspections, a several-year-old Cessna 152 can provide a reasonable modicum of performance and utility in the $7,000-$17,000 "sport plane" category. But the prospective 152 purchaser who thinks he's merely getting a modernized, "improved" Cessna 150 may need to think again. A fancy 150, the 152 is not.

History

"Operators of the 150 told us they wanted a training airplane that would burn 100-octane fuel, while producing lower noise levels, better fuel consumption and more payload," Cessna's vp Bob Lair remarked at the time of the 152's debut in spring of 1977. What operators got was an airplane that was—and is—subject to severe lead fouling, while delivering performance about equal to that of the Cessna 150—at a cost that made some operators wince. The original 1978 Cessna 152 (introduced in May 1977) listed at $20,635 with Nav Pac.

In changing from the 150 to the 152, Cessna gave its trainer a 110-hp Lycoming engine (with 2,000-hr. TBO) to replace the previous 100-hp Continental (1,800-hr. TBO); a McCauley "gull wing" propeller; an oil cooler as standard equipment; a 28-volt electrical system; and flaps limited to 30 degrees (instead of the previous 40). For all these changes, the 152 owner got 40 pounds more useful load than was available in the original 1958 Cessna 150 (and about 60 pounds *less* than a 1948 Cessna 140 could carry).

After 1978, relatively few important model changes were made to the basic 152. Those that *were* made point to the original airplane's mechanical shortcomings, some of which were quite notable.

In the 1979 model year, for example, Cessna incorporated impulse couplings on both magnetos— rather than just the left one, as before—to improve the 152's conspicuously lousy starting characteristics. (Likewise, direct priming to all four cylinders was made standard.) In addition, a split cowl nose piece was conjured up (retrofittable under a service bulletin), to enable shops to remove the whole cowling without first taking off the plane's propeller. (If you intend to buy a '78 model, be sure it has this feature.) An improved brake master cylinder, with fewer parts, first made its appearance on 1979 models.

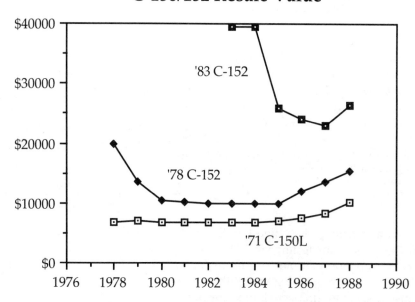

C-150/152 Resale Value

'83 C-152

'78 C-152

'71 C-150L

Starter Fix

In 1980, again addressing the airplane's poor startability, Cessna went to a slower-turning starter (the applicable armature is retrofittable under Service Letter SE79-

43), which allowed the impulse couplings to do their job better; and the plane's float carburetor got an accelerator pump as standard equipment. (Before, apparently, owners had been pumping the throttle to prime the engine, not realizing that without an accelerator pump, no fuel was coming from the carb.) Dual windshield defrosters were offered, and an even-more-expensive type of 24-volt battery (a "manifold" type) was made standard, eliminating the battery box.

In 1981, Cessna made the enlightened move of putting a spin-on oil filter on all 152s as standard—not optional—equipment. Larger battery contactors, with appropriate current capacity to eliminate contact welding, were instituted (to keep owners from having to replace so many $230 batteries after contactor fry-ups); and an avionics cooling fan became part of every avionics installation. Also in

1981, the 152's list price took a 25-percent jump, the largest single jump ever, to $30,175 equipped.

Most significant change on the 152 was a more powerful Lycoming engine designed to burn 100 LL with less grief. But lead fouling continued unabated.

For 1982, Cessna added a quick-drain to the standpipe below the fuel selector (at the belly of the airplane), to allow drainage of sediment and water from the fuel system's true low point. This modification can be—and should be— retrofitted to all 150s and 152s (an STC'd kit is available for only $19.95 from C-Mods, P.O. Box 506, Morrisville, N.C. 27560; Cessna wants $82.20 for its version of the kit).

Finally, for 1983-model 152s, Cessna went to a 108-hp O-235-N2C engine that better tolerates the lead in 100-octane avgas; the avionics cooling fan was improved; a panel vacuum warning light was made standard; and the gyro panel was redesigned to allow removal of gyro instruments from the front of the panel.

Investment Value

It generally takes four years for a new plane to bottom out on the depreciation curve—and that point was reached in 1982 for the oldest 152s. However, trainers have been known to continue depreciating much longer than "normal" aircraft. Nonetheless, it is interesting to note that the 1978 models, after losing some 55 percent of their value in the first four years, had recouped all but 25 percent of their original value by early 1988.

As it turns out, this up-swing in prices is not limited to 152s, but affects even 10- and 15-year-old 150s, which are also now commanding several thousand dollars more per plane than they did a few years ago. (Piper Tomahawks have not done as well.) Still, training activity remains strong in many of the nation's flight schools, and replacement training aircraft have to come from somewhere. Demand for used 152s at the FBO level continues to increase, driving resale prices higher.

Performance and Handling

In terms of cruise performance and payload, the 152 enjoys no real advantage over its Beech and Piper peers (the Skipper and Tomahawk), or the old C-150, for that matter. Top speed for the 152 is listed by Cessna as 109 knots, the same as for the Tomahawk and 150M (two knots more than the Skipper); likewise, the 152 Trainer's standard useful load of 528 pounds very nearly matches that of the Skipper (572 lbs.) and Tomahawk (542 lbs.). Some of the earlier 150s (E/F/G models) topped 600 pounds in load-carrying ability, however. But the useful-load

issue is made moot by the 152's optional fuel capacity of 39 gallons—33 percent greater than the Skipper's 29 gallons or the Tomahawk's 30. In range and payload flexibility, the 152 thus enjoys a slight edge over its competitors—although you may well have to sacrifice a passenger (and/or baggage) to take full benefit of the 152's longer range.

Runway performance for the 152 is good. The Cessna simply gets off quicker—and stops shorter—than Brand B or Brand P trainers (a reflection of the 152's fortunate lack of a T tail). If short- or rough-field operations are contemplated, the 152

On '76 and later models vertically adjustable pilot seats were offered. Through the years in attempts to make the cabin more comfortable, Cessna bowed out the doors and cut away floor pans for footroom.

wins hands down over its T-tail peers. Figure on an unstick distance of 725 feet for a fully grossed 152 at sea level (versus 780 and 820 feet for the Skipper and Tomahawk); and set aside a mere 475 feet for landing roll (vs. 670 or 707 ft. for the T-trainers). The 152, incidentally, lands about 10 percent longer than the 150—apparently due to the 152's 30-degree flap-travel restriction.

So where does the 152 really shine? Its confidence-inspiring slow-flight characteristics and straightforward Cessna-like handling provide the key. The plane stalls well and with plenty of warning. (Power on, you can get zero-knots indicated before approaching the burble.) Stability in all axes is outstanding. The barn-door flaps—electric, alas—are monstrously effective (but watch out for the pitch-up on initial deployment). The 152's light wing loading makes it a bit uncomfortable in more than very light turbulence; otherwise, however, it flies very much like a miniature Skyhawk. Which is just what Cessna wanted, of course.

The 152, like the 150, also comes in an Aerobat version—which the Skipper and Tomahawk don't. (Only about one in 20 152s is an 'A' model, however.) If loops and hammerheads are your cup of pekoe, the A152 will grudgingly comply. But don't expect Pitts-like—or even Citabria-like—performance, and forget about sustained inverted flight (the engine dies).

Comfort

Although significantly better than, say, a Luscombe or Taylorcraft, the 152's cabin comfort is nothing to brag about (and in fact takes a back seat to that of either the Skipper or Tomahawk). Visibility is poor, noise level is high, and shoulder room is almost nonexistent. Thicker seat padding became standard with the 1979 models (the previous cushions taxed the endurance of even the most hardened CFIs), but even so, pillows are highly recommended for cross-country work.

Ventilation (via the wing-root pull tubes, and air leaks around the doors) has always been good in 150s and 152s, even, unfortunately, in the dead of winter. To add insult to misery, Cessna located cabin-heat and carb-heat pickoffs next to each other on the muffler shroud. (Even with carb heat turned off, the carb-heat plumbing provides a sizable plenum for the escape of desperately needed cabin BTUs.) In 1979, Cessna released a service letter, SE79-12, describing a kit to relocate the carb-heat source to the number-four exhaust riser. This allowed the muffler's total heat output to be utilized for cabin heat, resulting in a 30-percent increase in cabin heat flow. All 1980 and later 152s were delivered with this cabin-heat mod. The first 4,100 airplanes off the line, however, did not get the deluxe heater kit, and most remain unmodified. Check for compliance with Cessna Service Letter SE79-12 before buying a '78 or '79 airplane.

Engine

In going from the 150 to the 152, Cessna switched from the venerable 80-octane Continental O-200-A to the somewhat more expensive (and powerful) Lycoming O-235-L2C. The rationale behind the engine change was threefold. First, with 80-octane avgas in increasingly short supply, more and more flight schools were reporting problems with lead buildup in their 150s' O-200 engines; Cessna wanted to give its dealers a trainer that could digest the higher-leaded 100-octane fuels. Second, the 150—which had seen empty-weight increases totaling nearly 150 pounds (or 15 percent) since 1958—was overdue for a horsepower boost. And third, Cessna— in accordance with proposed FAA and ICAO noise standards— wanted to see a reduction in the 150's internal and external sound levels. The high-compression Lycoming O-235-L2C, delivering 110 horsepower at 2,550 rpm instead of the O-200's 2,750, seemed a natural answer to all three requirements.

Many operators say that the switch to the Lycoming engine was a mistake. Although it did rid the Cessna trainer of the O-200's starter-clutch woes (the small Continental uses a $600 starter adapter that can fail frequently and without warning), the Lycoming O-235 brought its own constellation of mechanical quirks. Parts prices were, in some cases, astoundingly high: The O-235-L2C's sodium-filled exhaust valves, for instance, listed for $213.08 each—versus only $64 for the O-200's solid-stemmed valves. (Likewise, a piston for the Lycoming engine cost about twice what the corresponding Continental piston cost.)

What's more, the O-235's cylinders may not be ground oversize during a top overhaul (since it removes the nitride layer), whereas the O-200's jugs can be

Cost/Performance/Specifications

Model	Year	Average Retail Price	Cruise Speed (kts)	Useful Load (lbs)	Fuel Std/Opt (gals)	Engine	TBO (hrs)	Overhaul Cost
150	1959-61	$7,100	105	554	26/38	100-hp Cont.O-200-A	1,800	$7,000
150	1962-64	$7,600	105	554	26/38	100-hp Cont.O-200-A	1,800	$7,000
150	1965-67	$8,500	105	554	26/38	100-hp Cont.O-200-A	1,800	$7,000
150	1968-70	$9,500	105	554	26/38	100-hp Cont.O-200-A	1,800	$7,000
150	1971-73	$10,000	105	554	26/38	100-hp Cont.O-200-A	1,800	$7,000
150	1974-77	$11,500	105	554	26/38	100-hp Cont.O-200-A	1,800	$7,000
152	1978-80	$16,500	107	568	26/38	110-hp Lyc .O-235-L2C	2,000	$8,000
152	1981-83	$22,500	107	568	26/38	110-hp Lyc .O-235-L2C	2,000	$8,000
152	1984-85	$35,000	106	568	26/38	108-hp Lyc .O-235-N2C	2,000	$8,000

ground over. And if an owner elects to salvage run-out cylinders by chroming, extreme difficulty may be had in finding piston rings for final buildup. Unchromed rings must be used in chromed jugs— and no one, at present, supplies unchromed rings for 0-235s.

Other service quirks that have not endeared schools or their shops to the 152's powerplant:

• As originally delivered, the Cessna 152 came with Slick 4000-series "sealed" (i.e., unrepairable in the field) magnetos. A rash of unexplained capacitor problems led to engine failures in Tomahawks using the same engine/magneto combo, but the 152 was mysteriously unaffected. Nonetheless, operators soon tired of spending hundreds of dollars on new mags every time their "throw-away Slicks" needed points or bearings. A black market in bogus 152-mag "repair kits" sprang up, and Slick finally introduced a field-repairable version of the mags.

• The O-235 is one of few recent aircraft engines that uses solid (not hydraulic) tappets. Valve lash in the O-235 thus varies with engine temperature, and O-235 valve-train clearances must be checked scrupulously every 100 hours, not unlike a motorcycle. Lycoming, in an attempt to minimize lash problems, devised hollow-aluminum pushrods with steel ball ends (the idea being that the aluminum, which expands more than twice as much as steel on heating, would tend automatically to readjust lash at higher temperatures). Such construction calls for very critical ball-end fit tolerances, however, and—unfortunately—Lycoming's pushrod vendor failed, initially, to meet the necessary specs. As a result, pushrod "mushrooming" (pounding of the steel ball ends down into the pushrod) became common. After a fatal accident related to pushrod shortening in November 1980, FAA issued an AD on this subject. All defective rods should by now have been taken out of circulation, but it bears mentioning that valve train clearances are critical and subject to frequent rechecking in the O-235.

With the '76 models came vernier throttles in place of push-pull plungers, and pre-select flap controls. At the top of the panel is a rear-view mirror.

• The O-235-L2C did not escape the inspection requirements of a 1981 AD (81-18-04) that called for replacement of iron oil pump impellers with late-configuration steel and aluminum ones. This caused many 2,000-hour engines to be summarily grounded.

Miscellaneous reports of low static rpm and uneven operation led Lycoming to issue a special bulletin for the O-235 (S.I. 1388C) outlining trouble-shooting procedures to restore full power. This service letter has gone through several revisions.

Lead Fouling

Lead buildup—not only in spark plugs but in nooks and crannies in the combustion chamber, and on valves—has been a persistent problem in O-235 engines. So much so, in fact, that Champion designed a special spark plug just for this engine—the extended-electrode 'Y' series (e.g., REM37BY). The long-prong plugs do not scavenge lead any better than standard plugs; they merely have electrodes that sit far enough away from lead incrustations to constantly "burn clean." Once filled with lead, the 'Y' plugs continue to fire.

(But they still must be replaced often.) Most operators find that even with judicious leaning, spark plugs must be cleaned every 25 hours in a 152. "Otherwise," remarks one A&P, "at 100 hours, you can throw the plug away—it won't even be cleanable." Lead buildup on the inside of the cylinder affects spark plug life: Lycoming found that lead can be redeposited from the combustion chamber to clean spark plugs in as little as 25 hours. Accordingly, in Service Instruction 1418, Lycoming outlines a procedure whereby O-235 cylinders can be blast-cleaned with walnut shells without removal for top overhaul. (Prior to this, some operators were finding that early top overhauls were needed to prevent lead from reaching excessive levels in O-235 jugs.)

Safety

Safety statistics for the 150 and 152 are quite good. (In this regard, at least, trainers have come a long way since Piper Cub days.) An NTSB study found the Cessna 150 series with the lowest fatal accident rate—at 1.35 per 100,000 flight hours—of any two-seater, and one of the lowest fatal crash rates of *any* single-engine aircraft, period. The total accident rate, at 10.3 per 100,000 hours, is also quite respectable, again bettering most trainers *and* four-place aircraft.

If there's one fly in the safety ointment, it's the 152's relatively weak showing against the Piper Tomahawk. A special study by *Aviation Safety* (covering the period January 1978 through April 1980) found the 152 with a 38-percent higher total accident rate than the Tomahawk. (Fatal accident rates were about equal.) As a percentage of total accidents, the Cessna 152 is involved in disproportionately more groundloops, overshoots, undershoots, and fuel mismanagement accidents than the Tomahawk. The 152, on the other hand, fares much better than its Piper counterpart in the proportion of hard landing accidents and stall-spins.

Overall, the 152 has a sterling safety record, bolstered by the fact that there has never been an in-flight breakup of the airplane (despite a fair number of IFR-weather encounters by low-time pilots).

Maintenance

Many of the 152's early maintenance foibles (the most serious of which have been touched on above) have now been laid to rest and should not pose recurrent problems for used-trainer buyers. The 152's most serious ongoing maintenance problem involves lead fouling, which (according to some owners) can be severe even with proper leaning, the use of low-lead fuel, addition of TCP concentrate (a lead remover marketed by Alcor) to 100LL, correct adjustment of idle mixture, and switching to Champion long-prong plugs.

All of these measures are unnecessary, of course, in a Cessna 150 operating on grade-80 avgas or unleaded automotive gasoline. But unfortunately, the 152's engine is restricted to 100-octane avgas for the foreseeable future. (In all fairness, private owners should experience fewer bouts of lead fouling than flight schools, since much of the 152's lead fouling is due to chronic overrich operation in the pattern.)

Prospective 152 buyers should check to see whether these important service bulletins have been complied with:

• SE82-23 required a one-time inspection of 152 starter and battery contactors.

• SE81-38 outlined brake master cylinder modifications for 1979 through mid-'82 Cessna 152s (and post-1966 150s).

• SE81-24 puts a fuel quick-drain in the belly of pre-'82 Cessna 152s (and post-1966 150s).

• SE80-96 (Revision 1) calls for recurrent inspections of certain Stewart-Warner oil coolers on a variety of Cessnas, including the 152. This was also the subject of an AD.

• SE79-7 modifies the nose cap to allow removal of the cowl without first taking the prop off.

• SE79-11 and -43 concerned mods to improve the starting characteristics of pre-1980 152s.

• SE79-12 reroutes carb heat plumbing to improve cabin heat.

• SE79-16 outlines flap cable clamp mods that must be accomplished prior to 1,000 hours in service. This was also the subject of an AD (80-6-3); so make sure it has been complied with on any airplane you intend to buy.

• SE79-46 describes periodic inspection requirements for 152 carburetor airboxes. In 1982, Cessna came out with a service bulletin (SE82-12) describing an airscoop mod for the 152, compliance with which is also recommended.

• SE79-49 mandates vertical fin hardware attachment inspections every 100 hours. This now carries the force of law, under an AD (No. 80-11-04).

SE79-57 describes a much-improved flap actuator mechanical stop for 1979 and earlier 152s.

• SE80-2: Another cabin heat mod.

• SE80-10 requires use of Loctite on certain starter screws, which have shown a tendency to back out.

We mentioned before the 152's bout with self-shortening pushrods (the subject of a late-1980 AD, and Lycoming S.B. 453). What we didn't mention is that compliance with this AD doesn't guarantee that you'll *never* see pushrod mushrooming in your 152's engine. There have been reports (not many, but a few), subsequent to the AD, of engines with the improved pushrods experiencing ball-hammering or mushrooming. Hence, along with a compression check, we'd recommend a check of valve clearances (or pushrod length) in any pre-purchase inspection of a 152.

Modifications

The Cessna 150 can be given half as much horsepower and turned into a pint-sized STOL machine, thanks to a brace of alterations offered by several companies. Firms providing the engine switch are MASA (Mid-America STOL Aircraft, Inc., Wichita, Kans.) and Avcon Industries, Inc. (also of Wichita). Those offering STOL alterations are R/STOL, Sierra Industries, Garner Municipal Airport, P.O. Box 5184, Uvalde, Tex., (512) 278-4381, and Horton, Inc. at Wellington, Kans.

Flying classroom for numberless pilots, the 150 is forgiving and always recoverable, but sharp-edged enough to demand precision.

MASA and Avcon install 150-hp Lycoming engines in place of the normal 100-hp Continental. This makes for a big jump (up to about 950 fpm) in climb performance, a fairly healthy increase in cruise speed (up to 145-150 mph) and a small loss in useful load (about 30 pounds). Avcon also notes that some extensive juggling of weight is necessary to accommodate the bigger engine, mostly involving shifting the battery from the engine compartment to the tail section.

R/STOL provides what appears to be the most elaborate STOL treatment to Cessna 150s. This includes a sophisticated flap-aileron interconnect system with drooping ailerons that work at different angles to match flap angles. Also part of the mod are recontoured leading edges, stall fences, conical cambered wingtips and, if needed, aileron gap seals. For less money Horton installs a leading-edge alteration, along with new landing light lens for wing- mounted models, stall fences on top of the wing, aileron fences plus "drooped" wingtips. The purpose of both STOL installations is to lower stall speeds and provide more controllability near and in the stall regime. For pilots who prefer taildraggers, Custom Aircraft Conversions, Inc. in San Antonio, Texas, can supply landing gear kits.

There are quite a few approved mods for the 152. Brackett Aircraft offers conversion kits for installation of wet-foam air filters on the 152 (replacement elements are only a few dollars for this type of filter, whereas Cessna gets about $25 for a new paper element). Brackett filters are available through any large FBO.

Avcon Industries holds STC No. SA1384CE for installation of a Lycoming O-320-E2D 150-hp engine in the A152 only. However, J&S Engineering, Inc., of San Antonio has an STC to install the 180-hp Lycoming O-360 in 150s as well as 152s, allowing a gross weight increase of nearly 100 pounds to boot. Also, nose-wheel amputation is available through Custom Aircraft Conversions of San Antonio. The tailwheel conversion is claimed to boost speed by eight to 10 mph, by eliminating drag and substituting prop thrust that would otherwise be blanked out by the nose gear. Details of the 180-hp engine conversion and the so-called Texas Taildragger mod can be obtained by calling Custom at 512-349-6347.

Better performance and a cleaner-running engine are the highlights of a powerplant conversion for some Cessna 152s offered by a Washington mod shop called Air Mods N.W. Sprightlier takeoff, climb and cruise performance results from installation of a new prop that can be spun up to 2,800 rpm, while a higher compression ratio helps prevent lead sludge from building up in the combustion chambers and in the oil. The extra pressure does have its dark side, though, in increasing the chances of destructive detonation if the engine is worked too hard or given an improper diet.

The conversion is made up of three separate STCs that turn Cessna 152s and Aerobats built from 1978 through 1982 with 110-hp Lycoming O-235-L2C engines into 125-hp Sparrow Hawks. One of the STCs (SE792NW) covers installation of slightly taller pistons, which raise the compression ratio from 8.5:1 to 9.7:1, and an adjustment in timing from 20 to 25 degrees before top dead center. According to Ken Blackman at Air Mods N.W., the modified engine is very similar to a version that Lycoming exported to Europe in the early 1970s.

A second STC (SA1000NW) simply allows installation of the modified engine into a 152 airframe with changes to the baffling to permit better flow of cooling air around the engine. The third certificate (SA1008NW) covers replacement of the stock McCauley "gull-wing" propeller with a more efficient Sensenich S6-series prop and spinner.

A Sparrow Hawk package costs $2,550 and includes the three STCs, instructions and drawings, four pistons and precut baffling material. Air Mods N.W., P.O. Box 8, Snohomish, Wash. 98290. (206) 691-7634.

Horton STOL-Craft in Wellington, Kans. provides a STOL kit consisting of wing leading edge cuffs, drooped tips, stall fences and aileron gap seals.

Organizations

Early model 152 had one-piece nose caps, preventing complete cowl removal with the propeller in place. Later models have two-piece nose caps—a definite maintenance bonus.

The Cessna 150-152 Club has been around for some years. The group's monthly newsletter (The Cessna 150-152 News), edited by Skip Carden, is an excellent clearinghouse of service-related information and info on new mods, discount parts sources, etc. Membership is $20/yr. domestic and Canada, $30/yr. foreign. Contact the club at P.O. Box 15388, Durham, N.C. 27704, or phone 919-471-9492.

As a special service to members, the club publishes a fat loose-leaf volume called *Hints 'n' Tips* with a wealth of information on operating 150s and 152s. Included are modifications, ADs, Airworthiness Alerts, along with a host of information on servicing the aircraft. Don't miss this volume, which is updated annually.

The other big organization providing excellent service to all Cessna owners is the Cessna Pilots Assn. located in Wichita, Kans., (316) 946-4777.

Owner Comments

It's been an amazing airplane. I'd parallel that with the J-3, almost. Problems? You have the usual matter of guys pulling out the starter cable. As for reports that the nosewheel shimmies, if you land really fast on it, it'll shimmy, as it might on any airplane. But that's par for the course with a trainer. I wouldn't say the maintenance is high. For the beating they take, they're excellent.

The only problem with the Cessna 150 as a cross-country machine is the way it reacts to turbulence. You really feel the bumps. You get jolted around, compared with larger four-place airplanes. Nevertheless, it's a lot of fun, and maneuverable.

Aside from a cracked crankcase, the only maintenance problem I've had is with the nose strut, which I had to have overhauled. I bought the aircraft from an FBO who used it as a training plane, but it really held up to the wear and tear pretty well. Aside from the time in the logbooks, you couldn't tell how much it had been flown, and how hard. It had 2,850 hours on it when I bought it.

• • •

One problem with the airplane is the way the fuel system feeds unevenly with the tank selector on both. One wing gets heavy, so you have to compensate with aileron. And with my airplane it's usually the right tank that feeds first, so if you're flying from the left seat, you have to compensate for your weight and the fuel in the left tank.

The birth of "omni vision" occurred with the 1964 model 150. The fuselage was chopped down behind the wing and a wraparound window placed there.

• • •

It spins okay, but winds up pretty fast; it really whips around compared with other planes I've spun in training.

• • •

Cabin size is very limited for two full-sized people. You're elbow to elbow. Visibility is all right, but if they'd put a C-172-type windshield in, it would be much better. And, of course, top visibility isn't that good. In all, it's fun to fly, and it's not that expensive in fuel consumption.

• • •

We had the Horton STOL conversion on our 150, and it worked out beautifully. It just makes a good, complete all-around plane, though my husband and I probably will go to a larger four-placer next time. We really don't need the STOL for short fields; we just feel it makes the airplane safer.

The only mechanical problem we've had with it was an alternator failure on a long trip, and we lost all our electronics, got lost in a midwestern dust storm and had to make an expedience landing. But I think Cessna makes a good airplane.

• • •

What I like about it is that the maintenance is relatively inexpensive. This is the fourth airplane I've owned, and the newest one. The one thing I don't like about it is that to me it is a very boring airplane. Also, I don't like the fact that every time you pull up to a gas pump people ask you if you are a student on a cross-country.

When you're paying money for an airplane, you like to have people say it looks nice when you pull into the pump. It's an ego thing.

I think the handling is fairly good, but I'd prefer lighter ailerons. My old Swift had lighter ones, for example. I like the way it spins for training. It's very predictable; it goes into a spin the same way every time. To avoid problems on a balked landing, I teach my students to use just 20 degrees of flaps, and about the only time I teach them to use 40 degrees is when they get real high on the approach.

My instructor taught me that, looking on 40 degrees as just an extra drag device. Electric flaps, especially on a balked landing, are a real problem since you don't have any climb capability with full flaps.

I didn't feel I had too much problem with it, but the new students might.

• • •

The noise level, as in most light airplanes, is unbearable, and I think that's an area where improvement could be made. I use it quite a bit for cross-country in addition to training, and it works out pretty well. It's got pretty good range. You can figure it is a three-hour airplane, and then you have 45 minutes' reserve.

I would like to have a little more top speed on the airplane for cross-country cruising. The nosewheel is a constant problem. That's one of the weak links in the airplane. I've had nosewheel shimmy ever since I bought the airplane, and though the shimmy damper was rebuilt and rebushed, it never helped. I've had no real problem with the strut, except that it deflates about every two months, but that seems to be normal.

• • •

The airplane has a really outstanding fuel system, with just one lever for both tanks. But the uneven feeding of the tanks is disconcerting. On a long trip, one tank will be on empty, and the other on half, and you sit there hoping the other one will start feeding pretty soon and they'll even themselves out. They always do, eventually. In terms of maintenance, when something goes wrong with the old pull starter solenoid system, that's a $70 replacement. When they went to the key starter system, that meant the replacement cost went up to about $250.

I bought one of the first C-152s, taking delivery June 3, 1977. I've had some good experiences and some bad experiences. I'll start with the bad first. Here's what happened the first week:

Nose wheel tire went flat. Nose strut went flat and had to be rebuilt. Radio failed. Left brake failed—mechanic found small cupful of trash in hydraulic lines. Aircraft wouldn't start. Battery went dead. The aircraft's starting problems continued to plague me for the next six months. The dealer could not get it started, nor could he get four of his own started. I burned out two starters the first six months and had to buy a new battery plus get an APU start ($10) everytime I wanted to fly, and even then the aircraft would not start on most occasions.

Cessna would do nothing about it except send me a starting procedure. Even after writing the president with my complaints all he did was send me a starting procedure.

I wrote the Birmingham GADO, and they replied that since it was not a safety problem they couldn't help me. I contacted the FAA in Washington and they said it was not their responsibility to get Cessna to do anything about it. Next I contacted the Consumer Protection Agency in Washington, but they stated it was not within their charter to resolve such problems. I then contacted Lycoming and they were of no help either—they stated that once they sell an engine to Cessna, it then becomes Cessna's responsibility.

But luck did out! In desperation I called the attorney general of the State of Alabama and explained my plight—and as luck would have it he was campaigning for Governor, and was very attentive to my problem.

Anyway, I don't know what his office told Cessna or Lycoming, but in no time at all I was bombarded with phone calls, letters and telegrams from both companies. About two days later, Lycoming flew a mechanic from the factory with a coffin box full of parts. What he did I don't know, but he did fix it!

Not a bad little cross-country cruiser, the 150 can carry as much as 35 gallons of usable fuel as an option. Speed is 106 knots with everything to the wall at altitude.

Later Cessna issued a Service Bulletin recommending a second mag impulse, which improved starting by cranking on eight spark plugs rather than four. I complied with this Bulletin at a cost of $425. I also complied with another Service Bulletin recommending a modification whereby all four cylinders are primed for start rather than two. Both these modifications are great and even low-time student pilots can crank the aircraft with ease. I can only say Cessna is the most hard-nosed company I've ever dealt with.

But my story does have a happy ending. After the first six months of trouble and expenditure of getting the aircraft straightened out, I can say the aircraft has performed beautifully since then. It's a great flying machine; it's a great trainer, and I love it. I now have 2,540 hours on it and I couldn't wish for anything better. The engine was top overhauled at 2,000 hours and also an AD was complied with at that time in which an oil pump shaft was replaced. Also at 1,400 hours I had to rebuild a cylinder due to low compression.

As for 100-hour and annuals, I have a working agreement with an AI whereby I do certain of the work under his supervision and thereby get a price reduction.

E.R. Ritch
Huntsville, Ala.

We have been operating Cessna 152s since 1978 and have had more than our fair share of troubles with them. Because they have required much more cranking to start, they tend to wear out batteries and starters quicker than the 150 (which are more expensive than those of a 150 because they are 24-volt). Plugs. Until we received the flyer from Lycoming, we kept the plug cleaning machines and mechanics busy. Suffice as to say, I'm sure that a lot of us have leaned the 152 a little too early and a little too much in order to prevent lead build-up. This, of course, eventually leads to internal (and expensive) cylinder problems.

Our own company 152 had a jug topped at 1,500 TT. Whereas, our 1977 150 went 1,050 hours over TBO without having one cylinder removed.

Now some of the good points.

1) From a safety standpoint, we feel that the elimination of the last 10 degrees of flaps was a good move. 2) We have seen an upward trend in the reliability of ARC radios and nose wheel shimmy dampeners. 3) The newer seats are more comfortable which is a nice plus for those CFIs sitting in them all day. 4) The schemes, quality and colors of paint are markedly improved.

Texas Taildragger mod adds a sporty touch to the 152 that hearkens back to C-140 days.

The question is . . . would I consider buying another one? Only if Cessna had equipped it with a 12-volt electrical system and a good old reliable Continental O-200A. Despite all my grievances, Cessna by far makes the world's most desirable training aircraft.

Reed D. Novisoff
Long Beach Flyers, Inc.
Long Beach, Calif.

My 1978 Cessna 152 has been leased to a flying club, so perhaps all of my comments and data may not be comparable to aircraft operated by private owners. In addition, I am an A&P mechanic and do almost all of the maintenance myself, so labor cost is not included in maintenance cost, except for the annual inspection. But I am a pilot, so general comments are relevant.

Handling and performance are good, and the aircraft is certainly satisfactory for training purposes. However, on cross-country flights comfort is average to poor because of lack of leg room for the taller pilot and skimpy seat padding. Seating width is poor for large people when both seats are in use. Power is adequate under all conditions (home field elevation is only 469 feet though).

Most complaints center around the rapid lead-fouling of the lower spark plugs which causes many flights to be cancelled after ground runup with a 200-300 rpm mag drop. Even using TCP and the newer Champion REM37BY plugs, the lower ones must be cleaned every 20-25 hours. Fuel availability is limited to 100 octane at the home field—no 100LL is available—so perhaps the plugs would stay clean longer with 100LL Nose wheel shimmy is a problem from time to time due to linkage wear and the pounding the nose gear takes from students and operation primarily from an unpaved runway. I am not too happy with the 24-volt electrical system when it comes time to replace the battery. Last year the starter shorted internally and the parts cost for starter (rebuilt) and a Gill battery was $500. Parts availability has not been a problem.

The way the aircraft is used in flight training makes it difficult to accurately check fuel consumption (takeoffs and landings, forgetting to lean the mixture, etc.) but it appears to be close to the numbers published in Cessna's Pilot's Operating Handbook. I hope your other readers will benefit from this information, and perhaps someone has a solution for the plug-fouling problem.

Norman J. Makowski
Fairport, N.Y.

We have operated four Cessna 152s for the past three and one-half years here in our flight school. Our most popular one (a 1980 model) is doing about 700 hours per year. Hourly maintenance cost is about five dollars per hour. They burn six gallons per hour if properly leaned, lots more if run hard or full rich. All have had lousy compression since new, and even after tops or overhauls; 65/80 is typical throughout the 2,000-hour TBO span. Valve clearances must be checked each 100 hours. We go 100 hours without cleaning the plugs or changing the oil providing they are religiously leaned and run up to 1800 rpm for a minute before shut down. The 24-volt electrical system is a pain in the neck requiring $239 batteries at least once a year. The RT-385A radios are also expensive to repair when the lights (digits) burn out or they quit cold.

Optional skylights on top, barely visible here, provide a bit of extra visibility inside steep turns.

All in all it is a good trainer and rental aircraft, but a few pet gripes of mine are:

1) Who the hell needs a cruise prop (and therefore a 104-knot cruise speed) on a primary trainer used to build hours of training and proficiency? 2) It's a gas hog. 3) Cabin is four inches too narrow. 4) I miss the 40 degrees flap setting. 5) Too noisy (I *always* wear ear plugs). 6) Cessna Aircraft Co. overprices CPC supplies, parts, etc. 7) It's too damned expensive. In 1979 I bought two for $30,000.

Despite the shortcomings, it is the best airplane around for my purpose but honestly, I'd rather have a C-150 if I could find lots of clean low-time late models. Our answer to the problem is an Aeronca Champ. We have *one*, but I hope it continues in popularity so we can buy another. In that Aeronca we can teach students how to really *fly* the airplane.

David B. O'Brien, Pres.
FBO Lakewood Airport
Bay Head, N.J.

Cessna 170

It's a good-performing, honest four-seater and also a lot of fun to fly. Like any other taildragger, though, it can bite. Though 170s still are quite affordable, prices have begun to climb. Cessna built 5,136 of the airplanes in a nine-year production run that ended more than 30 years ago. But time has taken a toll. Today, less than half of the airplanes are still flying; and recent accident records show that ground loops and hard landings are continuing to thin out the 170 fleet at quite a clip.

Prices for 170s, like this 1955 B model (which has modified, fiberglass wingtips), are rising fast. There's no need to rob Fort Knox to buy one, yet; but you're still likely to come out ahead, budget-wise, getting an early-model 172 and converting it to a taildragger.

Still, there are many who turn a veiled eye on the taildragger's safety record and dismiss the tricycle-gear 172—the 170's successor—as a giant step backward in airplane design. Attesting their viewpoint are the growing popularity of tailwheel conversions for 172s and the rapidly increasing prices for Cessna's original light four-seater. Cessna 170s typically are fetching substantially higher prices than other comparable four-seaters of the same vintage, including the much faster Piper Tri-Pacer. Also, the price tags on many 170s outstrip those on vastly better-equipped and newer 172s.

Though they cannot be classified as bargains, 170s still are affordable family-movers. Figure paying anywhere from $11,000 to $15,000 for a good one. Owners characterize operating and maintenance costs as relative pittances, and they like to compare the performance and load-carrying capabilities with new four-seaters that cost a king's ransom. However, it is inevitable that the airplanes can show signs of their age, in the form of corrosion and fatigue. Though some parts are hard to find, help in the care and feeding of Cessna 170s is available from a supportive owners' group.

History

When Cessna started building 170s in 1948, it had only four other airplanes on its assembly lines. They were the svelte, two-seat, 85-hp 120 and 140 models, and the big, four-seat, radial-engine 190 and 195. The 170 actually is a stretched, four-seat version of the 140, powered by a six-cylinder, 145-hp Continental C145-2 engine (later to be redesignated the O-300A) and a two-blade McCauley propeller. A total of 714 Model 170s were built in 1948, and there are about 357 of them still around today.

The original 170, built only in 1948, can be distinguished from its descendants by its fabric-covered, constant-chord, round-tip, V-strutted wings and by the absence of a dorsal fin. Inside the wings are three 12.5-gallon tanks (one in the left wing, two interconnected in the right), providing a usable supply of 33.5 gallons.

In 1949, the Model 170A made its debut with a dorsal fin and all-metal wings supported by a single strut on each side of the fuselage. Outboard of the struts, the wings taper out to their squared-off tips. The A-model's flaps and ailerons are a bit larger than the 170's, and the hinged flaps can be extended to 50 degrees (whereas the 170's flaps are limited to 30 degrees). The dorsal fin is identical to the one on the Model 195 and was added, supposedly, to improve directional stability. There's only one fuel tank in each of the 170A's wings, and maximum usable fuel capacity is 37 gallons.

While the original 170 is affectionately referred to, for obvious reasons, as the "ragwing," the A model sometimes is called the "straight wing." That's because unlike the 170, which has about one degree of dihedral, and the 170B, which has nearly three degrees, the 170A has no dihedral.

Para-lifter

In 1952, after building 1,522 Model 170As (about 621 of which have survived), Cessna introduced the 170B. This model has what Cessna called "Para-lift" flaps—relatively large, slotted, semi-Fowler designs originally used on the Model 305 military observation plane, which blue-suiters dubbed the L-19 Bird Dog. Early B models have only four flap settings (zero, 20, 30 and 40 degrees). Those built after 1954 have an extra notch for 10 degrees of flap, which many pilots favor for takeoff.

In addition to being cranked up to nearly three degrees of dihedral, the 170B's wings have more twist than their predecessors'. The B model also has control balance weights that make its elevators a bit lighter to the touch.

Upper engine cowls on 170-series airplanes built before 1953 are hinged; those on later models are full pressure types with fairly large hatches that open onto the battery and oil dipstick. Airplanes built before mid-1953 also have straight, interchangeable main gear legs; later 170Bs have bowed and more acutely tapered legs, which cannot be swapped from side to side. Other changes in 1953 included addition of extra heating outlets for passenger seats and a windshield defroster, and replacement of piano-key type panel switches with push-pull knobs.

Airplanes built after 1954 can be distinguished by a cosmetic touch to their windows and by a different tailwheel-steering setup. The aft portions of their rear windows are flat, rather than round, and the airplanes have cables, rather than a rudder horn/spring system, for their tailwheels.

Tri-ing Times

Influenced, no doubt, by Piper's success with the Tri-Pacer (originally introduced in 1951 as a tricycle-gear option for the Pacer), Cessna introduced the Model 172 in 1956. But production of the 170B was not terminated right away. Some 72 were built in 1956, and three dozen rolled off the line early the next year (though, for some reason, they are called 1956 models).

The last B models off the line differ from earlier 170s in having molded-plastic interiors, rather than cloth; an un-openable right-door window; and only one engine-cowl hatch, which opens onto both the oil dipstick and the battery. (The battery had been moved from the right to the left side of the engine compartment in 1954.) Of the 2,900 Model 170Bs built, about 1,500 are still flying today.

Performance

A properly rigged 170 will cruise at 104 knots true at around 2,400 rpm (65 to 70 percent power) while burning between seven and eight gallons of fuel an hour at altitudes below 8,000 feet. Fuel can be drawn from either wing tank or from both of them at the same time (the latter is required for takeoff and landing). Direct-reading fuel gauges are located in the wing-root areas of the cabin.

Though its cabin generally is noisy and drafty, a 170 can carry four adults and full fuel. Extra heating outlets were added in 1953 to make the cabin tolerable in frosty air.

Lead Problems

The Continental engine was designed to operate on 80/87-octane aviation fuel, which is increasingly becoming hard to find in many areas of the country, and many 170 owners have experienced problems on 100LL. Some have invested in exhaust-gas temperature (EGT) gauges for their airplanes and alleviate the problems by leaning aggressively. Others have sought relief from lead-fouling problems and the higher prices of avgas by operating their airplanes on premium unleaded automobile gasoline with STCs available either from the EAA Aviation Foundation in Oshkosh, Wis., or from Petersen Aviation in Minden, Neb.

Generally, book performance numbers are achievable, according to owners. But some claim the takeoff figures in 170 POHs are conservative, at best. The book indicates that, under standard conditions, a 170 will require 1,820 feet for takeoff, 2,190 feet to clear a 50-foot obstacle. Subtract about 200 feet from those numbers if 20 degrees of flaps are used for departure. However, some owners say they regularly use up about half that amount of real estate getting aloft. The POH also shows that 1,145 feet are required for a normal landing, 1,210 feet to get in over an obstacle.

Best rate-of-climb speed is 77 knots, and climb rate diminishes from a sprightly 690 fpm at sea level to a leisurely 370 fpm at 7,000 feet. The airplane stalls at about 50 knots, clean, and 45 knots with full flaps.

Comfort and Loading

Visibility is excellent on the ground and in the air, due to the low panel and sloped engine cowl. Two wide doors and relatively big assist steps make it easy to board the airplane. Inside, there's plenty of room for four people, but 170 cabins tend to be rather noisy, and even the improved heating systems in late-model 170Bs are hard-pressed to deal with northern climes.

Unlike many other single-engine airplanes with four seats, most 170s can carry full fuel, four adults and their baggage. Maximum useful load of 170s and 170As with standard (that is, Spartan) equipment is 1,015 pounds; 995 pounds for the B model. Up to 120 pounds of baggage can be carried behind the rear seat but must be loaded through the front doors, since none of the airplanes was built with an external baggage hatch. External hatches have, however, been STC'd for the airplanes.

Handling

It would seem that, with the various changes made during the course of 170 production, there would be marked handling differences among the models. But pilots who have flown all three models say there is little difference.

Some idiosyncrasies arise from the different flap designs. The 170's are relatively small and limited to 30 degrees extension (at 90 mph, max). Though its flaps are not as effective as those on its successors (which can be extended at 100 mph), the original 170 can be slipped quite effectively. Slips with full flaps are prohibited in the A and B models, because their barn doors can block the air flowing over the tail, causing the nose to pitch down suddenly and severely. Another difference, mentioned earlier, is the lighter elevator control forces experienced in the 170B, due to its mass balance weights.

Owners seem to be split on whether three-pointers or wheelies are better for takeoff and landing. On one hand, they say, wheelies require longer ground runs and rolls, and higher airspeeds. On the other hand, the main gear legs are rather stiff, and three-pointers tend to give the tailwheel a good beating (and the occupants a good bouncing) if technique isn't perfect or the field is rough.

Swapping Ends

One long-time 170 pilot summed it up this way, "The 170 is one of the easier taildraggers to land, but any taildragger will bite you." Indeed, in a comparative study of 33 single-engine airplanes a few years ago, NTSB found 170s to be involved in a relatively high rate of ground-loop accidents. With 10 such accidents per 100,000 hours of flying time, the 170 came in fourth place. At the head of the list of ground-loopers was the Cessna 195, with a whopping 22 end-swaps per 100,000 hours. Then came the Stinson 108 and the Luscombe, each with a rate of about 13.

Close behind the 170 were its two-seat stablemates, the 120 and 140, with about nine ground-loop accidents per 100,000 hours. As might be expected, tricycle-gear airplanes fell to the bottom of the ground-loop list. The PA-22 Tri-Pacer placed in mid-range (15th, actually) with a rate of nearly three; the 172 was 29th with a rate of one ground-loop per 100,000 hours.

Studying more recent records, we found loss of control during takeoff or landing accounted for more than half of nonfatal accidents (40 out of 70) involving Cessna 170s during the past six years. Though many occurred with low-timers at the controls, quite a few involved pilots with hundreds of hours in type. Also, several of the accidents involving loss of control and those involving collision with objects during takeoff or landing (there were nine of these) occurred in such formidable operating areas as country roads, rough fields and sand bars. A number of accidents were precipitated by broken main landing gear axles and wheels.

Of the 12 accidents involving either fatalities or serious injuries during the past half-dozen years, four involved stalls and spins; four occurred during buzz-jobs or low-level aerobatics; and two involved continued VFR flight into instrument weather conditions (one pilot wasn't instrument-rated, the other was but the airplane wasn't suitably equipped). Two other pilots lost control of their 170s: one after the prop separated; one after a rusted rudder cable broke inflight.

Maintenance

Corrosion and fatigue cracks are the most frequent subjects of service difficulty reports filed with the FAA during the past six years. Affected components include flight control cables, main landing gear support brackets, vertical stabilizer attachments, bulkheads and engine attach brackets. There is one report of severely corroded wing spars in a 170A that had been parked outside and not flown for three years.

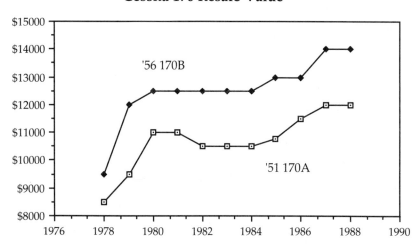

Cessna 170 Resale Value

Only a few airworthiness directives have been issued in recent years. The most recent, as of this writing, is 87-20-08 (Revision 1), requiring inspection and repair of seat tracks and locking mechanisms. Repair of slipping shoulder harness adjusters was the subject of AD 86-26-04. Another AD, 82-07-02, called for holes to be drilled in crankcase breather tubes to prevent moisture from building up in them, freezing and causing oil to be pumped overboard.

Due to similarities between the 170 and the 172, parts are not a big problem. The International Cessna 170 Association frequently arranges to secure quantities of critical parts from Cessna Aircraft Corp. and other suppliers. The group recently pooled its resources to have Cessna produce a supply of solid ("ski") axles. Two other types of axles used in production of 170s were hollow designs; and service difficulty and accident reports show that they are prone to break under excessive side loading. The association also was able to bring the price of seat tracks down substantially by placing a quantity order with Cessna. At press time, the group was working with Univair on a big order for engine cowlings.

Modifications

Nearly 100 STCs have been approved, including dozens for installation of skis and floats. Many floatplane operators have opted for larger engines. Avcon and Bush, both in Udall, Kan., offer 180-hp Lycomings and constant-speed propellers for A and B models. Turbotech in Vancouver, Wash., has a 220-hp Franklin conversion for the 170B. Flap and aileron gap seals, and complete STOL modification kits are available from Horton STOL in Wellington, Kan., and from Avcon and Bush. Davids Aviation Services in San Andreas, Calif., also offers gap seals, as well as a thorough aerodynamic cleanup, complete with wheel pants, landing gear cuffs and fairings. Ponk Aviation in Camano Island, Wash., recently obtained an STC for beefed-up landing gear brackets.

Owners' Group

Efforts by the International Cessna 170 Assn. to secure needed parts for the airplanes already have been mentioned. In addition, the group publishes a monthly newsletter and four quarterly magazines containing tips on maintenance and safety, and conducts regional fly-ins and an annual convention. Velvet Fackeldey is the association's executive secretary: P.O. Box 1667, Lebanon, Mo. 65536, (417) 532-4847.

In addition, 170 owners are represented by the two big Cessna owners' groups: the Cessna Pilots Assn. in Wichita, Kans.; and the Cessna Owner Organization in Birmingham, Ala.

Conclusions

Tailwheel airplanes are great for nostalgia, but they do require some special skills that largely have been lost among today's pilots. Those who want a vintage four-seater but not the hassles attendant to a taildragger might find a Piper Tri-Pacer a more attractive proposition (on paper, if not aesthetically). Not only is the third wheel up front, a PA-22 will cost three or four thousand dollars less than a 170 of the same vintage and fly about 15 mph faster on the same fuel. A Tri-Pacer's useful load, however, is a couple hundred pounds less than the Cessna's.

Those who want a four-seat taildragger, and are willing to develop and hone the necessary skills, might want to consider buying an early-model 172 and having it converted to tailwheel configuration (see the Nov. 1, 1987 issue). This could actually cost less than buying a 170.

In an attempt to escape lead-fouling problems, many owners have switched to autogas with STCs from EAA or Petersen. Others have found that EGTs and aggressive leaning help their 80-octane engines cope with 100LL.

But the 170 is in a class by itself, and those who want the real Mccoy aren't going to be bridled by a few extra dollars here or there. Since prices are going up, purchase can be seen as a good investment. And, as mentioned earlier, a 170 is a true four-seater with performance (if not mission flexibility) rivaling that of current production singles and acquisition and operating costs putting the brand-new airplanes to shame. Too, there's one very obvious fact: the 170 is a very handsome airplane.

Owner Comments

When I purchased my 1954 Cessna 170B in June 1987, I was looking for a taildragger that could carry my family, 100 pounds of baggage and fuel for 350 miles with reserves. The Stinson 108 and the Piper Tri-Pacer/Pacer meet the requirements about as well as the Cessna 170B, and I fully expected to end up with a PA-22 and

convert it to tailwheel configuration. My 170B just happened to become available locally, and even though it cost $3,000 more than a good Tri-Pacer, I am pleased with my choice.

The plane is a nice blend of classic looks and practical utility. It runs fine on auto fuel, burning eight gph at a cruise speed of 115 mph. At altitude, it will produce true airspeeds in the 135-mph range.

Though my pre-purchase inspection showed three cylinders with compression in the 60/80 range, after putting 75 hours on the plane in three months, compression was 74/80 or better in all cylinders. The plane was in need of some TLC. It was out of rig and needed a wheel alignment. Working with my mechanic, I did most of the annual inspection myself. The only serious problems discovered were worn rudder cables, which were replaced, and a bent rod on the elevator trim actuator, which was straightened. The inspection revealed that the right wing is from a 1959 C-172, but the log has no comment as to why it was changed.

A low panel eyebrow and sloped engine cowl afford excellent visibility. Owners say S-turns aren't necessary while taxiing.

The 170B will land much shorter than it will take off. With two on board and full fuel, it is no problem to land and stop in 300 feet. Takeoff is not so impressive but noticeably better than a 172 with the same engine.

Visibility is very good for a taildragger. Taxiing can be done without S-turns, and the nose is very low in level flight. In fact, the low nose attitude in climb was my greatest problem in transitioning to the plane. Unlike most taildraggers, the runway ahead is in full view during climbout. This would fool me into raising the nose too much.

The only operational problem I have had is a stuck exhaust valve. After the second occurrence, the valve guides and stems were cleaned and I changed to Mobil AV1 synthetic oil. I had been running AeroShell 15W-50. A Continental engineer I spoke with was very high on AV1. He felt the extremely long oil change intervals Mobil has experimented with (500 hours, plus) were risky, due to lead build-up in the oil, but he cited very good experience with 100-hour oil changes in his Cessna 150 club airplane. A nice side benefit of the AV1 oil is the way minor leaks dry up, leaving the engine dry and oil-free.

The International Cessna 170 Assn. is an excellent club. It provides advice on maintenance, places to fly, etc. Members even pool their resources and get Cessna to make up a supply of parts, such as solid axles and seat rails. For $15 a year, membership is a bargain.

I compared the specifications in the recent article on the Archer and Tobago (May 1, 1988 issue). They are really in a different class, but the lack of major performance differences is notable. With the exception of range, the 170B compares very well with these new, higher-powered airplanes. Besides, the value of the 170B is going up at a very nice rate.

Gary B. Collins
Cincinnati, Ohio

I have owned a 1949 Cessna 170A for just under two years and have found it to be reliable, great fun and cheap to operate; there have been no surprises or unexpected expenses. Total time is 2,300 hours on the airframe and 860 on the engine. Last year's annual, with me helping, cost $117.

Operated according to the EAA's autogas STC, the airplane burns 7.5 gallons of unleaded regular an hour. I have not had some of the problems that other owners seem to have encountered using autogas (soot in the exhaust, etc.). I do lean aggressively, though, and keep away from higher octane autogas to avoid the toluene additives. When I have to use 100LL avgas, I always add TCP.

The airplane is noisy, but addition of a voice-activated intercom solved that. It cruises around 115 to 120 mph at 2,450 rpm.

Figure maintenance to be the same as a 172. Parts are still available, though some, such as some body parts, are no longer available. I had an entire front cowl remade locally for about $1,100.

As with buying any used airplane, a pre-purchase inspection could avoid later problems. Be especially wary for corrosion and cracked axles on some of the earlier aircraft. The International Cessna 170 Association is a great place to start if you are interested in buying one of these classics.

The airplane is just plain fun. It attracts attention wherever it goes. I use it mainly for grass-roots type fly-ins and for cross-country trips up to 500 miles. It doesn't go fast, but it's a fantastic way to rediscover the countryside; and at under $10 an hour for direct operating costs, you get to see lots of country.

Ron Adams
Germantown, Tenn.

My 170, a 1950 A model, has been in my family for the past 20 years. I feel the 170 is an excellent airplane that has extremely docile handling qualities, excellent load-carrying capabilities and reasonable speed at very reasonable operating costs. The airplane is a sought-after classic that keeps increasing in value.

I feel that Cessna took a giant step backwards when they phased out the 170 in

Cost/Performance/Specifications

Model	Year Built	Average Retail Price	Cruise Speed (kts)	Useful Load (lbs)	Fuel Std/Opt (gals)	Engine	TBO (hrs)	Overhaul Costs
170	1948	$11,000	106	1,015	33.5	145-hp Cont. C-145-2	1,800	$6,500
170A	1949	$11,500	106	1,015	37	145-hp Cont. C-145-2	1,800	$6,500
170A	1950	$11,800	106	1,015	37	145-hp Cont. C-145-2	1,800	$6,500
170A	1951	$12,000	106	1,015	37	145-hp Cont. C-145-2	1,800	$6,500
170B	1952	$13,000	106	995	37	145-hp Cont. O-300A	1,800	$7,000
170B	1953	$13,500	106	995	37	145-hp Cont. O-300A	1,800	$7,000
170B	1954	$14,000	106	995	37	145-hp Cont. O-300A	1,800	$7,000
170B	1955	$14,500	106	995	37	145-hp Cont. O-300A	1,800	$7,000
170B	1956	$15,000	106	995	37	145-hp Cont. O-300A	1,800	$7,000
170B	1957	$15,000	106	995	37	145-hp Cont. O-300A	1,800	$7,000

favor of the 172. I normally cruise at 118 mph, true, on 7.2 gph. Even the 172 taildragger conversion can't match these numbers.

The airplane is great for flight training and as an all-around family airplane. The 170 is a logical move up for owners of smaller 140 Cessnas who don't want to lay out the large investment required to purchase and operate a 180.

The 170 has an unusually good field of view for a taildragger. Visibility from the cockpit, both on the ground and in flight, is excellent (better than the 172). This is due, primarily, to the low-cut panel, down-sloped cowling and the close proximity of the front seats to the leading edge of the wing.

It also is an easy airplane to maintain, due to the absence of complex systems and its commonality with the 172. The O-300 Continental is an extremely dependable and very smooth-running engine and gives the 170 adequate power under most conditions. There are several STCs available to convert to 180 and higher horsepower, but I personally prefer the 145 Continental.

As Parts and Maintenance Coordinator for the International Cessna 170 Association, I find the majority of parts for the airplane still pretty easy to obtain. Cessna has been very helpful in supporting us when they were able to. The 170 association is one of the finest type-clubs, offering lower insurance rates, an inside track on maintenance and parts tips, and the comradeship of some of the friendliest and most helpful people I know.

Fuselage-mounted venturis keep the gyros spooled up. Lacking accessory pads and dampened crankshafts, most 170 engines cannot accommodate vacuum pumps.

All models of the 170 have excellent characteristics, but I feel the older ragwings and A models, in many cases, have been unfairly overshadowed by the later B models. A potential 170 owner who is shy on conventional gear time would be well advised to seek several hours of dual from an experienced taildragger-qualified instructor to acquaint himself with the peculiarities of conventional-gear aircraft.

Although there are other four-place airplanes on the market that are faster or may carry more, I don't feel any offer the all-around "mission mix" that is found in the 170. When this is combined with the airplane's classic good looks, I truly feel that it makes the Cessna 170 certainly one of the finest, if not *the* finest four-place airplane ever built.

Tom Hull
Hollywood, Md.

We've operated a 1954 C-170B in our business for general utility purposes and as a backup for a P210 photo ship since 1968. The aircraft was originally outfitted as a floatplane, with interior corrosion-proofing and lift rings installed above the fuselage, but it never actually has been on floats.

We converted the 170 with a Lycoming O-360 and constant-speed prop in 1981. It made the plane a terrific performer compared to the standard Continental 145-hp version. A couple years after the conversion, we relocated the battery to the rear fuselage, which markedly improved the balance of the plane, particularly on solo flights. We also installed a camera hole in the floor.

The aircraft has proven to be reliable, with no vicissitudes in either flight operations or maintenance. Cross-country, we plan on 105 knots at 55 percent power, with fuel consumption about 7.8 gph. The O-360 can rapidly deplete the plane's modest 37-gallon fuel capacity at high power settings, so we tend to go high and throttle back, and hope for a tailwind. Another negative is the high noise level and drafty cabin. Our plane's hands-off stability is poor.

Annuals have been running about $900 to $1,000. The plane is a bargain compared to the P210.

In conclusion, the Lycoming power greatly increased the utility and productivity of the classic old 170 airframe. It's hard to imagine a better combination for the price.

Stephen J. Power
Vacaville, Calif.

I have owned a 1952 Cessna 170B since July 1978 and have found it a very inexpensive and virtually vice-free aircraft. I do my own maintenance and very seldom have to do more than routine servicing during annuals. I also did some modifications, including an Avcon 180-hp engine conversion 750 hours ago, and changed the interior using Airtex carpets and side walls. The kits were outstanding and fit with no reworking or modification.

In 1953, hinged cowls gave way to full-pressure types with large hatches opening on to the battery and oil dipstick.

There are two drawbacks, however. First, the 37-gallon fuel supply is not enough for the Lycoming conversion. I wish someone would make a retrofit kit that would add another 15 gallons. Second, the instrument panel becomes a mess when you have a couple of modern radios and a set of gyros.

On cross-country trips, I flight-plan conservatively for 115 knots and 10 gph. The airplane will carry just about anything you can close the doors on and still get out short and fly high.

Tom Schad
Del Rio, Tex.

I bought a Cessna 170B in 1964. Originally, three doctors owned the plane, but I am now the sole owner. All of us learned to fly in Cessna 120s, so this plane was absolutely no problem. A 1955 model, the plane now has almost 6,000 hours TT.

Like most Continental O-300s, my plane's engine has been overhauled "a few times." Quite a few hours have passed since the last one, but the jugs have been overhauled on an as-needed basis. As a result, I have two spare cylinders ready to go to save down-time.

Many years ago, the Goodyear brakes were replaced with Clevelands off a wrecked 172. This was probably the first significant update ever done on any old Cessna.

The plane is flown at least once a week, unless I'm out of town or the weather is bad. In the past few years, I rarely have taken trips of more than a hundred miles each way. At one time, though, I had two kids in college in Santa Barbara and ran a weekly commuting service for myself and other parents of students who were neighbors and friends. There was minimal LAX hassle in those days.

A cable tailwheel system, rather than a rudder horn and spring, distinguish airplanes built during the last two years of production.

It is difficult to establish the exact cost of maintenance, since the plane is a hobby and much of the maintenance is done when the mechanical or aesthetic problem is first noticed or the AD is first published. I would say the annual inspections have run about $200 in the past few years, though the last annual included a lot of cowling repairs and repainting of gear legs and was about $500.

Oliver R. Nees, Jr.
Long Beach, Calif.

I've owned a 1948 Cessna 170 since 1976. The aircraft has 3,986 TT, 970 hours since a Feb. 1973 overhaul and 303 hours since a 1982 top overhaul. Other than the top overhaul, which cost $2,500 initially and about $1,000 more over the next year to correct the rebuilder's mistakes and defects, the aircraft has been inexpensive to own. Maintenance costs about $600 a year, including an average of $300 for an annual.

A Ceconite fabric job in 1975 was poorly done, and I'll have to have it redone this year. Quotes, including paint, have run from $4,000 to $5,000. Shop rates for most car or aircraft repairs in the bay area are $40 to $50 an hour (higher for cars than aircraft).

The generator has been replaced twice, the voltage regulator once. I had to have a fuel tank repaired because water had collected and corroded the bottom of the tank. The rudder bellcrank broke when the plane was hit by heavy wind while parked four years ago; flap hinges also have been damaged by wind about every three years.

I've used autogas legally since 1983. The airplane burns eight gph on short flights, 7.5 gph on cross-countries. The Cessna 170 has no bad habits. It's easy to slip, three-point and wheel-land. It slow flies at 57 mph at 1,950 rpm, cruises at 117 mph at 2,450 rpm.

The 170 is a very forgiving aircraft, though the flaps are essentially useless (unlike the Fowler flaps on the C-170B). The heater also is useless (again, unlike the 170B), but it isn't needed much in the bay area. The aircraft is easy to handle in crosswinds, though I did have one 45-degree crosswind at 30 knots where I had to use wing-walkers to park the aircraft.

In summary, the ragwing C-170 is an attractive aircraft. It is inexpensive to own and maintain, easy to fly, gentle in a stall and hard to spin. The current market value of, maybe, $10,000 versus $8,500 purchase cost 12 years ago reflects the fact that most buyers seem to prefer the metal-wing C-170B with Fowler flaps.

Joseph J. Neff
Newark, Calif.

I owned a Cessna 170A (1951 model) for six years. In 700 hours of flying, I found performance to be adequate, even with four people aboard; cruise was about 100 knots on nine gph.

The airplane had excellent inflight handling qualities, but the small flaps on the A model left something to be desired. Ground handling was fair, with steering accomplished more by differential braking than with the tailwheel. I never did like the "soft" landing gear legs on the 170 and 170A, which would cause a teeter-totter effect when taxiing, especially in a crosswind. Later B models had stiffer gear legs, like those on the Cessna 180.

For a taildragger, over-the-nose visibility on the ground was excellent—much better than either the 120/140 or the 180. Because of inadequate heat and poor door sealing, cabin comfort was poor in New England winter weather. The back seat stayed close to OAT in flight.

Big, curved rudder is a hallmark of the breed.

Annuals ran between $400 and $600, and I never had any problem securing necessary parts through a variety of sources. At 1,300 hours SMOH, the O-300A engine swallowed a valve at 3,000 feet, resulting in a forced landing. An annual inspection had been performed shortly before, and compression checked okay on all cylinders.

One thing I strongly recommend is that 170 owners purchase and carry in the plane a spare main leaf for the tailspring, as they will break at the most inopportune times.

My overall opinion of the airplane is favorable. However, for what some of these 170s are selling for, I would be more inclined to get a more recent vintage airplane and experience less nickel-and-dime breakdowns, as was the case with my 30-year-old airplane.

Robert S. Andrews
Claremont, Calif.

Considered easier to handle than some other taildraggers, a 170 can still bite an unpracticed hand. Ground-loops and hard landings are paring the fleet at an alarming rate. Less than half of the 5,136 airplanes built are still flying.

Cessna Skyhawk 172

Even today the Cessna 172 continues to be the airplane most commonly associated with general aviation. It's been built in such numbers that the word ubiquitous seems hardly sufficient when describing this commonest of commonplace singles. The 172's characteristic high-wing shape, docile, dependable performance and pleasant handling have introduced thousands to flying.

History

The 172 and its little brother, the 150, both appeared on the market in 1956. The new 172 spelled the end of the line for its taildragging older cousin, the venerable Cessna 170. It did this

World's most popular airplane. Who ever thought they'd stop building it?

by outselling the 170 by a 10-to-one margin (1,170 to 174) in that first production year. Flightline planespotters can easily identify those first-edition 172s by the straight tail and "fastback" cabin. A peek under the cowl will reveal a 145-hp Continental engine, standard on the 172 line until 1968.

Changes in the 172 line were slow in coming. The year 1960 saw the introduction of a swept back tail in the "A" model; the 1963 "D" model featured "Omni-vision" rear windows. The 172E boasted electric flaps, to the chagrin of many pilots who considered them more a handicap than an improvement. Since that year, the 172 airframe has been virtually cut in stone with no significant changes to speak of.

What is probably the most important single improvement made to the 172 line came in 1968, when the 150-hp Lycoming replaced the old Continental engine as standard equipment. The following year's model was available with a 52-gallon fuel tank option, and by 1973 Cessna had re-designed the wing leading edge for supposedly better stall characteristics.

By 1974, Grumman American's Traveler was cutting deeply into the 172's market. Cessna countered with modifications to the wheelpants and cooling airflow, picking up some seven miles per hour in cruise speed.

As the ancient adage says, "If it ain't broke, don't fix it." Cessna ignored that advice in 1977 when the company shot itself in the foot by introducing the infamous 160-hp Lycoming O-320-H camshaft-and-valve-train-eating engine to the 172. The O-320-H episode lasted four years, and is remembered by both Cessna and Lycoming as a major embarrassment. (More on that in the "Engines" section to follow.)

Again, not content to leave well enough alone, Cessna opted for a 28-volt electrical system in the 172, a change that has meant problems for landing lights and rotating beacons.

Even these troubles have not done much to damage the 172s "generic airplane" image, although aircraft from the troubled '76-'81 period must be viewed with a jaundiced eye.

Used Skyhawks

With over 24,000 172s out there, the used market in Skyhawks is one of the busiest. A recent issue of *Trade-a-Plane* contained 220 ads for more than that number of 172s, since some ads offered more than one aircraft. With this much give-and-take in the market, prices tend to be rather steady, without much variation. An aircraft that's a true "steal" is unlikely because demand is so high. On the other hand, the supply is so great that no seller can get away with an exorbitant asking price.

However, used Skyhawk shoppers shouldn't waste too much time trying to pinch the penultimate penny; their time would be better spent thoroughly checking out the mechanical condition of the aircraft, hopefully with the help of an experienced A&P.

Resale Value

In 1981, when *The Aviation Consumer* first reviewed the Cessna 172 line, we predicted that the older pre-1968, O-300-powered C-172s would not be able to hold onto their value due to the fact that replacement engines and parts would become more and more expensive and harder to find. According to the *Aircraft Bluebook Price Digest*, this is just what happened.

A C-172D Skyhawk sold for $14,751 new in 1963, and was listed in the 1988 spring *Digest* at $13,000, a decrease of $1,751. This doesn't seem at first glance like that much of a decline after 22 years, but when the effects of inflation (the Consumer Price Index has more than tripled since then) are figured in, the weakness of this investment becomes readily apparent. The fact that prices are as high as they are reflects the relatively scarce supply of good condition 1963-model 172Ds, of which 1,027 were built.

If the 172D's price hasn't dropped tremendously, the cost of overhauling its O-300-D powerplant has risen to an average of $8,300 (TBO 1,800 hours), $800 more than the 150-hp O-320-E2D. While unusually low resale values for post-1977 model 172s have yet to appear, the listing in the *Aircraft Bluebook Price Digest* bears an ominous asterisk, followed by the words, "Price assume engine fixed—see notes below." The notes continue to say the stated price is for a 172 in compliance with ADs 77-20-7 (tappets) 78-12-9 (replace crankshaft) and 78-12-8 (replace oil pump impellers). More about pertinent ADs later.

Performance

The Skyhawk's performance is not exactly spectacular. Loaded up to gross weight, the 172 is lethargic, and we wouldn't want to try any hot-day, high-field takeoffs in a heavy airplane. The 1977 and later models with their 160-hp engines are, however, noticeably more energetic, with a book-climb rate about 20 percent higher than the 145- and 150-hp versions. Cruise speed at 75 percent power is a modest 104 to 113 knots under most conditions, with a fuel burn of about eight gph. The post-'73 models are faster by four knots or so because of generally cleaner aerodynamics. The 38-gallon standard usable fuel supply provides about four hours of flying with a small reserve, enough for about 500 miles or so if you really want to stretch it.

Optional 52-gallon tanks (48 usable) extend endurance to over five hours, enough for 600 miles or so. Of course, payload is reduced when 52 gallons of fuel are hoisted aloft; count on three medium-sized adults and no baggage, at best.

Although the Skyhawk has an excellent overall safety record, much attention has been focused on making sure the pilot's seat is secure to prevent it from sliding back on takeoff and causing loss of control.

Handling Characteristics

In a word, the Skyhawk's handling is stable, even positively benign. Rather heavy controls inhibit pilots with Chuck Yeager fantasies, but these same steady controls make instrument work a pleasure. Elevator forces are heavy, meaning that stalling is extremely difficult. The Skyhawk's handling characteristics are spectacularly average—for the simple reason that the airplane's universal popularity has helped make it the standard against which other aircraft are judged. Almost by definition, the Skyhawk is the average airplane.

If all this makes the 'Hawk seems a little lackluster, there is one flight regime in which the 172 positively excels: short-field performance. A skillful pilot can plunk a Skyhawk down in not much more runway than a so-called STOL specialty machine like a Rallye or Maule. At light weights, takeoffs can be nearly as short. The Skyhawk's huge flaps allow it to make steep, Space Shuttle-style approaches, and we wouldn't hesitate to pit a 'Hawk against either a Rallye or Maule in a slow-flying contest.

Safety

A big part of the Skyhawk story is its superb safety record, pure and simple. In an FAA study of accidents involving 48 different aircraft types between the years 1972 and 1976, the C-172 posted the best overall accident record of any four-place fixed-gear single. Its fatal accident rate also was excellent. In fact, out of the 32 most popular single-engine airplanes, the C-172 ranked in the top, or safest, 10 in eight out of 10 accident categories. It had the lowest engine failure rate and in-flight airframe failure rate of any lightplane.

The areas in which the Skyhawk is only average are mid-air collisions, presumably a result of the aircraft's poor visibility, and overshoot accidents.

A search of NTSB accident reports involving 172s in 1982 turned up a total of 98, of which nine resulted in fatalities, with 20 deaths. Six of these deaths occurred in five VFR flights that continued into IFR conditions. A total 177 people came away with minor injuries or none at all. Seven people were killed in two midair collisions (there were five people in one of the airplanes involved). The 172's good safety record is likely due to a variety of factors shared by all Cessna high-wing aircraft. High elevator forces and low stall speeds discourage killer stalls. Stalls accounted for just six of the 1982 mishaps and one of the fatalities.

The Skyhawk's fuel system is simplicity itself, with a well-placed selector that has only left, right, off and both positions. It takes a perverse form of determination to foul up the 172 fuel system, especially if pilots simply leave the selector on "both," as most do. Even more simply, the high-wing gravity-feed system requires no fuel pumps.

Debates have raged for years among high-wing vs low-wing fans, with claims made on both sides for visibility, handling qualities, aesthetics, and the like. And while the 'Hawk's big, strut-braced wing may look old-fashioned, a fatal in-flight airframe failure in a Skyhawk is a great rarity. The durability of that wing was evidenced by a June 1982 mishap in which a 172 struck and severed a number of powerlines, each a half inch in diameter. Afterwards, the airplane managed to return to its home field. Damage inspection revealed that three of the four left wing strut attach rivets were sheared, the entire engine cowling torn loose from the firewall attach points, and prop tips bent *forward* about three inches.

Sliding Seats

One nasty problem that surfaced to plague the line, and other Cessnas as well, affected not the basic airframe, but the cabin seats. It turned out that unless the seat tracks were appropriately fitted and notched and in good condition, pilots might have a problem locking the seats securely before takeoff. Of course, it was at the worst possible time on lift-off and climbout that the seat would be likely to slide back as the aircraft rotated nose-up.

Official concern about slipping Cessna seats dates back to 1981, when the NTSB called attention to the potential for a seat to wedge against a door jamb in its full-forward position and not lock properly. Such a situation existed when a flight instructor took off alone in a Hawk XP near Indianapolis in 1980. During lift-off, the unlocked seat slid back, and the board believes the pilot may have held onto the yoke and throttle as her seat slid rearward in the cockpit. Witnesses saw the airplane pitch up sharply and heard the power diminish to idle shortly before the

Cost/Performance/Specifications

Model	Year	Average Retail Price	Cruise Speed (kts)	Useful Load (lbs)	Fuel Std/Opt (gals)	Engine	TBO (hrs)	Overhaul Cost
172	1956-59	$11,800	108	940	37	145-hp Cont.O-300-A	1,800	$8,300
172A,B,C	1960-62	$12,000	114	940	42	145-hp Cont.O-300-C,D	1,800	$8,300
172D,E,F	1963-65	$13,800	114	970	42	145-hp Cont.O-300-D	1,800	$8,300
172G,H,I	1966-68	$15,800	114	985	42	145-hp Cont.O-300-D,E2D	1,800	$8,300
172K,L	1969-71	$16,800	115	985	42/52	150-hp Cont.O-200-E2D	2,000	$7,500
172L,M	1972-74	$19,000	115	965	42/52	150-hp Cont.O-200-E2D	2,000	$7,500
172M,N	1975-76	$23,200	120	965	42/52	150-hp Cont.O-200-E2D	2,000	$7,500
172N	1977-78	$24,800	122	770	43/54	160-hp Cont.O-320-H2AD	2,000	$7,500
172N	1979-80	$29,700	122	770	43/54	160-hp Cont.O-320-H2AD	2,000	$7,500
172P	1981-82	$38,200	122	770	43/54	160-hp Cont.O-320-D2J	2,000	$8,000
172P	1982-83	$43,000	120	680	43/54	160-hp Cont.O-320-D2J	2,000	$8,000
172P	1984-86	$56,000	120	680	54/68	160-hp Cont.O-320-D2J	2,000	$8,000

airplane hit the ground, killing the pilot. Citing that accident and 20 others in the previous decade involving seat-slippage in Cessnas, NTSB recommended the FAA take action. Culmination took place when the agency issued an AD in October of 1987 mandating repetitive inspection of tracks, roller assemblies, seat pins and springs on both pilot and copilot seats at annual inspections for any plane with more than 1,000 hours. Anything broken or worn out must be replaced or repaired.

Engines

While the basic 172 airframe has changed little over the years, the 'Hawk has been powered by three basic powerplant designs. Which one of these three engines lurks under the cowl of the used 172 you buy will play a starring role in how happy you'll be with the airplane. Our advice on engine choice can be summed up as follows: 1968-76 'Hawks, terrific; 1956-67 models, fair; 1977-80 models, awful; 1981 through present models, again, fair.

The Lycoming O-320-D2J engine that replaced the troubled H2AD has had a fairly ordinary maintenance history, marred only by a service letter dealing with stuck valves. The problem seems to center on a buildup of gunk in the valve guides. This gunk inhibits valve movement when the engine is cold, causing rough running on startup. As the engine heats up, it smooths out. This so-called "morning sickness" in the D2J is a symptom that valve guides need to be checked.

For 12 years, new 172s trundled down runways and into the skies propelled by six-cylinder 145-hp Continental O-300s, an engine little more than a four-banger O-200 (used in the C-150) with an extra pair of cylinders tacked on. The O-300 has an adequate reliability record, but the combination of comparatively low 1,800-hour TBO and $7,500 overhaul cost makes it a costly antique. "The problem is you've got six of everything to replace instead of four," one overhauler told us. "An old engine like this can be a real can of worms."

Parts for the O-300 are available factory-direct, although their price adds to a total upkeep cost for the engine that is, in the words of one overhaul firm, "not commensurate with the cost of the aircraft. It's just not worth it to put $8,500 worth of work into an aircraft with a value of only $13,000, which is about what one of those early '60s Skyhawks costs today."

The Lycoming O-320-E2D engine climbed aboard the 172 in 1968, giving the airplane an extra five horsepower. That same engine costs $7,500 at its 2,000-hour TBO time, $1,000 less than the O-300 with its 200 hours shorter TBO. This four-cylinder engine carries a reputation for going well beyond TBO with careful maintenance. Flight schools who put 100 hours a month on their airplanes and pay attention to maintenance regularly get 3,000 hours. "There's no better engine," one mechanic told us. The O-320 seems to handle 100LL with ease, as well as autogas, although careful leaning is recommended.

Messing with Perfection

As 80-octane avgas went the way of the nickel newspaper, Cessna ordered a redesigned O-320 from Lycoming. Dubbed the O-320-H2AD, it was a hard-luck powerplant, a disaster and major embarrassment for both Cessna and Lycoming and the first major engineering blunder to mar the Hawk's record. Hundreds of

1977 Skyhawks suffered serious camshaft and valve train damage, at a cost of thousands of dollars borne by their owners. What's more, there were a dozen or so abrupt engine failures caused by sheared oil pumps and accessory drive gears. Admitting its error in April of 1978, Cessna recalled all 1977 and 1978 Skyhawks for major engine repairs.

Oil pump and drive gear problems were fixed at that time, but camshaft/tappet problems continued unsolved through the 1980 model. Lycoming tried three different camshaft/tappet mods. None of them worked. Cessna finally admitted defeat in 1981 and changed to the O-320-D2J.

After Cessna switched engines, Lycoming belatedly came up with a fourth major mod, featuring an enlarged crankcase, which it hoped would solve the problem once and for all. The modified engines have slowly worked their way into the fleet through attrition, replacing the original faulty equipment. This mod will be found on engines with serial numbers 7976 and above. It seems that this fix may not have cured the valve train problems, but at least has alleviated them somewhat. Trouble is, if a 172 owner is willing to spend the roughly $2,100 extra at TBO time for the so-called O-320-H2ADT mod, opting for one of the extra-horsepower engine conversions may prove more cost-effective over the long run. More on them in the STC section of this article.

Our Opinion

We would not advise the purchase of a Skyhawk with an O-320 engine serial number below 7976, except at an extremely low price, low enough to allow for possible premature engine replacement. After 7976, the odds improve, but the engine is still far from a sure thing, in our opinion. Other factors to consider are that aircraft based in warm weather appear to have suffered less from the problem, and inactive aircraft are more likely to experience difficulties.

One overhaul firm, Mattituck Aviation, on Long Island, N.Y., recommends a pre-purchase inspection that includes careful checking of the camshaft, tappets, oil and oil screen. The average cost is $150, which has to be considered cheap insurance.

Back in the dim past, the 172A looked like this, with a blunt spinner and no rear windows, but it did have a new sweptback tail.

To what extent are the T Mods immune to drive train perils? Service difficulty reports on the O-320-H engine for a period from early 1981 to July 1987 showed a dozen reports on T-modded -Hs, 11 of which resulted from tappet/camshaft damage from spalling, with metal contaminants found in the oil and oil filter. And recall that the SDRs usually represent just the tip of the iceberg, or only about 10 percent of actual problems in the field.

In 1981 Cessna had a special 2,000-hour, pro-rata warranty period. Under this, if a Skyhawk was purchased with 900 hours and the engine failed 100 hours later, Cessna would provide a new or remanufactured engine at half price. By now, of course, most 'Hawks have flown enough to make the pro-rata discount academic.

There is a Way Out

For 172 owners who would prefer to avoid the maintenance headaches of both the O-300 and -320-H, there are alternatives. Unfortunately, they're quite expensive, with costs approaching the value of the airplane itself in many cases. RAM Aircraft Modifications, Inc., based at Madison Cooper Airport, Waco. Tex. 76708, (817) 752-8381 can put in a 160-hp O-320-D2G for between $10,000-12,000, depending on the model. That's 100 percent of the book value of a 172 built from 1956 to 1961.

A couple of firms offer upgrades that would make for a peppy Skyhawk with the addition of a 180-hp Lycoming O-360 engine, but again, it's an expensive improvement. The most popular mod has been the Penn Yan Aero Service Superhawk conversion, which replaces the 320-cubic-inch engines in the I through P models with a 180-hp Lyc. O-360-A4M, -A4A or -A4N engine and the McCauley prop with a Sensenich.

The mod also includes a gross-weight increase for the N and P models only, to 2,550 pounds. Kit prices are $2,295 for the I through M models and $2,595 for the newer Skyhawks, which get their gross weights boosted. Each kit includes a prop, drawings and installation instructions, material for the air box and exhaust mods, and a POH supplement with new weight and balance data. Good luck on finding a used engine, though, because there aren't many O-360s available. However, Penn Yan is a Lycoming dealer and can provide a factory-new O-360-A4M for $12,549. List price of that engine is $20,255.

Penn Yan Aero Services is located at Penn Yan, N.Y., (315) 536-2333.

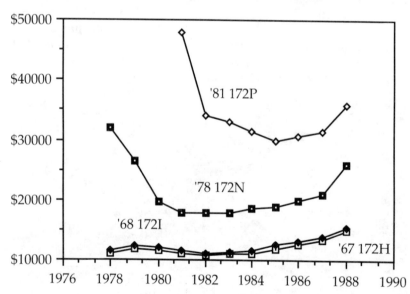

Cessna 172 Resale Value

Cost for an Avcon Industries installation complete with constant-speed prop comes to $17,260 for C-172s built before 1967, with the mod on 'Hawks built after that date amounting to $16,935. If owners prefer to cut their own deal on an O-360 engine, installation kits (less prop governor and engine) for pre- and post-1967 'Hawks are available for $2,875 and 2,750 respectively. Avcon Industries' address is P.O. Box 654, Udall, Kan. 67146. Phone: (316) 782-3317.

Taildraggers, Too

Aircraft Conversion Technologies in California and the Udall twins, Bush and Avcon, have kits to turn Skyhawks into taildraggers. The taildragger mods are, however, more complicated than any of the engine changes or STOL conversions, and they are expensive. The main gear has to be moved forward, requiring fabrication of a new gear box in front of the old one. Also, the rear fuselage must be strengthened to accept the new loads.

ACT, which acquired the Texas Taildragger STC in 1987, says that any A&P can do the work, but he'll need 160 hours to complete the job. Conversions by ACT mechanics in Lincoln are running an average of 130 hours. The ACT kit, with 100 pieces, costs $3,195; a factory conversion adds $3,150 to that. For the money, you get 10 to 12 more mph in cruise, a 100-fpm quicker rate of climb and a shorter takeoff run, the company says. Aircraft Conversion Technologies is located in Lincoln, Calif., (916) 645-3264.

The Avcon/Bush mod is almost identical to ACT's, except for some details of the rear-fuselage beef-up and tailwheel installation. Also, ACT's conversion is approved for all Skyhawks, but the Avcon/Bush mod does not include the P model. The Udall companies estimate 80 to 120 hours for a field conversion. Their kits cost $2,795, and either Bush or Avcon will do a turnkey conversion for $4,550.

High Plains Eagle

Mike Kelley Aircraft has an STC that allows installation of either Lyc. O-360-A4A and -A4M engines and Sensenich props, or O-360-A3As and -A2Fs with McCauley props on I- through N-model Skyhawks. A gross weight increase to 2,550 pounds also is approved for the N model only. Calling its conversion the High Plains Eagle, Kelley claims increases of 15 to 18 mph in cruise at 75 percent power and 300 to 400 fpm in climb. The High Plains Eagle costs from $2,195 to $2,495, depending on the model Skyhawk. Mike Kelley Aircraft is at Wellington Municipal Airport, Wellington, Kan., (316) 326-8581.

Factory-equipped ARC avionics tended to be troublesome on most Cessnas. This 1976 Skyhawk had the old-style flap control. A couple of years later the aircraft had flap position preselect. Fuel selector switch allows use of "both" tanks, a safety feature of no small importance.

If you want rocket-propelled performance and have a very large wad of cash burning a hole in your pocket, go for the 220-hp normally aspirated or 250-hp six-cylinder turbocharged Franklin conversion offered by Turbotech, Inc. in Vancouver, Wash., (206) 694-6287. The engine transforms a stock 172 into "a little hot rod," in the words of someone who has flown one. It should, considering the cost is $5,000 and $7,000 respectively for the kit, with the engines themselves another $11,495 and $12,995 respectively. Since there are parts problems for the Franklin engines, which are now built in Poland by Pezetel, conversions involve some risk.

Thousands of 172s built between 1977 and 1982 stood a good chance of developing an insidious illness that in extreme cases could lead to making the airplane unairworthy. We're talking about filiform corrosion, and it may affect the majority of the 25,000 airplanes built at Cessna's Pawnee Division plant in the years 1977-82, including over 8,000 Skyhawks.

Hopefully, it will have manifested itself by now and been corrected in many instances. What happened is that Cessna apparently disregarded the advice of DuPont, maker of Imron polyurethane paint, in preparation of the metal surface to block filiform corrosion. DuPont recommended using a combination of Alodyne and epoxy primer surface treatment. But Cessna opted for wash primer, a less expensive and much quicker-drying surface prep that may have saved Cessna many man-hours of labor and plant space, but cost owners in the long run. Therefore it still pays to check any used 172 around rivets and seams, where corrosion usually begins. Mostly the filiform problem has been localized to warm, humid coastal areas—ironically, the opposite of O-320-H engine spalling problems.

ADs, SDRs

The 172 line has enjoyed a comparatively quiet AD history, aside from the -H engine episode. Our check of Service Difficulty Reports on the aircraft, compiled from 1984 through April 1985, noted problems with stuck valves, including 19 reports on bent pushrods and bad guides on the older O-320-E2D powerplants. Other reports covered problems with brakes—chiefly cracked wheel hubs and brake housings; leaking, chafing and worn fuel lines on M, N, and P models, and Slick magnetos.

Maintenance

Hidden under the cowl of this 1980 Skyhawk lies possible trouble in the form of the notorious O-320-H2AD engine. Cold weather and inactivity increase the risk of encountering valve train problems.

Economy and low maintenance costs have always been the Skyhawk's strong suits. With the post-1968 four-cylinder engine, fixed-pitch prop, fixed gear and no cowl flaps, the average Skyhawk owner should survive on low annual inspection costs. Not that the Hawks are without their weak points. Late model '77 and '78 Skyhawks with 28-volt electrical systems tended to burn out their landing lights at a fantastic rate. Comments from one owner claimed an expenditure of $323 for landing light bulbs over the last 212 hours of flight, working out to $1.52 per flight hour, just for landing lights. Cessna came out with a "landing light improvement kit." Cessna owners have reported similar problems with beacon bulbs, claiming they last a mere 100 hours and cost $40 a pop to replace. A remedy to this costly bother is offered by Aeroflash Signal Corp., Chicago, Ill, (312) 342-4815., Aeroflash sells beacon bulbs carrying a 750-hour warranty.

Older Skyhawks tend towards problems with the nosewheel, particularly those flown by students and novices who land fast and hard. Nosewheel problems can produce damage to the firewall where the nosewheel strut joins it. This should be checked before purchase. Mechanics tell us that Cessna nosewheels are notoriously chintzy and soon succumb to minor punishment. Nose gear shimmy can also be troublesome. Flap, actuator jack screws have a dicey history, and are subjects of an AD in pre-1973 models.

Avionics

We usually don't talk about avionics in a used-plane article, but in Cessna's case, we really must make an exception. This is because of the generally poor reliability of the ARC avionics inflicted on virtually all 172s since 1974. ARC had serious management, production and quality control problems in the late 70s, and the result was a plethora of customer problems. The years 1977 and 1978 seemed to be especially bad.

If your search for a used C-172 turns up a '74 or later model with Collins, Narco or King equipment, you may save yourself future avionics headaches by buying it instead of an ARC-equipped airplane. If you must accept ARC avionics with your Hawk, demand documentation of repairs and past problems.

Owner Comments

I'd have to say the Skyhawk is the greatest of the all-time greats and is already a legend in its own time. In time to come it will be in the same league as the DC-3 and other bigger-than-life aircraft. I'm a part owner of a C-172 in a club where we also have a C-152 and a Comanche 260B. All three are popular, but the 'Hawk outshines them all and not only pays for itself, but sometimes has to support the other two.

Pilots love it, and it's a joy to instruct in. You can park it alongside any other comparable aircraft and pilots will fly it two to one. It's easy to fly, is not a greenhouse in the summertime, and its high wings act as a shelter in the rain. The high wing eliminates problems getting in and out. The aircraft is so stable you don't need automatic pilots, and since most students train in a C-150/152, a C-172 is a natural step-up. It's no wonder it's the world's most popular airplane.

As for performance, handling, maintenance, comfort and parts availability, I would have to rate it excellent in every category. One fly in the ointment is that ordering a small part, like a knob or something similar, from Cessna is impossible. And trying to get a dealer (if you can find one) to order it is an even bigger impossibility. Just how Cessna can build the world's greatest airplane, then do such a sorry job on small parts is unforgivable.

As for maintenance, we get 100 hours as well as annuals, and since there is so much variation between inspections, it's difficult to get any accurate average, but I'd say it's in the neighborhood of $300 each time. Let's hope Cessna doesn't goof up and try to improve the old metal bird and ruin it.

E. R. Ritch
Huntsville, Ala.

The plane (a 1981 model 172 P II) has, in general, been good to us. It now has 1,800 hours on it with no major engine problems or work to date. We've gone through more Slick mags than seems reasonable, including one that died shortly after being installed. I was so mad about that (it happened over mountainous terrain) that I demanded an explanation. Slick wrote back saying they don't normally explain themselves, but it was a quality control problem and they were upping their vigilance.

We were very fortunate to have purchased an '81, the year they went back to the 0-320-D2J engine. My partners and I were unlicensed, uninitiated, blind, dumb, and lucky when we bought the plane. It could just as easily been the valve-eater engine. The radios are, of course, ARC. Never again. We had more than a bit of trouble with them at first, though they've been stable in the last two years. We installed a used 400 series DME. Two visits to the factory and about $1,500 in repairs later, it began working right. It should. They replaced every circuit board in it. Not exactly a bargain by the time we got done.

What can you say about Skyhawks? Reliable, easy to deal with, dependable, friendly, gentle. Not fast, not great load haulers. Ours has taken us to the tip of Baja, to Santa Fe, New Mexico, and to lots of places great and small. It has done so without causing missed heartbeats, and without the need to fly 50 hours a month in order to stay competent to cope.

The Skyhawk is a good, honest three-person airplane if you're really traveling somewhere far enough away to require baggage. As equipped, ours will haul 620 pounds, and full fuel. Four at 150 pounds plus the pilot's flight case just about gets you there. Three of us plus baggage sufficient for a one-week journey through Baja almost read tilt.

It's disappointing to see that on a $50,000 piece of equipment, the best we can get for air vents is two tubes that push in and out about the pilot and co-pilot's head and can never be tightly closed. This contributes a continuous source of both noise and cold air. The noise is never welcome, and the cold air may or may not be, depending on the season. This arrangement makes the description "Mickey Mouse" seem like an improvement.

We're suffering filiform corrosion, for which I do not expect Cessna to run forward and claim responsibility. I'm certain they'll tell us it's absurd to expect to have an airplane parked within five miles of the ocean and not have it converted to aluminum dust by corrosion. I just wonder why they don't mention that possibility (necessity? inevitability?) *before* you buy?

I took my private and instrument instruction in the plane, and am glad I did. Life was a lot more comfortable there than it would have been in a 152, and I think it made getting through a lot easier and a lot more fun. The plane isn't perfect, but it performs pretty much as advertised. For a first plane, I don't see how anyone can go too wrong with a Skyhawk, though I'm also not too certain how anyone can afford one anymore. I can only afford the payments on an '81 with the help of two partners and a leaseback, and then just barely.

Brian Weiss
Santa Monica, Calif.

I am a CFII who no longer instructs. I am also a long-term Skyhawk owner. I have owned several models—1975, 1976, and 1966. By far and away, I find the 1966 model to be the best I have owned. Airframe maintenance is much less (one-half) of what I have spent on the 1976 and 1975 models.

Fuel cost is less with the 0-300 than the 0-320. Detailed records reveal the 0-300 averages one-and-a-half gallons less per hour at 75 percent power than the 0-320. Overhaul costs are about the same. The 1966 model is four knots slower than the 1976 and 1975 model. That is a small price to pay for increased reliability and a stronger airframe. I use unleaded autogas and find it much superior to aviation gas.

Every year or so I decide to step up, but when I compare what I get at the price I must pay, the only decision I can make is to keep the Skyhawk. Most common maintenance problem is the nose gear. Average cost of repair is $20 once or twice a year. Annual inspection runs around $200 per year. One dollar per hour is more than enough to cover maintenance. Two dollars per hour covers overhaul. Fifty cents per hour covers avionics maintenance. We have had many maintenance problems with the 1975 and 1976 models we do not have with the 1966, such as landing lights.

Dennis Teal
Canton, Tex.

In a streak of good fortune we bought our 1975 Skyhawk 172M as new in April 1977 at a discounted price since it had the old 80-octane "E" series Lycoming engine instead of the modern "H" series engine. We had minor warranty items including an out-of-balance propeller, all of which Cessna took care of with no quibbling. The only major service item in the 800 hours since has been a muffler flame tube replacement.

Nosewheel and nose-mounted landing lights have a reputation for giving problems in various model C-172s.

We stayed away from 100LL fuel, and are now running auto fuel almost exclusively. Aggressive mixture leaning gives us only 6.7 gallons per tach hour fuel consumption at 55 percent power for about 18 statute miles per gallon.

The engine has been very smooth and has been troublefree, including accessories. Oil consumption has been only one quart in 40 hours. The oil stays green for 20 hours and the oil temp. seems cold-blooded, suggesting the rings are in excellent shape with little blowby. No valve sticking or ignition roughness has been noticed, probably due to the low lead diet. Some say that this Lycoming rarely ices up, but I disagree. Ours frequently ices up slightly on all types of fuel, although it seems to load up only to a certain limit most of the time.

The ARC navcom has been troublefree. We've burned out only one landing light (from good propeller balance?), but the tail beacon bulb has been replaced a couple of times. We participate in our own supervised annuals, keeping them to about $100 per year with typical minor routine items. Several years in a Continental-powered 172H make the Lycoming-powered 172's performance seem very adequate, even at gross. Handling is superb, if not exciting or fast.

Features I like include the gravity fuel system (especially with auto fuel), the 12-volt electrical system, the big flaps, the ability to handle short unimproved strips; and the powerplant, along with the aerodynamic and structural integrity for which this airplane is known. It is sad to note all the problems Cessna encountered after building the 172M. I wouldn't think of trading it "up."

Niel R. Petersen, P.E.
Hopkins, Minn.

Cessna 177 Cardinal

Clean good looks with a full cantilever wing in an airplane that has finally won the market respect it deserves.

Cessna's 177 Cardinal is one of the few cult airplanes that lives up to its followers' hosannas. It's an airplane with an intriguing history: launched with great expectations but not much engineering, an early flop in the marketplace, its problems quickly fixed, but an initial bad rep that never went away. After a troubled 10-year career, it was finally replaced in Cessna's lineup by the Hawk XP, an airplane inferior to the Cardinal in virtually every way.

Genealogy

The Cardinal was first introduced in 1968. It was designed to be the Skyhawk of the future, building on the Skyhawk's classic traits as a reliable easy-to-fly 150-hp basic four-seater, but with snazzy good looks, more cabin room, better visibility and the latest in aerodynamic trendiness, a one-piece stabilator. Cessna was so confident that the Cardinal would be a winner that it shut down the Skyhawk production line in anticipation.

Unfortunately, the hardware didn't meet the expectations. That first 150-hp 1968 Cardinal, although good-looking and roomy, was a odd-handling, underpowered dog. Cessna had sold the Cardinal as a Skyhawk replacement, but it lacked the forgiving, safe, easy flying qualities that had been the Skyhawk hallmark. Such flying qualities may have been acceptable in a bigger aircraft, but Cardinal buyers expected the Cardinal to fly like a Skyhawk. But it didn't, and the plane's poor reputation was born.

In its optimism, Cessna cranked out 1,164 Cardinals in 1968 (nearly double Skyhawk production for the year), and the dealer organization managed to sell most of them before the word got out.

Reputation Justified

Most of the 1968 Cardinal's bad reputation was justified. The wing was a "high-performance" NACA 6400 series airfoil, the same one used in the Aerostar and Learjet. But that airfoil tends to build up drag quickly at high angles of attack and low speeds, which is not a good trait in a plane flown by low-time step-up pilots. Stall speed was higher than the Skyhawk's, too. Although the book numbers for stall and rate of climb didn't look too bad, they turned out to be wildly optimistic. The 1968 Cardinal climbed very poorly under the best of conditions, and if the pilot got the nose up a little too high, drag built up quickly, and climb rate sagged even more.

To make matters worse, the Cardinal had 50 pounds less useful load and bigger fuel tanks, so it was very easy to overload.

The 1968 Cardinal was quite sensitive on the controls, particularly in the pitch mode. The stabilator could stall in the landing flare, resulting in a sudden loss of tailpower and a sudden whomp of the nosewheel onto the runway. Porpoising and bounced landings were commonplace. Overall, its tricky landing traits, overloading tendency and doggy rate of climb made it a real handful for the Skyhawk-type pilot for which it had been designed and marketed.

Correcting the Problem

Cessna quickly realized it had made a major gaffe with the Cardinal. It restarted the Skyhawk production line and set to work fixing the Cardinal's problems. Under the so-called "Cardinal Rule" program, it retrofitted stabilator slots to Cardinals already in the field. This reduced the stabilator-stalling problem. Cessna also revamped the 1969 model calling it the 177A. Major change was the move to a 180-hp engine and a 150-pound increase in gross weight. The stabilator slots were incorporated, and the stabilator-to-wheel control linkage was changed to improve the pitch characteristics.

Despite the improvements, 1969 sales nosedived to about 200, while Skyhawk sales rebounded to their former league-leading levels.

A New Airfoil

In 1970, Cessna made more major improvements and called the Cardinal the 177B. The 6400 series airfoil was changed to a more conventional 2400 series similar to the Skyhawk's, and a constant-speed propeller was added for better takeoff and climb performance. More stabilator changes were made as well. At last, the Cardinal had all the makings of a good airplane.

From 1971 on, the Cardinal got only minor changes. In 1973, a 61-gallon fuel tank became optional, and cowling improvements boosted cruise speed from 139 to 143 mph. In 1974, a 28-volt electrical system was added. In 1975, speed went up again, but this was merely a bit of paperwork legerdemain by Cessna. Cruise rpm limit was increased so that 75 percent power could be obtained at 10,000 feet instead 8,000 as before. At most altitudes, side by side under the same conditions, a 1975 Cardinal is no faster than a 1974 model. In 1976, the Cardinal got a new instrument panel.

Despite Cessna's successful efforts to fix the original Cardinal's quirks, the plane continued to be a slow seller. It was the only Cessna single that didn't lead its category in sales. (Piper's Cherokee 180 beat it handily, as did the upstart Grumman Tiger.)

In 1977, Cessna finally gave up on the Cardinal. While jacking up the Cardinal's price dramatically, it introduced at the Cardinal's old price the Hawk XP (same performance, uglier, worse handling, noisier, more cramped, much higher fuel consumption and engine maintenance, lower engine reliability and TBO). Customers preferred the Hawk XP by a four-to-one margin.

In 1978 Cessna made one last-ditch effort to save the Cardinal. It spruced it up with some fancy interior appointments and radio packages (along with an absurdly high price tag) and called it the Cardinal Classic. Buyers weren't fooled, however, and the Cardinal Classic went over about as well as New Coke.

Used Plane Marketplace

Cardinal owners prize their craft, but the general public apparently didn't until recently. Prices used to generally run several thousand dollars less than a comparable 180-hp Cherokee, but recently they've come within $500 or so. (The Archer in '88 was going for $30,500, the Cardinal for $30,000). The Cardinal also commands more than the Grumman Tiger ($26,300) or Beech Sundowner ($20,500).

(Remember that "bluebook" retail prices are like automobile sticker prices; the actual selling price is usually somewhat lower.)

Many 1968 Cardinals have been converted to 180-hp engines and constant-speed propellers. This mod essentially turns the 177 into a 177B (except for the airfoil and different stabilator linkage), and commands a premium of several thousand dollars over a straight 177. In effect, a modified 1968 177 should be priced like a 1970 177B.

Performance

The Cardinal's performance is middle-of-the-road for 180-hp airplanes. Book cruise speeds range from 139 to 150 mph, while the 150-hp 177 is listed at 134 mph. Those numbers are nowhere near as good as the Grumman Tiger (160 mph), about comparable with the Cherokee 180/Archer, and better than the pathetic Beech Sundowner.

Owners report real-world performance reasonably close to book figures, except for the 1968 model. Typical figures: 140-145 mph on 9-10 gph. The 1968 model, judging from owner reports, is fortunate to cruise 120 mph.

Climb rate is about average for this class of aircraft—again, with the exception of the 1968 airplane, whose owners universally complain about its lethargic climb performance.

Payload-Range

Owners typically report useful loads in the 850-950-pound range, depending on installed equipment. That's slightly less than the Cherokee 180 or Grumman Tiger, and not enough to excuse the owner from careful consideration of weight and balance.

Assuming a fairly typical 900-pound useful load and 49-gallon tanks, the Cardinal has about 600 pounds for people and bags once the tanks are filled. That's three FAA-standard people and 90 pounds of luggage. If you want to carry four full-size people and 100 pounds of luggage, you'll be limited to perhaps 20 gallons of fuel—barely enough to fly anywhere safely. Weight limitations make the Cardinal essentially a three-passenger airplane, or at best a two-plus-two (adults and kids).

With full tanks, the Cardinal has good range. The 49 gallons usable and typical 10-gph fuel flow allow the Cardinal to fly four hours with reserve, and cover more than 500 miles. The 60-gallon tanks available on post-1973 models boost endurance by an hour and range by 150 miles—but at the expense of 66 pounds payload. A typical 60-gallon Cardinal with tanks full can carry just 540 pounds of cabin load. The 1968 150-hp Cardinal (2,350 pounds) has a gross weight 150 pounds lower than the 177A and 177B (2,500 pounds). Empty weight is only a bit less, so the 177's equipped useful load may be as low as 750 pounds. Put in four 170-pounders and 70 pounds of luggage, and there's zero—that's right, *zero*—left for fuel. (You could ride around behind a towtug, though. Wouldn't that be fun?)

Legally speaking, the 177s converted to the 180-hp/constant-speed setup are even worse, since useful load may not be legally increased while the new engine/prop are about 50 pounds heavier. But most pilots of the 180-hp 177s fly as if they have 177As or Bs. From the performance point of view, they're perfectly safe doing that. (As far as the landing gear and wing spar go, we're not so sure.)

Creature Comforts

A major design goal of the Cardinal was interior comfort, and the goal was achieved. The cabin is fully six inches wider than a Cherokee's, and puts its sibling Skyhawk to shame. Baggage compartment is huge. From the pilot's point of view, the Cardinal feels very spacious as well, since the wing sits higher and farther back, allowing excellent visibility out of the panoramic windshield. Unlike the Skyhawk and the high-wing Cessnas, the pilot's vision up and to the side is not blocked by the wing.

One Cardinal owner reports, "It's enormous in there...I often take the rear seats out and stand up a couple of ten-speed bicycles...the legroom in back is worth boasting about...the general spaciousness makes you feel like you're riding in the back of a limousine." Overall, the Cardinal is probably the roomiest four-place airplane made (not counting semi-six-seaters like the Bonanza).

A wide welcoming door—on both sides of the cabin—is one of the hallmarks of the Cardinal line. It's probably the easiest plane ever built to get in and out of.

It's also probably the easiest plane ever built to get in and out of. The doors are as wide as a soccer pitch, and there's no wing strut to get in the way. The floor sits lower to the ground than other high-wing Cessnas, so the step up is a small one. Tall people, however, will have to duck a bit to get under the low-slung wing.

Handling Qualities

The Cardinal generally wins praise from owners for its handling qualities. Even the odd pitch characteristics of the early models are typically excused by owners in a macho sort of way ("It may porpoise in the hands of the typical wimpy pilot, but hey, a superstud like me has no problem at all. Just a matter of technique, babe.")

In truth, the pitch sensitivity and porpoising tendencies of the Cardinal have never really been completely tamed. Pitch control forces are light (particularly compared to the notoriously nose-heavy Skyhawk and Skylane), and Skyhawk pilots are sometimes surprised by the responsiveness and pitch authority.

As one forthright Cardinal owner put it, "My own flying techniques and the Cardinal's characteristics on landing don't coincide very well. I feel like I run out of elevator effectiveness at recommended approach speeds, and thus land faster than I would like to. The very compliant landing gear saves my face a lot of times." Another owner writes, "It will porpoise for the inexperienced pilot. No problem for the owner-operator, but for this reason it is not a good aircraft for rental."

Cessna 177 Resale Value

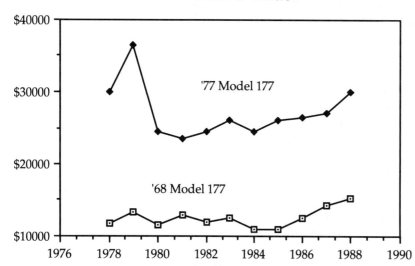

In flight tests by *Aviation Consumer* pilots, however, we've never had any problems, and frankly prefer the Cardinal's handling qualities overall to those of the Skyhawk. (Technique, babe.)

On takeoff, the Cardinal must be rotated for takeoff with firm wheel pressure, at least with two people in front and flaps up. (The pilot sits well ahead of the wing.) Dropping 15 degrees of flap for takeoff, however, will fly the Cardinal right off the runway without major yanks on the wheel.

In cruise flight, the Cardinal is a good steady IFR airplane—if you can get it trimmed out laterally and keep the fuel balanced. Several owners reported gross fuel-flow discrepancies when the fuel selector is on "both," with all fuel flowing from the left wing. Left-right switching every half hour may be necessary to maintain lateral trim.

Maintenance

Owner reports and service difficulty files suggest the Cardinal is a fairly simple, low-maintenance airplane. (Ironically, the retractable-gear 200-hp Cardinal RG is a real maintenance bear, with almost four times the rate of service difficulty reports on file as the fixed-gear airplane.) Annual inspections typically run $350-500 for the basic once-over. The engine and airframe have no major flaws that we're aware of. (The 180-hp Lycoming engine, in fact, is one of the most reliable of all.)

But there are some things to watch out for:

• McCauley prop inspection. It must be overhauled every five years or 1,500 hours. Check compliance on any airplane considered for purchase.

• Oil pump gears. Pre-1976 Cardinals should be checked for compliance with AD 75-08-09 on the oil pump gears. The Cardinal's engine model was not specifically called out in the vaguely-worded AD, and some mechanics may not be aware that the AD applies. Semantic hair-splitting aside, make sure this AD has been done.

• Other generic ADs that apply to many aircraft. Stewart oil coolers, Cessna fuel caps, vacuum pumps, ELT batteries, etc. etc.

• Water leaks through the windshield and door. Many owners reported being plagued with leaks. Check the sealant and any water damage.

• "That #@%*&# Bendix mag", as one owner put it. The 1975-78 Cardinal unfortunately came with the notorious Bendix dual magneto.

• Some Cardinals, particularly those in humid coastal areas, have been afflicted with corrosion. See service bulletin SE 80-02 for details. Also, Cardinals built in 1977 and 1978 have slick polyurethane paint jobs. A nice idea, but unfortunately Cessna failed to alodyne and prime the metal properly, and there's been a rash of filiform corrosion on painted surfaces.

• Engine and fuel gauges. These are proving troublesome, and unfortunately the instrument manufacturer has gone out of business. Cessna's replacement gauges (hideously expensive, of course) are not internally lighted and therefore almost useless for night flying.

• Clunking nosewheels. These can be cured with shims and/or new O-rings. Find a mechanic who knows Cardinals to do the job. The nosewheel is like no other Cessna nosewheel.

• High engine temperatures. Owners sometimes report their CHTs run near redline in warm weather. (One says the number three cylinder runs especially hot.) This can be cured with an aftermarket exhaust pipe fairing that improves cooling air flow and reportedly drops temps by 75 degrees. (See the Mods section.)

Owners gripe that the cowling is hard to take off and needlessly runs up their annual and repair labor bills.

One other major maintenance factor: ARC radios. Virtually all Cardinals have avionics manufactured by Cessna's onetime captive ARC company. Starting in the mid-1970s, quality of ARC radios began to fall, reaching a nadir about 1977 or 1978, the last two years of Cardinal production. ARC gear, virtually across the board, rated dead last in our avionics owner surveys during that period, and there were big shake-ups at the ARC factory at the time. An ARC panel is a major liability in any 1974-78 Cardinal, in our opinion. Check reliability and repair records carefully in any aircraft considered for purchase.

In 1975, the Cardinal got aerodynamic refinements (like this wheel pant fairing) that helped boost cruise speed to 130 knots.

Safety

The Cardinal has an average accident rate—not great, not terrible. We have no recent statistics, but an NTSB study for the years 1972-76 shows the Cardinal to have a fatal accident rate of 2.4 per 100,000 flight hours. This is about average for four-place fixed-gear aircraft. (By comparison, the Skyhawk had a superb 1.5 fatal rate over the same period.)

In the various categories of accidents studied by the NTSB, the Cardinal showed only two unusual traits. It ranked very poorly (29th out of the 33 aircraft tabulated) in landing accidents, and very high (best of the 33 airplanes, in fact) in landing undershoot accidents. The hard landing rate is almost certainly related to the

Cardinal's pitch sensitivity and unusual control feel in the flare.

According to the NTSB, the Cardinal ranked slightly worse than average in stall accidents. An *Aviation Consumer* study also ranked the Cardinal a bit below average, and well below the leaders in the four-place class, the Skyhawk and Cherokee.

Checking more recent accidents, we confirmed the patterns of the NTSB study. In 1979 alone, for example, there were seven Cardinal hard landing crashes, five involving 1968 models. There were also a bunch of takeoff accidents involving stall/mushes or impact with rising terrain—both a reflection of the aircraft's poor climbing ability. Again, most involved the 150-hp airplane with the 6400-series airfoil.

The lessons to be learned from the accident files: be very careful about overloaded takeoffs on short runways, at high density altitudes or with rising terrain (or heaven forbid, all three).

One of the Cardinal's best features is its spacious interior. The cabin is six inches wider than a Cherokee's.

And practice those landings. (Both warnings go double for the 1968 model.)

Modifications

The most important modification for Cardinal fans is the 180-hp constant-speed engine conversion for the 1968 model, which essentially converts it to the 177B configuration. Hundreds of 177s have been converted this way.

The conversion is quick and easy, basically a bolt-on job. Two different STCs are available from Avcon (316) 782-3317 and Bush (316) 782-3851. The two are very similar; both cost in the neighborhood of $17,000 (less a trade-in allowance on the old engine) for the complete job. Both sell STC paperwork and kit parts if you want to buy an engine and prop elsewhere and do the labor yourself. Avcon's kit price is $1,365; Bush's $1,100.

Avcon also has an STC to convert the fixed-pitch 177A to a constant-speed prop.

Horton Industries in Wellington, Kans. (316) 326-2241 offers a STOL kit for the Cardinal consisting of a leading-edge cuff, drooped wing tips and vortex generators on the vertical fin. The above-mentioned Bush also offers an STOL mod for the Cardinal. One owner characterized the Horton kit as "totally worthless," reporting stall speed was only two mph lower.

There's a burgeoning business in Cardinal speed mods. A Canadian named Roy Sobchuck came up with most of them, but they are now marketed in this country by C2 Enterprises, 3707 Pinehill Rd., Omaha, Neb. 68123 (402) 292-9327. The mods include a nose strut fairing (and a claimed speed gain of 8 mph), tailcone fairing (177B only, 7 mph) exhaust stack fairing (2 mph, 75 degree drop in engine temperature). The company also sells landing light covers, cowl cheek fairings, fuel drain fairings, ADF loop covers and mainwheel pants for which minor speed increases are claimed. The C2 mods are not STC'd, but may usually be signed off on a Form 337. (Check with your AI and FAA man before installation.) The company quotes no installation times due to wide variations in skill and experience in working with fiberglass.

Owner Clubs

Cardinal owners have a choice of two clubs. The Cessna Pilots Assn., Wichita Mid-Continent Airport, 2120 Airport Rd., P.O. Box 12948, Wichita, Kans. 67277, (316) 946-4777, is the biggest, and publishes much useful technical info. However, most of it applies to other single-engine Cessnas, so the Cardinal owner may feel lost in the crowd of Skyhawk and Skylane buffs. For the true Cardinal fan, there is the Cardinal Club, 1701 St. Andrew's Dr., Lawrence, Kans. 66046, (913) 842-7016. It tends to be more of a rah-rah social club, with newsletters focused more on fly-ins than technical problems and solutions. We'd consider both worthwhile for any Cardinal owner.

Owner Comments

We have generally found the Cardinal to be a very reliable airplane. This is particularly true since Cessna made modifications to the early Cardinals under the Cardinal Rule program. In many respects, the original 1968 177 Cardinal is a different airplane, in both handling characteristics and performance, from the later 177A and 177B. This is primarily due to the different horsepower and airfoils.

We are beginning to see some parts difficulties. They can take many, many months to arrive from Cessna, and will certainly cost many, many dollars. Because fewer than 3,000 fixed-gear Cardinals were built, salvage yards generally don't have a ready supply of Cardinal parts.

One thing that has really been a thorn in the side of Cardinal owners is the instrument cluster. These gauges, which include fuel quantity, oil pressure, oil temperature, cylinder head temperature, etc., were manufactured by Leigh Corp. Leigh went out of business, however, and Cessna's solution to the gauge problem was to recommend replacement with individual Stewart-Warner gauges. This is

Cost/Performance/Specifications

Model	Year	Average Retail Price	Cruise Speed (kts)	Useful Load (lbs)	Fuel Std/Opt (gals)	Engine	TBO (hrs)	Overhaul Cost
177	1968	$15,300	113	935	49	150-hp Lyc. O-320-E2D	2,000	$8,000
177A	1969	$17,000	118	1,060	49	180-hp Lyc. O-360-A1F6	2,000	$8,500
177B	1970	$18,000	119	1,025	49	180-hp Lyc. O-360-A1F6	2,000	$8,500
177B	1971	$19,500	119	1,020	49	180-hp Lyc. O-360-A1F6	2,000	$8,500
177B	1972	$21,000	119	1,015	49	180-hp Lyc. O-360-A1F6	2,000	$8,500
177B	1973	$22,500	124	1,005	49/60	180-hp Lyc. O-360-A1F6	2,000	$8,500
177B	1974	$24,000	130	995	49/60	180-hp Lyc. O-360-A1F6	2,000	$8,500
177B	1975	$25,500	130	995	49/60	180-hp Lyc. O-360-A1F6	2,000	$8,500
177B	1976	$27,500	130	967	49/60	180-hp Lyc. O-360-A1F6D	2,000	$8,500
177B	1977	$30,000	130	967	49/60	180-hp Lyc. O-360-A1F6D	2,000	$8,500
177B Classic	1978	$32,000	130	857	49/60	180-hp Lyc. O-360-A1F6D	2,000	$8,500

very expensive. Also, the S-W gauges are not internally lighted and require post lighting. (The Leigh gauges were internally lighted.) However, we have been able to find a shop that can repair the Leigh gauges. The Cardinal was built differently than other Cessnas, and for this reason it's important to find a mechanic who understands the airplane. For example, Cardinal nose gears are known to develop a clunking sound. This can be cured by the use of an O-ring or by installing a shim at a certain location. This is not generally known by Cessna mechanics because the Cardinal's nose gear is not like other Cessna nosegears.

One of the more popular subjects among Cardinal owners these days concerns speed-up kits. The most popular one is marketed by C2 Enterprises, 3707 Pine Hill Rd., Omaha, Neb. 68123, (402) 292-9327. This modification, which includes a nosewheel pant, and various fairings, is claimed to give a 15-20-mph speed increase, and some users back up this claim. C2 also sells an exhaust pipe fairing, and we have received many positive comments about its ability to reduce engine and oil temperatures. Most people are able to install these mods under a Form 337 approval, although other FAA offices refuse to allow this.

The Cardinal was not overwhelmingly popular during its production run, despite having reasonable performance numbers, good interior space and very attractive appearance. However, since production has ceased, it seems to be gaining in popularity. In fact, Cardinal owners seem to be so fanatical about their aircraft that they could almost be considered a cult. Due to lower horsepower, the 1968 177 sells for less than the later models. Owning a Cardinal can be a real pleasure if one is willing to put up with the minor inconveniences of an aircraft built in small numbers and out of production for eight years.

John Frank
Executive Director
Cessna Pilots Assn.
Wichita, Kan.

I own a 1974 C-177B with 1,300 hours on it. It's IFR-equipped and has speed mods. Fuel burn is 37 liters/hr (that's 9.8 gph. —Ed.). Average speed with mods is 155 mph. I fly 100-150 hours per year and do my own maintenance. Average maintenance cost (not counting my own labor) comes to about $450 Canadian per year.

Very stable airplane, lots of room. Excellent cross-country machine. Up here in Canada, it gets cold in the back seat during the winter. I have fixed that with a heating modification—now people complain that it's too hot. Lots of water leaks around the doors and windshield. They have been repaired with new sealant under the wing root fairings, and new door seals. It's now quieter, and no more leaks.

The plane is very roomy. With a child seat, we carry the whole family. It looks funny as all the people unload with their baggage. People ask us, "Where did they all come from?"

Roy Sobchuck
Brandon, Manitoba

Having been trained in a Cessna 152 and wanting an inexpensive, simple and comfortable plane of my own, I figured a third-hand 1969 Cardinal with 1,400 hours time was a perfect solution. In the last four years I have averaged about 60 hours per year. It is a very easy plane to fly, but it doesn't fly itself: you must pay about as much attention as when driving on a freeway. Too much attention to the sectional can result in some unusual attitudes. My Cardinal cruises 130 mph on 10 gallons an hour, and I can count on a 500-plus mile range with ample reserves. My only problem has arisen from inexperience with landing peculiarities. Failure to crank the trim down sufficiently can lead to porpoising or crow-hopping that makes a carnival ride seems tame. Landing too fast can cause endless floating in ground effect.

To take advantage of the 1,200-foot grass strip I built on my farm, I had a Bush STOL kit installed in Udall, Kan. (Excellent craftsmanship and fast work.) The results are well worth the price. Power off, the airplane will not stall if the wings are kept level; it just mushes down. With full flaps, one can land very slowly and steeply, with no fear of dropping in. For short-field takeoffs, put down 10 degrees of flaps, rotate at 45 mph and leap off the ground. This is a perfect plane for family flying, but one must not be tempted to overload, which can happen because of the cabin size and luggage space. Mine has IFR equipment and some extras. With full fuel it can carry 700 additional pounds, which means four substantial males and their toothbrushes, or two average couples and goodly luggage.

Cardinal (background) was replaced by the Hawk XP, an aircraft inferior to the Cardinal in virtually every way.

Maintenance items have included tires, battery, brake discs and pads. Unanticipated expenses have included replacement of carb heat and flap control cables, new gaskets in the nose strut, corrosion in the tail cone, new starter Bendix, new compass, and new directional gyro. Annual inspection is $450 plus parts and extra fixes required. Overall, mine has been remarkably trouble-free.

I am very satisfied and do not want any other airplane.

John Merserau
Dexter, Mich.

We purchased a new 1968 Cardinal 177 to move up from a 172 Skyhawk. We were disappointed with the 150-hp engine's rather anemic takeoff and climb. We opted for the Doyn 180-hp conversion a year later. Performance was good, as long as the pilot took reasonable care and attention to density altitude. The Cardinal is a good IFR platform, stable and solid. We file 115 knots, and it handles turbulence well. The Cardinal Rule mod program by Cessna corrected tendency for stabilator to stall and drop nose on landing.

No major repairs until 2,578 hours, when we did a major overhaul on the engine at a cost of $2,700 (some years ago). Only other major cost was inspection and maintenance of Hartzell prop. Plane was repainted in 1983 and looks sharp. Now has 3,100-plus hours. My biggest complaint is Cessna's obsolete cowling, which takes too much time for removal during inspections and maintenance.

William Tyson
KIngsville, Md.

Early Cardinal instrument panels were stylish, but lopped off the right corner, sacrificing avionics space.

I bought my 1973 C-177B in 1984 for $15,000. It had not been well maintained, and my initial maintenance figures are misleading. The McCauley prop had not been overhauled in seven years (five years or 1,500 hours is the TBO time), and I had to replace the hub as well as pay for the overhaul, for a total cost of $1,500. The carb heat box fell off into the bottom of the cowling. New muffler was $220. One of the fuel filler necks was badly rusted and had to be replaced for $325. The interior Royalite is doing what old Royalite does—falling apart after drying out and getting brittle. The plastic wingtips, stabilator tips and rudder tips are also cracking.

My biggest problem is the weird C-177 fuel-feed system. I have a real problem with drainage out the overflow vents on the wingtips. I have lost as much as 12 gallons of gas in a week due to siphoning overboard. The plane sits level, and this occurs regardless of the fuel selector position. It is absolutely imperative to check fuel level before every flight if the plane has been sitting—even overnight.

I also do not get any fuel feed from the right tank when the selector is on both. I have landed after a two-hour flight with the selector on "both" and found the right tank still completely full. No wonder it flew right-wing-heavy. When the selector is on "right," however, the tank feeds fine. Lest one think from the foregoing that the Cardinal is a dog, nothing would be further from the truth. The wide doors and spacious cabin will allow a lady to enter while wearing a dress and still be a lady. The cabin has more room than most twins.

Cruise speed at 5,500 feet is usually about 122 knots, according to the DME (in still air). Fuel consumption varies from about 8.5 to 11 gph depending on throttle and mixture. I normally set it up for about 10.2 gph, which allows the engine to run cool at about 72 percent power. I normally operate at 23 inches and 2300 rpm at about 5,000 feet. The Cardinal has a yellow band on the tachometer between 1,700 and 1,900 rpm. This caution range must be adhered to religiously. My plane's logbooks show that it once threw 10 inches of one prop blade off in flight. According to my mechanic, it had been operated in the yellow arc range, and apparently there is a harmonic vibration with a node about 10 inches from the tip.

Cardinal handling is solid. The big stabilator is powerful and likes to stay right where you trim it. Cardinals have a bad reputation for nasty landing traits, but this has not been my experience. It sits lower on the ground, and because of the low landing position there is a tendency to flare high. The Cardinal's nastiest landing bugaboo is the porpoising you'll get into if you land too fast and don't flare enough.

Parked by a Skyhawk or a Cherokee, it looks like a Corvette next to a sedan. My wife likes that!

C.S. Stanley
Jackson, Miss.

We've owned a 1968 Cardinal for the last 12 years. It has been modified with the Avcon 180-hp conversion and cuffed leading edge STOL kit.

Comfort is excellent. With 45 inches of shoulder room, it is significantly more comfortable than almost anything else. Two adults can sit in a Cardinal without rubbing elbows with each other or the vibrating airframe. You can slam the door without hitting yourself. The large doors open fully, unimpeded by a wing strut. Because the Cardinal sits low enough to back into (and then swing your feet up into the plane), I sawed off the entry step. The doors have to be the largest in the industry, with the back seat more accessible than any other single-engine plane.

With the '76 model the panel was enlarged. But ARC avionics remained to plague owners.

As for visibility, unlike most other single-engine designs, the wing is located rearward so that a pilot can lean forward for complete visibility. The ability to see the leading edge is a great comfort when the plane starts icing up. We've found maintenance to be stone simple. Annuals run $150 for the AI fee and $30-$60 for consumables like oil, filters, gaskets, etc. We open and close up the plane for inspection and do all the cleaning, lubrication and other maintenance that the owner is allowed to do. The Hartzell AD cost $605 in 1983. Brake pad wear from rusting discs and rain leaks past the fuel caps ended when I got into a T-hangar seven years ago. We do some of the avionics trouble-shooting ourselves, with my partner's oscilloscope and $40 worth of manuals and test harnesses. In one case, we found a failed potentiometer. Cessna wanted $125 for the part, but we replaced it with a with a superior part with a more stringent mil-spec from a local electronics supply house for $3. Autopilot removal from the wing is a fine example of perverse service engineering—a difficult and frustrating task for a contortionist in a good mood.

Performance is right on book for a 1974 177B, which is essentially what you get with the Avcon 180-hp conversion. I have flown the same plane hundreds of hours with both the 150-hp and 180-hp engines, and frankly I didn't notice anything different in the way it handles other than rate of climb and a modest improvement in speed. The ability to get quickly to the smoother, cooler air at altitude is an important factor in passenger comfort. Overgrossing is easily accomplished because the Avcon 180-hp STC did not increase the gross weight as the factory did when they put in the larger engine. Our useful load is 815 pounds with all the avionics.

I believe that the Cardinal is one of the great undiscovered treasures in the used aircraft fleet. It is underpriced relative to more recently built planes of older design.

Timothy J. Kramer
West Bloomfield, Mich.

Cessna Cardinal 177RG

By many accounts, Cessna's 177 RG Cardinal has survived the ravages of time and a defunct production line quite well. It perhaps now can even be considered the queen of the used economy retractables, at least in terms of near tag sale prices.

It is less doggy in performance than similar aircraft like the Piper Arrow and Beech Sierra, and though still 10 knots or more slower than the Mooney 201, costs a small fortune less. For example, where a 1978 Mooney 201 recently was going for a handsome price of around $47,000, a '78 Cardinal RG could be fetched for a relatively paltry $34,500 or so, according to *Aircraft Bluebook Price Digest* figures.

Cardinal RG owners don't seem to complain too much about parts availability, though the line was closed down in 1978 after only eight years of production. And they rave about its looks and novel design features. They even seem rather inured to the aircraft's Achilles heel—its trouble-plagued landing gear system. Owners who reported to us this time sounded off a lot less bitterly on the gear problem than they did for our initial call for user feedback on the 177 RG in 1980.

Peer Pressure

In comparison with the Piper Arrows, Mooneys and Beech Sierras that have the same 200-hp powerplant, the Cardinal RG is fastest, except for the Mooney, of course. It is roomiest, except for the Sierra. And it can carry the best useful load of all of them, by a small margin. In terms of price, it recently was $1,000 cheaper on the average than the Arrow on the used market (for a '78 model), though it actually surpassed the Sierra by about $4,000, at last look. Incidentally, in the last few years, the Cardinal RG has been picking up ground on the other two. It gained $2,000 on the Mooney and spurted up several thousand dollars to pass the Sierra in resale value.

Although the 75-percent book cruise speed for the Cardinal RG is supposed to be a sizzling 148 knots/170 mph, in the real world most owners talk about speeds closer to 140-145 knots/161-167 mph. But on the other hand, they boast of economy gas burns of eight to nine and a half gph. And with a generous 60-gallon fuel capacity on all but the '71 RGs, range is superb.

Owners report the Cardinal RGs ride well in turbulence, have nice-handling controls, provide a "stable instrument platform" and behave well in slow flight. "It is like driving a sports car compared to the cumbersome Skylane," said one owner. "Handling is superb."

Cabin Load and Comfort

As a safety-enhancing corollary to the spacious cabin, owners say the aircraft is almost impossible to load out of the cg envelope. But the baggage compartment is a strange one, since it is bisected by the hump that accommodates the retracted landing gear. This means suitcases that fit through the horizontally mounted baggage door then must be finessed into one of the two vertical slots on either side of the wheel well hump.

Said one owner, however, "The much maligned baggage compartment swallows an enormous amount of luggage, despite the hump. A useful load of 1,025 pounds works out to four adults, 120 pounds of baggage and enough fuel to fly four hours with IFR reserves. It is a true four-place single."

Whistling in the Wind

The four-foot wide cabin doors are everybody's pride and joy for ease of access, and they can catch the wind like sails to open a full 90 degrees to the fuselage. (Watch out.) Along with the benefits come some drawbacks, however, since owners still complain about door sealing problems. One said he solved the problem by simply removing the "hardened original seals" and replacing them with new ones.

But we remain skeptical in the light of comments by Bob Fields (of Bob Fields Aerocessories in Santa Paula, Calif.). Instead of providing inflatable seals for what we figured would be the ultimate solution to the problem, Fields told us he threw up his hands in frustration at getting any seals to work on the Cardinal RG, even though numerous owners came to him for help. "The variation in space between the doors and the fuselage is terrible," he said. Some portions of the doors fit too tightly, others too loosely, so when you get one part of the seal to inflate properly, another is pinched off. Fields attributed the awful fit to poor quality control.

Wet and Wild

If the doors can leak air, it stands to reason they can leak water. And so owners testify. The windshields tend to leak as well. But then Cessnas as a class seem prey to leakage problems. One Cardinal RG owner said he solved his leaky windshield problem simply by applying a bead of clear RTV around the outside of the windshield. As a final line of defense for the pilot, however, he suggested covering the pilot's left leg with a plastic chart.

Many aircraft also are noted for poor heating of rear seats in winter. The Cardinal RG tackled that problem by running heating ducts in back through the big doors. Alas, owners report little hot air makes it as far as the rear seats.

History of Model Changes

The aircraft has experienced a few modest changes through its eight-year production life. Though none is terribly significant alone, perhaps the collective improvements through the years to the landing gear system and its many idiosyncrasies amounts to something. The 1972 model gained a few knots in cruise and a slightly better climb rate thanks to a new prop. Also, the fixed cabin steps were dropped. They tended to expose the bottom of the fuselage to even more grief when the aircraft landed gear-up (as they did with some regularity). Instead, small foot pads were placed on the main gear struts. In addition, landing and taxi lights were mounted in the nose instead of the wing.

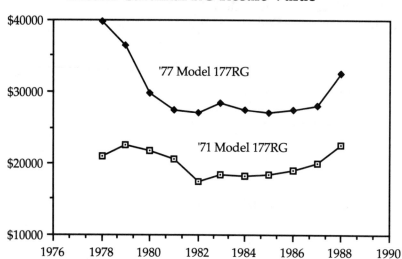

Cessna Cardinal RG Resale Value

The '73 model received a slightly redesigned nose cowl and an extra 10 gallons in usable fuel—up to 60 gallons. The fuel selector system was changed from one limited to "off" and "both," to one that also provided "left" and "right" positions. The problem on the earlier model was that one tank could be depleted more rapidly than the other, since the pilot could not select either a right or a left wing tank. This often meant unbalancing the aircraft.

In 1976 the instrument panel was redesigned and enlarged, and a simplified landing gear hydraulic system was offered, along with a stronger nose gear trunion. For the '77 model, the aircraft received a fuel selector that gave it commonality with other Cessna singles, had a more positive detent and was supposed to be more easily maintainable.

And finally in 1978 the aircraft received a 28-volt electrical system and an improved gear retraction power pack that cut retraction time in half to six seconds.

Resale Value

Despite inflation, the Cardinal RGs on the whole exhibited rather mundane resale curves, never soaring up as highly valued aircraft do. Instead, they merely sagged to a certain level in the standard four years after new, then remained pretty much on a plateau through the years. Thus, the original '71 model dropped from about $31,000 to around $20,000 and remained within a couple thousand dollars of that through the years. The last model, the '78 ship, dropped from about $54,000 to $29,000 in the classic four-year span, and only recently has begun to climb fairly well.

Safety Record

A study of accident rates in the decade 1972 to 1981 by *The Aviation Consumer* gave the Cardinal RG an excellent ranking in terms of fatal accidents and a slightly better-than-average rate in total accidents. In fatal accidents, the Cardinal RG came out third best after the Cessna Skylane RG and the Beech 33 Bonanza/

Debonair and tied with the Beech 36 Bonanza with 1.5 fatal accidents per 100,000 hours. In total accidents it was seventh out of 17 with 7.8 accidents per 100,000 hours.

What kind of accidents predominate among Cardinal RGs? A study of NTSB accident records for the years 1979-1980 by our sister magazine *Aviation Safety* showed the most—slightly over 37 percent—involved engine failures. But there seemed to be no particular pattern. Of those in which the problem could be determined, the most—three—occurred after breaks in oil hoses, but all different hoses going to different parts of the aircraft. One engine failure occurred when the oil pump impeller gear broke. This was later the subject of an Airworthiness Directive, but we noted in a three-year runout of the FAA's Service Difficulty Reports (up through September 1981) at least a dozen problems involving broken oil pump gear teeth.

Landing accidents accounted for the next highest category, with nearly 12 percent, with hard landings and groundloops leading the way in unpleasantness.

Gear Nemesis

As for the traditional nemesis of the Cardinal RG—landing gear problems—the two-year study showed it only third in the rankings along with a host of other problems like fuel management, takeoff accidents and weather-related problems. Nevertheless, failure of the gear to extend or actuator failure brought three RGs to grief.

Giant double doors open a full 90 degrees. But pilots report tricky problems getting doors to seal well. Squarely in the middle of the luggage compartment is a big hump that houses the retractable main gear. But load carrying remains topnotch.

Our earlier detailed study of 78 Cardinal RG accidents covering the five-year period from 1973 to 1977 showed once again that engine failures predominated, with about 34 percent of the accidents. These were seldom fatal. That time, though, gear-up landings and gear collapses and retractions accounted for second place or about 20 percent—or a total of 16 accidents. Some of these were pilot error, however.

Stall/spin/mush accidents in the Cardinal RG were fairly infrequent. In the five-year period there were two in-flight airframe failures. One occurred in bad weather and was fatal. In the second the pilot overstressed the aircraft and bent the wings, but actually managed to land safely. In general, despite the lack of wing-strengthening struts, the aircraft has a good record of in-flight airframe failures.

Maintenance

Powerplant accessories and brakes were the main problem areas reported on our most recent feedback from Cardinal RG owners. But most seemed to feel that maintenance required for the aircraft was reasonable, in general. A maintenance survey yielded average hourly maintenance costs for the Cardinal RG of around $17 an hour and annual inspection costs averaging a bit under $800. Unscheduled yearly airframe and engine costs together averaged about $600.

We received nowhere near the litany of complaints we did on our last survey several years earlier, when owners railed about chronic maintenance problems. Biggest problem areas then were alternator failures, Bendix magneto breakdowns, cracking exhaust pipes, malfunctioning fuel quantity gauges, breaking alternate air induction doors, leaking fuel caps, hot-running engines, landing gear horn malfunctions and malfunctioning landing gear mechanisms, especially hung-up nosegear.

The 1976 models, like this one, received a simplified landing gear hydraulic system. Early years of the model's history saw it plagued with gear problems. The main gear retracts into a notch in the rear fuselage without doors.

A check of Service Difficulty Reports from 1979 through most of 1981, however, suggested some troublesome areas. A few were: stabilator problems such as loose bolts, worn bushings and cracked brackets; cracked and broken prop spinners; cracked crankcases; broken engine oil pump gear teeth (mentioned before); Bendix magneto failures; and throttle cable malfunctions.

Focus on Landing Gear

Though some owners this time around reported problems with the notoriously quirky landing gear system, the complaints were by no means legion as before. It would appear that the constant focus of attention on the problem by pilots and maintenance shops, and by Cessna's own progressive series of fixes, have diminished its impact significantly. And this comes in the face of the '81 SDR breakdown showing page after page of gear problems. (One must temper this finding, however, with appreciation for the fact that so many of Cessna's *other* retractable-gear aircraft through the years have experienced more than their share of gear problems.)

Through the eight years of its production, the Cardinal had four different landing gear systems, as Cessna strived to correct all its quirks. The first, most problem-plagued one on the '71 and '72 Cardinal RGs, was a Rube Goldberg combination of electrical and hydraulic components whose weakest link was its electrically actuated main gear downlocks. The '73 Cardinals got hydraulic downlock actuators that improved reliability. Then on the '74 aircraft the gear selector handle itself was turned into a hydraulic valve and hydraulic pressure was routed not directly but through a panel-mounted valve controlled by the handle. This system also eliminated the remote electrical control unit.

Finally, with the '78 models the 12-volt Prestolite hydraulic power packs were eliminated in favor of a 24-volt power pack of Cessna's design. This has proved to be the most satisfactory of all the systems and, of course, would be the one to choose if cost considerations permit. At any rate, potential buyers should check to see which, if any, of Cessna's recommended service instructions have been applied to which ever model they are looking at. There are at least eight of them, including numbers 71-41, 72-26, 73-28, 74-26, 75-25, 76-4, 76-7 and 77-20.

Modifications

Among the STCs published for the Cardinal RG are the following: Wing leading edge cuffs and vortex generators on the vertical stabilizer, by Horton STOL Craft, Wellington, Kans.; chrome-plated brake disc installation, by Engineering Plating & Processing, Kansas City, Kans.; installation of an air/oil separator, by Walker Engineering Co., Los Angeles, Calif.; and recognition lights on the horizontal stabilizer, by DeVore Aviation, Albuquerque, N.M.

What to Join

Cardinal owners have a choice of two clubs: The Cardinal Club, 1701 St. Andrew's Dr., Lawrence, Kans. 66046, (913) 842-7016; and the Cessna Pilots Assn., P.O. Box 12948, Wichita, Kans. 67277, (316) 946-4777

Owner Comments

The average cost over the life of my '74 Cardinal RG (purchased when it was one year old) is about $40 to $45 an hour. (That includes direct operating and fixed costs, flying about 175 hours a year.) This may be higher than average, but I spare no expense on maintenance. The aircraft is maintained by Howard Aircraft Service, at Craig Field in Jacksonville, Fla., and Bob Howard is a real nitpicker. My annuals run from $1,500 to $2,000. My hourly maintenance cost for 1984, the highest ever, worked out to $28.06.

Mechanically, the aircraft has presented only one major problem. Following a fast, no-flap landing, the nose gear collapsed as the aircraft turned off the runway. An improperly adjusted nose gear linkage was found to be at fault. Apparently the aircraft left the factory in that condition and flew for two years before the accident. At normal landing speeds, the hydraulic system apparently could overcome the air pressure on the nose gear. At high speeds this was not the case. Result: a new prop. Brake pads also were a constant problem. I should have installed chrome disks years ago. Parts, however, are no problem.

I flight plan for 140 knots at about eight to nine gph. It is a fine cross-country

Cost/Performance/Specifications

Model	Year	Average Retail Price	Cruise Speed (kts)	Useful Load (lbs)	Fuel Std/Opt (gals)	Engine	TBO (hrs)	Overhaul Cost
177RG	1971	$22,500	125	1,170	50	200-hp Lyc. IO-360-A1B6	1,800	$10,000
177RG	1972	$23,500	129	1,155	50	200-hp Lyc. IO-360-A1B6	1,800	$10,000
177RG	1973	$25,500	129	1,140	60	200-hp Lyc. IO-360-A1B6	1,800	$10,000
177RG	1974	$26,500	129	1,140	60	200-hp Lyc. IO-360-A1B6D	1,800	$10,000
177RG	1975	$28,500	129	1,120	60	200-hp Lyc. IO-360-A1B6D	1,800	$10,000
177RG	1976	$30,500	129	1,093	60	200-hp Lyc. IO-360-A1B6D	1,800	$10,000
177RG	1977	$32,500	129	1,093	60	200-hp Lyc. IO-360-A1B6D	1,800	$10,000
177RG	1978	$34,500	129	1,106	60	200-hp Lyc. IO-360-A1B6D	1,800	$10,000

machine for my purposes. I usually fly the aircraft with an average of two people aboard. The handling characteristics are outstanding. The controls are firm, crisp and effective. The aircraft has the feel of a much heavier machine, more like a 182 than a 172. The stalls are mild with prompt recovery. The placement of the wing is one of the characteristics of the aircraft that I dearly love, since you are forward of the leading edge, which gives you outstanding visibility.

The avionics are ARC. What more can I say! One of the avionics people that worked on the radios said, "You really have to be wealthy to fly with ARC equipment," and I believe her. I had two problems: finding someone who would work on them, then finding someone whose repairs would hold up until I got back to my home base. I am going to install new avionics following completion of the new paint job.

All in all, I am very fond of the aircraft. Frankly, I don't find any of the aircraft of the same class being marketed today comparable to a Cardinal RG.

John D. Shea, Jr.
St. Augustine, Fla.

Early in 1980 I read *The Aviation Consumer's* Used Aircraft Guide on the Cardinal RG, and decided the aircraft had the performance and range I was looking for. Later that year I bought a 1973 model which had been operated by a flying club in Wisconsin. I selected this particular craft, which had about 2,300 hours on the airframe, because someone had the good sense to install a complete Collins Microline avionics package. This has proven to be a reliable set of equipment during many hours of IFR cross-country flying.

After purchasing the airplane, I gave it new paint, new interior and a zero-time engine and prop. Also, I replaced the horrible plastic instrument panel cover and glove box door with a hardwood panel. The cheap plastic panel does make a good template for laying out its replacement.

The airplane pretty much meets book speeds and delivers 165 mph cruise at 70 percent power. I always plan nine gph from takeoff to touchdown. Sixty gallons works out to six and a half hours of fuel on board. I was surprised that with two on board, it is relatively easy to get to 14,000 feet if you just increase the rpm to 2700 during the climb after leaving 8,000 feet. The book permits this power setting from sea level. There seems to be a lot of additional power in the last 200 rpm, which is also nice when the bird starts to collect a little ice. It sees a lot of IFR and is a good IFR aircraft. I installed a Cessna 300A autopilot a couple of years ago, and it works very well.

On two occasions, the gear down-and-locked indicator would not illuminate without a few cycles of the landing gear. After spending hundreds of dollars at repair stations where they found nothing, I was looking at the connections to the microswitches in the end of the main gear struts during an annual, and found the inline connectors to be loose on the wires. After five minutes with a soldering iron, there have been no more gear indicator problems. I suggest examining these little connectors whenever you have a chance. I was a little concerned about the retractable gear after reading your 1980 article, but it goes up and down every time I move the switch.

I've spent some time trying to reduce the noise level in the airplane even though it is fairly quiet for a single-engine machine. I found that some thin cork with adhesive backing made by Sound Coat of Santa Ana, Calif. applied on top of the glareshield running to the windshield was more effective than other sound absorbent material on the floor or in the ceiling panels, etc. The airplane is pretty quiet now.

The door noise problem was solved by removing the hardened original door seals and replacing them with new seals. The doors will stay a lot tighter if you keep the door latch screws tight. Most of the water problem from the windshield can be solved by applying a bead of clear RTV around the outside of the windshield. The residue can be controlled with a plastic chart on the pilot's left leg. I had a Walker Engineering Air/Oil Separator added to the engine breather, and this has helped tremendously in keeping the bottom of the airplane clean. Maintenance on the airplane is not too far out of line. The aircraft has settled into about an $800 annual, with no big surprises during the year except maybe an alternator—due, I feel, to the vibration of the IO-360. Small inspections throughout the year and a hangar have done a lot to keep maintenance costs down.

I was considering moving to a T210 for more speed and the ability to climb up through the clouds here in western Oregon, but the Cardinal RG is much more economical, very comfortable, and has been pretty darn reliable—in five years only two delayed trips—so I plan to keep it for some time.

John Desmond
Vice-president Engineering
Flight Dynamics, Inc.
Hillsboro, Ore.

In my opinion, performance of the Cardinal RG is outstanding: 140 knots at just under 10 gph. Although the book says 148 knots, I have never been able to duplicate those numbers. Handling is superb. It is like driving a sportscar compared to the cumbersome Skylane. It is a total departure from the other Cessna singles, rides fairly well in turbulence and is rock solid even at 80 knots—a good IFR machine.

As for maintenance, I purchased my '74 model in 1984 with 1,125 hours since new. Low time on a 10-year-old airplane doesn't mean much, so I bargained for a

The 1973 RGs benefited from an extra 10 gallons of fuel and a new fuel selector system that allowed the pilot to select left or right tanks. Also, the nose cowl was redesigned.

low price and expected the worst. And that's exactly what I got—chunks of metal in the oil within the next 40 hours. The engine was overhauled at one of the leading shops in central Florida. I replaced the ARC radios (just awful) with Narco and installed an Arnav loran. I also replaced the rusted and badly pitted brake discs with Cleveland chrome. In 150 hours of flying I have replaced the vacuum pump, an alternator belt, one EGT probe and a squat switch. No other gear problems to date, although a gear-up landing is noted in the logs back in '76.

The cost of operation, including fuel, maintenance and reserve for engine and prop overhaul is about $29 per hour. Maintenance costs thus far have been $4 to $5 an hour, based on 120 hours a year. My last annual was just under $500. Some of the nagging problems have been grossly inaccurate fuel gauges, a damp cabin when flying in rain and a gear horn sounding off at cruise. (You play with the throttle position to make it stop.)

Cessna solved the problem of where to anchor the shoulder harness by locating it in the ceiling ahead of the wing spar. Geometry is not ideal for crashworthiness, however.

As for comfort, it is a very roomy single, even for rear-seat passengers. It's a pleasure boarding and exiting with two huge doors and no struts or wings to step over. The much maligned baggage compartment swallows an enormous amount of luggage, despite the hump. A useful load of 1,025 pounds works out to four adults, 120 pounds of baggage and enough fuel to fly four hours with IFR reserves. It is a true four-place single. Cabin noise level at cruise is less than most other singles I have flown. I really love my Cardinal. The good points far outweigh the problems. I am a CFII and have owned four other airplanes in 11 years. Considering the outrageous costs of today's new singles and the performance this airplane affords, the Cardinal RG can be the steal of a lifetime for a careful shopper. Truly this airplane could be the best single Cessna ever produced.

Vince Veltri
Sarasota, Fla.

I have owned and operated a '75 177RG for about four years. The cost of flying and maintaining it has been very low. I have flown it for about 600 hours with only one unscheduled maintenance problem, and that was for a voltage regulator. Annuals average about $250 to $350, and only routine procedures have been necessary this far. The airplane averages 145 knots on about 67 percent power, at about 9.5 gph. I have flown it on long cross-countries and find it very comfortable and quiet. In short, I think it's the best retractable that Cessna ever built. (I also have owned and flown T210s, P210s and 182RGs.)

Milton Killebrew
Victoria, Tex.

We bought our '74 Cardinal RG in '75, so now have nearly 10 years of experience to report on. The aircraft may have suffered a certain amount of abuse during its first year with a commercial charter operator. The total time at purchase was just over 400 hours, and during our first two years of ownership we ran into a number of irritating snags and repairs—none major. Since that time the RG has operated reliably, with very little unscheduled downtime. During nine and a half years, we've flown about 1,600 hours and installed a factory reman engine at the TBO of 1,800 hours. The original engine ran perfectly till the last day—and the only major repair was one piston and valve at about 1,200 hours. At 1,800 hours the engine was still giving us two hours to a quart of oil, with good compression. We also lost one alternator and one vacuum pump, fortunately not during IFR. Much has been written about gear problems with the Cardinal RG. In almost 10 years, we've encountered two incidents, both fairly minor. On one occasion the gear refused to lower, but was pumped down manually without difficulty. The problem turned out to be worn brushes on the pump motor. Recently, one of the hinge brackets on the forward nose gear door sheared off, causing the door to twist about 45 degrees. I discovered this during the ground check, but it could have resulted in a jammed nosewheel.

The aircraft is stable and easy to fly, with low landing speed for an aircraft of its type, yet it provides reasonable cruise speeds (nothing like a Mooney, of course) and excellent range. You can fill the tanks and still take four average adults, or three and baggage without going over gross. There is no such thing as a cg problem under any normal loading situation. Endurance is up to nine hours at lower power settings, which can give tremendous range with a good tailwind.

I normally flight plan for a cruise of 135 knots. We use the RG for a combination of personal family travel and business. It's ideally suited for trips up to about 500 miles, with plenty of reserves and reasonable block time. Cessna's book figures for cruise performance are quite realistic. Since installing the factory reman engine, I find speeds with one or two knots of published value.

I don't know how Canadian operating costs equate to U.S. costs, but our overall cost per hour, including fuel, hangar, insurance and maintenance, based on 175 hours per year, runs about $68 per hour, equivalent to about $50 U.S. The Canadian equivalent of a U.S. annual is a C.C.I plus a 100-hour on the engine, and runs $1,000 to $1,200 ($730 to $880 U.S.). Hourly cost of maintenance, not including engine reserve or avionics runs $17.50 an hour ($12.80 U.S.). Among the few negative comments I could mention are the cabin heater, which is very marginal. In winter with temperatures below zero F, the front seats are barely comfortable. Anyone sitting in back would freeze in short order. The ducts in the doors, which are supposed to carry heat to the rear, are next to useless.

The cabin is moderately noisy, and conversation is not easy. Seals are not too good. This contributes to the noise level, and in heavy rain there are leaks. The fuel gauges are unreliable. When the tanks are about half empty, the gauge indications wander all over. The gear warning horn is Mickey Mouse. For a year it either wouldn't work at all, or would blast away when the throttle was set for 18 inches in descent. After years of trying to adjust it, our FBO finally came up with some minor mods that appear to have cured the problem. The original paint stood up well, but eventually some cracking and fading occurred. The plastic interior and upholstery, while certainly not deluxe, is durable. It still looks good. We paid C. $36,000 in 1975, and it's worth about the same now, with a low-time engine. Too bad Cessna stopped production. I think this is the best and smartest-looking single (except for the much costlier Centurion) Cessna has ever produced.

R.G. Shelley
Toronto, Ont. Canada

Cessna Skylane 182

This 1972 Skylane was touted as Cessna's 100,000th airplane. With room for four and plenty of fuel and baggage, the Skylane dominated the "high-performance" fixed-gear scene for decades.

Even if the Cessna 182 hasn't been around as long as the Old Testament, it sometimes seems like it has. The third most popular lightplane in history, the Cessna 182 has long been the keystone of Cessna's step-up marketing philosophy, bridging the gulf between Cessna's low-profit 150/172 entry-level airplanes and the higher-profit, higher-performance 210 and light twin aircraft.

A decade earlier, this '62 Skylane marked addition of a rear window, though blunter than later models. Swept-back tails came a couple of years earlier.

Today, more than 30 years after the 182's introduction in 1956, the aircraft is still *the* basic enhanced-performance aircraft, an economical flying machine capable of hauling four people, bag and baggage, a reasonable distance, in comfort, and at a reasonable speed.

The first Skylanes rolled off the production line the same year as the first 172s. Together, the duo marked the beginning of Cessna's 20-year dominance of the single-engine market. The basic 182 design was cut in stone in those days and both airframe and powerplant have remained fundamentally unchanged ever since. The overall effect is generous, with a fuselage of ample size, topped by a big slab of a wing.

In 1958, Cessna introduced the "Skylane," a 182 fitted with enough amenities and creature comforts to raise the gross weight approximately 100 pounds, and therefore decrease useful load by roughly the same amount. Those 1958 Skylanes including rudder trim and a ratchet click elevator trim device, along with optional autopilot. Later Cessna bestowed the Skylane name on the 182, and made the marginally upscale version of the same plane the "Skylane II."

Dependable Engine

The 230-hp Continental O-470 has proved a dependable performer through the years, despite some break-in problems reported in the later O-470-S model. Those first 182s used the O-470-L engine, which featured larger cast shell cylinder heads, thinner and more numerous cooling fins, and an engine mount improved over the early O-470-K installation in the Cessna 180 design.

Cars with enormous swept tail "fins" were all the rage in the late 1950s. Eventually this vogue found its way into airplane styling, with Cessna sweeping back the tail on the 180 in 1960. Basic fuel capacity was increased in 1960, from 55 gallons to 65, with long-range 84-gallon tanks introduced as an option. Later Skylanes would boast a 92-gallon capacity.

Two years later the airplane got a rear window and electric flaps. The year 1971 witnessed an alteration to the 182 in the form of its so-called camber lift wing. The wing was given a constant radius droop—a downward curl. The aim of the droop was to provide better low speed handling and stall reaction. Combined with the aircraft's washout, the result is good lateral control even while deep in the stall zone.

Gross weight has grown steadily over the years, from the original 2,550 pounds to 2,650 in 1957 to 3,100 for the last ones built. Empty weight has also increased, although not quite as fast as gross, so that useful load numbers for the 182 have not increased dramatically, starting at 1,010 pounds in '57, and topping off at 1,377. Overall, however, the 182 design has gone through remarkably few changes over the years.

Built for Comfort, Not for Speed

Book speeds have remained in the 139 to 143 knot range through the years with evolutionary aerodynamic refinements making up for the speed penalty of higher gross weights. Most owners report such speeds are possible in the 182, but prefer to drone along at lower power settings to save fuel, with 130 knots a commonly mentioned figure. One owner reported burning 12.5 gph to get 140 knots at 75 percent power. Another said his 182, burdened with a "full load" cruised at 135 knots at 75 percent between 6,500 and 8,500 feet, while consuming a quart of oil every four hours. Performance like this may seem pokey for an airplane driven by a 230-hp engine, and it is. The Mooney 201, albeit a retractable, slips through the air 30 knots faster than a 182, while using less horsepower.

The first-edition 182, a 1956 model with squared-off tail and no wheel pants. It was destined to become the third-best-selling lightplane in history.

While no one ever said the 182 was a racer, the airplane does climb, with 1,000 fpm easily obtainable at heavy weights, and 1,500 fpm at lighter weights (both from sea level, of course).

If the 182 doesn't get you there particularly fast, it treats you kindly along the way, thanks to a spacious interior. It's a real four-seater, the kind that allows the back seat mob to abandon the fetal position and stretch out. Two wide doors ease entry and exit. On the negative side, cabin noise levels approach brain-damage thresholds, and can make long flights fatiguing without a good pair of earplugs or headsets.

Handling

In a word, the 182 is stable. Most pilots praise it both as an IFR platform and as a reasonably comfortable aircraft in turbulence. Nonetheless, in the air, as on the ground, there ain't no free lunch, and this stability is paid for with rather heavy control surfaces.

To use another word, the 182 is ponderous, especially in pitch. With full flaps and two people aboard, flaring to land takes maximum muscle and maximum back trim. This heaviness of control is the price paid for the 182's vast cg envelope. Trying to stall the 182 with power on is probably the nearest anyone will come to aerobatic maneuvering in this staid aircraft. It will buck and shake like a bronco until the pilot either relaxes back pressure to lower the nose or settles for a pronounced wing drop.

Such performance will never come as a surprise, however, because the 182's humungous elevator forces make the airplane virtually impossible to stall by accident. Slow-speed maneuvering in a Skylane builds confidence; there's no feeling of flying right on the edge. On the other hand, aileron control at low speeds is relatively clumsy, and gusty crosswinds can prove challenging.

Loading

Unless you're transporting ingots of solid neutronium, the 182's load limits are pretty tough to bust. It's acknowledged as one of the few airplanes in which you can almost always fill all the seats, all the tanks, stuff the baggage compartment to capacity, and still be legal (and safe). Admittedly a well-equipped 182 with long-range tanks might require a degree of fuel/passenger tradeoff, but on the whole, Skylane pilots don't fuss much with weight and balance. If it fits, it's probably legal. Cg balance is also generous. One Skylane owner reports he can put himself up front, load a pair of 200-pounders in the back, fill the baggage compartment to the max, and still be with CG limits.

Safety

The Skylane has a good safety record—well above average as measured against the GA fleet overall. Both accident and fatality rates come in below the norm. FAA records from 1980-81 list 41 fatal accidents for the 182 fleet, with over three million hours flown during that period.   The Skylane has among the best stall/spin accident rates of any aircraft. In both a 1972 stall/spin study from the NTSB, and a 1984 study conducted by our sister publication *Aviation Safety*, the 182 scored among the lowest in both accidents and fatalities attributed to stalls or spins.

Thanks in part to the airplane's megalithic pitch performance, in-flight structural failures are virtually unheard of. It's nearly impossible to pull hard enough on a 182 to overstress the airplane. That high-drag fuselage and fixed gear also limit speed buildup in an unintentional dive. This is in keeping with the fact that when measured overall, Cessna designs featuring wing strut braces have an excellent record of holding together when the going gets tough.

The Skylane also excels in the area of fuel management. Its no-frills fuel system consists of a high-wing, gravity-feed system, and an idiot-proof left-right-both fuel selector.

Deadly Fuel Cells

By far the most disturbing AD to emerge from the FAA's regulatory woods, AD 84-10-1 has caused thousands of Cessna owners to delve deep into the innards of their fuel-bladder equipped wings for potentially deadly water-trapping wrinkles. For years the problem eluded detection during the traditional sump-draining preflight because the water trapped by wrinkles could also be kept isolated from the quick-drain openings. Such a tank could be sumped, and no water would show in the sample.

Buyers should check for damage to the firewall, the result of hard or nose-low landings.

A simple attitude change, such as that encountered in takeoff, would spill the water out of its wrinkle containment area, through the intake, and into the engine. Too often, this water was more than the three ounces that can be stopped by the gascolator. Result: engine stoppage at the worst possible time, just seconds after takeoff. AD 84-10-1 affected all 182 models built between 1956 to 1978, at which point Cessna changed over to a wet-wing design.

A worthwhile discussion of this AD requires some background. In an *Aviation Safety* examination of accidents from 1975 through 1981, 396 accidents in various types of aircraft were found in which water- contaminated fuel was cited as a cause or factor. A total of 155 (about 39 percent) of these accidents involved Cessna aircraft, and 39 of those mishaps involved Cessna 182s. What's more, 25 of the 39 C-182 accidents involved the P-model, the 182 model in production from 1972 through 1974. In those days, the rubber fuel bladders installed at the plant were made of Goodyear BTC-39. The passage of time revealed that BTC-39 bladders deteriorated rapidly, becoming brittle, "cheesy," and eventually leaking copiously. An AD mandated their replacement with bladders made of stiffer BTC-67, a urethane material.

The extra stiffness of BTC-67 seems to be the contributing factor to the wrinkle problems that were to be discovered later. As Bob Stevens, then FAA manager of Standards and Evaluations, put it, "There's two ways to install a tank like this. If the tank is put in on the assembly line as the airplane is built, that's fairly easy. The tank just fits in before the butt rib. It's installing the tank in the field as a replacement where the trouble starts. As delivered in the field, these tanks aren't too wrinkled. The procedure to install is to soften the BTC-67 tanks in warm water, and then wad them up and stuff them into the wing. That's where I think the wrinkles come from."

Smoothing and Blending

The AD required an inspection of the bladders, "smoothing and blending" of any wrinkles found, and installation of new quick drains on aircraft in which the "smoothing and blending" process requirement involved movement of the drains. The chief target of the inspection is a water-trapping wrinkle that commonly extended at a 45-degree angle across the inboard rear corner of the fuel tank floor. Such a large wrinkle can trap quite a bit of water. More than a few 182 owners reported discovering their tanks harbored as much as a quart, sometimes more.

The entire "smoothing and blending" process is something akin to eliminating the wrinkles in a carpet. Stomping on one wrinkle can make it vanish, only to reappear somewhere else on the carpet. Often what's needed is to take up the whole carpet and lay it again. In the fuel bladder case, this move required relocation of the drains. Cessna has provided a quick-drain kit for $89 (part number SK-206-24 and 25).

The 1972 through 1974 models in particular seemed to be afflicted by mishaps stemming from water in the fuel. Fuel caps and wrinkled bladder tanks bear much of the blame. This as a '73 model.

Rock n' Roll!

Another move mandated by AD 84-10-1 is the famed "rock n' roll preflight." The aircraft is sumped normally, on level ground. Then the tail is lowered to within five inches of the ground while rocking the wings 10 inches up and down at least 12 times. Then the sumps are drained again, checking for any water that may have been shaken out.

After the main wrinkle has been eliminated, the AD specifies that the amount of fluid trapped by any other wrinkles must be determined. If this trapped fluid measures more than three ounces, the aircraft is placarded with the "rock n' roll preflight" procedure, making those moves mandatory before flight. The wording of AD 84-10-1 has been criticized as vague. For example, it's unclear whether these "rocking and rolling" moves have to be done simultaneously, something clearly beyond the ability of just one person. Plus, pilots of petite stature would probably find the tail-lowering maneuver impossible. And it's unclear as to just how owners of float-equipped aircraft are supposed to perform these moves.

As more and more 182s come into compliance with this AD, some evidence is emerging that it has been effective. Life-threatening wrinkles have been detected and corrected. However, there have also been reports of heavy labor costs for airplanes with particularly convoluted wrinkles.

What Else Can You Do About Water?

People often tend to overlook the matter of where the water comes from that puddles in the wrinkled fuel tanks. Answer: from leaking fuel caps. Stop water from coming in there, and you eliminate most of the problem. Unfortunately, the flush caps that were in use from mid-1959 until 1984 had great potential for leakage. The solution to the problem is use of so-called umbrella fuel caps similar to those used on Skyhawks. Cessna has kits for these costing $45.30 each. They can be one of the best investments a Skylane pilot can make.

Some other devices intended to prevent undrainable water from reaching the engine seem to us worthwhile. One consists of two small reservoir tanks located near the fuel system low point in the aircraft's belly. They fit under the 182's cabin floorboards. Designed by Skylane pilot Rodney Gross, who experienced a water-contaminated engine failure on takeoff in a 182. These tanks allow water that was not drained during pre-flight sumping to settle, and are equipped with quick drains of their own, so that water can be eliminated from the system.

Gross's system has received a revised STC, and cannot be installed until the rest of the fuel tank AD has been complied with. "These tanks are just an insurance policy," Gross said. "They don't solve the problem."

Priced at $330, the system is available from Saturn Components Corporation, 15268 Earlham Street, Pacific Palisades, Calif. 90272, (213) 454-6714.

Plastic Tanks

Another way of eliminating wrinkled fuel tanks is to install more rigid plastic ones offered by Monarch Air and Development. The tanks are made of fiberglass impregnated with a vinyl-ester resin developed by Dow Chemical. According to Monarch head William Barton, the material is the most corrosion resistant in the plastics market today. Tanks made of the resin have been used in refineries for years to process aromatic compounds and are now being used, in fact, for underground storage of aircraft fuel.

Walls of the tanks are about 0.0075 inches thick. Replacing fuel bladders with Monarch's plastic tanks requires the wings to be taken off and rivets removed from the inboard ribs of both wings. Then a section of each fuel bay must be removed to make way for a new sump (which, unlike Cessna's, Barton says, "really is at the lowest point of the tank..."). Finally, the ribs are re-riveted and the wings re-mated.

A set of standard-sized Monarch tanks costs $1,600; larger ones cost $200 more.

Cost/Performance/Specifications

Model	Year	Average Retail Price	Cruise Speed (kts)	Useful Load (lbs)	Fuel Std/Opt (gals)	Engine	TBO (hrs)	Overhaul Cost
182A	1956-57	$14,700	117	1,010	55	230-hp Cont. O-470-L	1,500	$9,000
182A,B	1958-59	$16,500	120	1,090	55	230-hp Cont. O-470-L	1,500	$9,000
182C,D	1960-61	$18,000	123	1,090	65-84	230-hp Cont. O-470-L	1,500	$9,000
182E,F	1962-63	$19,300	123	1,190	65-84	230-hp Cont. O-470-R	1,500	$9,000
182G,H	1964-65	$20,250	123	1,190	65-84	230-hp Cont. O-470-R	1,500	$9,000
182J,K	1966-67	$21,300	123	1,175	65-84	230-hp Cont. O-470-R	1,500	$9,000
182L,M	1968-69	$22,750	123	1,175	65-84	230-hp Cont. O-470-R	1,500	$9,000
182N	1970-71	$24,500	121	1,310	65-84	230-hp Cont. O-470-R	1,500	$9,000
182P	1972-74	$17,300	125	1,169	61-80	230-hp Cont. O-470-R	1,500	$9,000
182P II	1975-76	$35,800	125	1,169	61-80	230-hp Cont. O-470-S	1,500	$9,000
182Q II	1977-78	$41,200	121	1,169	61-80	230-hp Cont. O-470-U	1,500	$9,500
182Q II	1979-80	$49,700	121	1,390	61-80	230-hp Cont. O-470-U	1,500	$9,500
182R II	1981-82	$61,500	124	1,373	92	230-hp Cont. O-470-U	1,500	$9,500
T-182R II	1981-82	$68,500	157	1,319	92	235-hp Lyc. O-540-L3C5D	2,000	$12,000
182R II	1983-84	$74,800	124	1,373	92	230-hp Cont. O-470-U	1,500	$9,500
T-182R II	1983-84	$86,800	157	1,319	92	235-hp Lyc. O-540-L3C5D	2,000	$12,000
182R II	1985-86	$95,000	124	1,373	92	230-hp Cont. O-470-U	1,500	$9,500

Installation time has averaged about 35 hours, according to the company.

One knowledgeable observer said he believed the plastic tanks should last as long as the airplanes in which they are installed. Bladder tanks typically begin deteriorating after five to nine years. Fuel stains underneath the wings betray the deterioration. Brand-new bladders cost about $1,200 apiece, though some can be reconditioned for from $250 to $450. Monarch Air and Development, Inc., P.O. Box 416, Oakland, Ore. 97462, (503) 459-2056.

Water Separator

Another product that emerged a few years ago appeared to be a sensible one to help eliminate engine water ingestion, assuming it got that far. This was the Silver-Wells water separator, which was basically an enlarged gascolator, so commodious that it increases the maximum permissible amount of water trapped by wrinkles from three ounces to a full quart under provisions of the AD.

The Silver-Wells separator cost $500 and had been marketed by TurboPlus, Inc. at Gig Harbor, Wash. But sales have been discontinued.

Seat Tracks

The Skylane was snared in the big AD (87-20-03) roundup of Cessnas needing seat track inspections. Aircraft with more than 1,000 hours must get them at every annual inspection, or every 100 hours if in commercial service. The purpose is to prevent the type of seat slippage that might lead to loss of control, especially in nose-high attitudes as on takeoff, when a pilot seat careening backward might be disastrous. An extra provision for preventing unwanted seat slippage is made in the form of a SAF-T-STOP that attaches to the seat rail behind the pilots' seats and is locked in place by the clamping action of a thumb screw. It sells for $29.95, or a few dollars less by the Cessna Pilots Assn.

Carb Ice

In figures released by the NTSB in 1977, an alarming number of accidents involving carb ice and 182s emerged. While the 182 isn't as prone to carb ice problems as some other designs (notably the C-150), anyone who regularly flies a Skylane in heavy weather should consider investing in a carb ice detector.

Crunch

When shopping for a used 182, examine the firewall carefully. The nose-heaviness of the 182, coupled with the airplane's heavy elevator forces, makes for frequent hard landings with a potential for gear-bending nose-low landings. The firewall is usually the first to suffer. Another casualty of the 182's nose-heavy handling is the nosewheel assembly, with buckling and shimmies the usual result.

In 1987 the Cessna Pilots Assn. reported it was investigating a number of landing gear strut failures that had occurred on 1963 C-182F models. The NTSB also was checking out the matter. Inspection of some failed struts indicated the failures occurred where there was fretting at the points where the strut comes in contact with the saddle and clamp. The association recommended the landing gear be checked for proper installation involving the 80 percent contact with the saddle, along with proper torque on the bolts, and if at all possible, magnaflux inspection.

Any landing gear strut showing significant wear from contact with the saddle clamp in the forward portion, said the association, "would seem to be suspect."

Overall

Plenty of power, a big wing, heavy pitch forces, solid handling and a simple, safe fuel system (providing AD 84-10-1 has been complied with) make the Skylane one of the safest buys around.

Maintenance

The 182 is a simple, robust aircraft, with a healthy, but normal appetite for maintenance as the fleet ages. When we evaluated this airplane in 1979, readers reported annuals in the $250-$300 range. Today's readers have cited annuals in the $1,000 to $2,000 neighborhood. Looking at those numbers, it seems to us that the 182 line hasn't become any less reliable mechanically, but that maintenance and parts costs have gone through the roof.

The Skylane shares the same McCauley/Hartzell prop AD that encumbers many aircraft designs, Cessna and otherwise, equipped with constant-speed propellers. With the exception of this and the fuel bladder problem, the AD scene for the 182 is relatively clear.

Powerplant

The Continental O-470 engine has a good record, although it doesn't seem to be as reliable as the four-cylinder carbureted Lycomings. TBO for the O-470 was 1,500 hours until 1983, when it was boosted to 2,000 for the O-470-U model.   A well-maintained engine should meet or exceed the TBO. The key to longevity on this engine appears to be a rigorous break-in period. "Firewall that sucker," is how one O-470 operator put it. The theory is that the heat of heavy initial operation seats the piston rings and valve seats firmly in place, cutting oil consumption and smoothing operation.

Chief virtue of all Skylanes: a big, roomy cabin tough to load out of the weight and balance envelope. It was one of many Cessnas affected by the seat track inspection AD, however.

Some 1975 and 1976 Skylanes had special engine problems that used airplane buyers should be aware of. Aircraft built in those years bore the 182 P II designation, and featured the O-470-S engine, which had a new ring design. Some of these engines had break-in problems, in some cases using as much as a quart of oil per hour. Despite its efforts, Continental apparently never really figured out what was wrong, and instead switched to to higher-compression O-470-U in 1977. The most plausible theory offered to date is that the S-series engines were babied in break-in by well-meaning owners. Check for tell-tale high oil consumption on these engines.

Valve Problems

A few years ago, Continental issued a mandatory service bulletin covering some

75 new and rebuilt O-470 engines evidently shipped with the wrong exhaust valves. It seems that soft, stainless steel valves were installed in the engines by mistake. This engine has hardened Nitralloy valve guides, which promptly chewed up the soft valves, a process resulting in stuck valves and metal particles wreaking havoc throughout the oil system. Proper valves for the O-470 engine carry part number 637781.

At roughly the same time, Continental sent out about 40 O-470 cylinder assemblies (P/N 646680) fitted with the wrong valves. By the time the problem was discovered, Continental had been sending these faulty assemblies out for almost a full year.

As of April, 1985, about 15 engines had been replaced due to extensive metal contamination of the oil. The rest were being reworked with the correct valves. During the valve replacement, valve guides must be reamed out to remove any metal build-ups.

Getting the Lead Out

The Skylane seems to have suffered less from 100LL problems than other 80-octane airplanes. Nevertheless, the proven process of careful leaning, plug rotation, and 50-hour oil changes is the best policy, along with use of TCP should lead fouling be suspected. Skylanes have paper induction air filter elements that can swell up in the presence of moisture and restrict airflow. Even worse, old paper filters can decompose to the point where they can be ingested by the engine. Such an ingestion was blamed as cause of a fatal Skylane crash leading to AD 84-26-02, which put a life limit of 500 hours on paper filters. The filter on the downed Skylane reportedly was more than 10 years old, and had accumulated 1,100 hours in the time of the crash.

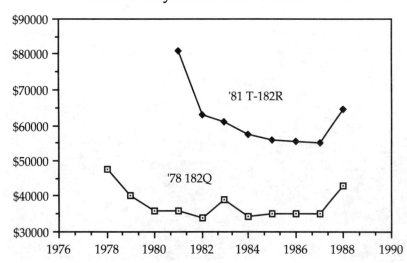

Cessna Skylane Resale Value

This AD did not include foam induction air filters such as those made by Brackett Aircraft Co., which recommends their filters be replaced every 12 months or 100 hours if one inch thick, and every 200 hours if two inches thick. Since paper filters range in price from about $20 to over $100, the Bracketts might actually be cheaper to use. They are priced from $10 to a little under $60, and replacement filters cost even less. Brackett claims its filters stop potentially damaging particles down to 15 microns for a longer period than paper filters.

Aside from water and dirt, another factor that can cause great distress to paper, and maybe even foam filters is a "backfire" in the manifold system that belches flame out into the filter. This flame can burn portions of the filter into ashes and cinders that do no good for the engine. Suggestion: next time a backfire is encountered on startup, shut down, get out, and check the condition of the induction air filter.

In 1980 Cessna introduced a turbocharged Skylane with a carbureted, not fuel injected, Lycoming O-540-L3C5D putting out 235 hp. Judging from service difficulty reports, it seems to be operating okay.

Modifications

The marriage between airframe and powerplant has been such a happy one in the case of the 182, that there have been relatively few STC'd mods. EAA and Petersen Aviation both hold the autogas STCs for the 182 series, with Petersen's usable for both leaded and unleaded fuels (see Owner Comments for more on the difference in fuels).

R/STOL by Sierra Industries at Garner Municipal Airport in Uvalde, Tex., offers an extensive STOL mod. Less elaborate systems featuring new leading edge cuffs, sealed ailerons and stall fences are marketed by Horton STOL-craft, Inc., Wellington Municipal Airport, Wellington, Kan.

The major slick-up mods offered for the 182 line come from Charlie Siebel's Flight Bonus, Inc., the rights of which were sold in 1988 to Horton, Inc. Kit parts formerly made from thermoformed ABS plastic are now made of fiberglass-polyester. Depending on the year of manufacture, Siebel's slick-ups promise to boost a 182's cruise speed from 12 to 20 mph.

In 1981 the Turbo Skylane came on the scene with a carbureted Lycoming engine.

C.S. Industries, an engine and accessory overhaul facility in Viola, Kan., (316-545-7158) has STCs to modify Skylane engines to add fuel injection and turbocharging. Overhaul and conversion to the O-470 costs about $24,500, assuming the engine is a normal run-out.

Owners' Group

Check out the Cessna Pilot's Assn., located at Wichita's Mid-Continent Airport at 2120 Airport Road, Box 12948, Wichita, Kan. 67277, (316) 946-4777.

Owner Comments

I own a 1981 Cessna Skylane 182R, and have put over 800 hours on it since new. There is a lot of good news about the plane, and a little bad.

First the good news: Performance. The Skylane is a terrific instrument platform, both stable and forgiving yet able to fly fast approaches when mixing it up with the big planes at major airports. Its outstanding range adds flexibility for hard IFR. Its short-field performance is exemplary, as are its load-carrying capability and, more important, its wide center-of-gravity tolerance. I can truly haul four people, full fuel, a panel full of avionics, and a little luggage, and be within both payload and cg limits.

Its controls, while not light, are balanced and authoritative, so that it handles crosswinds and turbulence very well. In fact, its smooth ride, coupled with generous inside space, make it a comfortable cross-country machine. The Skylane's speed is consistently better than book, flying at over 140 knots at most altitudes and weights. Fuel burn is as advertised—12.5 gph at 75 percent.

There's plenty of room on the panel and in the payload for a full complement of avionics (King, Stormscope) and other options (standby vacuum pumps, carb ice detector). It's noisy; headphones and intercom are a must.

Now the bad news: Cost. While parts availability and backup have presented no problems, I've had too many opportunities to find out. Annuals have cost from $500 to $1,800, even though painstaking maintenance is performed at every 50-hour oil change. Operating cost, exclusive of hangaring, insurance, and allowance for overhaul, exceeds $40 per hour. All three left-side cylinders needed rings and valves at 600 hours, although the subsequent reduction in oil use (from 4.5 hours per quart to nine) indicates there may have been a problem from the beginning.

Now the worst news: Reliability. I'm on my seventh alternator control unit. It's no fun while IFR suddenly to be reduced to battery power, but it has happened so often that I carry a spare ACU so that at least when (and if) I land, I can get an immediate repair. Neither Cessna nor my repair shop has found a solution.

In summary, the Skylane offers balanced performance, with a cost penalty. Buy a clean used one, but if the alternator control unit is over 10 months old, replace it immediately before venturing into a cloud.

Dr. Stephen J. Browne
Cambridge, Mass.

I bought my 1981 C-182 new for $58,500 complete with the Skylane II package and Narco DME. I wanted a full four-passenger fixed- gear that I could move into immediately after getting my license, as well as one that would be a stable IFR trainer. I got my instrument ticket in the plane, and my wife (she's also a pilot) and I have owned it for four years.

Total time is 450 hours and we have perceived no engine problems. I knew that huge oil consumption was a possibility, and true to form I use a quart every four hours—always have. I change the oil and filter every 50 hours and have an oil analysis done at every change. It shows normal.

Fuel economy has not been outstanding at 12-13 gph but it is outweighed by the 1,300 pound payload and 92-gallon tanks. My bladder is out well before the six-hour range. The comfort level is quite good, and coupled with headsets for all four seats, a four-hour trip to Mexico is quite pleasant at 142 knots true.

Besides the usual ARC radio glitches, squawks have included a broken carb heat control cable (my wife's heavy hand!) at 400 hours, a turn coordinator out at 410 hours, a new battery at 375 hours, three new tires at 390 hours, as well as new landing lights every 30 hours. Other than these items, we have been trouble free.

An annual inspection without any major problems runs a very healthy $1,500+.

I've been told that late-model 182s normally run half this amount, but I've never seen it. As a result, my hourly maintenance costs clock in at $25 per hour.

My wife and I are happy with our airplane and have no plans for upgrading. We have a neighbor who has owned his 1962 Skylane since new and loves it still. We fly to our mountain home, where the airport elevation is 6,000 feet, a dozen times each summer, and have never had a problem taking off from the 3,000-foot strip even at gross. For us, the Skylane has lived up to our expectations beautifully. I'd buy another one!

Dr. Tom Bales
Novato, Calif.

With Charlie Seibel's full-speed equipment I cruise 160-165 mph at 10,000 feet on 2,250 rpm and 18.5 inches at about 12 or 11.5 gph and use a quart of 50-weight Shell every three to four hours. With RSTOL strips, 1,500-foot takeoffs are easily manageable.

Instrument panel is big and imposing, though ARC radios are not. This is from a '72 model. Extra little complexities for a fixed-gear aircraft are cowl flaps and variable pitch prop.

Granted, it is a little ponderous compared to my Bonanza, but it's a wheels down grandpappy airplane and rock solid for IFR—very predictable when flying the numbers for climb, descent, approaches, etc. Baggage compartment gets wet in medium rain or more, otherwise it's tight, warm in winter and, being a high wing, cooler than a low wing in summer.

Maintenance has been very predictable—no surprises, but then I'm meticulous. Nothing's too small for attention; therefore my $2,000 annuals are high. The 25-hour checkup and oil change is around $250 with no problems with either parts availability or backup.

My wife and I spent three weeks plus in the airplane last summer going to British Columbia, Alaska and the west, having plenty of room throughout—though packed stem to stern with camping, living and survival gear.

Henry G. Wischmeyer
Dallas, Tex.

We have owned a 1979 Skylane since 1981. This aircraft was purchased with 700 hours on it. It has an all ARC panel with the exception of a King 62A DME and a Sigtronics four-station intercom. In four years we have had minor navcom trouble four times—trouble that takes about $100 and three days to be corrected each time. No trouble at all with the 300 A/P or KN62A. We average 100+ hours of pleasure flying per year. Annuals average about $350. One went to $600 because a jug had to be reworked at 1,000 hours. Seems Continental used a hammer to seat an exhaust valve guide. Other than that, the cylinders always hang in there at 72 to 76.

Our useful load is 1,146 as equipped. With a full load and 75 percent power at 6,500 to 8,500 feet we true at 135 knots. A light weights we reach 145 knots. It burns 12 gph and a quart of oil every four hours. For local flying we can get the burn down to nine gph.

Generally speaking, we like the overall performance and big plane feel it has over, say, a 172 or Cherokee. On the downside, we might wish for a little better fit and finish All of the door-to-airframe fits are atrocious, with very bad air leaks. We had a bad spell of water leaks which we finally stopped on our own through judicious use of silicon sealant. I can say that after four years the paint and interior have held up real good. We keep it hangared.

There is one mod we were really interested in: the Seibel speed mod. But another Skylane owner at our airport did it, and the only good thing he had to say about it was that it didn't slow his plane down, which was kind of disappointing because we just know that the ol' 182 could be Mooney-ized a la 201.

Bob Billa, Jr.
San Antonio, Tex.

The six-cylinder Continentals have a pretty good record, in general, and seem to suffer less from 100LL than other 80- octane engines. They also are approved for autogas. But watch out for carb ice. Another disadvantage: a relatively low 1,500-hour TBO.

I purchased my 1979 Skylane II in the summer of 1983. The airplane has reportedly been hangared since new. The two navcoms, ADF, and encoding transponder are ARC equipment. The ARC radios have naturally given me some difficulty, but a nearby shop knows them well and repairs them at what I think is a reasonable cost. I have also replaced a fuel gauge and sender unit. I have replaced the EGT gauge and have had the clock/timer rebuilt. I've also noticed that the static eliminators "spontaneously" break, and naturally I wonder. I've also noticed areas where the paint is peeling along with areas where filiform corrosion is appearing under the paint.

There was a problem with the control-mounted microphone switch wire, and I've replaced some panel lights which are outrageously priced by Cessna. Watch out for the Gill battery. I replaced mine. Gill has changed designators, and although Aircraft Components, Inc.'s catalog says the Gill 242 replaced the previous battery, in fact it's the Gill G243.

My annuals cost from $375 to $450. The first one uncovered some problems while last year's found nothing significant. I also have 100-hour inspections done, and I have oil analysis done when the mechanic remembers to submit the sample. I change the oil every 50 hours.

I love my 182. My wife, at all of five feet tall and 83 pounds, finds it too big an aircraft to handle. My flight instructor suggested electric trim might help a small person like her.

Although the 182 leaks like a sieve, I don't plan on leaving it outdoors or flying it in the rain anyway. I burn about a quart of oil every two hours. I get a lot of oil under the fuselage. I was told not to fill it to the nine-quart level unless I am going on a long trip. I do this and I have never seen the oil level go below eight quarts. I've wondered if the engine would quit using oil altogether if there were only eight quarts in the crank case; however, I'm not going to try that out.

It may seem strange that there appear to be so many faults with this aircraft; I've not named them all, yet I like it so much. I'm very picky.

John S. Ford, M.D.
Texarkana, Tex.

In 1977, I bought a 1974 Skylane with an O-470-R Continental engine. There was only one previous owner. The tach indicated slightly more than 400 hours at that time. I have kept the airplane hangared and provide meticulous maintenance. It has been a delight to fly, and is particularly stable for IFR conditions. Annuals have generally been $600 to $1,000, although one annual was $200 when I worked with the mechanic.

After initially flying the Skylane for about 100 hours from time of purchase, I encountered a significant engine problem. The oil was found to be contaminated with metal particles during a routine oil change. This resulted in an expensive early major overhaul. It was discovered during the overhaul that a normally floating wrist pin had frozen and was rubbing on a cylinder wall, creating metal flaking. The wrist pin had apparently frozen due to overheating.

It is my understanding that Cessna tightened the cowling in 1972. This resulted in slightly higher speeds, but apparently insufficient air was provided to cool the engine. The problem was improved in 1975 when the O-470-R engine was replaced by the -S model. The -S engine has additional oil passages that squirt oil on the back sides of the pistons. Heat is then relieved through the oil cooler.

The overhaul was performed by Lynn Quackenbush, located in Boeing Field, Seattle, phone: (206) 763-1912. In addition to the overhaul, he converted the -R engine to an -S engine at that time. Lynn is a fine craftsman and has the special equipment for the -S conversion. He has the reputation as one of the best mechanics in the Northwest.

The engine has performed flawlessly for several hundred hours since Lynn did his magic. I highly recommend that anyone with an -R engine have Lynn Quackenbush perform an -S conversion when the engine is disassembled for overhaul.

I encountered a more recent problem with the use of automobile fuel. About a year ago, I purchased the EAA auto fuel STC. Unleaded autogas ate the foam carburetor float and dislodged black particles from the bladder tanks. The EAA felt that the problem was due to alcohol in the fuel, but testing did not indicate the presence of alcohol.

I believe the problem is due to aromatics in unleaded fuel. I have subsequently switched to the Petersen Aviation autofuel STC that allows both leaded and unleaded auto gas. Regular leaded automobile fuel has been used for the last year with no difficulty.

Ben Prince
Richland, Wash.

Cessna Skylane RG

The Skylane RG has won favor in the used-plane market as an economy retractable that is strong on room, load and comfort and quite a bit less expensive than the bellwether Mooney 201. It is, however, nagged by mechanical and airframe shortcomings that warrant close inspection.

Most prominent of these is the landing gear system, which, judging from the FAA's Service Difficulty Reports, carries on a long Cessna tradition of retractable-gear bedevilment manifested in both its singles and twins. Prospective buyers should also be on the lookout for airframe quality control shortcomings like leaking windshields and doors.

Despite a sizable proportion of prangs due to gear problems, the airplane has an excellent safety record compared to other aircraft in its class when it comes to fatal accidents.

History

The aircraft has undergone no major changes over the years since it was introduced in 1978. But there have been lots of little ones that are significant in correcting a myriad of glitches. Buyers should make a close check of service bulletins that were complied with, or ignored, on this airplane—especially those concerning the various components of the landing gear system.

The biggest changes to the line occurred in 1979 when the bladder tanks (and all their well-known problems) were dropped in favor of integral fuel tanks of larger capacity. Also, that year the turbo model was brought out. Among the smaller changes made through the years were—in 1980—a new door latch and pin system designed to help seal the doors better, an electric fan for the avionics, to help cool the radios while taxiing, and redesigned wing root ventilators. (Some owners of '79 models complained that these would simply pop open during high-speed flight.)

In 1981 the Skylane RGs got improved battery access along with a new muffler for better heating (rear-seat passengers complain about cold feet in '79 models) and an improved fuel selector valve with more positive detents. (At least one fatal crash was reported where the pilot had the selector positioned between tanks.)

In 1983 the extension speed for the first 20-degrees of flaps was raised from 95 knots to 120 knots, as an aid to slowing down the aircraft. A low-vacuum warning light was offered, as was an electric six-cylinder primer system replacing the manual one for easier starting. Also, the landing gear "up" indicator light was replaced with a red "gear unsafe" light. This goes on whenever power goes to the gear pump motor, or when the gear is in transit.

In addition, the nose gear doors were redesigned so the door skins overlapped the lower cowl skin, eliminating butt joints. Service Difficulty Reports show three instances where the nose gear doors interfered with proper operation of the gear.

Thankfully, the main gear has been spared door problems—because it has no doors.

In 1984 the Skylane RGs received new "improved" composite fuel caps, and rear-seat shoulder harnesses were made standard equipment instead of options. (The SDRs suggest that leaking fuel caps have been a problem with the R182s.) Also, the copilot got a standard control wheel and rudder pedals, so these would not have to be purchased as extra-cost options.

Performance

Since the Skylane RG is most often compared with the Mooney 201, it should be noted up front that although the Mooney can be expected to beat out the Cessna in a flat-out, full-power heat at altitude, it won't do so by an embarrassing margin. In fact, when the Cessna 182RG is lightly loaded, it will give away only maybe three to four knots to the low-winger.

Big loads, on the other hand, seem to have a more significant retardant effect on the Cessna than with other aircraft. One owner plotted the phenomenon as giving the Skylane RG a boost of two knots for every 100 pounds it was below gross weight.

The Cessna by no means is completely overshadowed by the Mooney 201. In a side-by side flyoff by *The Aviation Consumer* between the two aircraft (when both had two aboard and about three-quarters fuel) the Cessna showed itself to have the better climb rate and to be much more adept at getting into and out of airports than the Mooney. On top of that it showed off much more agile ground handling.

Owners of the nonturboed R182s talk about getting a healthy 150 to 160 knots at top cruise (75 percent power), burning 12 to 14 gph. Turbo owners report getting 160 to 165 knots at 9,000 to 13,000 feet with about the same fuel burn. One turbo owner reported getting 178 knots on 66 percent power at 19,000 feet with light weights.

With its 235 hp, the RG also climbs well. Full power is available on the turbo all the way to 20,000 feet. One turbo pilot said he got a 1,000-fpm climb all the way to 20 grand with full power and could pull 750 fpm nicely on a cruise climb. Said another, "I have climbed through 14,000 feet with an inch of ice at 900 fpm, and I'm here to tell you this is the true value of a strong turbocharged engine."

Range of the Cessna is nothing to sneeze at, either. With 81 gallons usable on '79 and later models, that's enough fuel for six hours of flying at high cruise speeds.

Handling

The aircraft is typical Cessna—i.e., heavy on the pitch controls, especially in the landing flare, but stable as a rock in cruise. Said one owner: "Once trimmed, it will stay put. I don't feel a real need for altitude hold on autopilot, even in hard IFR." Said another, "I lift weights for a hobby, but still had trouble holding full aft control wheel in a full stall." But he added that as an aerobatic pilot he felt he had completely explored all its flight characteristics and found them to be "fault-free." Nevertheless, the big, effective flaps do create pitch changes that require retrimming.

One flier summed it up: "It makes no unusual demands on pilot ability. It is a very safe, forgiving and rugged aircraft."

Cabin Load and Comfort

Skylane RG pilots rave about the ability of the aircraft to haul people and baggage—in spades. And they love the roominess. One six-foot-four pilot whose wife is six-two said, "We are able to stretch out and be comfortable even with four people in the plane. Even the A36 Bonanza cannot match the Skylane in interior comfort on a long trip, in my opinion." They talk about a loading envelope that would be hard to exceed and mention useful loads with IFR-equipment of over 1,100 pounds. On top of that, the double doors allow easy entry for front and rear seats, and headroom is good both front and rear.

Struts and all, the RG clips along at 155 knots or better. Light weights give a disproportionate speed boost.

The handicaps on the RG, on the other hand, are a loud cabin din, occasional leaky doors and windows, cold rear seats and, as we mentioned before, wing root air vents that sometimes pop out at higher speeds and provide unwanted air conditioning. Some RG pilots also complained of uncomfortable engine vibration at cruise.

Safety Record

During the first five years of production, the Skylane RG logged a marvelous safety profile compared with other single-engine retractables in its class—when it comes to fatal accidents. When stacked up with 17 other aircraft, the RG came out best by far, eclipsing even that longtime safety star, the Beech 33. The one fly in the statistical ointment, however, is that the Skylane RG has not flown enough hours to compare with others of the group like the Piper Arrow or Bonanza.

And in the last few years fatalities have been chipping away at the RG's clean record. We tallied 23 fatal accidents through 1985. But most of these resulted from factors that couldn't be blamed on aircraft shortcomings. Nine were weather related and three stemmed from medical problems—heart attack, stroke, alcohol.

Another two were blamed on buzzing, and details from three others were still missing. Equipment failure apparently caused another fatal crash after the pilot departed IFR with a defective gyro horizon and later lost control on a missed approach. And we mentioned above the accident involving the fuel selector.

The total accident record of the Skylane RG is not, however, so golden. The Beech 33 comes out better in this category. Our survey of accident causes shows that landing gear problems were major factors in the greatest proportion of nonfatal RG accidents. We counted 21 of these from 1978 through 1985.

The greatest number involved the failure of the gear to extend, or a collapse on landing or takeoff. On only a small portion of these was the pilot blamed for inadvertently retracting it during touch-and-goes. And, interestingly enough, we noted no instances where the pilot simply forgot to extend the gear on landing.

Next largest nonfatal accident category for the RGs involved hard landings. We tallied 15 of these. The typical scenario involved a bounce, damaging the prop and possibly running off the side of the runway. On almost half of these the nosegear eventually collapsed.

Third biggest category was engine problems—we counted a dozen. Over half the stoppages occurred after takeoff. Three were blamed on magneto problems—the cam screw coming loose—and an Airworthiness Directive was issued to address the matter. Three others were related to internal malfunctions, one to water ingestion, and another quit after changing tanks on letdown. It's worth noting that none of the engine failures resulted in a fatal accident in the RG.

The next largest accident category involved fuel exhaustion—eight cases were noted. In a couple of cases fuel had siphoned out because of "unsecured" fuel caps.

Maintenance Considerations

The Skylane RGs are plagued with a sizable number of problems that merit buyer attention. Here's a list gathered from owner reports and FAA Service Difficulty Reports:

• Landing gear malfunctions. The litany of problems with the gear chronicled by the SDRs almost defies description. It's actually difficult to isolate any one or several main causes. Whereas most SDR problems usually can be tallied in singles or maybe tens, we counted over nine pages full of gear-related problems—with about a dozen cases on each page. Consider that maybe only a tenth of the cases in the field even get reported to the FAA, and you have some idea of the apparent magnitude of the Skylane RG gear problem over the years.

Some examples: main landing gear actuator bolts loose, broken or sheared; chafed hydraulic line completely failed, pilot unable to lower gear and lock; rudder cable rubbed hole thru emergency hand pump gear down line; control cable to carb heat rubbed thru hydraulic line to power pac; nose landing gear actuator hose ruptured in flight; downlock actuator leaking, found piston rod assy. scored; relay became intermittent, causing landing gear to fail to operate either up or down; landing gear failed to extend due screw missing from gear motor circuit breaker; hydraulic hose on nose landing gear actuator has a tendency to kink in the crease and stop the flow of fluid; solenoid stuck closed, causing hydraulic pump to run continuously until circuit breaker popped; nose landing gear door grabbing on fuselage skin when it tried to open, etc. etc., *ad nauseam*.

• Shimmy dampeners. Problems were legion, involving broken clamp pins, broken attach bolts, worn bellcrank bolts, cracked barrels, etc. At least one Cessna Service Bulletin (80-67) was aimed at correcting the problem with a modification kit. Two pilots, however, said they found a cure to nosewheel vibration by increasing tire inflation to 55 psi.

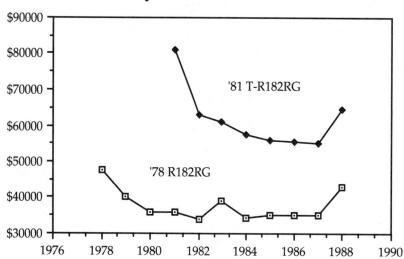

Cessna Skylane RG Resale Value

'81 T-R182RG

'78 R182RG

• Balky throttles. At least five different service bulletins and mod kits were put out to cure the problem, and any used RG should have them installed.

• Instrument panel "eyebrow" lights that flicker out quickly. Multiple replacements seem to be the rule. Said one owner, "I buy them by the dozen. If anyone can figure out a fix, I'll happily buy the STC."

• Cabin air and water leaks. Service bulletins address the chronic Cessna problem of leaks around the windshield and wing roots. "Repeated applications of silicone only retuned the sound of the air leak," said one owner. "Finally, they removed the windshield to discover about a six-inch gap in the sealing gasket."

• Other problems noted included turbos leaking oil, vacuum pump drive shafts shearing, aileron hinge cotter key holes badly aligned, Bendix starters failing, exhaust stacks cracked and alternator mounting bolts worn.

AD History

Despite the arduous roster of problems tabulated above, the Skylane RG has managed to get by with relatively few Airworthiness Directives, so far. And most of those that were issued affected engine accessories like the Bendix magnetos (six ADs called for inspections and mods) and the Slick magneto (one AD). An inspection was also required of the Stewart-Warner oil cooler for leakage.

Much-publicized ADs called for inspection of fuel tank caps for leakage, and for inspection of bladder fuel tanks on '78 RGs for wrinkles and installation of quick drains. Others required inspection of aileron hinges for the correct location of cotter pins. Replacement of certain Marvel-Schebler carburetors and Airborne vacuum pumps was called for—as it was on many other aircraft.

Modifications

R/STOL Systems, of Sierra Industries has taken over the full list of Robertson mods. They are at P.O. Box 5184, Uvalde, Tex. 78802, (512) 278-4381.

Resale Value

After an encouraging rise in equity for RG owners in 1981, the aircraft disclosed a desultory curve in resale value to 1985, but then began to rebound. Interestingly, they overtook and exceeded the cost of the Mooney 201 in recent years. Hence, a 1980 RG goes for about $58,000 according to the *Aircraft Bluebook Price Digest* vs. about $56,500 for the Mooney 201. Just a few years ago the Mooney cost several thousand dollars more on the used-plane market.

Owner Organization

Check with the Cessna Pilots Assn. at Wichita Mid-Continent Airport, P.O. Box 12948, Wichita, Kans. 67277, (316) 946-4777.

Owner Comments

We have owned and operated three 182RGs—one normally aspirated and two turbos. We have found them to be among the best aircraft to put on our rental line of all those Cessna has built.

But magnetos tend to cause ignition noise on radios. The engines vibrate a fair amount and cause general loosening of parts, including beacons, landing light bulbs, alternator filters and avionics. The starter Bendix is weak engaging, particularly in cold weather. The windshields leak around the base during flight in rain, and the black instrument deck covers warp. Despite the above, we recommend the aircraft highly.

Field Morey, President
Morey Airplane Co.
Middleton, Wisc.

The only problems I have had so far on my one-year-old Skylane RG are the electric flap switch and the No. 2 comm radio—both repaired under warranty. I have been very well pleased with this aircraft. The strong points are the roomy, comfortable cabin, excellent stability in rough air and smooth, six-hour cruising range, easy cold-weather starting, good load-carrying ability, a great-performing Lycoming O-540 engine and excellent short-field performance.

On a low pass for the camera, the R182RG looks like this with the gear retracted. It also looks like this sometimes when the gear won't extend for landing.

Also, it makes no unusual demands on pilot ability. It is a very safe, forgiving and rugged aircraft.

On the down side is the rather poor visibility, a too noisy cockpit that requires either ear plugs or a headset, mediocre Sperry avionics and heavy pitch forces—especially in the landing flare. It must be properly trimmed in all flight attitudes.

It cruises at 140 knots true at 65 percent power, burns 11-12 gph and uses one quart of Aeroshell 15-50 each 10 hours. Insurance is $2,000 per year and includes liability, property damage and hull. I felt the $930 cost of a recent annual was rather excessive for a new aircraft with no serious glitches.

T. Gorman
Yarmouth, Me.

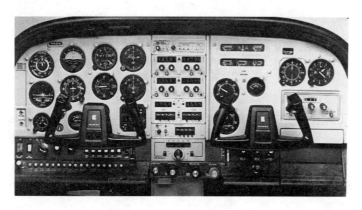

Fail-prone instrument panel eyebrow lights are a constant source of frustration for some RG owners. ARC avionics in later years receive more passable ratings from users.

My '79 Skylane RG has been highly reliable and quite comfortable, especially on long trips. I am 6'4" and my wife is 6'2", and we are able to stretch out and be comfortable even with four people in the plane. Even the A36 Bonanza cannot match the Skylane in interior comfort on a long trip, in my opinion.

Maintenance has run about $1,000 to $1,300 a year, including parts. I do my own oil changes and have assisted on annuals several times. In five years I've got about 1,100 hours on the plane. I've had to replace a flap motor, the brake drums with chrome discs, the turn-and-bank indicator and the vacuum pump. I am now on the third battery; they seem to die at about 18 to 24 months, despite my best efforts. I've also had the DG go out in the first 500 hours. And the Bendix starter broke this past month and cost about $250 to get fixed.

The plane has Cessna radios. Both navcoms have been reliable. The ADF has had an intermittent problem that's been worked on four times over the years. It worked reliably for the last two years, but is now back in the shop for a fifth time. The transponder has required three trips to the shop.

Kenneth B. Carpenter, M.D.
Knoxville, Tenn. 37939

Dealer warranty support on my 1979 Turbo Skylane RG was good, as far as the factory would allow. Cessna's support was fair for some things, but poor on others. Parts availability has been poor some of the time, and the prices often seem unrealistic.

We normally like to cruise between 9,000 and 13,000 feet and use 2300/23", which is 65 to 73 percent, depending on temp. Fuel consumption will be 12.5 to 14 gph and TAS from 155 to 165 knots a near gross. Performance has been good right up to maximum operating altitude of 20,000 feet.

As equipped (with a full panel of King digital avionics and a Century IIB autopilot), the useful load is 1,160 pounds. With full 88 gallons of fuel, that leaves 630 pounds payload. As with all Skylanes, the loading envelope is good, and it would be hard to exceed with normal people and cargo loads. Range with full fuel and comfortable reserves is more than 700 nm.

I'm a big person (6'3" and 200 pounds) and enjoy the large roomy cabin with plenty of headroom. The doors allow easy entry for both front and rear seats. The full articulating front seats adjust to tall and short as well as giving comfortable positions for long flights. Rear-seat headroom and legroom is good. Noise level is fairly high. Cessna's doors and windows are not fitted and sealed very well. The ventilation system is good; however the front wing root vents tend to come open unexpectedly at high speeds. (It was a good system for 120-knot Skyhawks.) Heating is okay for front seats, marginal in back, especially with the air leaks and high, cold altitudes. Carry a blanket.

Handling is typical Skylane—very stable with moderately balanced controls. Once trimmed, it will stay put. I don't feel a real need for altitude hold on autopilot, even in hard IFR.

It has very effective flaps both for extra lift and high drag. They do produce pitch changes which necessitate retrimming. Rudder control is adequate for pretty heavy crosswind landings.

The Lycoming engine requires much different procedures than the Continental O-470 in the fixed-gear Skylane. Throttle linkage and adjustment is very critical for the turbo model, to operate both carburetor and wastegate properly and smoothly. The modification kit available from Cessna took three or four times as long to install and adjust as Cessna estimated. The air intake flange on the carburetor air box broke off at about 300 hours while in flight, resulting in loss of turbocharging and drop in mp. The replacement box has a riveted flange rather than a crimped one and should hold up better.

Be really careful about using carb heat on the ground. The box with the flapper valve has big holes that can allow solid matter to enter, then go into the turbo when carb heat is applied. Cessna disputes this and wouldn't pay for a new turbocharger.

Incidentally, as long as I operate at high enough power settings to keep turbocharger activated, I have not had any carb ice problems. Engine temperatures normally run on the cool side of the green. Even at 18,000-20,000 feet and high

Cost/Performance/Specifications

Model	Year	Average Retail Price	Cruise Speed (kts)	Useful Load (lbs)	Fuel Std/Opt (gals)	Engine	TBO (hrs)	Overhaul Cost
R182	1978	$42,000	157	1,200	56/75	235-hp Lyc. O-540-J3C5D	2,000	$10,000
R182	1979	$45,000	157	1,200	88	235-hp Lyc. O-540-J3C5D	2,000	$10,000
TR182	1979	$47,000	173	1,150	88	235-hp Lyc. O-540-J3C5D	2,000	$11,000
R182	1980	$50,000	157	1,200	88	235-hp Lyc. O-540-J3C5D	2,000	$10,000
TR182	1980	$53,000	173	1,150	88	235-hp Lyc. O-540-J3C5D	2,000	$11,000
R182	1981	$57,000	157	1,200	88	235-hp Lyc. O-540-J3C5D	2,000	$10,000
TR182	1981	$61,000	173	1,150	88	235-hp Lyc. O-540-J3C5D	2,000	$11,000
R182	1982	$69,000	157	1,200	88	235-hp Lyc. O-540-J3C5D	2,000	$10,000
TR182	1982	$72,000	173	1,150	88	235-hp Lyc. O-540-J3C5D	2,000	$11,000
R182	1983	$82,500	157	1,200	88	235-hp Lyc. O-540-J3C5D	2,000	$10,000
TR182	1983	$86,000	173	1,150	88	235-hp Lyc. O-540-J3C5D	2,000	$11,000
R182	1984	$94,000	157	1,200	88	235-hp Lyc. O-540-J3C5D	2,000	$10,000
TR182	1984	$102000	173	1,150	88	235-hp Lyc. O-540-J3C5D	2,000	$11,000
R182	1985	$106000	157	1,200	88	235-hp Lyc. O-540-J3C5D	2,000	$10,000

cruise powers the temperatures stay low even with cowl flaps closed. I have had no vacuum pump problems yet, but will likely install the cooling kit available from the Cessna Pilots Assn.

We have had no gear problems, and so far no evidence of corrosion under paint. (The aircraft is hangared in Sacramento, Calif. with hot, dry summers and cool, damp winters.) The fuel caps are still sealing fine, but I will replace with vendor-produced new metal caps this winter as a precautionary measure.

We're on the third alternator control unit. This one, however, has been operating for about 350 hours. The windshield had a bad air and water leak when delivered. Repeated applications of silicone only retuned the sound of the air leak. Finally they removed the windshield to discover about a six-inch gap in the sealing gasket. Annuals and other engine/airframe maintenance runs about $1,200 to $2,000 per year.

In summary—the Turbo Skylane RG is like all Skylanes—a big, comfortable four-seat airplane. It loads easy and flies easy. It handles dirt and sod strips almost as well as the fixed gear, but has the additional speed and altitude capabilities. I like the airplane and basically have been pleased with performance and reliability of most systems.

James W. Elliot, D.D.S.
Sacramento, Calif.

Stacked up against the Mooney 201, the RG falls short by a few knots in a race at altitude despite its extra 35 horses. But in airport performance it outshines the low-winger. In recent years, the Cessna has also caught up in resale value.

In the 15 months that I have owned my '78 Skylane RG, the average price for a similar airplane has appreciated about $4,000—not bad for an investment, although the last new equipped price (when they were making them) was about $120,000, which makes used planes very attractive. Cost per hour in the last year, including engine, hangar, insurance, replacements, repairs and maintenance comes to $22.65 per hour.

The Lycoming O-540 engine is simply great. It has 1,620 hours on it and I haven't put a dime into it, and the lowest compression reading taken recently was 75 over 80. It burns a quart in about 10 hours.

The high performance and low stall speeds make it a safe airplane for people who don't fly professionally. The minuses are the usual Cessna leaky windows and doors and the average interior and appointments. The nosewheel gave me a periodic chatter problem on landings and takeoffs, with constant bushing replacements required, until I realized that we mistakenly kept the air pressure in the tire too low. Increasing tire pressure to 55 psi seems to have solved that problem. The other problem is the constant need to change nav and red panel lights.

Donald S. Prusinski
Hales Corners, Wisc.

My 1982 Skylane RG is every bit as good as your publication—maybe better on a cool, clear day. It is the roomiest four-seater in the sky, with kidney-busting range. Loaded to maximum gross weight, it regularly makes the trip from Miami to Beech Mountain, N.C. in four hours and 20 minutes (plus or minus wind) with well over an hour of fuel remaining. I cruise between 7,000 and 12,000 feet with the throttle wide open at 2350 rpm, regularly see 155-160 knots true (depending on weight), and average 12.5 gph.

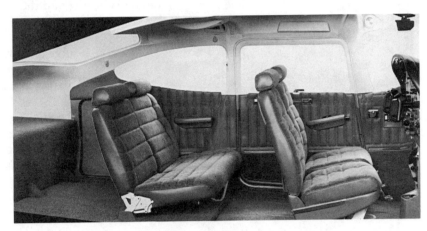

Because the airplane has integral wing tanks, no reservoir tanks, and a fuel drain at the fuel selector valve, the fuel system does not hide water that will drown you after takeoff, as many Cessna high-wings do. (The fuel selector valve should be placed on "both," however, before preflight draining.) I consider it the safest single-engine retractable around.

Just to make sure, however, I added an Aero Safe standby vacuum system (which I heartily endorse); a low-vacuum warning light (which is now available from Cessna as an inexpensive retrofit); a carb ice detector (which, now that I am able to monitor the venturi, seems to have proved itself largely unnecessary); a graphic engine monitor (which provides an enormous amount of information and much peace of mind); new old-style fuel caps, with restrictors (also available in an inexpensive kit which took three man hours to install, and which appears to have eliminated all traces of water from my tanks); and a Terra TRA-2500 radar altimeter.

The RG cabin is roomy and comfortable, but doors and windows may leak. Gear door hump impinges on the baggage compartment.

Its Imron paint job is holding up nicely, and even though it is tied down outside in southern Florida, filiform corrosion is not a significant problem.

Every silver lining has its cloud, of course. There are times when I feel like I am supporting a small army of A&Ps and ETs in the southeastern U.S. The normally aspirated Lycoming O-540 has so far purred like a big cat—but it is a cat which eats all manner and kinds of exhaust gaskets. I've tried them all, and none of them work very well. I left the cowling in place for a while once, and a blown gasket went undetected long enough to cause erosion requiring removal of a jug and resurfacing of the mating surfaces. That was an expensive lesson. Frequent inspections of the exhaust gaskets are highly recommended. When the jug was off, we also found that the stem of the exhaust valve had a chunk missing from it.

Lead fouling ceased to be a problem when I began using TCP. On balance, I am pleased with the engine.

Although I do a lot of night flying, every light bulb in the airplane is original issue, except the four glareshield eyebrow lights. I buy them by the dozen. If anyone can figure out a fix, I'll happily buy the STC. The main gear legs are also a problem; they attract rust. I've had them stripped and repainted twice so far, and they require constant attention. The rubber step-pads on the gear legs were poorly glued, and trapped a lot of moisture. I did not discover the damage until one of the pads came off. I recommend that the pads be removed, the damage corrected and a rectangle of wingwalk compound be painted on as a substitute. I also had to replace all four door hinges at 500 hours because of virulent dissimilar-metals corrosion where the hinge fingers grasp the pins. The job was labor intensive, and the new hinges were not cheap. I now keep the hinges bathed with LPS-3.

The nose gear shimmy damper and the strut collar to which it attaches are weak links. Any leaks should be corrected at once. After some initial problems and failures, I have had good success at removing the vibration it is designed to damp simply by keeping the nose gear tire fully inflated at all times.

The wing fuel tank access plate sealant deteriorated to uselessness at 350 hours, and a complete resealing of all eight covers was required. Stainless steel screws should be substituted when this inevitable project is encountered. The steel hardware securing the rotating beacon lens clamp should also be replaced with stainless, or a loss of the entire assembly is predictable.

Like most Cessnas, the 182RG exhibits good short-field and low-speed handling performance.

Surprisingly, my factory-issue ARC avionics have been much more reliable than I had any right to expect.

Annuals run around $800. My operating cost per hour (which includes fuel, scheduled and unscheduled maintenance, tiedown, lots of insurance, etc.) is approximately $60 to $65 per hour, depending on flight hours. Parts are readily available, and Cessna support has been exemplary. Maintenance costs notwithstanding, I would not trade the airplane for your cramped (but sexy) Mooney, even if you threw in a 10-year subscription to *The Aviation Consumer*.

Joel D. Eaton
Miami, Fla.

Prior to my Skylane RG ownership I bought a 1979 Cessna 180 Skywagon. The most noticeable difference between the 180 and the 182RG was in engine roughness. The O-540 Lycoming was rougher and louder than the Continental O-470. It had a "beat" at cruise that caused the visors, compass and panel to vibrate. I flew another RG of the same vintage (1978), and it did the same.

In spite of careful leaning, I was never able to get the fuel consumption below 14 gph except at high altitudes (10,000 to 12,000 feet), when it would pull only 18" mp and 13 gph. After the contamination scare, I went to Shell semi-synthetic "W" oil and the consumption decreased dramatically. As an engineer, I am doubtful of miracle cures, as well as an engine that doesn't use oil, but I didn't add more than one quart between 50-hour changes afterward.

My main recollection of the engine, however, was its hard starting characteristics. I heard the same from other owners. (I moved up to a light twin after 500 hours and two years with the RG.) We blamed the sidedraft HA-6 carburetor—too many cubic inches for the carburetion, etc. Lots of throttle pumping usually did the trick, but after the easy-starting O-470U engine, I had my doubts about the big Lycoming. Cessna and Lycoming people were no help. According to them, the problem didn't exist. I left it at country airports on two occasions because of this.

I had the carburetor overhauled to comply with the metal float AD, the primer lines and nozzles checked repeatedly, and careful spark plug gapping and maintenance. All to no avail. Upon selling the plane, the mechanic doing the pre-purchase examination noted that the impulse coupling was worn. It was replaced, and the engine started easily. So much for my local mechanics' diagnostic abilities.

Despite the starting stubbornness, however, the engine ran strongly, and gave a measure of reassurance in those heavy weather and dark night excursions that it would keep running as long as it got its share of 100LL. I never have had problems with carb ice as I did with the O-470 Continental. Overall the Skylane RG is hard to beat. I'm going on to a Baron, but know if I have to come back in the future, it will be like welcoming an old friend once again.

Charles D. Haynes, P.E.
Tuscaloosa, Ala.

My '79 Skylane RG had some filiform corrosion when I got it; so I invested in a new paint job, complete with the epoxy primer it should have had all along. I also put on chrome brake discs. I specifically shopped for a '79 or later to avoid the fuel bladders.

The maintenance has been entirely reasonable. The most recent annual, with my assistance, was $650. This included a starter drive gear and a seat rail. I budget $10 an hour for maintenance, and put in lots of my own time on preventative items.

I have already purchased the new-style fuel cap kit ($73 for both sides). Your article on that subject was correct; it will be a lot of labor to install them, involving draining the tanks and removing access panels, since the new adaptors install from inside the tank. However, in a six-year-old airplane like this the adaptor necks for the flush-style caps are getting rusty, and would need replacement soon, regardless.

Keyhole slots on the underbelly enclose the retracted landing gear without doors, which presumably reduces the malfunction burden somewhat. Smaller-than-usual tires fitting into those slots, however, make the RG less suitable for rough strips than the standard Skylane.

The turbocharged Lycoming O-540 engine shakes at idle; it runs so rough at runup that one wants to taxi to the nearest mechanic, but it is remarkably smooth and quiet at the top of the green (2400 rpm). It would appear that the turbo is a very effective muffler. I always cruise at 2400 rpm, and any attempt to reduce the cruise rpm below that results in a noticeable increase in vibration. My point of reference is the Continental O-470 in my '74 Skylane that idled very smoothly but was an ear bruiser at cruise.

It appears that the turbo throws a small amount of oil into the induction air stream. This shows up as an oil leak at the junction of the induction duct and the carburetor air box. When I first got the plane, I had the turbo rebuilt to eliminate this, but it did not help. So I sealed the joint with silicone, and now the oil passes into the carburetor instead of onto the belly.

Later this week my wife and I are leaving on our fourth trip to the Bahamas in this plane. I can imagine no other plane (within my means) that I would rather have for this trip.

Peter F. Hebb
Peterborough, N.H.

I purchased a 1979 Turbo 182RG with 1,050 hours on it. Although redline is 31 inches mp, I normally take off with about 28 inches. This allows the turbo to spool up, which may increase manifold pressure. Only knowledgeable pilots can fly this plane because it can be **easily** overboosted. However, I have had no problems learning how to fly it. In adverse weather (possible ice) I have been able to do a full-power climb (31"mp, 2400 rpm) up to 17,000 feet with two passengers and baggage and maintain a constant 1,000 fpm climb the whole way up. Normally, a cruise climb setting will give a very respectable 750 fpm.

I flight plan with 70 percent power for 150 knots true. The big cowl flaps, coupled with the engine's low turning speeds, keep the engine within all temperature limits in climb. Only once, when I was in south Georgia at 10,000 feet with the OAT at 70 degrees, did I have to open the cowl flaps to keep the engine cool in cruise. In descent, this plane is fast and can go to the top of the green if not careful. Since the gear can be extended up to 140 knots indicated, I have never had a problem getting down to pattern altitude (when cleared to descend by ATC).

My only complaint is getting the plane slowed down enough (to 95 knots IAS) to lower 20 degrees of flaps. The nose will pitch up with flaps. You must be prepared for this and push on the yoke even if you make a power reduction. If Cessna had any sense, they would have cleaned this plane up (as they did the 210) and taken Mooney on head-to-head. With the full fuel payload, range, altitude capabilities and terrific accident record, this plane is a sleeper.

Ronald Z. Mason
Columbus, Ohio

Good lines, good balance, good speed and load carrying. The Skylane RG has it all, except for good attention to details. Appropriately parked beneath a water tower, bladder-tank-equipped models suffered from water in the fuel.

Cessna 195

From out of the past rumbles one of aviation's all-time classic beauties. A vision in metal modeling with living room comfort and a reputation as a groundlooping-Lena, the Cessna 190-195 sets up great internal stresses among potential buyers seeking a satisfying balance between practicality and a touch of class and mystique.

History

Cessna cranked out some 1,200 of the 190s, 195s and military LC-126s between 1946 and 1954. The main distinction between the four different models built is the engine configuration. The C-190 came with a Continental radial putting out 240 hp. The C-195 had a 300-hp Jacobs, while the A and B models had a 245-hp and 275-hp Jacobs respectively. There was plenty to choose from that first year since all but the 275 were offered concurrently.

Elegant and trim, with a cantilever wing, the aircraft was one of the last radial-engine models.

The C-195B came out rather late in the production cycle, but its R755-B2 engine is generally considered to be the most reliable of the group, even though all three of the Jacobses have the same displacement. The 300 received a deeper intake manifold to get its extra 25 horses, but this seems to make it more susceptible to case cracking. The other significant changes were slightly larger flaps along with a modified horizontal tail at serial number 16084. And in 1953 the Goodyear crosswind gear was offered as standard, along with a lighter, springier set of main gear struts.

Performance and Handling

Owners report they get from 117 to 140 knots on the various models with a fuel burn of 12 to 19 gph. With 76 gallons of usable fuel on board, that means a range of from 500 to 800 nm. With the 275-hp Jacobs, count on a cruise of a bit over 130 mph, burning about 13.5 gph, with a comfortable no-reserve range of about 600 nm.

The aircraft is described as having "authoritative" pitch and rudder control, but ailerons are a bit on the heavy side. One owner characterized handling as similar to a Cessna 210, except for the "more ponderous" aileron control. Stalls are gentlemanly. Although the aircraft is commonly described as an excellent, stable instrument platform and cruise ship, it possesses an annoying tendency to wander in pitch in a mild never-ending phugoid. One pilot bemoaned the lack of a more capable autopilot to counter this characteristic than the "old, heavy Lear L2," which he said was the only one approved.

Another comment shed some doubt on the "stable instrument platform" characterization. Said one flier, "Since it has no dihedral, it is impossible to trim the airplane to fly hands off."

Suggested ways to land the C-195 without groundlooping it are, naturally, legion. The Cessna owner's manual suggests doing it three-point, and many owners subscribe to this philosophy. Others swear by the wheel landing technique, if only in crosswinds or gusty wind conditions.

But everybody agrees that the pilot must keep highly alert throughout the entire landing process. Said one reader: "Airspeed control on final is the key to good three-point landings (70 knots or less), and the pilot *must* remember to look straight down the runway until the airplane has slowed to a walking speed. Taking your eye off the runway to glance in the cockpit is inviting a groundloop. It must be remembered that this is a relatively heavy taildragger with the c.g. located well behind the main gear. Allow a swerve of more than 10 or 15 degrees to develop, and you don't have enough brake to stop it. A groundloop in this airplane will usually cause major damage to the gearbox, fuselage and wing."

The Shaky Jake with the cowling off. The entire engine swings out on its mount. The oil filler aft of the engine takes a whopping five gallons. The right type of spinner makes for better cylinder cooling.

Cabin Load and Comfort

Roominess is the aircraft's strong suit, with space for four comfortably, or five cozily. The useful load on an IFR- equipped 195 goes around 1,200 pounds, which allows full fuel and four 170-pound adults plus about 29 pounds of baggage.

The view out the cabin is really nothing to brag about, since the windows are long, but not terribly deep, except for a monster skylight right above the pilots' heads. Many 195 pilots say visibility is quite good in cruise (though abominable in taxi and on the landing flare), while others say they live constantly in fear of a midair because the pilot's head is lodged just about in the wing root.

In cold weather the 195 offers instant cabin heat thanks to a Southwind gas heater located right under the rear seat. One pilot had an interesting adventure thanks to this configuration when a spare can (a cardboard can, actually) of oil he'd tossed in the back rolled around and made contact with the heater, generating a bit of cockpit IFR.

Investment Value

With the passage of years, inflation, and perhaps their reputation as classics have slowly brought the resale value of the 195s up to their equipped price when new. Tracking a 1952 B model, we noted a big trough in the 1960s and early 1970s when the aircraft was selling for only about $6,000. Then in 1973 the price took a jog upward to about $9,000, and in 1976 commenced a steady climb until in 1979 it peaked out at $20,000. Since then it has risen steadily to about $23,000 according to the *Aircraft Bluebook Price Digest*, following the general trend of most aircraft to climb in the last couple of years. The various models range in average *Bluebook* price from about $19,000 to $23,000.

Safety Record

According to the National Transportation Safety Board's special study of single-engine aircraft accidents between 1972 and 1976, the Cessna 195 enjoys the unhappy distinction of being the worst groundlooper of all 33 aircraft compared. It was worse than even the Luscombe 8. The aircraft also came away in that report with the stigma of having the second highest overall accident rate—just behind the Luscombe 8, incidentally. Things improved somewhat in the fatal accident rate, with the C-195 coming out 11th worst.

And although the aircraft experienced only two in-flight airframe failures during the period studied, that brought the rate up to fourth worst among the 33, based on flying hours.

We understand that during the period 1964-1977 there were five fatal in-flight airframe failures. One of these seemed to involve pilot incapacitation due to carbon monoxide, another was a spin in the clouds, one a wingtip failure, another an empennage separation.

Cessna 195 owners are justifiably proud of the fact that so few Airworthiness Directives have been issued against the aircraft through the years since it was introduced. But one of them requires an inspection of the wing spar and addition of a steel reinforcement kit. It was issued following a fatal accident involving what was believed to be fatigue failure of the front wing spar fuselage carry-through lower cap. According to Dwight Ewing of the the Intl. 195 Assn., however,the rear wing spar had not been bolted in the wing root, so the problem wasn't fatigue failure at all. But the AD was never revoked

Misdirectional Control

As we mentioned earlier, by far the greatest number of accidents and incidents tallied by the NTSB and the FAA on the Cessna 190-195s concern groundlooping this taildragger. We counted 43 of these in the six years on printouts made for us. Damage was to pride, airframe and pocketbook in each case; no injuries were reported.

Fatal accidents in this period were caused by engine failures in three cases. In one, the aircraft had lost oil from a fractured rubber hose from the oil sump to the main screen, with the pilot making an emergency descent in bad weather. In the second, water was found in the fuel after the crash. Two other nonfatal accidents were also caused by water in the fuel. The third fatal accident occurred after the number one piston disintegrated. The aircraft was reported to have an oil leak from the vicinity of the oil cooler prior to departure.

Another nonfatal engine failure and forced landing was blamed on carburetor ice, and quite a few C-195 pilots report great care has to be taken to avoid this problem, because the engine is quite prone to build carb ice. Yet another engine failure, this one in the traffic pattern, resulted from fuel starvation because engine vibration caused the fuel selector valve to move to the off position.

Another pair of fatal accidents stemmed from problems on climbout or go-around. One took place in high density altitude conditions in the Grand Canyon when the pilot made a steep turn and stalled. In the other, the pilot attempted a go-around late but neglected to move the prop pitch to the takeoff range.

A final fatal accident involved a float-equipped C-195 which the pilot attempted to take off in wind gusting to 35 knots with an unbalanced fuel load. The wingtip dug into the water, and a passenger drowned.

Many of the groundlooping accidents were caused simply by pilot inability to keep the aircraft going straight down the runway during the landing, sometimes in gusty crosswind conditions. However, a fair number were blamed on faulty brakes. Even though some pilots said it was impossible to nose over the big bird by hard braking on the landing roll, even after a wheel landing, in several instances pilots did just that, and even flipped the aircraft over on its back. The Goodyear brakes the aircraft came with are often described as inadequate, with Cleveland brake conversions making a big difference.

At least one pilot claims that groundlooping problems can be corrected by the use of the proper tailwheel tire: i.e., a channel tread.

For some help in managing the aircraft, Larry Bartlett of Pagosa Springs, Colo., makes videos on how to fly and land C-195s.

Landing Gear Struts

In some groundloops involving Cessna 190 and 195 aircraft, more than embarrassment results because one of the landing gear struts is torn off. Reader Larry Bartlett has some information on that topic:

"Two types of spring steel gear legs were installed. The later type, on the '53 and '54 models, was thinner and weighed about 20 pounds less. It is often referred to as the 'Wasp' or 'Spider' gear, or sometimes as the 'light' gear. The earlier 'heavy' gear is much stiffer, and I think causes more damage in a ground loop since it generally tears out of the fuselage, whereas the 'light' gear will spring or spread out and remain intact. I have no empirical data to support this, but all totaled 195s that I've seen that were groundlooped (and I've seen a few) had the 'heavy' gear."

A never-ending debate rages on the use of cross-wind wheels for the taildragging Cessnas. Some old, experienced pilots maintain that only fools fly without them; others maintain that with a little care and experience, a pilot will have no problems.

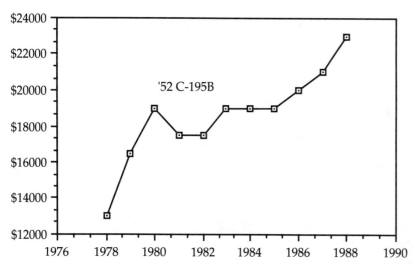

Cessna 195 Resale Value

'52 C-195B

The Goodyear castering gear was installed as standard equipment in 1953, and about 75 percent of the aircraft currently flying have them. Bartlett, for one, dislikes them. "I guess they do reduce the possibility of a groundloop and cover up for sloppy pilot technique, but I hate the looks of them," he says. "Aesthetically, the airplane needs wheel fairings, and they will not fit over the crosswind gear."

Another C-195 pilot said the narrow nine-foot track of the main gear adds to the problem of landing the 28-foot-long aircraft. "Once you let the tail wheel swing outside the track of the mainwheels on rollout, even with full differential braking, you will probably groundloop," he reported.

Short-field Performance

In the accident listing for the past six years only four patently obvious cases were reported of C-195s getting into trouble with short fields. In one instance already mentioned, the pilot attempted to land on a short private field, overshot, then attempted a go-around too late and stalled (with coarse prop pitch). In the other, the pilot stalled on takeoff in a high-density altitude situation. In two other cases the pilots landed long while attempting to cope with strong crosswinds.

For a Cessna the aircraft has uncharacteristically modest flap "power." The aircraft has a strange-looking set of split flaps that project down from the bottom of the wing, not from the trailing edge, but several inches forward. Naturally, they provide no lift, just drag.

This was the last 195 to roll off the Cessna line, in August 1954. It belongs to Dwight M. Ewing, president of the International 195 Club.

Said one pilot, "Slow-flight is a dream, and as a result you can make very short landings with it. Unfortunately, the lack of a Fowler-type flap keeps it from being a true short-field airplane. The split flaps are good speedbrakes, but provide no lift."

Judging from the NTSB's big study of single-engine accidents, however, the C-195 has a comparatively rotten record in overshoots. Its accident rate in this category was second only to the Grumman Traveler. Note that because of the number of hours flown by C-195s, there were only five overshoot accidents.

A set of slightly larger flaps was added with the B model along with a shorter-chord horizontal stabilizer and modified trim tabs. But some pilots say the bigger flaps don't really affect performance in a beneficial sense that much. In fact, they seem to make it more difficult for a solo pilot to land three-point, according to Dwight Ewing, president of the International 195 Club.

Maintenance

Naturally, maintenance on these old birds is something of a chore because they're rather rare, and not too many mechanics nowadays are familiar with the old radial engines. Owners say, however, that the parts situation is really not too bad these days. But a glance at the 195 Club's newsletters shows that scrounging, upgrading and trading of parts is a matter of continuing concern.

The engines go about 1,000 to 1,200 hours on the TBO, with frequent oil changes recommended (at around 25 to 30 hours). An overhaul or an exchange will cost $13,500 from the Jacobs Service Co., depending on the engine and number of accessories. Working on the old radials is made easier by an engine mount design that allows the powerplant to be swung out from one side, as on a hinge.

One common problem with the 195s is leaking tail struts. Owners through the years have resorted to various cures, including installing Chevy valve springs. But some believe Granville Strut Seal might be the answer.

Old heads advise potential buyers to feel the fuselage skin in front of the main landing gear struts for smoothness, because it's hard to disguise rupturing of the gearbox, as it's called, by groundlooping. Owners are wont to extoll the grand old birds by claiming that only one solitary Airworthiness Directive has been issued during the entire history of the bird. And of course that was the big one concerning the wing truss. But the records show three others on the 190 and two others on the 195.

One required inspection of the rudder cables to detect premature fraying at the forward pulley. Another called for inspection for cracking and failures of the cowl mounting ring channels, until new channels and stiffening angles were installed. A third required inspection for fatigue cracks in the elevator spar webs at the outboard hinges until reinforcing doublers were installed. A final one, shared with many other Cessnas, involved checking the electrical system to prevent in-flight fires.

Electrically operated split flaps generate drag, but no appreciable lift. They at least tend to point the nose of the aircraft down on approach.

Parts and Service

Despite the fact that these days Cessna provides little more than moral support to the some 720 Cessna 190s and 195s still registered, owners report the parts situation is not too bad. In fact, it should even improve, thanks to a whole new enterprise devoted to building and overhauling the Jacobs engines.

The Jacobs Service Co. in Payson, Ariz. acquired the type certificates, tooling, drawings and parts inventory from Page Industries. It also received PMA approval, and does overhauls as well as provide exchange engines. Check with shop foreman Jim McCracken at (602) 174-2014.

A west-coast maintenance and repair facility that is characterized as "excellent" by the International 195 Club is Ray's Aircraft (run by Ray Woodmansee) at Porterville, Calif. Ray's bought out Andy Brennan of Brennan Formed Sheet Metal Parts, which manufactures sheet metal parts for the C-195. And they shipped the whole facility from Torrance, Calif. to Porterville.

Out in the East, Air Ads of Dayton at the Moraine Air Park is well known for its repair and service work on 195s. Down south in the Florida panhandle, John Hambleton of Gulf Coast Air Service in Fort Walton Beach does the same. And in the Illinois area, Phillip Van Reeth and his son, of Lombard, Ill. have developed an FBO serving the aircraft.

Operating Characteristics

Along with the panache of the big radial-engine Cessna comes a healthy dose of fussing—even before you can start the grand old bird. Since oil collects in the bottom cylinders if the aircraft has been sitting more than a few hours, the pilot must pull it through five to 12 blades, depending on whom you talk to. This will allow the start to generate less of a smokescreen.

The pilot is not home free once he gets taxiing, either, since many of the old radials begin to heat up with prolonged ground operation. This is one reason C-195 pilots like to avoid big, busy airports with long rides to and from the active, and much sitting in line waiting for takeoff. Some owners even install double oil coolers to diminish the problem.

And the type of spinner installed has an effect on the cooling efficiency of the aircraft—though presumably only after the aircraft is airborne. The so- called Cessna "floating" bullet spinner is generally regarded as the most efficient. But some owners have used BT-13 spinners because they were more easily available.Though the engines are designed for 80 octane avgas, quite a few C-195 owners report they have used autogas with success.

Modifications

Although owners say only one autopilot, the Lear L2, is approved for the 190-195s, we note that Brittain had an STC for its B2C system.

Judging from the comments of owners, one of the most useful conversions is from the troublesome old Goodyear brakes to Cleveland brakes, which are many times more effective. Some say they're almost too effective and take a cautious touch or they can get the pilot into trouble. Also, of course, the airplane can be equipped with floats and is regarded as a marvelous seaplane whose squirrelly groundlooping tendencies have been purged.

We understand also that a number of 195s have 330-hp Jacobs L6MB engines that came from surplus World War II stocks in Canada and were installed with a modified cowl to accept the larger engine. Some 195s also received 450-hp Pratt & Whitney powerplants. And a 350-hp turbocharged version of the Jacobs was developed by Page,using an AiResearch turbo. Also, the Jacobs Service Co. is developing a 325-hp fuel injection mod for the 275-hp engine that not only should reduce fuel consumption and even out fuel flow to the cylinders but eliminate the specter of carb ice.

Organization to Join

The International 195 Club takes good care of members and publishes a slick-looking bulletin. Contact Dwight Ewing at the club address of P.O. Box 737, Merced, Calif. 95340, (209) 722-6284.

Rationale

The airplane obviously oozes aesthetic appeal. It has to be one of the all-time sculptured beauties. And at $19,000 to $23,000 or so, can it really be matched in a broad-shouldered contemporary ship of similar performance? As one owner

Cost/Performance/Specifications

Model	Year	Average Retail Price	Cruise Speed (kts)	Useful Load (lbs)	Fuel Std/Opt (gals)	Engine	TBO (hrs)	Overhaul Cost
C-190	1947-53	$16,000	139	1,335	80	240-hp Cont. W-670-23	1,000	$7,000
C-195	1947-53	$19,000	148	1,300	80	300-hp Jacobs R-755-A2	1,000	$8,500
C-195A	1947-53	$18000	139	1,320	80	245-hp Jacobs R-755-9	1,000	$8,500
C-195B	1952-54	$22,000	143	1,300	80	275-hp Jacobs R-755-B2	1,000	$8,500

comments: "In summary, the Cessna 195 is a five-place all-metal airplane which will produce an honest 139 knots on 15 gph. No AD hassle, easy maintenance, easy to fly. Have we really made any progress in 30 years?"

Answer: maybe not in looks and classic aura, but in safer, easier ground handling, certainly anything with tricycle gear excels. And for a similar investment, something on the order of the 1964 to 1974 Skylane will offer fairly similar cruise speeds and load- carrying ability with better parts availability, and a pretty decent cabin size. But as they say, love is blind.

Owner Comments

The Jacobs engine is a very reliable unit and does not have any unusual maintenance problems, but it does have some quirks. Smokey starts are common, more so than most radials, and it must be pulled through 10 or 12 blades to clear oil from the bottom cylinders if it has been sitting more than several hours. The engine will produce carburetor ice faster than an ice maker, and in cool, moist air it should be flown with partial carb heat, using the installed carburetor air temperature gauge.

Many times in flight in clear air the engine will cough or sputter momentarily, leading many to believe the mixture is too lean. But the "Shakey Jake" is merely swallowing some ice. A major difference between the Jake and other engines is that instead of two magnetos, it has one mag and a battery distributor just like a car. You might say it has a one-and-a-half ignition system instead of a dual system because the loss of the generator will soon have you operating on one mag.

The airframe is solid; you might say it was built like a tank. Parts can usually be found for most anything. The hardest parts to find have been cowling sections and the gearbox.

Good brakes are essential on this airplane. A Cleveland conversion is available and it does a great job. It is expensive, but well worth it. The only problem with the Clevelands is that they provide more braking action than the gearbox was designed to handle. I've seen two cases of popped rivets in the gearbox due to hard braking with the Clevelands installed. You have to really bear down on the Goodyears, but a light touch will do the job with the Clevelands.

Larry Bartlett
El Paso, Tex.

The best feature is the large internal volume. In the front you sit up in chairs off the floor, as at your kitchen table, and in the back you can stretch your legs out as in a Cadillac Limo.

The worst feature to me was the visibility to the sides in level flight. The pilot's head is located in the wing root; hence, to scan, one must duck down in an uncomfortable position, or lean forward.

Paul Taipale
Bellevue, Wash.

Flying machine and art object, this was John W. Duff's aircraft. When the cabin door is opened, a retractable entrance step lowers automatically. Under the aft seat was a gas-fired heater.

The biggest problem with the plane is the air-filled tail shock unit, and I found few who flew the plane who had not had a large spring installed inside the shock and used that to reduce the vibration. I tried for a long time to keep the darn shock filled, and most of those you see are sitting down low on the wheel, indicative of the fact that their tail shock doesn't work either.

It is a smooth-flying machine—easy to fly, wonderful and stable platform, big and comfortable. I can't remember having difficult landings, and always made wheel landings to keep pressure off the tail and its poor shock.

The flaps don't do anything for all practical purposes as far as slowing you down; but they do pitch you forward so you can see to land.

Art Brothers
Salt Lake City, Utah

It has been a most satisfying aircraft. It is as steady in all types of weather as you can expect a single-engine civilian craft to be. In the air, it feels much like a Cessna 210, except it is more ponderous in aileron control.

Its one big drawback initially is its ground handling. Visibility over the nose in three-point attitude is nil, the slow-turning prop (2200 rpm at takeoff while delivering 300 hp) provides plenty of torque to contend with. All of this adds up to what is probably one of the most difficult civilian aircraft to handle on the runway. On landing, it is worse. For the first few months of ownership, the local airport wags will sell tickets to your landings. However, once you master the aircraft, the feeling of accomplishment is tremendous, and more of a thrill than you will ever get with any modern tricycle-gear plane. The only real annoyance is the tendency to overheat on the ground. Despite twin oil coolers, the tightly cowled Jake will run near the top of the green arc at cruise in the summer, and takeoffs and landings are out.

If you buy a 195, buy it in the winter, when you can get your 100 takeoffs and landings for your checkout at a rate of more than one per day. On normal operations, the handbook even suggests you do part of the runup while taxiing as "fast as safely possible" to the runway. You can live with it, but crowded airports need careful planning.

You can find modern aircraft that go faster on less fuel, but if you are willing to pay for your enjoyment, for sheer classic elegance, panache, *joie de vivre*, return to the challenge and romance of flying, you can't beat the 195.

Carlos R. Diaz
Clinton, Md.

My 195 receives more attention from lookers, gawkers, askers, admirers than any aircraft I have seen. And the roomy, solid comfort will impress you. The best 195 combination is a 275-hp Jacobs engine, Cleveland wheels (no crosswind gear), IFR radios and nice paint and interior. You'll love it. It is the Cadillac of all Cessna singles.

Tail strut leakage is a chronic problem, but Granville Strut Seal seems an effective antidote.

Thomas J. Schmid
Roseburg, Ore.

The engine was susceptible to carburetor ice, the fuel system had a tendency to collect water, and flight in icing conditions was hazardous because the fuel tank vents had a tendency to ice up.

Twice during flight in turbulence my rear door opened in flight. This unnerved my rear-seat passengers, but didn't seem to affect the flight characteristics adversely. I was able to close the door after I cranked down the left front window. I found that wheel landings were consistently better than three-point landings. You can brake a 195 as soon as the main gear is planted on the ground, so wheel landings require no more distance than three-pointers.

David M. Baker
Huntington, W. Va.

The horror stories about groundloops can be corrected by the simple use of the proper tailwheel tire—a channel tread.

Reports of engine oil overheating can in all cases be traced to improper type of spinner and elimination of cowling cooling rings. Many owners use a blunt bullet spinner, then wonder why they have to add oil coolers. The bullet spinner deflects the airstream outside the cowling while the original Cessna spinner directs the airflow to the cylinders.

Several propeller seal modifications are STC'd and are available at a reasonable price to eliminate prop oil leakage permanently. Cylinder head bolts should be tightened ever 250-300 hours. And exhaust valve clearance should be checked at that time. If the engine is equipped with valve rotators, no adjustment of valves will normally be necessary.

I could not get the comfort, speed and safety at double the price of my aircraft.

Harry E. Reed
Baldwinsville, N.Y.

Cessna
Centurion 210

To use a sports analogy, the Centurion is like the brawny fullback who can outrun everybody. But he's had knee surgery and maybe even a bypass operation. You've got to respect his speed and heft, but naturally have a few reservations about his durability.

The C-210 in many ways is a truly remarkable airplane, one that evokes expressions of awe and respect from owners. Even with the normally aspirated models you're talking about cruise speeds around 170 knots/195 mph, coupled with useful loads of about three-quarters of a ton, equipped, that defy belief.

Add to that cruising ranges of 1,000 nm and better with full tanks, and you have an airplane to be reckoned with when shopping for a fast aerial U-haul.

Historical Perspective

The aircraft is the classic case of the "grandfather clause" carried to extremes. Certified way back in 1959 as a 2,900-pound airplane with a strut-braced wing and a redline speed of 174 knots, it's evolved into a 4,100-pound 325-hp pressurized behemoth with a 200-knot redline, designed to fly above 20,000 feet in icing conditions.

Big and brawny and an astonishing hauler, the 210 nevertheless has been afflicted with more than its share of mechanical problems.

And all this has been accomplished under the certification standards of the old CAR Part 3 rather than the more stringent current FAR 23. Cessna reports that with later models it has conformed to newer criteria, but of course it is under no obligation to prove this. The matter has been a debating point in connection with the C-210's in-flight airframe breakup rate. (More about that later.)

Landing Gear Gripe List

The aircraft owes its origin to even earlier sources, since it sprang, like Adam's rib, from a Cessna 180 airframe. One of the interesting challenges posed to Cessna engineers way back then was to figure a way to retract the gear into the fuselage, since the wing, perched on top of the fuselage, did not lend itself to housing the retraction mechanism. Their efforts were not crowned with glory. The results, through a series of attempted upgrades, have bedeviled 210 owners ever since. Even to this day Service Difficulty Reports shows landing gear problems remain at the top of the gripe list among owners and mechanics—by far.

As the years went by, a series of changes were also made to cabin, wings and powerplants. In 1962 the cabin was enlarged a bit and outfitted with rear windows. Then, in 1964 engine power rose from 260 hp to 285 hp, and in 1965 a turbocharged model was introduced that went on to outsell the normally aspirated model by nearly two to one.

In a side-by-side race at altitude with the A36 Bonanza, the 210 could more than hold its own, and carry a bigger load, to boot.

In 1967, presumably to counter the scoffing of competitors, Cessna replaced the strut-braced wing with a cantilevered one, at the same time boosting the fuel capacity from 65 gallons to a whopping 90. However, since the airframe breakup rate of cantilever models way exceeds that of strutted ones, some critics question the wisdom of that change. (The retractable Skylane RG retained its struts, by comparison.)

In 1970 Cessna made a big change in the cabin, boosting the seating from four places to six—to accommodate four adults and two dwarfs, and adding extra baggage space, all the while raising the gross weight by a significant 400 pounds to 3,800 pounds. Then, in 1971 takeoff horsepower was boosted once again, to 300.

Gear Improvements

In 1972 Cessna made an important effort to improve the landing gear mechanism, by replacing the old engine-driven hydraulic system with an electro-hydraulic one. Taking the process one step further, in a dramatic stroke Cessna in 1979 simply did away with gear doors and all the extra mechanical bother they represented. (Mod shops today will do the same for owners of older aircraft, for a price.) There seems to be negligible if any speed sacrifice.

Also in 1979 Cessna raised the gross weight to 4,000 pounds with the 210N model, and in 1985 raised it once again to 4,100 pounds for the 210R.

Since the Centurions were highly desired as instrument-flying ships, the specter of loss of instruments from simple accessories like alternators and vacuum pumps led Cessna in 1982 to offer optional dual alternators and vacuum pumps. The dual pumps became standard with 1983 models as turbo ships were certified for flight in icing conditions. Pneumatic boots naturally imposed an extra burden on the vacuum pump system.

Also on the 1983 models, Cessna began installing new Slick pressurized magnetos to prevent misfiring at high altitudes. And in 1984 engine TBO went up from 1,400 to 1,600 hours, and shoulder harnesses were made standard equipment on all seats.

Performance & Handling

As we mentioned before, the C-210 series aircraft go like bats. Pilots note cruise speed is easily 160-170 knots, climbout around 750 fpm at 120 knots indicated, though one owner boasted he could do an "easy 1,500 fpm" with two people on board.

With an IFR-equipped payload of about 970 pounds after full fuel, a late-model Cessna 210 can haul the astonishing load of five adults and about 22 pounds of baggage for each rider. No other single comes close except the Piper Saratoga, which is still about 30 pounds shy. Furthermore, the Centurions have an unusually broad center of gravity envelope that tolerates loading extremes that would cause aerodynamic chaos in other airplanes—like the Bonanza for instance.

The airplane does not have well harmonized controls. Though ailerons are delightfully quick for such a big airplane, pitch pressures are heavy, as in the Skylane. The other side of the coin, as one owner noted: "Although somewhat built like a truck, with controls to match, nevertheless it is a most dependable IFR platform in adverse weather."

Thanks to limited elevator travel, the big Centurion is tough to wrangle into a full-stall break, so there's nothing sneaky or nasty about stalls. Since it's the heaviest airplane in its class, it must naturally be handled with respect, especially on landing. Judging from the number of hard landings, swerves and runway overruns and gear collapses on the accident reports, this is a matter to be reckoned with.

Although most Cessnas have an excellent reputation for short-field operation, the C-210 on paper anyway does not shine in this category in comparison with its peers. Minimum runway over a 50-foot obstacle tallies out at a little over 2,000 feet, which is close to the figure given for the Beech A36 Bonanza, but longer by several hundred feet than for the other Bonanzas and the Piper Lance/Saratoga in the big-single class. Nevertheless, one pilot who had stepped up from a Skyhawk to a '78 T210 told us: "The biggest surprise has been the superb handling qualities in the pattern. When there are a half dozen jetliners lined up on final to Phoenix Skyharbor, the 210 can slip in between them on a tight, short approach just like the C-172 could. True, the stick forces are high at slow speed, but judicious use of the electric elevator trim alleviates that problem."

Cabin Comfort, Finish

With a cabin width of 44 inches in the middle and a height of 47 inches, the aircraft has a roomy interior for four adults and perhaps two kids. Wrote one happy owner: "It's been a family machine, comfortably carrying, for example, four skiers averaging about 165 pounds, skis, boots, poles, banjo, guitar and clothes for a week." Another summed up his attitude toward the fifth- and sixth-seat arrangement: "The back seats are really only for short trips or small people."

Although in the past we received quite a few complaints about the "cheap" Royalite instrument panels, our latest call for reader feedback did not turn up any derogatory comments along this vein. We also did not receive any complaints of leaking windshields this time around, though one pilot said his baggage compartment leaks "with all precipitation."

He also complained that the rear cabin has a serious heating deficiency. "The difference between the N and R models (he's owned both), is that the '86 model is a flying freezer for anyone behind the pilot. The pilot roasts; the midseat passengers require full winter gear, and water freezes behind them." He noted he'd complied with service bulletins on the matter. "But my family remains reluctant to fly again this winter," he added.

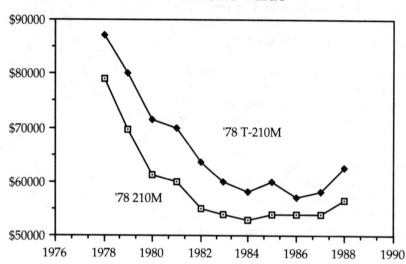

Cessna 210 Resale Value

'78 T-210M

'78 210M

In this context, we noticed Cessna has issued Service Bulletin SEB87-5, designed to improve the cabin heating system. It includes a heat exchanger seal to prevent outside ram air from entering the exchanger, and the simple artifice of a removable insulated cabin curtain to separate the cabin passenger area from the baggage compartment. Cessna claims these provide a "significant increase in cabin temperature."

Maintenance

Most of the owners offering feedback on 210s reported an average maintenance burden and what we figured were rather low prices for the annual inspection for an aircraft of this size and complexity; i.e., from $800 to $1,500. (We've been averaging a lot more for our Mooney 201, incidentally.)

Though production of 210s has ceased, owners reported decent parts availability, but high prices. One owner said he was exasperated, however, with Cessna's policy of selling parts only through dealers, with no drop shipping, even if purchased through a dealer. This, he said, meant that in his part of the country (the Greater Philadelphia area), parts had to come from one of several dealers 50 to 100 miles away, meaning the aircraft was AOG at least once a year for an extra week "with bureaucratic supply delays, often for trivial parts (e.g., landing gear relay, etc.) being purchased through a third party who is not working on the plane and may not order what is requested."

Landing Gear Malaise

A number of owners reported problems with gear doors on their 210s, and a survey by *The Aviation Consumer* of FAA Service Difficulty Reports from the years 1985 through October 1988 showed that, indeed, landing gear problems dominated the list, by far—with 131 reports. (Traditionally, of course, the FAA estimates SDRs represent a 10% tip of the iceberg.)

Sample comments: "Unable to lower gear, landed gear up." "Gear failed to extend. Hand pump did not help. Landed gear up." "A forced gear-up landing was accomplished due to lack of hydraulic pressure . . ." "Aircraft made a wheels-up landing when landing gear failed to lower." And so on.

Among the various components blamed for gear problems: Thermal relief valve in power pack unseated; landing gear door valve failure; hydraulic reservoir depleted from chafing by control cable; filter housing ruptured in flight; power pack pump failed, causing continuous running and overheating; power pack motor burned, etc. We tallied quite a few more gear-up landings on the SDRs than were reported in the accident briefs for the same period.

Blazing Saddles

The historic nemesis of the older Centurions, cracking landing gear saddles, has apparently not abated completely. We counted 25 reports of cracked saddles in the latest run of SDRs. All 210s built from 1960 to 1969 live under the shadow of this problem, involving fatigue cracks. With luck, the cracks are found during annual inspections. If not, the saddles eventually break, and the pilot discovers his problem when one landing gear leg hangs up in the half-way position.

AD 76-14-07 issued in 1976 to deal with the problem calls for dye penetrant inspections at 1,300 hours and at annual inspections afterwards. But mechanics have found cracks sooner in the life span. Saddle replacement was required for 1960 and 1961 models, but even they must be replaced every 1,000 hours at a cost of $1,000 to $1,500. Buyers should check the saddles and replacement times on these aircraft.

The 1962-67 models had the same original defective saddles, but differences in the retraction system allowed an improved saddle to be retrofitted. But even they have not eliminated the cracking problem. Later, 1968 and 1969 model 210s came with the "improved" saddles as original equipment, but they must be inspected at 1,200 hours and annually thereafter, and still run the risk of eventual cracking.

And finally, the landing gear system was redesigned in 1970, and this apparently rid the 210 line of the cracking saddle scourge.

Magneto Problems

Mag failures came in second worst in our tally of Service Difficulty Reports, with 72. These involved Slick magnetos on not only pressurized and turbocharged 210s, but normally aspirated ones as well.

The FAA issued an AD late in 1988 (88-25-04) calling for inspection of pressurized

A major cabin modification in 1970 yielded six adult seats and extra baggage room. The aircraft is notable for its broad center of gravity envelope.

mags for moisture contamination within the next 50 flight hours, and at each annual thereafter for Part 91 operators. But the SDRs suggested that contamination represented only part of the problem with the Slick mags. Others called out failures from a variety of causes such as bearing failure, worn brushes, partially disintegrated distributor blocks, worn gear teeth, broken impulse coupling, broken mounting flanges, to name some.

We talked with Slick Aircraft Products to see if they could explain the problem, and they said they believed it occurred when pilots flew through visible moisture, and was a function of the "plumbing" design on the C-210, taking air from the induction manifold. They suggested the problem was not as great in other aircraft

like the turbo Mooneys and the Piper Malibu, which also use pressurized Slick mags.

As for other types of magneto problems, a Slick representative suggested some might be related to improper maintenance in the field. In particular, extensive improvement and changes in Slick magneto components since 1980 mean that some critical parts must be mated, and this means a mix-and-match use of cannibalized parts by some mechanics can pose a real problem.

The first models had strut-braced wings, no rear windows, only 260 horses and a pronounced hump under the nose.

Buyers might make it part of their pre-purchase exam to try to ascertain whether the magnetos have been inspected with a case opening at 500-hour intervals, so major problems may be forestalled.

Cylinder Cracks

Third highest on the list of Service Difficulty Reports was cylinder cracks, with 36 of these called out. Pressurized and turbocharged 210s dominated the roster with this problem, but it occurred on normally aspirated 210s as well. One mechanic ventured as the probable cause overheating due to overleaning and improper cooling procedures with turbocharged powerplants.

In 1986 Cessna brought out a service bulletin (SEB86-3) tagging, in turn, a Continental SB (M86-7) calling attention to "unexplained" cylinder barrel cracking that had caused instances of head to barrel separation. Inspections were required, to be repeated every 100 hours, on certain serial number IO-520 and TSIO-520 engines.

The Continental engines on C-210s were also prey to a number of crankcase cracks (we counted nine reports), though we usually think of this as the main province of Beech Bonanzas and Barons. In addition, those old bugaboos of any aircraft—vacuum pump and alternator failures—took their toll on C-210s as well, with 35 of these reported.

Potential buyers should also take care to check out the horizontal tail for a variety of problems, including stabilizers and brackets for cracking. Cessna brought out several service bulletins (SEB88-3, SNL87-18 and SEB87-2) aimed at strengthening various tail components. And make sure the elevator skin itself has not become corroded thanks to water absorbtion by the foam filler.

Filiform Paint Problem

Check used 210s built between 1977 and 1982 and based in hot, humid seaside areas for possible filiform corrosion.

Safety Record

In our last major survey of accident rates among single-engine retractables in 1984, the Cessna 210 came out with a very poor rating in total accidents and a slightly worse than average rating in fatal accidents. To be specific, it was the third worst out of 17 aircraft compared in total accident rates between 1972 and 1981 and eighth worst in fatal accidents. (These figures do not include the P210, which came out with a better score in both categories.) Only the old Piper Comanche and Beech 24 Sierra had worse total accident records for that period.

Our close-up inspection of accident data for 1975 and 1976, along with 1985 through 1987 highlights two areas of biggest concern through the years: engine failures for mechanical and other reasons and fuel mismanagement.

During the latter period ('85 through '87) fuel mismanagement claimed by far the greatest number of nonfatal accidents (see the nearby chart), with engine stoppage in second place. Time and again the National Transportation Safety Briefs report C-210 pilots for some reason simply running out of fuel—exhausting every drop of usable gas in the tanks. But some also flame out because they fail to switch to a tank with fuel remaining. It's worth noting that not until 1982 did the line receive a "both" tanks fuel selector position along with the left and right tank choices. This has turned out to be nearly infallible in Cessna Skyhawks.

Since there is a generous 89 gallons of usable fuel available—enough for five to six hours at high cruise speeds—it's astonishing that so many pilots "flame out." A possible factor on older 210s might be location of the fuel gauge on the right side of the instrument panel. But in 1978 Cessna relocated the gauges on the lower throttle pedestal directly above the fuel tank selector switch.

It never ceases to amaze how many fliers with complete engine stoppage manage to get the aircraft down dead-stick without killing themselves. But C-210 fuel mismanagement resulted in only two fatal crashes compared with 25 nonfatal prangs in the three-year period between 1985 and 1987.

By the same token, only three fatal crashes resulted from engine failure, compared to 15 nonfatals. The biggest cause of fatal accidents in the three years: bad weather, accounting for eight crashes.

Engine Failure

What causes C-210 engines to give up in flight? The accident briefs identified a broad mix of problems, such as: oil lube block to connecting rod bearing, with resulting rod failure; main bearing moved; bad overhaul; fuel lines loose; connecting rod bolt failure; crankshaft failures; P210 mag arcing; piston separation; fatigue failure of an exhaust valve; bearing journal failure, starving oil to the conrod; carburetor ice; oil starvation after overhaul, on a test flight.

This 1966 model shows the slightly enlarged cabin with rear windows introduced a few years earlier. It also has the bigger 285-hp engine.

The specter of engine stoppage from vapor lock seems to have receded, if we interpret the latest data correctly. At the end of 1981 Cessna introduced kits designed to eliminate vapor lock by installing vapor return lines. Service Bulletin

SE 81-33 dealt with the matter, applying to 1976-1979 T-210s and P210s, which Cessna believed had the worst of the vapor problems. The kits are similar to the fuel system in the 1962-1962 aircraft, which have had few vapor lock problems.

Then in 1988 the FAA rescinded AD 80-04-09 that had required installation of

insulated fuel lines ahead of the firewall (per Cessna Service Letter SE79-60) on some 3,000 T-210s and P210s, to combat the fuel vapor problem. Why after all these years would the agency take such action? A spokesman told us that apparently one aircraft had fallen through the regulatory cracks, so to speak, but in view of the fact that the vapor lock problem— so prominent in the early 1980s—had apparently "gone away," they felt there was no need to enforce installation of the mod on that aircraft.

POHs now advise pilots encountering fuel fluctuations to switch on their aux fuel pumps, taking care, of course, to adjust the mixture at the same time, to avoid flooding the engine. But we should note that a number of engine stoppage accidents were unexplained, and the engines worked after the accidents, so the possibility of vapor lock should not be excluded.

The instrument panel is so tall that when the average pilot has his seat positioned high enough to see over it, he can't see out to the left without ducking his head under the window jamb.

One pilot reported he had experienced a catastrophic engine failure in a 1960 C-210 and crashed into the surf off California after part of the engine and prop separated from the airplane, chopping off part of the right wing in the process. He blamed the failure on hydrostatic lock during starting. A bent connecting rod, he said, caused failure of the wrist pin and connecting rod and crank shaft, in that order. The fuel injectors on the IO-470, he noted, were located over the valve stems, and while the plane was parked, a leak in the fuel distribution valve allowed fuel from the overhead tanks to drip onto the stem. It flowed down the valve into the cylinder causing the lock. We had no other reports of this phenomenon on the 210s.

In-flight Airframe Failures

In recent years considerable attention has been focused on the rising rate of in-flight breakups of Centurions. However, our last check of statistics on breakups between the years 1977 and 1983 showed the 210 to be only third worst among the four big retractable singles in this category. The Piper Lance had the poorest record with 6.5 breakups per million hours, with the Beech 35 models second with 4.8 and the C-210 third with 3.3 The Beech 33/36, incidentally, logged the best record in this area, with a rate of only 0.5.

We tallied three fatal airframe failures in C-210s in the three years 1985-1987, all involving apparent encounters with dangerous weather such as thunderstorms.

There was some concern that aileron flutter might have contributed to several 210 breakups. Cessna beefed up and rebalanced ailerons starting with the 1985 models, and mod shops now provide retrofits for older aircraft.

Wrinkled Bladders

Watch out for Cessna 210s with fuel bladders. These aircraft were manufactured until the late 1970s. The bladders are expensive to replace, and may have water-trapping wrinkles.

Modifications

Quite a few Centurion owners have good things to say about intercooler mods as a means of cooling off engines and giving extra performance. Three companies specialize in retrofitting this STC'd equipment, or selling kits so it can be done by local mechanics.

One is Aircraftsman, 2870 E. Wardlow Rd., Long Beach, Calif. 90807, (213) 427-4423. Their kit is priced at $4,995, and they'll do the installation for $500. Others are Riley International Corp. at 2206 Palomar Airport Rd., Carlsbad, Calif. 92008, (619) 438-9089 with a kit price of $3,950 and Turboplus in Gig Harbor, Wash., (800) 742-4202. Their kit price is $4,495.

We noted one comment on the Turboplus installation in the Cessna Pilots Assn. newsletter that changing the the oil filter takes extra effort because a portion of the intercooler system has to be removed to get at it. Aircraftsman's and Riley's intercoolers are less complicated in this context, the C-T-210 owner reported.

Speedbrakes

Turboplus also sells speed brake kits for $3,995. Precise Flight has received an STC for electric speedbrakes, which replace hydraulic ones offered in 1984. Price is $2,495, with 25-hour installation time. Precise Flight, 63120 Powell Butte Rd., Bend, OR 97701, (800) 547-2558. And to fill out the roster of speedbrake mods, Thompson Aero Products, P.O. Box 3375, Sunriver, OR 97707, (503) 593-1484 sells a distinctive kind of speedbrake for $3,495, basic. The entire kit costs $4,640, not including installation.

Autogas

Petersen Aviation, Route 1, Box 18, Minden, NE 68959, (800) 352-3232 has an STC allowing 91 octane autogas to be used in IO-520 engines when modified with their alcohol-water injection system. It's also available for 80/87 octane engines.

Petersen's so-called ADI (anti-detonation injection) system costs $4,245 for the C-210 and comes with a mod to prevent vapor lock, which is more of a problem with autogas.

Flint Aero in Santee, Calif., (619) 448-1551, can provide wingtip tanks for the cantilever wing 210s, adding an extra 33 gallons. The price is $4,250.

R/STOL by Sierra Industries, Inc., in Uvalde, Tex., (512) 278-4381, has taken over the Robertson mods and can install them for $7,950. One of the most elaborate STOL kits available, it includes drooped ailerons when flaps are down, recontoured wing leading edge, stall fences and gap seals.

If you fly your 210 in hot climates, Parker Hannifin Corp.'s Airborne Div. in Elyria, Ohio, (216) 871-6424, will sell you an air-conditioning kit for $6,283.

If you are concerned about oil spilling out all over the belly of your Centurion, consider contacting the Cessna Pilots Assn. for a free (for members) set of so-called Baylock drawings (named after the fellow who devised them) that reposition the crankcase breather line.

And if you don't mind spending $800 or so and another 10-15 hours of installation time, you can get rid of the gear doors and associated hydraulic paraphernalia on your 1970-78 210 with a Uvalde gear door removal kit from the Uvalde Flight Center of Sierra Industries.

Three's company, six is not too much of a crowd, even with baggage, thanks to a monster useful load.

To prepare for the unpleasant possibility of loss of vacuum pressure, a number of companies have STCs providing auxiliary vacuum pump systems. Parker Hannifin Corp. has one; Allison-Coffer, Azle, Tex. has an STC for an electrically driven pump as a standby. Also, Precise Flight, Sunriver, Ore., (503) 593-1484, offers a standby vacuum system that works without any external pump.

To ease fears of aileron flutter, a place with the interesting name Airplane Help, in Carlsbad, Calif. (619) 931-8788, makes updates to meet 1986 210R factory specs. They are 100 percent mass balanced and contain new ribs for stiffening. O&N Aircraft Modifications in Factoryville, Pa., (717) 945-3769 does work not only on the 210 ailerons but on the rudder and elevator. Complete kit price is $1,850 for all three. The kits insert new rib assemblies in the rudder and aileron and add balance weights to 100 percent mass balance elevator, rudder and ailerons.

Petersen Aviation of Minden Neb. (800) 352-3232, well known for its autogas approvals, has a fuel system mod for 210s to correct fuel vaporization problems.

Societies

The National 210 Owners Assn. is located at 9959 Glenoaks Blvd., Sun Valley, Calif. 91352. Contact Bill Kitchen at (213) 875-2820. They publish a quarterly newsletter. Another good source of information is the Cessna Pilots Assn., Wichita Mid-Continent Airport, 2120 Airport Rd., P.O. Box 12948, Wichita, Kans. 67277. John M. Frank, (316) 946-4777, is editor of the association's slick, four-color monthly newsletter.

Owner Comments

The small company I own uses a 1978 210M with non-turbo engine to deliver maintenance to motion picture theaters in the eastern half of the United States. I have 800 hours in the aircraft.

The 210's "heavy-on-the-controls" reputation is well deserved. When learning the 210 transition, the increased P-factor during max. performance takeoffs made me reconsider the purchase. In cruise (consider that is 98 percent of the flight) the heavy control feel becomes a virtue. The only handling downsides are: smaller pilots *must* use the trim to fly the elevator, and during the approach-to-landing phase it is possible to develop a quite-pronounced sink, leading to a hard landing. This is particularly irksome, considering that when loaded in the front seats only, the elevator does not seem to be very effective. The cure, of course, is not to remove the last two inches of power until over the runway.

Maintenance: We will dispense with the usual comments about ARC avionics. We fly serious IFR and removed them all before attempting it. Electrosonics of Columbus, Ohio installed, over time, a complete King package with HSI, Stormscope and intercom. We have had only one failure in four years, and that was in the box and rectified by mail.

Engine: No engine work has ever been done to this plane although it is at 1,640 hours. I am using Phillips multigrade. The usual batch of vacuum pumps, prop overhauls and starters, and every solenoid has been replaced.

Brakes: It is likely that during maintenance a brake line can be positioned so that during gear cycling it will "pop" back into contact with the drum. Care must be used.

Nosewheel: Overpumping the nosewheel cylinder will make ground steering nearly impossible. We have removed the gear doors since fatigue cracks dictated door replacement. We lost two to four knots, and acquired a hollow, "air-over-Coke bottle" sound. It's safer, though.

Problems: Not many really; just a lesson learned. I had complained of the throttle

Cost/Performance/Specifications

Model	Year	Average Retail Price	Cruise Speed (kts)	Useful Load (lbs)	Fuel Std/Opt (gals)	Engine	TBO (hrs)	Overhaul Cost
210, A	1960-61	$20,000	165	1,600	65, 68	260-hp Cont. IO-470-E	1,500	$10,500
210B, C	1962-63	$23,300	160	1,220	65/84	260-hp Cont. IO-470-S	1,500	$10,500
210D, E	1964-65	$24,800	166	1,260	65/68	260-hp Cont. IO-470-E	1,500	$10,500
210F, G	1966-67	$27,800	166	1,435	65/84, 90	285-hp Cont. IO-520-A	1,700	$11,500
T210F, G	1966-67	$29,500	194	1,350	89	285-hp Cont. TSIO-520-C	1,400	$13,000
210H, J	1968-69	$29,800	167	1,440	90	285-hp Cont. IO-520-A, J	1,700	$11,500
T210H, J	1968-69	$32,000	194	1,350	89	285-hp Cont. TSIO-520-C, H	1,400	$13,000
210K	1970-71	$32,000	167	1,552	90	300-hp Cont. IO-520-L	1,700	$11,500
T210K	1970-71	$35,000	190	1,620	90	285-hp Cont. TSIO-520-H	1,400	$13,000
210L	1972-73	$36,500	164	1,552	90	300-hp Cont. IO-520-L	1,700	$11,500
T210L	1972-73	$39,500	190	1,620	90	285-hp Cont. TSIO-520-H	1,400	$13,000
210L	1974-75	$42,500	164	1,552	90	300-hp Cont. IO-520-L	1,700	$11,500
T210L	1974-75	$45,500	190	1,476	90	285-hp Cont. TSIO-520-H	1,400	$13,000
210L, M	1976-77	$49,000	171	1,552	90	300-hp Cont. IO-520-L	1,700	$11,500
T210L	1976	$51,000	197	1,476	90	285-hp Cont. TSIO-520-H	1,400	$13,000
210M, N	1978-79	$59,000	171	1,552	90	300-hp Cont. IO-520-L	1,700	$11,500
T210M	1977-78	$60,000	197	1,476	90	310-hp Cont. TSIO-520-R	1,400	$14,000
210N	1980-81	$72,000	170	1,580	90	300-hp Cont. IO-520-L	1,700	$11,500
T210N	1979-80	$72,000	197	1,476	90	310-hp Cont. TSIO-520-R	1,400	$14,000
210N	1982-83	$100,000	170	1,580	90	300-hp Cont. IO-520-L	1,700	$11,500
T210N	1981-82	$95,000	221	1,700	90	310-hp Cont. TSIO-520-R	1,600	$14,000
210N, R	1984-85	$151,000	170	1,580	90	300-hp Cont. IO-520-L	1,700	$11,500
T210N	1983-84	$134,000	221	1,700	90	310-hp Cont. TSIO-520-R	1,600	$14,000
210R	1986	$190,000	170	1,580	90	300-hp Cont. IO-520-L	1,700	$11,500
T210R	1985-86	$188,000	221	1,780	87/115	325-hp Cont. TSIO-520-CE	1,600	$14,000

cable being very hard to push when I was low time in the aircraft. So 10 to 12 mechanics tried it, and none seemed to think anything was unusual. I went flying at zero degrees F, with ground wind at 30 mph and found myself high on short final, reduced power to zero. And when it came time to add two to three inches on short final, I could not move the throttle cable and landed in the snow about 500 feet ahead of the runway. Fortunately, the grass and snow were nearly as well packed and level as the runway (very short) and so no damage, other than to the throttle cable, was caused. I consider this a serious problem, especially in 210s— enough so that I check other 210s on the ramp even at the risk of offending the other pilot. Feedback indicates that when checked out, about half the aircraft had problems in this area. Apparently grease buildup is one problem, and grooving of the core when in the full off position is the other culprit.

Overall: I am considering a large twin. However, I will not sell the 210. Once used to it, you find it easy to fly and an honest, simple, fast aircraft. Runway length of 2,000 feet or more is safe with any legal load. It handles *better* when fully loaded. Before purchase, I had considered many aircraft, but decided on the 210 because of cost, speed, loading and method of loading. We carry a lot of heavy equipment, and I don't want to carry it over the wing.

Hot starts: We use the boost pump just enough to see the fuel pressure move, push throttle, prop and mixture to the firewall and crank. Within 10 blades, the engine catches and the throttle is reduced immediately. This works 100 percent.

The notch on the lower aft fuselage is a wheel well for the main landing gear when retracted. With the 1979 models, Cessna dropped the gear doors and the extra nuisance and complication they represented. Speed, however, was not compromised.

Fuel system: I have reason to believe that it may be possible to unport a partially empty tank in the air. This may be the reason for some power losses attributed to vapor lock. On landing rollout with hard braking and a quick left turn, with the right tank selected, it is possible to stop the engine 100 percent of the time. Likewise in reverse. For that reason, after hard braking, I lead with some throttle before making the hard turn. Maybe this is an irrational worry, but when landing in a crosswind, I always allow the fuel to feed from the higher wing tank. The fuel selector does not have a "both" position.

Louis Bornwasser
Louisville, Ky.

I own a 1973 Cessna 210L with one partner. In our opinion, the aircraft is, without a doubt, the best six-place single on the market for the money. We have had relatively low maintenance except for the gear doors, which we recently brought up to new standards. The 210 really does fly with six passengers and a small amount of luggage. We can cruise at 160 knots and burn 13 gph at 9,000 feet.

Handling qualities of the 210 are heavy compared to a plane like the Mooney or Bonanza, but the other qualities of speed, payload, fuel, etc. make up for this one factor. I handles well in weather and is very stable in flight. We are presently insulating our plane like the Riley models and upgrading the windshield to one-quarter inch thickness. We intend to keep our 210 for a long time.

Alex Lancaster
Sarasota, Fla.
I own a 1981 210N, fully IFR equipped and with Rnav, S-tec two-axis autopilot and Horton STOL conversion. Last year the annual was $800, with no problems. This year it was $2,200 due to a $1,200 propeller charge caused by acid eating the prop under the boots from a previous prop cleaning.

The plane is a pleasure, comfortable, indicates 150 knots at 23/23 and will climb at any speed you wish. It handles four people and all the baggage you can stuff in. Range will outlast any bladder. Holds 90 gallons usable, and the overall average is 13-15 gph on fuel.

I cannot imagine anything better in a single-engine.

Sidney F. Shapiro
Memphis, Tenn.

I purchased a used 1976 T210 in 10/86 for $40,000. Since then I have invested another 40 more in paint, interior, King Silver Crown, Northstar loran, Riley intercooler, S-Tec A/P, Shadin fuel flo, odds and ends—1200TTSN, 50 SPOH.

Performance: After adding the intercooler a year ago, I saw a 10-knot increase, run at 27 inches MP, true airspeed of 180 knots at 11,500, and a loran GS of 175 knots. This is with four adults (720 lbs), full gear/luggage, two miniature Schnauzers and 65 gallons of fuel. Engine is the TSIO-520, 285 hp. I am very happy with these numbers for my needs.

Handling: The T210 has the reputation of being "yoke-heavy," but this never was a bother to me. I transitioned from a 172 to a 182 to the 210. However, since adding the electric trim and the S-Tec (w/alt. hod, climb and descend functions) with the 300 Navomatic, handling is a dream, allowing more time for the pilot to "see and be seen."

Maintenance: Since I've been told that 40 percent of everything involving general aviation costs is tacked onto the prices as "liability insurance costs," owning and maintaining any airplane "ain't cheap." Annuals have run around $950 if I do the inspection plates. Parts availability has been okay, but getting them may take a while. Seems these days if you want anything done, the plane's down two weeks. I don't really feel the T210 is that expensive to maintain.

Idiosyncrasies: I continue to hear about the "gear-door problems" and the need to beef up the ailerons, elevator and vertical stabilizer. I had to replace one up-switch on the gear doors, but I've had no actuator trouble, which can easily be detected if leaking. I had the able to the spring-loaded step, which retracts with the gear, break, but I simply wired up the step permanently. I've received varying opinions as to having the "mod" done. I know that Uvalde claims, but one commercial pilot with 15,000 hours, mostly in 210s and jets, told me he prefers the doors left on. "It's cleaner looking, and you don't lose five knots cruise, and I've owned them both ways." So up till now I've kept the doors. I've yet to be convinced that the beef-up mod is absolutely essential also.

Conclusion: Weighing all the pros and cons of owning a 210, I feel for my needs—

a big family and big loads, with a need for decent speed—I know of no single-engine airplane for $40,000 to $80,000 that can do all that.

Ken LLoyd
La Crescenta, Calif.

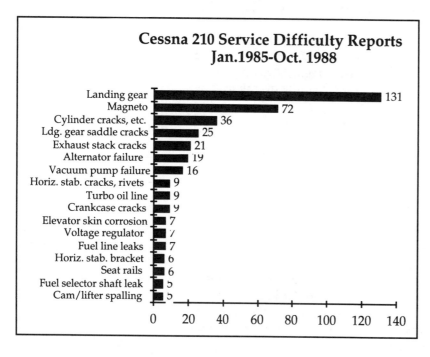

Cessna 210 Service Difficulty Reports Jan.1985-Oct. 1988

Landing gear	131
Magneto	72
Cylinder cracks, etc.	36
Ldg. gear saddle cracks	25
Exhaust stack cracks	21
Alternator failure	19
Vacuum pump failure	16
Horiz. stab. cracks, rivets	9
Turbo oil line	9
Crankcase cracks	9
Elevator skin corrosion	7
Voltage regulator	7
Fuel line leaks	7
Horiz. stab. bracket	6
Seat rails	6
Fuel selector shaft leak	5
Cam/lifter spalling	5

A chart plotting user reports of problems with C-210s shows the landing gear by far dominates the list.

My two flying partners and I have owned a 1978 C-210M for about three years, and have put on about 450 hours without any serious mechanical malfunctions. We have averaged around 15 gph and gone through a quart of oil abut every 10 hours.

Total maintenance has run about $2,500 a year, about three-fifths of that for the annual inspection.

Realistically, our total cost (fixed and variable, mortgage, incidentals, etc.) comes out to about $100 per hour, but the plane has been a reliable aerial "pack horse" and is much more adaptable to various requirements than our previous C-182.

Although built somewhat like a truck, with controls to match, it is a most dependable IFR platform. With the exception of some rather costly small parts (i.e., a retractable step which costs over $350 to replace), we haven't been hit with very many unpleasant maintenance surprises. We are, however, thinking of getting the gear door modification for peace of mind during those cold Minnesota winter landings.

All in all, we have been very pleased with our regular 210 and see no reason to move up to a turbo. The plane adapts to all our various demands, and we look upon it as a big old friendly station wagon.

Bruce A. Norback, M.D.
Edina, Minn.

Our 1982 model has the dual vacuum system installation, which takes care of the one difficulty we experienced with the previous aircraft—relatively frequent vacuum failures—about four in five years of operation.

The aircraft is in a class by itself for load carrying capacity and efficient operation. It will carry six people, full fuel and luggage, although the back rear seats are cramped.

W. Thompson Comerford, Jr.
Winston-Salem, N.C.

*This page left
intentionally blank.*

Cessna P210

As a used airplane buy, Cessna's pressurized P210 is a tantalizing paradox. The plane has one of the worst reputations of any airplane in recent years—and deservedly so, for it has plagued owners with a seemingly unending series of mechanical problems. As a result, value of the P210 on the used- plane market is relatively low.

In fact, we saw an ad a few years ago placed by a P210 owner who wanted to trade his six-place pressurized P210 for a four-place non-pressurized Mooney 231—and he was willing to trade even. However, because of the P210's depressed value, a canny buyer can get a good bargain if he finds the right airplane. After years of trial and

Enlarged air inlet alongside the spinner helps identify the much- improved P210R model, which had intercooling, a longer wing and tail.

tribulation, it appears Cessna finally made enough changes so that it's possible to get a reasonably trouble-free P210—but only if the buyer chooses carefully.

Troubled History

The P210 is a pressurized out-growth of the ancient 210 line. It first appeared in 1978 as the only pressurized single on the market. (It held that distinction until the Piper Malibu arrived on the scene in late 1983.) The P210 was heralded as a great daring leap in technology, and its later problems were excused by many on the grounds that, "Well, that's the price you pay for advancing the state of the art." This is a major misconception. The P210 was indeed a daring marketing leap, but technologically it was nothing new. The airframe was a quarter-century old, the basic TSIO-520 engine had been around for years, and the pressurized system was lifted straight from the pressurized Skymaster. "New" features like the fixed-point controller for the turbo wastegate were in fact technical steps backward designed to cut costs.

But the marketeers certainly had done their homework; the P210 sold well from the beginning. Nearly 400 were built the first two years, and most owners seemed happy. Things looked good for the P210.

Then, during the summer of 1980, two P210s crashed after engine failures resulting from detonation. The FAA issued emergency ADs requiring ultra-rich mixtures to keep the engines cool, along with other performance-robbing anti-detonation measures. There followed a long period of technical turmoil at Cessna which only died down after some years. A new turbocharger was fitted, and announced with much hoopla as the "Performance-Plus" package that would solve the detonation problems. That it did, but the "Performance-Plus" label was rather farcical. Performance in fact declined dramatically, and most P210 pilots found they could not maintain manifold pressure or cabin pressurization above 16,000-18,000 feet.

Months of Frustration

For six months, P210 owners screamed and fumed in frustration, while Cessna tried vainly to come up with a solution. Finally, in late 1981, Cessna announced its fix: A new air induction system, retrofitted free by Cessna, restored the lost performance. The P210's original induction system, it turned out, had been poorly designed all along.

During all the detonation/turbocharger goings-on, P210 owners were reporting all sorts of other engineering and quality-control problems: leaky, warped exhaust systems, failed vacuum pumps, overheating avionics, engine surging due to vapor lock, and landing gear malfunctions. Many pilots also complained about poor instrumentation that left them ill-equipped to operate the complex high-performance aircraft correctly.

Choice of model year (except for the drastically changed -R model) shouldn't be a major concern for the P210 shopper; most important mods have been retrofitted to the older models, making all pre-'82 airplanes essentially identical, except for the landing gear. The 1978 P210 had gear doors, whereas on later models Cessna dropped main-gear doors altogether, thereby cutting manufacturing costs (and maintenance costs for the owner). The loss of gear doors did not affect cruise speed—although gear-lowering speed did go up a whopping 25 knots in the doorless post-'79 birds, to 165 KIAS

The 1982 and 1983 models (actually they're all 1982s; the 1983 P210 is a leftover 1982 airplane with a new paint job) did get some major non-retrofitable (for the most part) improvements that deserve attention. Among them:

• New turbo controller. The "fixed-point controller" on 1978-81 aircraft is an economy measure that maintains an upper deck pressure—the pressure between the turbo compressor and the throttle butterfly—of 35 inches, even when the engine only needs 25 inches. This causes the turbo to work a lot harder than it has to, which results in more exhaust back pressure and hotter induction air. Both sap performance and reliability. The 1982-83 P210 has a "slope controller" that maintains deck pressure at a steady two inches above manifold pressure, and takes a lot of unnecessary load off the turbo.

• New fuel system. The vapor-lock-prone system of earlier P210s was discarded in favor of an excellent left-right-both system with proper vapor-return lines.

• Engine improvements. The valves, rings and valve guides were improved, and the engine designation changes from TSIO-520-P to TSIO-520-AF. In the process, TBO went up 200 hours, to 1,600 hours.

• Dual vacuum pumps and alternators were made available as options.

• Cowl flaps were improved to reduce the chances of overcooling on descent.

• A TIT (Turbine Inlet Temperature) gauge was added, along with a restriction of

1,650 degrees TIT. This serves to limit leaning and keep exhaust temps down.

A Major Redesign

Then, in 1985 Cessna performed a major redesign job on the P210. It put in a more powerful engine with an intercooler, added longer wings, more fuel, new tail and better handling qualities. This was the P210R, hopefully nicknamed the "Malibu-eater" by Cessna executives. (Little did they know the Malibu would eventually "eat itself" in a series of technical disasters that rivaled the P210's.)

Part of the P210's problem may have been Cessna's odd division of engineering and management between the Pawnee and Wallace Divisions. Wallace designed and built the big-iron business airplanes—the jets, turboprops and big piston twins. Pawnee designed and built the little stuff, the price-sensitive airplanes aimed at cost-conscious owners—the 150s, the Skyhawks, on up through the Skymaster twin.

Although Cessna's Wallace Division had built thousands of turbocharged, pressurized aircraft, the P210 was engineered by the Pawnee Division. Pawnee's only previous pressurized aircraft had been the P-337, a disaster of such magnitude that the first year's production had to be returned to the factory for a major overhaul of engines and systems.

Intracompany Schism

Smaller windows come with the pressurized cabin, which at a differential of only 3.35 pounds, is the lowest of any current pressurized airplane. There is no rate controller. The cabin is quiet, however.

Communication between the two divisions was apparently minimal. Pawnee apparently paid little heed to the lessons learned at Wallace over the years about intercooling and exhaust systems in pressurized airplanes. After literally years of vain attempts to fix the P210 within Pawnee, Cessna apparently had a change of philosophy. In effect, the P210R was taken out of the hands of the Pawnee Division, and soon after Cessna reorganized its engineering and management to eliminate the Wallace/Pawnee split.

The intercooled -R engine puts out a tad more power than the -N engine (325 hp compared to 310 at 2700 rpm), but the extra power comes at the cost of extra manifold pressure: 37 inches on the new airplane compared to 35.5 on the old one.

The P210R flies much faster than the older P210s, fast enough to breathe down the neck of the Malibu. Max cruise is listed at 213 knots at 23,000 feet, at best power mixture and mid-cruise weights. That's a good 20-plus knots faster than the year before. Under more realistic conditions—65 percent power, 20,000 feet, best economy mixture—book cruise is still an excellent 190 knots. That's only four or five knots slower than the Malibu under the same conditions.

Besides the intercooler, the major change in the P210R is the horizontal stabilizer.

It's a full three feet wider in span than the old one, and aspect ratio is about 40 percent higher. The new stabilizer does its job so much more efficiently than the old one that Cessna was able to eliminate the downsprings and bobweights required in the control systems.

Much-Improved Handling

The new tail produced a smooth, responsive, nice-handling airplane. Pitch forces are much lighter; takeoff rotation, steep turns and landing flare can all be managed with one hand. Also, the new wing tips, adding more than two feet of wing span and 10 square feet of wing area help climb performance. And since the new tips contain an extra 30 gallons of fuel together, they bring total capacity up to a generous 120 gallons. The tips feed by gravity into the mains, and there is no pumping or switching required. From the pilot's point of view, it's all one big tank.

Summing up, there are three kinds of P210s: the "Mark I" airplane built from 1978-81, the "Mark II" that appeared in 1982 and the -R introduced in 1985. P210 buyers should make every effort to find a 1985 -R model first, if the pocketbook allows, or 1982 or 1983 model as a less expensive, (and less desirable) alternative.

Unlike most Cessnas, the P210 has only one cabin door, on the left side. A double window panel hinged from the top swings open on the right side of the cabin, however, for emergency egress. Baggage goes into a separate, unpressurized rear compartment.

Used-Plane Market

Prices have climbed from a few years ago. In 1983, a 1979 P210 could be bought for about the same price as a comparable T210 or even a normally aspirated A36 Bonanza of the same vintage. In effect, the pressurization came free on the used-plane market. The used-plane buyers thus could benefit from the huge depreciation loss suffered by the poor fellow who bought it new. But now the P210 (take an '83 model as an example) is worth about $35,000 more than a T210 of the same year and about $13,000 more than a normally aspirated Beech A36 Bonanza.

However, the P210 is outclassed by the turbo 36 Bonanzas in price. The '83 P210, for instance, has a Bluebook value of only $158,000 vs. $177,000 for the B36TC. The '79 P210 exhibits an even greater, humiliating margin beneath the A36TC: $82,000 vs. $112,000. Current P210 prices run from about $74,000 for a 1978 model with ARC avionics and no de-ice equipment to $134,000 for a 1982 model. This is an improvement since 1983, however, when one P210 owner sadly confirmed a $100,000 ceiling price; he tried to sell his loaded 1981 model (it had even been updated with the dual vacuum and alternator systems) and the best offer he could get was $95,000—precisely half what he paid for it new one year earlier.

Performance

The performance of the P210 can be considered from two angles. Compared to other big, turbocharged, single-engine airplanes, it has adequate performance. But compared to other pressurized aircraft such as the Cessna 340A or Baron 58P, it falls well short. Because of the power drain of pressurization, P210's performance is slightly less than that of the T210,which has the same airframe and power. Maximum certified ceiling of the P210 is 23,000 feet, but owners report that because of the mediocre climb performance, cruising altitudes above 20,000 feet are impractical unless the plane is very lightly loaded and the trip a long one. Time-to-climb to 23,000 feet is listed as 31 minutes at max available power, but a more reasonable figure is the 39-minute climb to 20,000 feet at normal climb power. That's a long time, and it explains why many P210 pilots prefer to stay in the 15,000-18,000-foot area.

Cessna P210 Resale Value

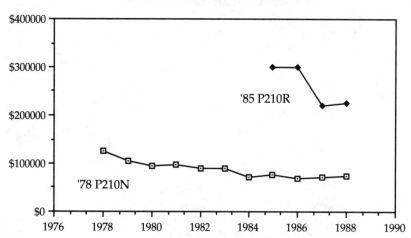

'85 P210R

'78 P210N

Cruise speeds range from about 170-190 knots, depending on altitude and power setting. However, one P210 pilot reports he gets over 200 knots consistently at light weights.

The 90-gallon fuel supply on the Pre-'85 models is not exactly generous. By the book, it's good for a range of about 700 nm with a 45-minute reserve at 70 percent power. Throttled back to 55 percent, book range climbs to over 800 nm. However, these range figures require leaning to rather high exhaust gas temperatures, and prudent P210 pilots prefer to run richer mixtures. This results in higher fuel consumption (by about two to three gph) and range deductions of about 100 nm. A good conservative rule of thumb is 20 gallons per hour, block-to-block, at high cruise speeds. With IFR reserves, that's only about three hours' cruising time.

Takeoff and landing performance is comparable to heavier twin-engined aircraft; about 2,200 feet is necessary to take off over a 50-foot obstacle at gross weight under standard conditions. Stall speed with flaps down is 61 knots, right at the FAA-imposed upper limit for single-engine airplanes.

Creature Comforts

Here, of course, is where the P210 shines. The pressurized cabin makes all the difference in the world above 12,500 feet, eliminating the need for cumbersome and uncomfortable oxygen masks. But once more, compared to pressurized twins, the P210 is rather anemic. Pressure differential is only 3.35 pounds, the lowest of any current pressurized airplane. The P210's pressure system has no rate controller; it simply starts to pressurize at the altitude selected by the pilot, maintains that cabin altitude as long as it can, and then maintains the maximum differential as the climb continues. As a result, pilot and passengers are subject to more ear-popping than they would be in, say, a Cessna 421. Such is the price of the "economy" pressurized airplane.

The front four passengers have reasonable—although not lavish—room. Cabin width is a modest 42 inches, but there is lots of headroom for the pilot to sit comfortably upright. The two rear seats, however, are quite cramped, and recommended on long trips only for children, midgets or contortionists. Cabin quiet is one of the P210's strong points. The turbocharger muffles the exhaust roar, and the tightly sealed cabin keeps out most of the slipstream noise.

Loading

The 210 series is renowned for its big load capacity and wide c.g. envelope. The P210 generally lives up to those traditions. When it was introduced in 1978, the P210 was the heaviest 210 of them all at 4,000 pounds, 200 more than the Turbo 210. (The T210 has since been boosted to 4,000 also.) Typical operating weights run around 2,500-2,600 pounds for well-equipped aircraft, including de-ice equipment. That leaves a healthy 1,400-1,500 pounds of useful load. With 90-gallon tanks full, there's still about 900 pounds left for payload. That's five standard 170-pound people, or four plus baggage.

The P210 pilot is more likely to find himself loaded out the front end of the center-of-gravity envelope rather than the rear, particularly on well-equipped airplanes with full panels and dual alternator/vacuum systems.

Handling Qualities

The 210 series is known for very heavy controls, and the P210 is the most ponderous of the 210s because control cables must be routed through tight-fitting air seals where they pass through the pressure vessel. The P210 will be perceived as a stiff-handling dinosaur, both on the ground and in the air, by pilots stepping up from smaller single engine planes. But on the other hand, the P210 is rock-solid in turbulence and IFR conditions, the environment in which it will presumably spend a lot of time.

Pitch control (except in the -R model) is particularly heavy. This makes landing with two people in front a challenge to the biceps, but it does have the safety plus of limiting the pilot's ability to apply high G-loadings and overstress the airplane. (The 210's record of overstress-induced in-flight breakups is surprisingly poor however—16 in the five years up to 1983.)

Safety Record

We have no statistics on P210 accident rates, but the 210 series in general ranks about average or slightly below when compared to other single-engine retractables during the period 1972-1976. The 210's fatal accident rate was 3.1 per 100,000 flight hours, in a group that ranged from 1.0 to 4.2.

Rear windows don't give much visibility to the stern, but lighten the cabin a bit.

A look at P210 accidents, however, reveals some unusual trends. A surprisingly large percentage of accidents are related to mechanical malfunctions, design defects or poor human engineering of the aircraft. Of 30 accidents reported by the NTSB during the period 1978-1981, only about a third were pure and simple pilot blunders. (Only one involved weather.) Thirteen of the 30 were engine failures. Of those 13, six were fuel mismanagement crashes. (These figures confirm our earlier findings of very high fuel mismanagement accident rates for the 210 series in general.) Of course, the pilot must take some blame in any fuel mismanagement accident, but the design of the fuel system plays a big role, too—and the P210's fuel system apparently needed the big improvements it finally got in 1982. Several accident reports mention misleading fuel gauges.

The other seven engine failures were your basic internal problems: two from detonation, with various other exhaust fires, cylinder blowoffs, and undetermined causes. The notorious vapor lock syndrome caused one crash, and another was triggered by excessive fuel from a runaway boost pump.

Another fertile ground for P210 accidents: landing gear problems. FAA accident/incident records show 19 P210 gear crunches of various sorts from 1978 through 1982, more than half of them due to mechanical malfunctions. The FAA records—which appear to be more complete than NTSB data—list a total of 75 P210 accidents or incidents since 1978. That amounted to about 10 percent of the fleet at that time

We tallied 10 fatal P210 accidents through 1982. Of those, three were in-flight breakups (one triggered by a vacuum system failure). One resulted from a cylinder blowing off the engine, another came after the pilot reported a loss of elevator control over the Gulf of Mexico.

Buyer's Checklist

The Turboplus intercooler exhausts air through a large vent on the right side of the engine.

We've covered the P210's myriad technical problems in detail in the past, and touched on them earlier in this article. Rather than describe the problems again, we'll concentrate on solutions. What follows is a P210 buyers' checklist which, if followed closely, will give the buyer a fighting chance at getting a safe, reliable airplane that won't drive him to the poorhouse.

• Exhaust system. Do not buy a P210 without the Inconel exhaust system. (Or at least plan to retrofit it immediately after purchase.) The P210 exhaust system is, in our view, an engineering disgrace, made of unsuitable material. As a result, the P210 exhaust system has been notoriously troublesome since the beginning and carries a 50-hour AD inspection for cracks.

• Fuel system. Ideally, one should buy a 1982 or later airplane with the redesigned fuel system. If not, make sure that the airplane is fitted with Cessna's vapor-return line fix. (See service letter SE81-42.)

• Vacuum system. We'd recommend the dual vacuum system, which can be retrofitted to all P210s. It is mandated by AD for any P210 equipped with the known-icing option.

• Dual alternator system. The 1982 aircraft were available with dual 60-amp alternators, and some 1980 and 1981 models were retrofitted at the factory. (That program was terminated in 1983, however, so it's too late to retrofit a plane after purchase.) Electrical redundancy is a must for an all-weather plane like the P210. We'd recommend the dual system. Some earlier P210s have a small emergency standby generator. This is better than nothing, but try to get the dual 60-amp system.

• Induction system. Don't buy a P210 without the bigger intake scoop and improved plenum chamber introduced in 1982. Most aircraft should already be retrofitted, since Cessna paid the bill for it.

• Avionics. Cessna's in-house ARC line reached an all-time low in quality and reliability in 1977-78, and although they seemed to be improved later, most people consider a panel full of ARC avionics to be a major liability in a P210. Look for King or Collins equipment. Also, consider retrofitting the improved avionics cooling fan introduced on Cessna's single-engine line. The previous cooling fan was poorly designed and very unreliable, and when it quits, the marginal ARC radios are even more likely to malfunction.

• Instrumentation. Standard factory engine instrumentation on 1978-81 P210s is, in our opinion, pathetically bad. We believe every P210 should be equipped with (1) a six-probe EGT with absolute temperature scale, (2) six-probe cylinder-head temp gauge, (3) Turbine Inlet Temperature (TIT) gauge, (4) accurate digital fuel-flow gauge. Look for a plane with this equipment (any serious pilot should already have it installed). If you can't find one, plan to install it immediately after purchase.

• Engine. The TSIO-520-P has a poor reliability record in the P210. Cylinder problems are common, partly a result of excessive heat. Check compression carefully, and have the mechanic inspect the condition of the valves and valve guides. Check the cooling baffles with great care. Look at maintenance records closely. The engine has a nominal TBO of 1,400 hours, but few engines have reached that mark without major problems.

• Cabin leaks. Poor quality control at Cessna's Pawnee plant has shown up in leaky cabins, particularly the door seals. These problems manifest themselves in reduced pressure capability and loss of manifold pressure. Check the outflow valve carefully; if it's defective, a replacement valve costs more than $5,000.

Modifications

In addition to the previously listed mods, which we would consider virtually mandatory, there are other aftermarket products available for the P210. Among them:

R/STOL Systems kit offered by Sierra Industries at Uvalde, Tex., (512) 278-4381. Drooped ailerons decrease the stall speed by about six knots, while stall strips and wing fences assure a gentle, controllable stall, according to R/STOL. A modified aileron control system with special low-friction pressure seals greatly reduces aileron control forces and increases roll rate by about 50 percent. R/STOL claims eye-opening takeoff performance improvements, but these are

Cost/Performance/Specifications

Model	Year	Average Retail Price	Cruise Speed (kts)	Useful Load (lbs)	Fuel Std/Opt (gals)	Engine	TBO (hrs)	Overhaul Cost
P210N	1978	$72,000	187	1,600	90	310-hp Cont. TSIO-520-P	1,400	$12,000
P210N	1979	$79,000	187	1,600	90	310-hp Cont. TSIO-520-P	1,400	$12,000
P210N	1980	$72,000	187	1,600	90	310-hp Cont. TSIO-520-P	1,400	$12,000
P210N	1981	$79,000	187	1,600	90	310-hp Cont. TSIO-520-P	1,400	$12,000
P210N	1982	$79,000	187	1,600	90	310-hp Cont. TSIO-520-AF	1,400	$12,000
P210N	1983	$79,000	187	1,600	90	310-hp Cont. TSIO-520-AF	1,400	$12,000
P210N	1984	$72,000	187	1,600	90	310-hp Cont. TSIO-520-CE	1,400	$12,000
P210R	1985	$79,000	212	1,629	85/115	325-hp Cont. TSIO-520-CE	1,600	$12,500
P210R	1986	$79,000	212	1,629	85/115	325-hp Cont. TSIO-520-CE	1,600	$12,500

apparently based on a takeoff speed five knots below power-off stall speed—not a wise procedure, in our opinion.

• Turboplus intercooler, speedbrakes. One way to help keep the engine running cooler is to have an intercooler installed by Turboplus in Gig Harbor, Wash. for a kit price of $4,995. The company also can install speed brakes on the aircraft. These will, conversely, help keep the engine from being overcooled on descent. Riley International Corp. in Carlsbad, Calif. also can install an intercooler on the P210. Aircraftsman at Long Beach, Calif. can do the same. See the C-210 article for details.

• Flint long-range fuel tanks. Two tip tanks add 33 gallons' fuel capacity and a couple of feet of wing span for better climb performance. Range is increased by about 250 nm. Cost of the kit is: $5,250, Flint Aero 865 Mission Gorge Rd., Santee, Calif. 92071, (619) 448-1551.

• Riley Turboprop conversion. Noted aircraft souper-upper Jack Riley has a PT6 P210 conversion. The Riley P210's cost is about $260,000, triple the value of any used P210 on the market.

• The Well's Aircraft fuel system mod to correct fuel vaporization problems is offered by Petersen Aviation in Minden, Neb.

• Rudder, elevator and aileron modification adding stiffening and mass balancing to improve the flutter margin, offered by O&N Aircraft Modifications at Factoryville, Pa. Airplane Help in Carlsbad, Calif. provides similar kits to bring ailerons up to 210R configuration.

Owner Comments

P210s can be approved for flight into known icing, with the proper equipment. Pod-mounted radar is one option, but Stormscope may do a better job than the smallish radar.

As a former owner of a pair of Model 33 Bonanzas, I must say that after 550 hours in a P210, it would be hard to give up the pressurization and icing capabilities. It is truly a comfort on long trips. We used to spend $10 to $20 to fill our oxygen tanks. Now I spend it for the extra fuel for the P210. Beech's A36TC costs the same or more than the P210, and offers no pressurization or de-ice capability. A used P210 with all the options is a good buy today.

Howard Hermel
Mankato, Minn.

I have experienced continuing heat-related problems and avionics malfunctions to the extent that, as of this date, I still have not had all avionics working at the same time. On the positive side, I am very impressed with the stability of the aircraft for IFR purposes and for landing. I have a Robertson STOL kit, which I'm very impressed with. The pressurization system makes flying much more comfortable than I had given it credit for.

Roger O. Weed
Anchorage, Alaska

Cessna
Skymaster 337

Cessna's push-pull twin, the 337 Skymaster, is a tantalizingly risky used-plane bargain. Suffering from a poor reputation among pilots, it can be bought at fire-sale prices well below the cost of other twins of similar performance.

But the potential downside is huge maintenance bills—particularly in the turbocharged and pressurized models—because of poor engineering and quality control at Cessna's Pawnee Division. On the other hand, for a pilot who knows the fine points, shops around carefully, and who doesn't object to some of the Skymaster's unique features, a used 337 can provide a lot of performance for a little bit of money.

Genealogy

The Skymaster first appeared in 1964 as the fixed-gear Model 336. With its front-rear engine layout, high strut-braced wing, and down-and-welded gear, the 336 was a radical departure indeed from the light twins of the day. But Cessna sold almost 200 336s that first year, and revamped it into the retractable-gear 337 Skymaster in 1965. The design evolved only a little over the years, progressing from the A model in 1966 through the 1978-80 H model, with minor refinements. The engines remained the same throughout the Skymaster's career: the 210-hp six-cylinder Continental IO-360.

A turbocharged version, the T-337B, appeared in 1967, but was dropped in 1972 with the addition to the Skymaster line of the pressurized P-337 version, with uprated 225-hp engines. The turbo was revived in 1978, but Skymaster sales had begun slipping by then, despite the great general aviation sales boom of the late 1970s. After selling between 80 and 115 Skymasters a year throughout the early and mid-1970s, Cessna saw sales drop to only 61 in the boom year of 1979 and less than 50 in 1980. Cessna pulled the plug following the 1980 model year, after a total Skymaster production run of 2,058, plus 332 pressurized versions.

Major model changes were few. Gross weight crept up over the years, starting at

4,200 with the 337A and increasing to 4,300 (B model), 4,400 (C model) and 4,440 (E model). With the 1971 F model, Cessna increased takeoff weight to 4,630 pounds, but max landing weight remained 4,400. (The P-337, with its 30 extra horsepower, had a takeoff weight of 4,700 pounds, and max landing weight of 4,465.)

Empty weight crept up as well over the years, however, and the useful load of the later versions wasn't all that much greater than the early models, although the 1971 model claimed to have 150 pounds more useful than the 1970 version.

In addition, the 1971 model had padding of the panel, door posts and seats for improved crashworthiness, plus an extra engine access door. In 1972 the electrical system—a long-time Skymaster trouble-spot—was improved. The 1973 model saw the replacement of the straight hydraulic landing gear system with the electro-hydraulic "power pack" gear, a change that turned out to be of dubious value. In 1974, the prop syncrophasers were improved. The 1975 model had more fuel capacity in the long-range tank option—148 gallons, up from 124. Radar was introduced as an option in 1977.

Cessna's last-gasp refinement efforts were, unfortunately, more cosmetic than real. The final 1980 version sported a "new instrument panel treatment including a burled elm wood grain panel cover that adds rich, attractive styling." Despite the irresistible lure of such features, almost nobody bought any Skymasters that year, the airplane's last.

Used Plane Market

To be blunt, the Skymaster is one of the worst dogs on the used-plane market. The older models go for only $15,000-20,000 in reasonable shape—barely half the price of a Twin Comanche of similar vintage. If the engines are due for overhaul, you could probably buy an old Skymaster for four figures. (Like many old, low-value twins with expensive engines, the value of an early-vintage Skymaster depends almost entirely on the engine condition. A double overhaul will run close to $25,000, not much less than the value of the plane with the new engines.)

Later models do better. A 1980 cream-puff IFR Turbo Skymaster might bring $60,000—only a bit less than a comparable Piper Seneca II, which uses the same engines. But the Skymaster still pales by comparison to a B55 Baron, for example, a 1980 version of which is worth close to $100,000. Not even a 1980 pressurized Skymaster would command anywhere near $100,000.

In terms of percentage resale value retained, the Skymaster looks pretty dismal. Assuming "bluebook" retail prices for a 1978 model, the Skymaster has retained just 40 percent of its original value. Comparable figures for other light twins range from 46 percent to 53 percent.

However, the Skymaster resale picture may be improving. Several people we talked to say that 337 prices have been rising recently, and one said he was having a hard time finding a decent P-model for under $80,000, much to his surprise. Like many aircraft that got bad reputations early (Yankee, Cardinal, etc.), the Skymaster may be starting to achieve a sort of cult status, with most of the planes eventually falling into the hands of people who like their peculiarities, which tends to keep the supply down and prices up.

Performance

The Skymaster lacks the sizzling performance of a B55 Baron, or the frugal efficiency of a Twin Comanche. But it doesn't look bad next to the generation of "light-light" twins (the Piper Seminole and Beech Duchess) that followed it. And the turbocharged models can put up some pretty decent cruise numbers if you take them high enough.

Book cruise speed for the normally aspirated Skymaster is about 165-169 knots. But, as one owner put it, "The manufacturer doesn't cheat any more than normal on owner's manual performance figures, and it comes pretty close to delivering the claimed performance when it is 800 pounds under gross." In the real world, typical Skymaster cruise speeds are around 150-155 knots, with the occasional optimist reporting 160 knots. One owner who also owns an A36 Bonanza reports that the two aircraft have almost identical cruise and climb performance.

Landing gear malfunctioning has been a chronic trouble point with Skymasters, and the biggest cause of accidents.

The turbo and pressurized models will push 190 knots at 20,000 feet, their maximum certified altitude. At the non-oxygen middle altitudes, 170-180 knots is a typical speed for the turbo models.

Reported fuel burns ranged from 16 gph to 22 gph, with 19-20 gph typical for a 150-155-knot cruise. For comparison, a Twin Comanche will do about the same speed on 100 less horsepower and a lot less gas. Efficiency is not a Skymaster hallmark.

Rate of climb ranges from a modest 1,300 fpm in the old 336 to a pathetically lethargic 940 fpm in the last 337H models. (Climb goes down as gross weight goes up.) We're unaware of any other twin-engine airplane with a book rate of climb below 1,000 fpm—even the old 150-hp Apache had a book climb of 1,250 fpm with both engines running.

Runway performance, on the other hand, is pretty good. Some owners even go so far as to claim STOL qualities at moderate weights. The Skymaster uses the good old Cessna formula—long, tapered wing and big flaps—to achieve stall speeds (and therefore takeoff and landing speeds) well below those of most twins. Stall speeds with flaps range from 63-70 mph, depending on the gross weight of the particular model—10 to 20 mph below conventional twins like the 310 and Baron.

As a result, a Skymaster will get off the ground in less than 1,000 feet at gross weight—a feat very few other twins can manage. Barrier performance is not quite so good, however; the lethargic climb rate brings the Skymaster's 50-foot takeoff figures down to the middle of the light-twin pack. Landing ground rolls are around 700 feet, also among the best of the twins.

Single-engine Performance

The single-engine climb rates of all the light twins tend to be very similar—200 to 300 fpm—because engine-out climb rate is a certification point around which the airplane is designed. FAA requires a certain minimum climb, figured by a formula relating to stall speed, and the manufacturers typically bump up the gross weight to the point at which the airplane just barely meets the FAA minimum. (Any excess engine-out climb capability is, in effect, wasted payload. And payload numbers sell airplanes.)

So it's no surprise that the Skymaster's engine-out rate of climb is right in there at 200-300 fpm on most models. What is surprising is the difference between the front and rear engines. Using the 1974 model as an example, rear engine climb is 320 fpm, but the front engine can manage only 270 fpm. The reason is apparently that when the rear propeller is turning, the airflow over the rear fuselage remains attached. But it separates when the rear prop stops, increasing drag.

Engine-out service ceiling is also typical for light twins—7,100 on the front engine, 6,100 on the rear (again, we're using the 1974 model as an example.) The turbo models naturally do a lot better; engine-out ceilings range from 15,000 to 20,000 feet.

Payload-Range

A Cessna press release from the 1970s describes the Skymaster as "a full six-place airplane with nearly a ton of useful load." This is utter bullpuckie. One owner accurately describes the two rear seats as "a joke, to say the least." And the press release conveniently forgets to mention that with the fifth and sixth seats installed, there is no baggage space whatsoever. (If you must carry six people and bags, an optional belly cargo pod was an option on later models.) Consider the Skymaster a nice four-placer.

Actual real-world useful loads run around 1,500 pounds—not bad at all, and several hundred pounds more than a Twin Comanche, for example. Standard fuel is 88 gallons, and that still leaves better than 900 pounds available for payload, more than enough for those four passengers and lots of baggage. Standard fuel is just barely adequate, however, unless you throttle way back—a little more than three hours with IFR reserves at fast cruise.

The long-range tanks—148 gallons in 1975-80 models, 123 in earlier models—solve the range limitations nicely, at the expense of payload, of course. One owner reports that with long-range tanks full, he has seven-plus hours at 150 knots with 650 pounds of payload (three people and bags). Not a bad compromise.

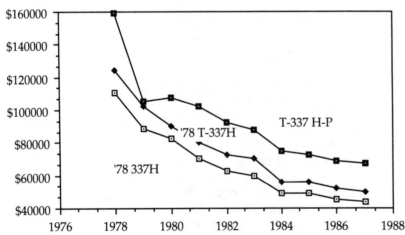

Cessna Skymaster Resale Value

'78 T-337H

T-337 H-P

'78 337H

Accommodation

As we said before, consider the Skymaster a four-seater, with two more available in an emergency if nobody has any baggage. Oddly, the P-337 may carry only five people; it was certified under different rules that require an emergency exit in a six-seat airplane. Rather than put in the exit, Cessna simply limited the seating to five.

The air-stair door is an attempt to give the Skymaster a "big-airplane feel," but it gets mixed reviews. "Cumbersome" is how one owner puts it.

The Skymaster is a roomy airplane. "Lots of creature comforts," reports one owner. "Good cockpit space," reports another. "I am comfortable with my six-feet-four, 200 pounds and very long legs. In other planes, like the Mooney, Cardinal and Trinidad, the yoke pins my left leg against the side bulkhead. Not the Skymaster."

Visibility is excellent, about as good as it gets in any light airplane, single or twin. The view down is unlimited, of course, and the wing is set far back enough that it doesn't block upward vision, as it does in most Cessna singles. The good visibility is not only a safety feature, but it adds to the feeling of roominess in the cockpit as well.

Windows became smaller through the years, as unpressurized models took on the tiny-window format of their pressurized stablemates, presumably for conformity of construction.

The Skymaster may be roomy, but it's noisy. Both engines are attached directly to the passenger compartment, and sympathetic vibration can be a problem, particularly without the prop synchronizers.

Handling Qualities

In normal flight, the Skymaster has typical Cessna handling: heavy in pitch, reasonably responsive ailerons. (The P-model has especially light ailerons.) Pilots praise its IFR stability. "It makes a stable instrument platform and handles turbulence well, without excess yaw," is a typical comment.

The noteworthy aspect of the Skymaster's handling—indeed, the whole reason for the airplane's existence—shows up when an engine fails. Instead of the normal yaw-roll-stall-spin scenario that too often follows engine failure in a normal twin, the Skymaster continues to fly straight ahead. An unprepared or rusty pilot can take his time and concentrate on the task of identifying and feathering the prop on the failed engine, without worrying about losing control. The Skymaster has no minimum control speed in the usual sense. The FAA considers the Skymaster so easy to handle with a failed engine that it doesn't even require a normal multi-engine rating to fly it. Instead, there's a special center-line-thrust rating.

One owner sums up the Skymaster design philosophy succinctly: "Much of my operation is mountain, IFR and/or night. I wouldn't feel safe in a single-engine plane, but since I only fly 100-125 hours a year, I don't feel I could stay as current and competent as I should be in a standard-configured twin."

Another owner, however, cautions Skymaster pilots against overconfidence. "I do think the plane has been oversold to low-time pilots. I was at or perhaps beyond my level of competence in the plane at 500 hours with 18 months of IFR experience. I am still not as smooth in controlling this plane as I would like to be. I believe that some of the blame for the Skymaster's high accident rate must be placed on the seductiveness of thinking that centerline thrust makes a twin just like a single. This is just plain not true."

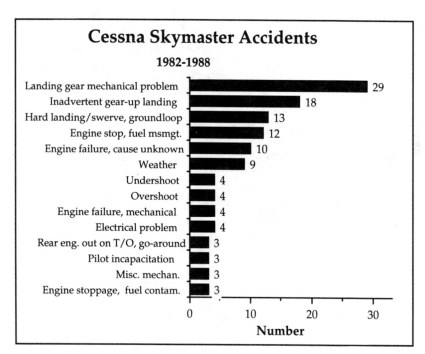

Cessna Skymaster Accidents

1982-1988

Category	Number
Landing gear mechanical problem	29
Inadvertent gear-up landing	18
Hard landing/swerve, groundloop	13
Engine stop, fuel msmgt.	12
Engine failure, cause unknown	10
Weather	9
Undershoot	4
Overshoot	4
Engine failure, mechanical	4
Electrical problem	4
Rear eng. out on T/O, go-around	3
Pilot incapacitation	3
Misc. mechan.	3
Engine stoppage, fuel contam.	3

Number

When Skymaster pilots aren't having mechanical problems with the landing gear, they initiate the trouble on their own by forgetting to lower it on landing. Accident causes with only one occurrence were not listed in this graph.

We heard from one Skymaster pilot who credits the airplane's engine-out handling qualities with saving his life. He had skipped the preflight before takeoff, failing to notice that (for reasons too complex to explain here) the left tank was full but the right one empty.

Shortly after takeoff, he found he needed nearly full right aileron just to stay level. Then the rear engine, feeding from the right tank, quit. "In any other twin, the flight would have terminated right then," he says.

But he was able to keep the Skymaster under control, restart the engine, climb to altitude, and burn off enough fuel to eventually make a normal landing. "No other airplane would have forgiven my oversight, singles included," he reports.

Another owner describes losing an engine in a P-337 shortly after reaching 19,000 feet on a long flight to do some quail-hunting. Not wanting to miss the fun, he simply descended to 15,000 feet and kept flying, arriving only a little behind schedule. He bagged his quail.

Safety

Despite the theoretical promise of the Skymaster's "safety twin" centerline-thrust design, and the occasional "I was saved by the Skymaster" anecdote, the sad fact is that the Skymaster has a lousy overall accident record. Even more ironically, its rate of engine-failure accidents is actually higher than most standard twins.

A 1984 *Aviation Consumer* study found that during the period 1972-1982, the 337 had 2.5 fatal accidents per 100,000 flight hours—16th worst fatal accident rate of the 18 twin-engine aircraft we studied. Only the Aerostar and Cessna 411 ranked lower. Median fatal rate for the group was 1.3 (nearly twice as good as the Skymaster) and the best of the lot, the Cessna 414, rated 0.8, which is three times better than the Skymaster.

For total accidents, the picture was similar. The Skymaster ranked 15th out of 18 with a rate of 9.5 per 100,000 hours. Median was 5.8; the lowest rate was 3.2.

Focussing on engine-failure accidents, the picture is even more puzzling. Despite its docile engine-out handling qualities and lack of minimum-control speed, the Skymaster ranked a dismal 16th out of 20 in a 1980 NTSB study of fatal engine-failure accidents in twin-engine aircraft.

Several of the Skymaster's fatal engine-failure crashes occurred when the rear engine quit on takeoff, and the pilot apparently failed to notice the failure and continued the takeoff. Such accidents have plagued the Skymaster for years; Cessna eventually added a warning light and revised the takeoff checklist to require advancing the rear throttle first for takeoff.

A look at two dozen Skymaster fatal accidents shows no other obvious pattern; the crashes are a fairly random assortment of weather, fuel exhaustion, stalls and ground impacts of various sorts—the usual mix.

Non-fatal accidents do show one pattern: fuel exhaustion. Cessna bragged about the reliability of the capacitance-type gauges in the Skymaster, but they were unreliable, and their location on the right side of the panel made them hard to read. Furthermore, a Skymaster with the long-range fuel system has only two gauges for four tanks; the pilot must turn a switch to make the gauge read either the main or aux tank for each engine.

In our judgment, this is a bad piece of human engineering that has caused fuel-mismanagement problems in other aircraft like the Bellanca Viking.

Several fuel-starvation crashes may have occurred because of poor design of the check valves in the vapor return line of certain model Skymasters. On 1975-80 model 337s with long-range tanks, the check valves are mounted horizontally, which makes them more likely to stick in the open position. Because the vapor return line runs to the manifold instead of the fuel tanks, a stuck valve allows some fuel to reach the engine even when the selector valve is turned off.

The problem is, if the pilot inadvertently turns the fuel selector off, the engine will continue to run at moderate power. That's fine, until the pilot goes to high power—for takeoff or go-around, for example. Then the engine quits, and the pilot has no idea why. (At least when the engine quits immediately after a fuel selector change, the pilot may think to check the selector.) One attorney investigating the problem believes at least eight Skymaster fuel mismanagement crashes may be related to this phenomenon.

Pressurized models like this one will push 190 knots at 20,000 feet, their top certified altitude.

Maintenance

Here's the potential Skymaster nightmare: runaway maintenance costs, particularly in the turbo and pressurized models. The Skymaster was the most complex aircraft ever engineered and manufactured by Cessna's Pawnee Division, which otherwise

built only the Cessna single-engine line. The evidence suggests the Pawnee Division simply wasn't up to the task, particularly in the 1975-80 period when production was growing rapidly and Cessna was plagued with an epidemic of design, engineering and production problems.

For example, the pressurized Skymaster was initially such a disaster that the first year's production was recalled to the factory for complete remanufacture and modification.

And listen to the plaintive cries of one owner who traded in his 1973 model for a brand-new 1978 337H in the hope that

Cruise speeds are a modest 150-155 knots. On an engine-out situation, the rear engine yields a better climb rate because of greater efficiency.

it might reduce the frequency of visits to the service department of his local Cessna dealer: "In the nine months and 130 hours since then, I seem to have experienced nearly all the standard joys of 337 ownership, including but not limited to: (1) inoperative synchrophaser (two times); (2) rear alternator shaft oil seal leaking (three times); (3) defective cabin door lock and problems with the door latching mechanism; (4) shaft twisted off rear vacuum pump; (5) cracking of rubber grooves of all three tires; (6) erroneous indication by left-hand fuel gauge; (7) rear EGT inoperative; (8) gas leak in right wing tank; (9) water leak around cowling cover at base of windshield.... There have been 35 other minor squawks . . . but I have my Skymaster blinders securely on, and am hoping that after this initial period of de-bugging I will be able to give up the more or less permanent spot which I have been occupying in my dealer's shop."

Most of the Skymaster's problems seem to be in the systems. The basic airframe is a stout one, with the rugged strut-braced wing. And remember that the military version of the Skymaster, the O-2 observation aircraft, did plenty of rough duty in Vietnam, often flying home with bullet holes and worse. "It took a hell of a beating," recalls one civilian Skymaster owner who had previously flown O-2s in Vietnam. (As a point of interest, he also mentioned that it was "a very stable rocket and gun platform.")

At least the used-Skymaster buyer has the chance to get a debugged airplane. Closely examine the logbooks and service records of any Skymaster considered for purchase. And keep a sharp lookout for these chronic Skymaster problems:

• Oil leaks in the rear engine. Loose rocker box covers, a chronically leaky quick-drain and a sloppy breather tube seem to be the main culprits (although one Skymaster buff claims the problem is entirely psychological, due to the fact that the bottom of the rear cowling is more easily visible than the front). Skymaster aficionados tell us it is possible to run a dry-belly Skymaster, but you'll have to keep the rocker-box covers tight, eliminate the quick drain and modify the breather tube to post-1975 configuration.

• Defective landing gear switches. Cheap plastic switches plagued the Skymaster during the mid-1970s (as they did other Cessna models). Actually, the entire landing gear system is a mechanic's nightmare; eleven—count 'em, eleven—hydraulic actuators in all.

• Aluminum wiring. Certain model Skymasters had aluminum wiring and cheap connectors, a certain recipe for electrical gremlins.

• Crack-prone engine crankcases in pre-1973 models. Engines remanufactured since then should have been retrofitted with heavier cases. Look for the "H" logo on the heavy cases.

• Water leaks around the windshield were a chronic problem in older models. Check for possible rain damage, and check the condition of the windshield sealant.

• Hot-running rear engine. Carefully check the cooling baffle seals in the rear cowling. Also check the rear temperature gauge. One Skymaster buff we talked to swears that the "hot rear engine problem" is a red herring due to defective gauge installations. He says he's installed precisely accurate digital six-probe CHT gauges in two Skymasters in which the standard Cessna gauges indicated a hot-running rear engine. In both cases, the better gauge showed that the rear engine actually ran

Cost/Performance/Specifications

Model	Year	Average Retail Price	Cruise Speed (kts)	Useful Load (lbs)	S.E. Service Ceiling (ft)	Fuel Std/Opt (gals)	Engine	TBO (hrs)	Overhaul Cost Ea.
337	1965	$18,000	167	1,565	8,300	93/131	210-hp Cont. IO-360-C/D	1,500	$9,000
337A	1966	$20,000	167	1,585	8,200	93/131	210-hp Cont. IO-360-C/D	1,500	$10,000
337B	1967	$21,000	167	1,685	7,500	93/131	210-hp Cont. IO-360-C/D	1,500	$10,000
T-337B	1967	$22,500	196	1,515	20,000	93/131	210-hp Cont. TSIO-360-A/B	1,400	$10,800
337C	1968	$21,500	166	1,750	6,800	93/131	210-hp Cont. IO-360-C/D	1,500	$10,000
T-337C	1968	$23,000	195	1,705	18,600	93/131	210-hp Cont. TSIO-360-A/B	1,400	$10,800
337D	1969	$22,000	166	1,745	6,800	93/131	210-hp Cont. IO-360-C/D	1,500	$10,000
T-337D	1969	$24,000	195	1,485	16,200	93/131	210-hp Cont. TSIO-360-A/B	1,400	$10,800
337E	1970	$23,000	166	1,820	6,500	93/131	210-hp Cont. IO-360-C	1,500	$10,000
T-337E	1970	$26,000	223	1,780	14,400	93/131	210-hp Cont. TSIO-360-A	1,400	$10,800
337F	1971-72	$25,000	166	1,935	5,100	93/131	210-hp Cont. IO-360-C	1,400	$10,800
T-337F	1971	$29,000	194	1,780	14,400	93/131	210-hp Cont. TSIO-360-A	1,500	$10,000
337G	1973-74	$29,000	169	1,517	6,900	90/150	210-hp Cont. IO-360-G	1,500	$10,000
T-337G-P	1973-74	$38,500	204	1,533	18,700	150	225-hp Cont. TSIO-360-C	1,400	$10,800
337G II	1975	$33,000	169	1,517	6,900	90/150	210-hp Cont. IO-360-G	1,500	$10,000
T-337G-P	1975	$45,000	204	1,533	18,700	150	225-hp Cont. TSIO-360-C	1,400	$10,800
337G II	1976	$35,000	169	1,517	6,900	93/131	210-hp Cont. IO-360-G	1,500	$10,000
T-337G-P	1976	$52,000	204	1,533	18,700	150	225-hp Cont. TSIO-360-C	1,400	$10,800
337G II	1977	$39,000	169	1,517	6,900	90/150	210-hp Cont. IO-360-G	1,500	$10,000
T-337G-P	1977	$59,000	204	1,533	16,500	90/150	210-hp Cont. TSIO-360-C	1,400	$10,800
337H II	1978	$48,000	169	1,687	6,900	90/150	210-hp Cont. IO-360-G	1,500	$10,000
T-337H II	1978	$49,000	200	1,608	16,500	90/150	210-hp Cont. TSIO-360-H	1,400	$10,800
337H II	1979	$50,000	169	1,687	6,900	90/150	210-hp Cont. IO-360-GB	1,500	$10,000
T-337H II	1979	$50,000	200	1,608	16,500	150	210-hp Cont. TSIO-360-H	1,400	$10,800
T-337H-P	1978	$67,000	204	1,533	18,700	150	225-hp Cont. TSIO-360-C	1,400	$10,800
T-337H-P	1979	$77,000	204	1,533	18,700	150	225-hp Cont. TSIO-360-CB	1,400	$10,800
337H II	1980	$60,000	169	1,687	6,900	150	210-hp Cont. IO-360-GB	1,500	$10,000
T-337H II	1980	$70,000	200	1,608	6,500	150	210-hp Cont. IO-360-G	1,500	$10,000
T-337H-P	1980	$89,000	204	1,533	18,700	150	225-hp Cont. TSIO-360-CB	1,400	$10,800

cooler than the front. The owner says he now climbs with the rear cowl flaps partially closed and temps well in the green.

• ARC 300 radios. These were notoriously shoddy and unreliable during the mid- and late 1970s. Avoid them if at all possible. If not possible, be prepared to spend a bundle keeping them going.

• Defective paint jobs. When Cessna switched to DuPont Imron on the Skymaster (as well as the other Pawnee models) in 1977, it ignored DuPont requirements for metal preparation and priming, using a cheap, quick wash primer instead of the required alodyne and epoxy primer. The result was an epidemic of filiform corrosion, particularly in warm, humid coastal areas. Check the geographical history of any 1977-80 Skymaster; if it's spent much time in Florida, the Gulf Coast or California, look scrupulously for filiform corrosion, And be suspicious of a recent paint job; in many cases, the corrosion comes right back after a year or two.

• Landing gear solenoids. Post-1974 models have improved solenoids, part number 9881201-1.

Inspection Costs

Owners typically report annual costs in the $1,000 to $3,000 range. Here's one owner's litany of annual inspection costs over a nine-year period: $1,487; $1,742; $1,777; $1,186; $1,686; $2,067; $1,403; $1,957; and $2,294. You get the picture.

Service Difficulty Reports

The SDRs reveal some familiar patterns. Leading the Skymaster breakdown parade are the landing gear system (36 reports over six years) and electrical system, especially the alternators (24 reports). The Continental IO-360 and TSIO-360 also came in for their share of black marks, most of them in well-known trouble areas: cracking crankcases, broken crankshafts (the 1979 and 1980 models have -CB engines with beefier cranks), bad connecting rods, and broken oil pump/tach drives. Cylinder problems were also widespread, with numerous reports of head-to-barrel separations.

Incidentally, the turbo and pressurized models accounted for more than half of all the service difficulty reports. Moral: complexity equals maintenance bills. (For example, the P-337's TSIO-360-C engine has more than 80 service bulletins issued against it. And its unique engine installation geometry can make even routine maintenance work a real chore.)

Modifications

STOL mods are popular on Skymasters, and you may find three different types on used Skymasters: the full-blown Robertson system, with drooped ailerons and flap-actuated elevator trim (now sold by Sierra Industries Inc., P.O. Box 5184, Uvalde, Tex. 78802, (512) 278-4381 at a price of $12,000, with a 10-15-percent discount available during the summer of 1988); and simpler systems involving only vortex generators and recontoured leading edges and wingtips from Horton STOLcraft, Wellington Municipal Airport, Wellington, Kans. 67152, (316) 326-2241 or (800) 835-2051 (price: $1,649 installed) and Bush Conversions, P.O. Box 431, Udall, Kans. 67146, (316) 782-3851 (price: $1,490 installed).

American Aviation at S. 3608 Davison Blvd., Spokane, Wash., 99204, (800) 423-0476 is now offering an intercooler installation for the pressurized Skymaster and the turbo models. By reducing induction air temperatures, the intercooler increases critical altitude, reduces manifold pressure required for maintaining power, and generally lets the engine run cooler and with less strain. Price is $7,900 for the kit, plus 35 man-hours installation in the field.

Owner Group

A font of Skymaster knowledge (and also Skymaster affection) is Dick Whitaker, Box 1950, Liberal, Kans. 67901. Whitaker publishes an informative Skymaster newsletter filled with tips, complaints and hosannahs from various Skymaster owners.

An experienced Skymaster service center is Liberal Aircraft in Liberal, Kansas (316) 624-1646. Art Downs is the man to ask for.

Owner Comments

My partner and I purchased our 1973 337G Skymaster in 1986. It had a total time of 1,050 hours, and we paid slightly under $20,000. The "bluebook" retail price at the time was $29,000. The 1973 model was the first year with the electric Power-Pac for the gear system, as opposed to the more troublesome hydraulic system on pre-1973 models.

Skymaster placement of fuel gauges way over on the right side of the panel is less than ideal in thwarting fuel mismanagement.

The clamshell door is cumbersome and the rear two seats are a joke, to say the least. They literally sit on the floor, and an adult has a great deal of difficulty sitting in these seats comfortably for any length of time.

From a pure numbers viewpoint, the Skymaster is an impressive plane. Single-engine performance is extremely docile, and on either the front or the rear engine, it will cruise about as fast as a Cessna Skyhawk. On both engines, its performance is very similar to my 1980 A36 Bonanza, which my partner and I routinely fly side by side. At 70 percent power, both aircraft stay right with each other. As most people already know by now, the Cessna avionics are for the most part best used as boat anchors.

The most appealing thing about the Skymaster is its value. The 1973 Skymaster was purchased for about one-third of the price of a 1973 Baron 58 that I previously owned. While the Skymaster certainly does not have the power, prestige or speed of the Baron, it could carry a slightly larger useful load. Operating costs are lower, too. Fuel burn is about 20 gallons an hour—not bad for a 190-mph airplane—and my last two annuals ran about $800.

One other advantage of the Skymaster over conventional twins: no Janitrol heater. That is an expensive, unreliable piece of equipment that requires regular costly overhauls. The Skymaster's Power-Pac unit does have to be overhauled about every 1,000 hours, however, at a cost of about $800.

Alden Buerge
Joplin, Mo.

I owned a 1967 337B Skymaster from 1972 until 1985. It gave us faithful service and we reluctantly traded it for a B55 Baron when we were faced with two engine overhauls. I still look back at the Skymaster as a special aircraft that deserves far more respect and popularity than it received over the years.

Since the Skymaster has no nose bay in which to place a large radar dish, a smaller one must be hung on a wing.

First of all, it did what it was conceived to do: add a margin of safety to twin-engine flying by eliminating Vmc. The airplane remains controllable on either engine right up to the moment of stall.

There are a number of other special features that I miss. The Skymaster is roomy and has more creature comforts for the pilot and passengers.The high wing lets you get in and out in the rain without getting wet. I greatly miss the superb visibility.

The performance was extremely close to the figures published in the handbook. We always flew at conservative power settings in the hopes of trading speed for engine life. With the tanks filled we cruised at 150 knots with 7.5 hours endurance and 650 pounds payload. Leaving the aux tanks empty gave 5.5 hours endurance and a payload of 885 pounds. Fuel burn was less than 19 gallons per hour. The Skymaster is a bit heavy in pitch on liftoff and flare, but otherwise there are no unusual flight characteristics.

The Skymaster flies quite nicely with gear down. The recommended procedure is to leave the gear down on takeoff until at least 500 feet, since the plane will still climb with gear down and either prop feathered. The gear retraction process is rather slow (about 14 seconds) and increases the drag quite significantly during that time.

Many aviation buffs think the Skymaster is ugly, and names such as Mixmaster and Skythrasher are familiar to all of us. But beauty is in the eyes of the beholder, and the Skymaster has a functional beauty that is most appreciated after owning one.

John Blalock
Winter Park, Fla.

Our company operates a 1978 T-337H, the turbocharged non-pressurized model. This is the second Skymaster we've owned, and we've been pleased with the performance, handling qualities and versatility of the aircraft. With six 170-pound adults, a fuel load of 460 pounds (77 gallons) can be carried. With this fuel, range with a 45-minute reserve is over 450 nm. With full fuel, range is over 1,000 nm, with a payload of 580 pounds.

The airspeed on the Turbo 337 varies greatly with altitude. At 5,000 feet, we average 170 knots. Upstairs at 20,000 feet, the airspeed is about 200 knots. At those speeds, fuel consumption is about 25 gph. At altitudes approaching 20,000 feet, a rate of climb of 500 fpm can be expected. (The engines can develop about 80 percent power at 20,000 feet.)

Maintenance costs have been within the order of magnitude of a complex twin. Our costs for annual inspection ranged between $1,500 and $3,500. Total maintenance cost for 1987 was $4,500. Problems with the landing gear power pack were a nuisance item that was finally resolved. On two occasions the green down-and-locked light would not illuminate. Other times, the gear would take up to 45 seconds to cycle. The problem was resolved by replacing the power pack. Another nuisance problem is oil seepage from the rear engine breather and rocker box covers. We find that the rocker box cover screws require tightening every 10 to 15 hours. Wiping oil from the rear cowling and stabilizer seems to be a regular pre-flight occurrence.

Even with these problems, the T-337H has been quite a satisfactory airplane for us. It's an excellent IFR platform. And for what it does, it's one of the best buys on the market.

Michael Kaplan
Van Nuys, Calif.

I own a normally aspirated 1966 Skymaster with 2,400 hours total time. The front engine is 350 SMOH, the rear 750 since new. I've now owned the plane for 30 months, through two annuals. The main problem I encountered was a persistent low-grade hydraulic leak, which required refilling the system every 25 hours or so. It has now been resolved, on the fifth try. My annuals cost in the $1,000 range. On one, we had to replace a cylinder on the rear engine because of low compression. No other major engine work has been required. One cowl flap motor had to be rebuilt, and I have replaced an alternator, vacuum pump, manifold pressure line, and oil temperature gauge.

My fuel burn is usually between 15 and 16 gallons per hour at a cruise speed of 150-155 knots. I generally fly between 8,000 and 12,000 feet. My operating cost of $100 per hour includes a reserve of $15 for engine overhaul. The operating cost is higher than a single, but I like the duplication of systems and the ability to maintain altitude in the mountains on one engine. I have experienced two engine failures in single-engine airplanes, a pair of experiences I might not have survived so well had I not been VFR and within gliding distance of an airport. The Skymaster's handling on one engine is gentle. It is a stable airplane, and makes an excellent instrument platform. Of my 700 hours, 250 are in the Skymaster, 10 actual IFR and 40 under the hood. I love the airplane.

Roger Howe
Mt. Shasta, Calif.

I'm on my third Skymaster. The first two were turbo models, and I now have a P337. I have about 1,000 hours in cross-country and in the Sierra Mountains and no downtime on any trip due to maintenance problems. I do not feel my maintenance problems have been excessive or unusual for a twin, except the cost of a good reman engine (TSIO-360C) can be high ($16,500-plus Victor used "cert." case and crank).

I added intercoolers three months ago and increased speed by 9-10% and climb performance by 20%. Also, the cabin is much cooler. Ventilation without the intercoolers is is very poor in the P models. Since adding the intercoolers, I'm very pleased with the result both in performance and comfort.

Name withheld on request

Cessna Crusader T303

Five years ago, the T303 was considered by many in the industry to be the prototype of a new family of aircraft that would leap the gulf between Cessna's two engineering and manufacturing companies—the Pawnee and Wallace divisions.

For a period of time, there was a third marketing and support organization: Cessna Citation, but it was brought into the fold as a part of the Wallace operation. This was considered beneficial, since in design and manufacturing techniques and philosophies, the two were so different that they did not seem to be arms of the same corporation. There apparently was little if any exchange of ideas or information.

The Crusader, as it was later named, would be the first application of lessons learned in aerodynamics, systems, human factors, materials, methods and manufacturing on the military T- and A-37 jets and the 500 series of Citations—many of which had led to significant changes in the 400 series of piston and turboprop twins—down through the rest of the line.

The mid-mounted horizontal tail: a thing of beauty designed to reduce propwash vibration and improve elevator effectiveness. But watch out for over-rotation on takeoff. Also, several fixes were needed to prevent rudder oscillation in icing.

Trickle-Down Hopes

More importantly for buyers, it offered hope that more modern design and construction was finally trickling down through the ranks towards the woefully derivative single-engine line. As successful as these products had been, they were variations on a theme that had been cast between the late 1930s and '40s, their growth in size, performance and capability more the product of bolt-on and paste-on adaptation than of engineering progress and general technological advance.

As is well known, the first Model 303 was a very different airplane from what was introduced as the T303 in late 1979 and which was finally put on the market in late 1981. It was still called the Clipper—the name change was forced by Pan American after the design was radically redone—but instead of a very light twin to compete with the Cougar, Duchess and Seminole, it was a turbocharged baby cabin twin. The company hoped to position it somewhat above the successful Piper PA-34 Seneca and Beech B-55 Baron and just below Piper's PA-31 Navajo and Cessna's own 400 series unpressurized piston twins.

To its credit, Cessna had recognized during the heady sales successes of the late

1970s that the small-twin market was not a large one, in part because the add-on systems necessary to give that category true utility could not successfully be carried on the diminutive twins and leave any room or power for payload and performance. Demand for a training/personal, nice weather twin was insufficient to pay back a development program. The existing 300 series twins, the 310, 337 and 340 (although the latter continued to be offered through the 1984 model year) were increasingly incompatible with the design, manufacturing and materials philosophies and techniques of the company.

Handmade

They were labor intensive to build. In fact, there was still a great deal of hand rather than tool or process forming involved. The 400 series had been transitioned to more modern airfoils and construction techniques as well as to much better-organized, less work-intensive systems and cockpits. None of the improvements were being added to the 300 series, particularly the venerable 310, and speculation had begun in the late 1970s that it had reached the end of the line.

So the T303, renamed the Crusader, should be considered both an end run around the bottom of the twin market philosophy of the competition and a hoped-for successor to the 310/320/340 family that would conform more closely with the new design and manufacturing direction at Cessna.

In the Beginning

Much of the coverage of the T303 has focused on it and the very light, "entry level" twins or between it and the PA-34. In those categories it does quite well. Considered as a 310 replacement, however, it is very much a mixed bag, to be generous. Despite the production economies of the T303 over the 310 airframe and the relative cost of the powerplants, the Crusader hit the market with a substantial price differential. In practically every performance category save runway requirements, the 310 outperforms the T303 by a hefty margin.

However, in ease of operation, including the transition time required to safely operate, and in design-induced traps, overall pilot workload, and—most important for many operators—passenger acceptance, the Crusader wins hands down. That is to be expected for a new design; but so are performance improvements.

In brief, Cessna's planners positioned the airplane in one segment of the market. The market positioned it a bit further down the line.

A Cabin Twin that Shrank in the Wash

The airplane has been thoroughly described in previous issues (February 1, April 1 and October 1, 1982; and a Used Aircraft Guide in the October 15, 1984 edition), so we will just highlight some features here.

At a glance, the T303 does not resemble any other Cessna, particularly anything produced at the Pawnee Division. On closer inspection, there are many features of the 500 and remodeled 400 series: bonded, clean wings incorporating integral, wet fuel tanks rather than the troublesome fuel bladders; and beefy-looking trailing beam or link main landing gear that smooths-out rough fields and less-than-perfect landings. One visible departure is the cruciform tail.

The horizontal tail is mounted approximately one third up the vertical stabilizer. The design objectives were to minimize vibration from the disturbed air generated by the propellers (one early claimed benefit is the ability to operate at low rpm— down to 2,100, at which speed noise and vibration are very low), improve elevator effectiveness and to minimize pitch changes with power or configuration changes. One trade-off is a tendency to over-rotate during liftoff. (Some observers think a cruciform tail would have more effectively solved the empennage problems of the 340, 425 and 441.)

Cessna design engineers, led by David R. Ellis, spent a lot of time tuning the aerodynamics and the relationships demanded by high and low-speed flight and clean and landing configurations. Solutions resulted in airflow control devices on the vertical tail, at the fuselage/wingroot juncture, the engine nacelles and on the upper flap surfaces. Designers also spent a fair amount of work on the airframe to improve service and maintenance access.

First Counter-Rotating

The T303 is the first Cessna twin to feature counter-rotating engines/propellers. As part of the weight-management program, Cessna selected a special variant of the Continental IO-520, the L/TSIO-520 AE, which saved 65 pounds each over the normal version. AiResearch turbochargers are bolted on at the Cessna plant.

In addition to being lightened, the Continentals were tuned to run at a fairly high compression ratio as aircraft engines go, 8.5 to 1, as part of the goal to reduce fuel consumption. One result of that is that maximum continuous power is established at 71 percent to preclude detonation. To calm fears in the marketplace over yet another light (read troublesome) engine, it was delivered with a recommended TBO of 2,000 hours, a full warranty for six months or 240 hours and pro-rata to TBO. Visual and aural fire warning detection systems were also standard (fire suppression devices were not). Cooling is by a variation on updraft; instead of cowl flaps, there are internal shutters to reduce aerodynamic drag.

The gear-actuating system is based on the electrically actuated hydraulic one that has caused so much grief for operators of retractable singles. (To get a bit ahead of ourselves, it has been comparatively trouble-free on the Crusader, in which a free-fall emergency extension mode has been incorporated.) Other good trickle-down systems include dual bus main and avionics electrical systems that include pull-off circuit breakers rather than the typical Cessna reset-only, lower cost version. The fuel system and fuel management is simpler (on, off, crossfeed) and located within easy reach and fairly easy sight on the base of the power quadrant.

Cockpit organization reflects much of the good planning established in the Citation and is a boon to pilot workload. There is enough room for an independent set of copilot flight instruments with its own pitot/static system.

Early Success

The market for new general aviation aircraft was well on its way to the worst crash ever when the T303 was introduced, but all things considered (and remembering the sales shot that a still-large dealer network represented to predictable orders for the company), it started breathing down the volume neck of the most popular twin selling, the Seneca.

According to official factory figures, 31 airplanes were delivered in 1981 (as '82 models); 131 in 1982; 57 in 1983; 65 in 1984; 11 in 1985; and 2 in 1986. Most of the aircraft delivered in 1984-86 were probably assembled in '83. A total of 297 aircraft have been delivered (although serial numbers through T30300315 were set aside. Whether those last 18 assigned serial numbers reflect aircraft built and put in storage somewhere, or whether production was terminated at 00297 is an interesting question.) Keep in mind that factory deliveries reflect distributor/dealer sales, not necessarily retail sales. Many Crusaders stayed in dealer inventory and were used as training/air taxi/charter aircraft.

Fore and aft baggage loading makes for flexibility. Crusader was the first Cessna with counter-rotating props. Nosegear shimmy has been a problem.

Light as in Flimsy

In any event, the new twin got off to a good start, particularly considering market conditions. However, the first year of field experience disclosed that light twin meant light (some would say flimsy) in some design, material and manufacturing elements. Typical of all manufacturers' general aviation aircraft, real-world use was disclosing some shortcomings. Certain areas, such as the turbocharger mount, copilot's door hinges, main gear shock struts and a few other bits and pieces of the airframe were beefed-up.

In its second model year, the Crusader also received known icing certification and a few operational options (one, fuel pressure limiting switches, was later made standard). An aft cargo door, which more than doubles the width of the opening and slightly increases baggage space (from 22.5 to 26.5 cubic feet) due to relocation of the aft cabin bulkhead, was also offered in 1983. In the first year of field experience, quite a few operators were mentioning that they liked the airplane, but it was spending too much time in the shop. One said that something seemed to break on practically every trip. This brought back echoes of the unfortunate 411 to many, and presaged the experience many people had with the Malibu in later years.

At first glance and first flight, most people were impressed with the diminutive Crusader, even line boys and mechanics who admired some of the service-oriented features. But despite the thousands of hours of testing and evaluation by the factory, real-life use was disclosing shortcomings in just a few hours. Quite a few of them were traced to poor performance on the assembly line, but increasingly design or materials defects were showing up.

To its credit, Cessna worked hard to support the product, but some fixes did not work or transferred problems to another part of a given system. Operators were becoming frustrated because many proposed fixes were not true fixes, and shortcomings disclosed early on were recurring.

Service history

In the first three years of service, operational experience with the Crusader resulted in more than 60 service bulletins and an even larger number of service letters and advisories. Service difficulty reports (SDRs) supported the field experience. Some of the problems identified back then have been continuing, as the 278 SDRs issued in the interim reveal. These include vertical fin attachment, main and nose landing gear, and turbo and exhaust mounting systems.

Cessna Crusader Resale Value

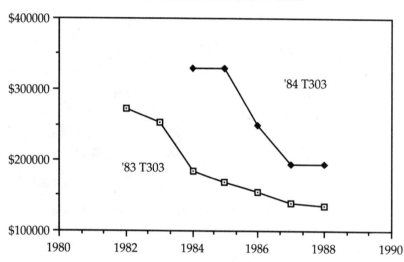

The service bulletins, kits and letters have continued to be issued, as well. Cessna has continued to try to resolve the problems. For instance, last year the company was working on a second totally new turbo and exhaust mounting system.

Landing gear and turbocharger-related problems are the biggest continuing issues on the T303. Magneto problems are next, followed by alternator troubles, especially a tendency to throw or break belts and instances of cracking cases. Maintenance people suspect a combination of poor alignment and vibration as the major factors in quite a few of the service difficulties experienced, including numerous reports of cracked engine mounts.

Quality Control Problems

Most of the others are traced to poor quality control. For instance, several reports of loose vertical fin attach bolts reported as a result of in-flight vibration were attributed to improper assembly and torquing at the factory. These resulted in an airworthiness alert.

The turbo/exhaust problems also triggered an airworthiness alert. They have also led to engine mount, turbo heat shield and mounting rust and corrosion problems and to quite a few other heat-related problems within the engine compartment. There has also been continuing difficulty in aligning the turbo exhaust outlet with the tailpipe.

A lot of people expected the lightweight engine to result in many difficulties, but it has performed surprisingly well. There have been some cylinder and valve corrosion and galling or spalling in the valve train. Most of the deterioration appears to be a product of aircraft stored without proper preparation of the powerplant. This situation is not peculiar to the T303 and TSIO-520 AE, as many purchasers of low-time or nearly-new aircraft from field inventory have discovered in the past few years. The only protection against this expensive headache is a thorough internal inspection before purchase.

Nineteen of the current batch of SDRs report cracking and failure in the main landing gear retraction arm and assembly; several others relate to side braces and downlock assemblies. The nose gear shimmy damper, actuator and its attach bracket, steering bellcrank and retraction stop have also experienced continuing difficulties. Cessna beefed up the main gear doors after several instances of cracks occurring at the hinge.

Shimmy Shock

One former operator of a fleet of five has a host of incident horror tales related to the shimmy damper. Its failure while in motion, particularly after landing, results in almost uncontrollable vibration that has broken instruments in the cockpit and, in one occurrence, resulted in the instrument panel flopping out onto the controls.

Some of the alternator-related SDRs suggest that electrical power demands of the systems, particularly with the smaller, 60 amp alternators, are too high (a shortcoming shared with the Seneca). T303 shoppers should put the larger capacity 95 amp alternators that are standard with deice-equipped models on the list of must-haves. Magnetos are troublesome items on most aircraft. Quite a few of the SDRs suggest that pressurized mags, while they cure some operational problems, may create new ones, particularly moisture contamination that leads to arcing and filter and other material breakdown, including bearing seizure. In turn, this suggests that regular inspection and replacement of filters should be part of the preventive maintenance program.

The roomy cabin and rear-entry airstair door get high votes from users.

Umbrella Needed?

Another headache that could result in a serious problem, particularly if you experience an emergency after takeoff, is a result of water leaks. There were five reports of circuit breaker disconnect traced to water leaking over and into the panel mounted on the side wall below the pilot's side window. In two of the experiences, the gear could not be retracted because the breaker had disconnected internally and could not be reset. (We have encountered this problem three times in 400 series Cessnas. In each case it was the gear circuit breaker that popped.)

Operators of aircraft that are regularly stored outside should be particularly alert to the problem, especially if they start a trip during or after heavy rain. Look for a trail of water from the ice window down the side wall to the panel. This is a place where the company should do a better job of sealing, or at least deflecting water.

Based on experience with other Cessna aircraft, there were surprisingly few squawks reported on the ARC avionics gear that was standard kit for it and most other Cessnas until just before the end of production, when some optional systems from other suppliers were offered.

ADs

Given the operational and service record of the Crusader, there have been surprisingly few ADs issued. There are a total of five, most of which relate to accessories (dratted magnetos and air filters, for instance). One was for a mandatory inspection for turbo-related problems. An early one covered the counterweight bolts on McCauley propellers. The big one (two, actually—85-11-5 and 86-1-1) lifted known-icing certification from properly equipped T303s. Cessna developed a fix and an associated kit that, together with some operational and configuration limitations, restored approval effective last October.

Trailing beam landing gear smooths landings, but the gear has had its share of mechanical problems.

Cessna documents describe the effect of ice accumulation at the juncture of the horizontal and vertical stabilizers as resulting in "...a mild oscillation of the rudder/rudder pedals when the airplane is configured for final stages of a landing approach...and possibly a slight nose down pitch change. The extent of this phenomenon varies with certain combinations of airspeed, power setting, flap deflection, sideslips and type of icing conditions." Pilots who have encountered the phenomenon may want to embellish that description a bit.

The airframe fix is the addition of more vortex generators below the horizontal stabilizer, a new fairing shape covering the leading edge of the stabilizers at the cruciform junction, a flow control fence at the bottom of the left horizontal stabilizer and a flow energizer on the vertical fin just below the horizontal tail.

Reduce, Reduce

Operational recommendations are to reduce airspeed, reduce power, reduce flaps and to coordinate flight (reduce slip). Operational restriction in the final fix is a maximum of 10 degrees of flaps, which makes sense when you are carrying a load of ice on any airplane.

Safety Record

The accident record is quite good, too. There were a total of 25, of which two were fatal (a total of six fatalities) and three involving injuries. The worst one, in terms of fatalities (five) was a result of flight into known icing conditions, during which the pilot reported heavy vibration.

Three non-injury accidents were attributed to gear failure, one during taxi because of a violent nose wheel shimmy and nose gear collapse. One horrendous incident that resulted in no damage was caused by a vacuum pump failure that led to loss of control and stall in the clag. The airplane fell out of the overcast in an inverted spin. At 500 feet agl, the pilot recovered and landed. The other accidents do not appear to bear any relationship to the nature and character of the design.

Is There a Bargain Here?

Average equipped list prices for the Crusader ranged from just under $275,000 in 1982 to about $318,000 in 1984. Current asking prices range from about $135,000 to $195,000. Average airframe time is right on 1,000 hours (the highest-time T303 we noted had a reported 1,600 hours on it, although there are undoubtedly some with more than that).

While we can't prove it, a higher-time copy might be preferable to a cherry low-time airframe/engine combination. If it has been carefully maintained and all the bulletins followed and fixes applied, that is. The theory is that most of the items that have been failing will have been corrected except for those that recur, in which preventive maintenance and careful inspection must be the rule.

Given the level of support Cessna has given to the aircraft, it appears that the Crusader might be a better bet than older, out of production aircraft. However, the prudent potential buyer of any aircraft not currently being built might better assume himself an orphan and secretly hope for a pleasant surprise. Given the availability and increasingly outrageous price charged for relatively simple bits and pieces, that would seem to be the safest strategy.

The good part

Pilots drawn to twins should be disabused of any belief that two is better than one, unless they are regularly trained to the highest possible level of proficiency. Only turbine equipment has the sufficiently high surplus of power needed to climb or accelerate-go out of an engine failure. And even if the engine goes during a comfortable cruise, good systems management and proper technique will extend the range of your landing options in a piston twin, nothing more. The accident record continues to suggest that the decision-making and technique skills required of piston twin operators are very high.

The Crusader is average, which means marginal, in single-engine capabilities and characteristics. What it has going for it is a well organized cockpit, good visibility (except at night, when reflections in the side windows from the panel are bothersome because of a skimpy glare shield), generally better designed systems that provide more options if something goes awry, and light, reasonably well-harmonized controls and good basic flying characteristics.

The trade-off of light control forces is more work in turbulence. While Cessna originally touted the good longitudinal stability of the design, it jiggles and twiggles a lot in rough air. Therefore, a yaw damper should be on your shopping list (check to make sure that everything is rigged right and the yaw damper hasn't gone to sleep in your pre-acceptance inspection).

Another of the nice big airplane features of the T303 is three-axis trim. But in our initial single engine work in the airplane several years ago, it was apparent that there was not enough rudder trim to remove the control pressure required to maintain minimum slip flight after an engine-failure. Your leg will get tired (and you need a big input at initial failure to keep the airplane headed in the right direction), as we can attest from a night, IFR, for-real engine shutdown.

In addition to its very nice all-around flying qualities, the design has high gear and flap speeds that make operations in high density areas, or quick descents, far

Cost/Performance/Specifications

Model	Year	Average Retail Price	Cruise Speed (kt)	Useful Load (lb)	Std/Opt Fuel (gal)	Engines	SE Ceiling (ft)	TBO (hr)	Overhaul Cost
T303	1982	$135,000	180	1,870	155	TSIO-520-AE	13,000	2,000	$12,500
T303	1983	$160,000	180	1,870	155	TSIO-520-AE	13,000	2,000	$12,500
T303	1984	$195,000	180	1,870	155	TSIO-520-AE	13,000	2,000	$12,500

easier to accomplish and far easier on the powerplants than in many competitive alternatives.

Loading Flexibility

The array of baggage places gives the operator considerable loading flexibility, both in terms of cabin clutter and weight and balance. The only caveat here is that the cubes far exceed the legal carrying capacity, and careless loading can lead to an out of cg condition.

As a light twin with a bit more panache and some very good operational features, the Crusader is a very real option. It would be even better if Cessna had definitely fixed all of the weaknesses that are the bad side of "light" twin and would finally learn something about quality interior materials and finish. Anyone in the market for a light twin right now should definitely put the Crusader on his list. But spend a few nights reading the volumes of service letters and bulletins, and ensure that your heart's desire had them all handled. P.S. Make sure your mechanic takes his borescope with him for the inspection.

Owner Comments

We have owned our Cessna 303 since January, 1986. As president, CEO and chief pilot of our company, I have flown the aircraft about 250 hours. The aircraft currently has about 880 hours with 880 on the left engine and 280 on the RE reman.

We had the latest "mandatory" service bulletin done (turbine mounts), at which time bolts on turbos were frozen in, and turbos were cracked getting the bolts out, resulting in two new turbochargers being required, which Cessna didn't pay for. The 400 radios have spent many hours on the bench and are the worst equipment on the plane.

The aircraft flies like a sweetheart—comfortable, roomy, stable (once you get past the hop on takeoff) and very forgiving.

Lost some compression on a few cylinders on the LE at the last annual (1/87). Exhaust valves not seating properly. Cause was valve stem worn excessively by valve guides. Continental's mechanic's comment was, "Yea, we changed that in the newer engines (reman doesn't have the problem), something to do with a difference in hardness between guide and stem, surprised you got that many hours out of them." Even though it took six months to get credit, Continental did pro-rate the cost of the fix.

Little things [on the aircraft] are junky. Tumbles on baggage compartment locks are "pot metal." You have to use lock-tite to hold a tiny screw that retains the locking arm that holds the tumblers in. I've dropped two over northern Mississippi (tumblers, that is). Air stair cables frayed and had to be replaced after 600 hours (how many openings and closings?). Ashtrays are all corroded. Little things, I know, for something that lists around $250 M, you'd expect a little more. Why cut corners on a 50¢ item? I normally cruise at eight to 10 M, top of the green on MP and 2200 rpm, get 155-160 TAS, and burn 25 gph. Climbout @ 2400 rpm and 115 knots IAS for about 700 fpm.

SE performance won't set the world on fire, but it is docile. No heavy rudder pressure required if you tip the right way, and will hold altitude and give some climb when you get it all cleaned up, but most important is that it's easy (no rapid

loss of heading, no heavy pitch up or down) to control. SE approach is easy, and the greatest danger seems to be delaying your descent to be conservative, and overflying the runway.

The fact that the wheels come down at 175 seems to help control temps—leave these rpms up, come down fast (approach control appreciates it), drop the wheels and land. Overall satisfaction—very good. Comfort—outstanding. Flyability—great. Electronics—poor. Little things—poor.

Pilots rave about high gear- and flap-lowering speeds. But overall performance is mostly eclipsed by its predecessor Cessna 310 twin.

Richard L. Kanary
Portland, Ore.

I have owned and operated my Crusader since January 1985. I purchased it as a factory demonstrator directly from Cessna with 214 hours on the plane. Terms of the purchase also included an annual inspection, which turned out to be the best thing that ever happened to me. When the annual was completed, significant corrosion was found on all cylinders on the left engine, and the compression rating on the No. five cylinder was just below 13 psi. The right engine also had light to severe corrosion on five cylinders. One was pulled from the left engine for a more detailed inspection, and a casting flaw on the engine block was also discovered, which necessitated a complete new left engine.

By the time everything was completed and the plane was back in flying order, I ended up with a completely new left engine and entire new "top" on the right engine. Total cost came to $50,272, of which Cessna and/or Continental paid $48,264. This covered all parts, engines, pro-rated labor, etc. I now have about 940 hours on the plane. Other problems I have experienced were as follows:

1) Replacement parts are extremely expensive. For instance, I had to replace a tachometer at 618 hours, at a cost of $1,560. This seems outrageous to me.

2) At 762 hours I discovered something which at the time caused me great concern, and still worries me. On an annual inspection it was determined that the left flap was unairworthy due to extreme heat damage. In trying to determine the cause of the problem, it became evident that the fuel tank drain valve is located immediately outboard of the exhaust pipe. When the system was installed at the factory, apparently a washer was missing, which caused a "minute" gas leak. At some time in landing configuration with full flaps extended, the heat given off from the exhaust system was sufficient to ignite a small amount of fuel from the drip, causing a blowtorch effect on the flap. As far as I am concerned, location of the

fuel tank drain valve directly behind the exhaust pipe is an extremely poor one, and incredibly dangerous. Total cost to replace the flap also amounted to approximately $3,000. In addition, the plane was grounded for almost one month.

3) At 775 hours during work on an exhaust system AD which necessitated pulling both turbochargers, it was determined that one of them had casting flaws, and cracks had developed. This required replacement of both turbochargers at a cost of $3,500.

In addition to the above items, I have had a continual recurring problem with the Slick pressurized magnetos on the plane. To date I have suffered four magneto failures, including one almost simultaneous failure of both mags on the right engine just after rotation with the plane at max gross takeoff weight and IAS + 10 conditions. Fortunately, I was on a 15,000-foot runway and was able to land straight ahead. Aside from the above problems, I thoroughly enjoy the plane. It is an absolute delight to fly and is extremely stable in all weather conditions.

 Being located in the Pacific Northwest, I log a significant number of IFR and night operations and have found that the plane flies well in all conditions. It has an extremely high gear and flap speed, which allows a lot of flexibility when getting slowed to landing configuration, and overall I am extremely pleased with the plane's comfort and reliability.

At the time I purchased the plane, the factory estimated that direct operating costs would be about $78.92 an hour. To date my figures have averaged $113.24 per hour. Fuel and oil have averaged $54.40 per hour, and maintenance costs $58.84 per hour. Maintenance costs are almost twice the cost of the factory estimate, but I believe this is due to the dramatic increase in the price of airplane parts since 1984. After factoring in replacement reserves of approximately $25 per hour, I end up with a cost per flight hour of $138. This compares to Cessna's estimate of $103 per hour based on 1984 figures.

 I maintain my plane to FAR 135 conditions, and normal 50-hour inspections run about $285 plus parts, while 100-hour inspections (annuals) have averaged $1,380 plus squawks. I have found the original factory performance estimates to vary in accuracy somewhat. I normally preflight based on a 170-knot cruise speed, while Cessna estimated 180 knots. I fly at 72% power with the mp and rpm at 24/24, and average 26 gph of fuel. I have found the range to be slightly better than book.

Overall, I have been extremely pleased with the plane and its performance. Its short-field characteristics are excellent, and the trailing link landing gear system makes it almost impossible to botch a landing. In addition, compared to other light twins in its class, the stairway entrance door, large cabin area and emergency exit located by the copilot's seat are real plusses.

The plane can also carry a tremendous amount of luggage, people, etc. and still remain safely within all CG and gross weight requirements. Overall, I would rate the plane a solid eight on a scale of one to 10, and other than having to pay the extremely high cost of replacement parts, I have thoroughly enjoyed the plane over the last 700 hours.

William J. Allred
Portland, Ore.

Cessna 310

You've talked it over with your accountant (and presumably your psychiatrist), and you've decided that the time has come to trade up: you want to be able to tote a ton of useful load from one Loran chain to the next, at speeds that will have ATC confusing you with heavy iron, and do it with (alleged) safety of two engines—all for less than the price of a late-model 182. The choices are few. You can buy a used Baron or Aztec (or possibly an Aero Commander, or a clapped-out Navajo). Or, you can do what more than 5,000 other light-twin buyers have done-and take home a Cessna 310.

As two-engine planes go, the 310 is singularly impressive-in appearance, if in no other category. (Who could fail to notice those Stabila tip tanks?) The George-Lucas-inspired design of the late-model (Roman-nosed) 310R leaves some pilots cold, admittedly. But despite the Baron-with-a-gland-problem appearance, the 310 proves itself a worthy contender in the six-place twin category, combining get-it-done-today performance, with surprising docile handling, not to mention the load-carrying capacity of a light armored vehicle.

For every Indian head, there's a buffalo, however, and the flip side of aesthetic over achievement (in this case) is mediocre Dutch-roll stability, high V-speeds, and generally unflattering runway handling. (As one owner puts it, "A one-time flight will endear few pilots to the 310.") But what the 310 lacks in cockpit charisma, it makes up for in raw verve: Cob it, and the mother scoots. Topping 174 knots is no problem. Single-engine ROC is a credible 330 to 440 fpm (depending on year/model), and the maximum two-engine climb rate will have you begging for ear surgery.

In production for a quarter of a century, the 310 tuna tank brigade proliferated and evolved into a heavy hauler with a distinctive personality.

Fuel consumption, maintenance, and insurance costs for the 310 are substantial, but the same is true for any six-place twin. Owners point proudly to the 310's beer-hall cabin proportions, extra-tall (and wide) wheelstance, superb cockpit visibility (especially in later models), and logical panel layout as reasons for preferring a 310 to a Baron or Aztec. Another reason: price. In any given model year, 310's tend to underprice Barons by 10 percent (and more).

Model History

As any Sky King fan knows, the 310 (Cessna's first low-wing aircraft, not counting the wartime UC-78 "Bamboo Bomber"—which was Sky King's first airplane) began life as a snub-nosed, straight-tailed, tuna-tanked wonder in 1955. Approximately 1,200 tuna-tank models were delivered before Cessna-intent on enhancing the 310's dihedral stability and sex appeal in one bold stroke-introduced the now-familiar slanted tip tanks on the 310G in 1962. Wing lockers (and an underwing exhaust system) appeared two years later with the "I" model. Total optional fuel was 133 gallons, carried in the tips (50 gals. each) and wing bladders.

The 310K-N models (1966-1968) were the first to sport double-wide "Vista-view" side windows. Optional fuel capacity increased to 143 gallons, flap speed (white arc) went from 122 to 139 knots, and the three-blade props were offered for the first time. With the 1969 'P' model, optional fuel went to 184 gallons; the nose gear geometry was altered slightly; and the IO-470-VO (the same as before, but with Nimonic valves, richer fuel injection, and piston oil cooling-all for better top-end life). A Turbo 310P model was offered as well, with more powerful TSIO-520-B engines (285-hp, versus the normally aspirated model's 260-hp).

The next big change came in 1972, when Cessna (wanting to rid the 310 of the "tunnel effect" that plagues many long-cabin aircraft) put a rear window in the fuselage of the 310Q. Rear passengers got three extra inches of headroom; the top of the one-piece windshield was extended a full nine inches aft; and the panel eyebrow was lowered. These changes brightenedthe interior environment, indeed. Optional fuel capacity became 207 gallons, and gross weight was boosted to 5,300 pounds (from 5,200 in the 310P).Buyers should note that while all 310s built from 1970 to 1974 are 'Q' models, the rear-window and cabin-brightening mods first appeared in 1972, and apply only to serial number 310Q-0401 and up.

Culmination of the line was the long-nose 285-hp 310R. Production halted in 1981.

The last, and numerically most abundant, of the 310 models was the 310R, introduced in 1975. With the 310R, 285-hp IO-520 engines (1,400-hr. TBO if turbocharged; 1,700 hours otherwise) became standard, and baggage capacity went to a forklift-busting 950 pounds, thanks to a new 350-lb. cargo hold in the NASA-inspired nose. Max fuel stayed at 207 gals. Gross weight was boosted to 5,500 pounds, but useful load, equipped, remained in the 1,900 pound ball-park-about 200 pounds less than full-fuel-and-cargo (never mind pilot/pax).

It should be noted that Cessna made hundreds of minor (but important) changes to the 310 over the years; the forgoing discussion is necessarily cursory, and outlines only the most major changes.

Production of the 310 was terminated in 1981, to make way for the T303 Crusader, a clean-sheet-of-paper design that Cessna felt would better serve the light twin market into the 21st century. Actually the 310's death was accidental; Cessna had not originally intended the T303 as a 310 replacement. Rather, the original T303 (neé "Clipper") was a 180-hp super-light twin aimed at the Duchess/Seminole market. Cessna wisely decided to withdraw from the "trainer twin" arena at the last minute, however, reconfiguring the T303 with 250-

hp turbocharged powerplants. By default, the present Crusader—a lesser airplane than the 310 in almost every performance category—took away the 310's niche.

Systems

In contrast to the Aztec, Aerostar, and Navajo, the 310 has no engine-driven hydraulics: Gear and flaps are all-electric, with juice supplied by 50-amp (standard) or 100-amp (optional) alternators on each engine. Cowl flaps are manual (unlike those on most Barons, which are electric). Brakes are Goodyear—which is to say, expensive to repair-and tires are odd-sized (6.50x10 on the mains-same as the Cheyenne), thus costly to replace.

It's perhaps worth noting that ARC 300-series avionics came as standard equipment on 310s (even the later models), although many owners have had King or Collins equipment installed. (Nonetheless, the 310 without an ARC autopilot is rare.) Check the black-box assortment before you buy, and price each plane up or down accordingly.

If the 310 has a serious systems sore-point (and it does), it's the ludicrously labyrinthine fuel system, with its plethora of pumps, pressure switches, valves, vapor return lines, and underwing drains. (With the 207-gal. system, you can count on draining no fewer than 10 petcocks each morning: one for each main tank, aux bladder, 20 gallon locker, crossfeed line, and sump/strainer.) The fuel selectors read "on, off, aux, crossfeed"—simple enough, you say—but thereby hangs an invitation to disaster. Aux fuel can't be crossfed, for example, in a single-engine emergency. Nor can wing bladder fuel be used in event of failure of an engine-driven fuel pump, since the boost pumps are inside the tip tanks. (Also in the tips are transfer pumps to ensure that fuel from the front of the tank can be gotten to the rear-where the pickup line is—in steep descents. These pumps are wired to the landing-light circuit breakers and constitute go/no-go items.)

New 310 owners are often amazed to learn that their wings aux tanks—31 gallons each—are good for no more than 60 minutes' use in cruise (sometimes a lot less). That's because excess fuel is returned by the engine-driven fuel pumps not to the aux tanks (whence it came), but to the tip tanks. Accordingly, one must burn 60 to 90 minutes' worth of fuel out of the tips before selecting "aux." Otherwise, return fuel, arriving at already full tip tanks, will be pumped overboard out the vents.

Lockers are another story entirely. Some 310s have but one locker tank, in which case the drill is to burn fuel out of the mains, activate the locker transfer pump (which sends locker fuel to the adjacent tip tank), then crossfeed as necessary to balance the main-tank load. With dual lockers, you simply engage the transfer pumps when the mains have burned down to 30 gallons remaining (or less), and wait for two idiot lights to come on when the lockers are dry. There are no quantity gauges.)

Obviously, the fellow who designed this system needs to have his bed made, and possibly his straps tightened. The rest of us, meanwhile, would do well to study the handbook carefully before (and after) buying or flying a 310.

Comfort and Handling

Interior comfort is excellent in any model 310 (assuming you can abide the outdoor-patio grade carpets and fade-faster-than-memory seats), although noise levels are high enough to sterilize mice. Pilot and copilot sit miles apart, and rear passengers are pinched neither for leg nor shoulder room (except in the 5th and 6th seats, which are best occupied by Billy Barty types). And thanks to a generous array of baggage compartments (even the short-nosed 310Q can take up to 600 pounds in the lockers and aft cabin), no one is obliged to carry groceries on his-or her-lap.

In terms of handling, the 310 offers typical "big mutha" control response, with few or no unpleasant surprises. The ponderous roll response for which the 310 is famous has been overplayed somewhat by the airport-lounge lizards. Roll and yaw damping are poor at lower airspeeds, it's true, due to the concentration of mass in the wings (remember each wing carries 600 pounds of petrol), and inexperienced pilots tend, as a result, to overcontrol on climbout or approach. The key is to keep a light touch. (One eventually learns to "husband" the plane's inertia, rather than fidget constantly with the yoke.) The 310 has a "wallow" mode, but so do other aircraft. More than one ATP has observed that "there's no better training for a future Learjet pilot than a couple hundred hours in a 310."

In cruise, the plane is a joy to fly. Stabila-tip models (310G thru R) exhibit little or no adverse yaw, and standard-rate turns can be done with feet flat on the floor. Extended hands-off flight does not result in tumbled gyros. Turbulence, however, produces a nauseous Dutch-rolling which can be quite pronounced at high fuel loadings, even in the post-1969 models with ventral-fin tail stingers. (This is where the $2,160 yaw damper option proves its worth.) Maneuvering speed (Va) is a high 148 knots.

Stalls in the 310 are preceded by bucking and shuddering (and steep deck angles, if any power is left on); the break and recovery, however, are straightforward and undramatic. Dirty, the stall comes at 63 KIAS; clean, 75.

Cessna 310 Resale Value

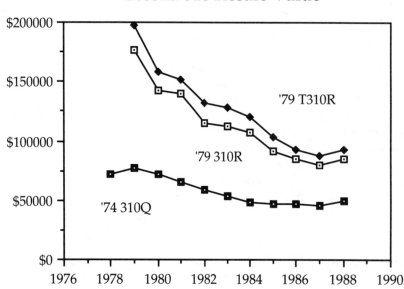

'79 T310R

'79 310R

'74 310Q

Flaps are of the DC-3 (split) variety, producing more drag than lift-which is perhaps just as well, since the 310 is difficult to slow down without chopping power (and TBO). The standard slow-down drill is to squeeze off a couple inches of manifold pressure, then apply 15 degrees of flaps at 160 KIAS or below (139 KIAS in early models); then wait. Initial application of flaps is enough to slow the plane down to gear speed (140 knots), and with the gear down, power can slowly be bled off until-established on final approach-17 inches of manifold pressure remain.

Landing a 310 with dignity calls for finesse (and, some would argue, retro-rockets.) Power is best kept at 17 inches until over the threshold, at which time the throttles can slowly be brought back and the elevator trim readjusted. (Yoke forces are high in the flare.) The airspeed decay with power reduction is dramatic, and the plane "pays off" quickly. At moderate weights, the best landings

Interior comfort is excellent in the big, beamy cabin—except for the fifth and sixth seats. Starting with the K models in 1966 a rear "skylight" window called Vista View eliminated a tunnel-view back seat. This is a 1976 model.

seem to come about nine knots above Vso, with some power still on. (If the stall horn sounds, you're in for a thumper.) At very light loadings, on the other hand, good "stall horn" landings are accomplishable with fair regularity. Just don't heave back heartily on the wheel after touchdown, or you're liable to pound the tail into the tarmac.

Performance

The 310 offers nosebleed-on-demand performance and thus is closer to the B55 Baron in all-around pep than to the Aztec. Owners of normally aspirated models typically claim 65-percent cruise speeds of 175 knots (at fuel flows of 22 to 26 gph) or 180 knots at 75 percent (burning 28 to 30 gph), at altitudes to 7,500 feet. Turbo models deliver blistering cruise speeds (up to 222 knots at 16,000 feet, burning 32 to 36 gph, at 75 percent), with top speeds of up to 238 knots—considerably better than the Turbo Aztec F (214 knots max) and dangerously close to Duke territory. Only one non-pressurized piston aircraft is faster than the Turbo 310-viz., the Baron 58TC.

Almost all 310s were ordered with auxiliary fuel, and many have the full 207- gal. complement, which presents interesting possibilities for trip planning. Fill the cabin (six seats), and you can go 690 nm with reserve-although you'll be limited to about 450 pounds in the cabin. Fill the cabin, the tanks, and the baggage bays, and you'll be 1,400 pounds over gross.

On one engine, the normally aspirated 310 climbs 330 to 415 fpm; the turbo models 390 to 440 fpm. (The Aztecs deliver about 100 fpm less.) Single-engine ceiling is 17,000-feet-plus in the turbo models; a Baron-like 6,650 to 8,000 feet otherwise (depending on year- model.) The 310s with the highest wing-and-power loadings (and therefore the lowest S.E. performance) are the 310K, L, N, P, and Q.

Safety

A special NTSB study of light twin safety covering the years 1972-76 showed the 310 ranking 10th in fatal accidents—and sixth-worst overall-out of 20 twin-engine planes studied. The 310 incurred 2.18 fatal accidents per 100,000 flight hours (versus 2.83 for the Barons and 2.60 for the NTSB's"Apache-Aztec" group, which unfortunately was not broken down further),while the total accident rate for the 310 came out to 9.81 per 10,000 flight hours (against 8.29 for the Barons and 7.54 for the "PA-23"). By comparison, the overall accident rate for general aviation as a whole, at the time of the NTSB's special study was 9.42.

A later (October 1983) FAA computer-search of 310 accident statistics showed a grand total of 694 write-ups in the computer, going back to 1959. Major categories (and the number of incidents pertaining thereto) included: wheels-up landings, 139; gear collapses, 183; gear retractions on ground, 23; collision with ground, (controlled), 26; collision with ground(uncontrolled), 28; stall, 31; spin, 1; fire in flight, 5; fire on ground, 6; "systems malfunction," 45.

Do you know how much fuel you have in which of up to six tanks? Fuel gauge in front of the copilot tells some, but not all.

Finally, an NTSB report analyzing accidents from 1978 to 1982 showed 213 total accidents in the five-year period, of which some 55 crashes—or 26 percent—were fatal. The single largest category of mishap (true to the plane's bag-of-bricks reputation): landing accidents. Some 45 pilots landed their 310s wheels-up in the five year period, many for reasons having to do with material failure and/or poor maintenance. Hard landings accounted for another 19 accidents (a surprising number of them non-injury); gear collapses totaled 26. There was some overlap between "hard landing" and"gear collapse" categories, since NTSB allows more than one line in its type-of-accident description.

Interestingly, as many as a quarter of the wheels-up landings happened in conjunction with engine failure or malfunction (despite the fact that either of a 310's alternators—on either engine—will suffice to power the all-electric gear up or down). A typical scenario has the pilot noticing an engine irregularity, and aborting a departure, just after breaking ground—and also just after selecting "gear up." The plane subsequently settles onto the runway under complete control, wheels retracted.

In several cases, maintenance personnel apparently forgot to reconnect nose gear doors to actuator arms after performing required inspections of combustion heaters (which in early model 310s are accessible only through the nose gear well). Jamming of the nose gear in the well-and/or breakage of retract arms-is the frequent result.

Many of the "hard landing" and "gear collapse" accidents involved arrivals in which the plane had accumulated some airframe ice; others happened as pilots unfamiliar with the 310 were being checked out by their instructors. In one case, a pilot making an ice-laden arrival," dropped hard on all three wheels," after which "the right wing outboard of the engine nacelle buckled downward until the right tip tank struck the runway and was dragged along the ground."

The high number of gear collapse incidents may be related to several factors, including poor maintenance, poor pilot technique, and outright underdesign of landing gear components in early (particularly pre-1970) 310 models. (Cessna issued numerous landing gear service bulletins in the late 1960s and early '70s.) An aggravating factor, almost certainly, is the heavy torsional loadings placed on the trunnions, struts, and brackets as a result of tip tank "oversteer" in taxi. (The inertia of the tanks is felt on the ground, as well as in the air.) Many gear-collapse accidents happen during high-speed turnoffs.

Engine failure or malfunction was a factor in 35 (or 16 percent) of the reported 1978-1982 Cessna 310 accidents, with fuel contamination, fuel exhaustion, and/or poor maintenance accounting, collectively, for over half the cases.

As light aircraft go, the Cessna 310 has a particularly perverse fuel system. Accordingly, one would expect the 310 to rate high in fuel mismanagement accidents. Not necessarily so, however: Only 13 out of 213 accidents (or a little over six percent of 310 mishaps) involved fuel-system-related brouhas has; and of these, several happened as pilots simply flew their airplanes beyond known endurance limits after exhausting all fuel from all tanks. In addition, fuel selectors were unaccountably found positioned between "aux" and "main" positions in several accidents.

Given the 310's high V-speeds, one might expect a disproportionate rate of stall-spin accidents. But the five-year record shows only eight such mishaps (out of 213 mishaps reported). By comparison, there were almost as many accidents involving marijuana overloads (some half a dozen in all).

Two of 55 fatal 310 accidents involved midair collisions. Another involved wake turbulence as a 310 attempted to land behind a Boeing 737 at Orange County Airport in southern California. There were no airframe breakups listed in the 1978-1982 printouts.

What kind of a pilot crashes a 310? PICs tend to be young (in their early 30s, most commonly)—but not inexperienced: Fully a quarter of all 310 accidents from 1978 to 1982 involved pilots with over 500 hours in type. (Only 54 of the reported 213 accidents came at the hands of pilots with fewer than 100 hours in type.) The vast majority—147 out of 213 (or 69 percent)—of aviators involved in 1978-1982 Cessna 310 crashes had more than 1,500 hours in their logbooks; 53 (24 percent of the total) had more than 5,000 hours, while 23 pilots—more than 10 percent-had logged 10,000-hours-plus. One 310 fatal accident involved a 69-year-old commercial

Cost/Performance/Specifications

Model	Year	Average Retail Price	Cruise Speed (kt)	Useful Load (lb)	Std/Opt Fuel (gal)	Engines	SE Ceiling (ft)	TBO (hr)	Overhaul Cost (each)
310A-B	1955-58	$17,500	178	1,740	133	240-hp Cont. O-470-B,M	8,000	1,500	$10,500
310C-F	1959-61	$21,000	191	1,795	133	260-hp Cont. IO-470-D	7,450	1,500	$10,500
310G-H	1962-63	$23,000	191	2,037	133	260-hp Cont. IO-470-D	7,450	1,500	$10,500
310I-J	1964-65	$26,000	194	2,037	133	260-hp Cont. IO-470-U	6,850	1,500	$10,500
310K-L	1966-67	$29,500	193	2,075	143	260-hp Cont. IO-470-V	6,850	1,500	$10,500
310N	1968	$31,000	193	2,075	143	260-hp Cont. IO-470-VO	6,850	1,500	$10,500
310P	1969	$37,000	193	2,086	184	260-hp Cont. IO-470-VO	6,850	1,500	$10,500
310Q	1970-71	$43,000	192	2,086	207	260-hp Cont. IO-470-VO	6,680	1,500	$10,500
310Q	1972-74	$44,300	192	2,086	207	260-hp Cont. IO-470-VO	6,680	1,500	$10,500
310R	1975-77	$61,000	194	2,047	207	285-hp Cont. IO-520-M	7,400	1,700	$11,500
310R	1978-79	$80,000	194	2,047	207	285-hp Cont. IO-520-M	7,400	1,700	$11,500
310R	1980-81	$106,000	194	2,047	207	285-hp Cont. IO-520-M	7,400	1,700	$11,500
T310P	1969	$40,000	226	2,108	184	285-hp Cont. TSIO-520-B	18,100	1,400	$13,500
T310Q	1970-74	$48,500	225	2,208	207	285-hp Cont. TSIO-520-B	18,100	1,400	$13,500
T310R	1975-81	$91,000	223	2,277	207	285-hp Cont. TSIO-520-BB	18,000	1,400	$13,500

pilot with 30,087 logged hours. The crash in question occurred on an IFR air-taxi flight. (The pilot apparently became disoriented during a 400-and-one approach in fog and rain.) "Pilot failed instrument check four days before accident," NTSB noted.

The moral: Don't underestimate the importance of proficiency and good maintenance in flying a 310 safely—regardless of the amount of time in your logbook.

For all-round single-engine safety, the 310 probably ought to be considered on a par with the Baron. The Aztec bests both planes for Vmc (69 knots vs. 75 for the 310, 81 for the Baron), but the 310 and Baron climb half again faster than the Aztec on one, and you don't have to reach to the ceiling to re-trim. The 310 and Aztec both have slow gear retraction times (about 13 seconds, versus the later Barons' four), which can be critical in an emergency. But at least the 310 has all-electric gear, and with an alternator on each engine you can be sure the gear is on its way up as soon as you hit the switch (conveniently and logically located above the upper left side of the power quadrant). Many Aztecs have but one hydraulic pump, on the left engine, and a port-engine failure means pumping the gear up by hand. Barons have fast-retracting electric gear, but the switch is in the wrong place.

The Aztec, Baron, and 310 all have emergency exits in addition to the entry door. In the 310, it's the pilot's side window; in the others, it's a back-seat window.

The 310 has one crashworthiness feature worthy of special note: namely, the tip tanks. Contrary to hangar mythology, aesthetics had little to do with locating the 310's main fuel tanks on the tips of the wings. According to one former Cessna engineer who was there at the time, Cessna felt in 1954 that many post-crash fires might be avoided if fuel were stored in detachable-on-impact external tanks. The 310, as a result, was graced with huge metal tunas, held on with quarter-inch bolts. The wisdom of this decision got an early test, as it turns out: One of the factory's first production prototypes crashed-landed wheels-up in a wheat field. The plane shed its tanks on touchdown; a major fire was averted; and the pilots walked away unscathed (and uncooked). External tanks remained a Cessna-twin trademark for many years thereafter.

Maintenance

Of the 310, Baron, and Aztec, the 310 is the clear winner in terms of the fewest number of Airworthiness Directives. Only eight airframe ADs affect the oldest 310s, and of those only one (on fuel-line inspection) is repetitive (every 50 hours). Turbo models have an additional repetitive-inspection AD of their own, requiring 50-and 100-hour look-sees of exhaust risers, slip-joints, ball joints, etc. (With the installation of Inconel parts, some of the 50-hour items are eliminated or rendered 100-hour items, however.) The Baron 58 has 14 airframe ADs; the Aztec, 24.

Some specific ADs to watch for include 69-14-01, which required installation of transfer pumps in the tip tanks of pre-1969 models; 72-03-07, inspection of main landing gear (the 310Q only); 72-14-08, the 50-hour fuel and oil hose inspection; and 76-04-03 and 78-11-05, requiring modification of ARC autopilot actuators.

A review of FAA Service Difficulty Reports on the 310 series going back six years reveals 1,300 reports covering a multitude of (mostly minor) sins. The single biggest category of complaint: landing gear problems (over 260 reports). Unfortunately, few generalizations can be made, as the reports refer to cracks in numerous locations (trunnions, torque links, rod-ends, brackets) on both main and nose gears, covering all models from 'A' to 'R.' One area that does stand out clearly is the nose gear idler bell-crank, P/N 08421022, which appears to break frequently on 310L-N models. (Also, nose gear drag brace doublers, P/N 081308930, crack on 310R models at upwards of 1,200 hours.)

Fortunately, the median breakage time of landing gear components appears to be fairly high in most cases. Be wary of airframes that have racked up thousands of Part 135 hours.

Other problem areas suggested by our SDR printout: aileron bearing seizure in 310Rs; aft spar corrosion (from exhaust gases) in all models up through the 310Q; battery box corrosion (all models); leaking bladder tanks (all models with aux tanks); exhaust mufflers, bellows, and ball joints (turbo models in particular); and defective bearings in Prestolite ALV 9047 alternators (on 310R models).

Stub-nose profile, as in this '71 aircraft, lasted until the R model. With it came extra baggage capacity and balance capability. Slanted "Stabila" tip tanks replaced the vertical ones in 1962.

Crankcase cracking appears to be less a problem with 285-hp 310s than with 285-hp Barons (the Baron 58 in particular). Our SDR listing showed up only 20 instances of crankcase crackage in IO-520-powered 310s in a six-year period, versus more than 50 such reports for Baron 58s (IO-520-C) in a little over two years. The Baron fleet is older, on average; but it is also smaller.

Thus it appears that the 310, by Baron standards, is relatively crack-immune. (Only four Turbo 310s showed up with cracked cases in our SDR printout.) The flip side of this coin is that the IO-470-powered 310 fleet, considered by many people "crack-proof," isn't. We counted no less then 10 IO-470 case cracks in the printout (most at or beyond TBO, however).

Modifications

The 310 was the plane, of course, that rocketed Jack Riley to stardom. In the early 1960s, Riley—having bought the Rajay turbo-charger line from TRW—built up a pair of 290-hp turbosupercharged Lycomings and installed them on a 310D (along with pressurized magnetos, three-blade props, one-piece windshield, pointy radome, and King Faisal control yokes) to create the original Riley Rocket.

Many of these 300-mph speedsters are still in service, and they occasionally pop up on the used market in the $29,000-35,000 price range. Most have been through the mill, however, and may be in need of considerable refurbishment. TBO is a short 1,200 hours.

Riley later outdid himself by putting 350-hp Navajo Chieftain engines on a few 1964 and later 310s, thereby creating the Turbostream.

If you have a Turbo 310 or 320 made after 1965, RAM Aircraft Modifications of

Waco, Texas (817-752-8381) has a 300-hp upgrade costing $46,300 installed with a series of options; and a unique 325-hp conversion that modifies the engines to Cessna 340 configuration ($91,400). RAM does first-quality work, and its STCs often include many worthwhile changes to ignition, cooling baffles, and exhaust systems; we can recommend their work highly.

If you own a 310F through Q (normally aspirated), and you want more power, but you don't want turbochargers, consider the Colemill Executive 600 conversion, which, for $42,500, gets you a pair of factory remanufactured 300-horse Continental IO-520-E engines with three-blade props. For $55,000 they'll give you factory new engines. This is another excellent mod to have for better single-engine performance. Call Colemill at 615/226-4256.

Finally, Sierra Industries in Uvalde, Tex. can give your 310G, Q, or R, or T310P/Q/R the runway performance (and Vmc) of an Aztec, roughly speaking, by replacing your split flaps with wing-widening Fowlers.

Owner Comments

Since 1978, I have owned two Cessna 310s—a 1969 Turbo 310P with Robertson STOL, a 1973 Turbo 310Q with a Colemill conversion. Overall, I think the 310 is an outstanding performer, with straightforward handling, excellent comfort, good parts availability and adequate factory support. Since my airplanes have been based at Crested Butte, Col., 8,850 ft. MSL, and the minimum enroute altitude to Denver is over 16,000 ft., high-altitude performance, especially climb performance, is vital in my operations. In this parameter the 310, especially the Turbo 310, performs admirably; however, at the cost of substantial maintenance expense.

A thorough 100-hour (or annual inspection) on a Turbo 310 by a shop experienced in maintaining turbocharged aircraft (and with all that complex, red-hot turbo exhaust machinery, you certainly want an experienced shop) always cost me at least $4,000. The cost of properly maintaining the Turbo 310 is what drove me to try the Colemill conversion, which replaces the normally aspirated 260-hp IO-470 Continentals with normally aspirated 300-hp IO-520 Continentals.

If you don't need the turbo, I strongly recommend this conversion. At mid-cruise

The Continental 520 powerplants enjoyed greater freedom from crankcase cracks than in other aircraft. Preflight ritual requires the cautious pilot to police a plumbing nightmare of 10 petcock drains.

weights, the Colemill will still climb at 500 fpm at 10,000-12,000 ft., MSL), and cuts the hourly maintenance cost of the turbo in half.

A couple of points: We have gotten excellent engine life by (I suppose this applies to any aircraft engine) using light power settings and extreme care on sudden temperature changes by gradual power reductions on descent. We have had no problems with cracking cases on the TSIO-520s. One of our cases is still an old "light case" and is performing very well.

The danger of overboost from cold oil is eliminated by using Aeroshell Multigrade. We fly into Truckee, Calif., frequently the coldest weather station in the U.S. Cold starts are easy and we suspect engine wear is considerably reduced. The 320E and F models have the heavier gear of the 400 Series. If you can locate a clean 320 in the E or F model, it can be an excellent buy.

John A. Linford
Oakland, Calif.

Our company has owned and operated Cessna 310s for 12 years-a 1967 "L" model for five years and a 1974 "Q" model with a Colemill conversion (IO-520-E) for the remainder.

It is my belief that normally aspirated engines in the close-cowled 310 should not be operated at over 65 percent power. The small increase in speed with the increased maintenance and higher fuel burn does not justify going to 75 percent power. Our 310 cruises at altitudes of 5,000 and 12,000 at 187 knots at 27 gph. I have operated the IO-470 and the IO-520 engines to TBO and beyond using 65 percent as a maximum.

Tank management in the 310 was designed by somebody with a sense of humor who hoped to keep the pilot alert on long flights. The improved fuel gauges in the "Q" model are not as accurate or convenient as the gauges in the "L" model. When flying on the aux tanks, approximately 10 gph will be returned to the main tanks.

The wing lockers may be Cessna engineering's greatest claim to fame. Four suitcases, four sets of golf clubs, and all sorts of miscellaneous baggage can be loaded in the locker, very close to the c.g.

The annual inspections of the "Q" model have averaged $2,875. These have been higher than I would have anticipated, but they included some heavy maintenance items: i.e., complete rebushing of landing gear, AD on heater, and corrosion problems on wing flap push rods. The problem with the push rods was simple, but the labor to remove and replace the rods was incredible.

The annual maintenance cost has been just above $7.50 per hour. Approximately one-half of this cost has been in the replacement of vacuum pumps (covered in an earlier issue of *The Aviation Consumer*) and three alternators that had to be replaced. I do not believe that there is any light twin available today that has the speed, good looks, and reasonable price of the Cessna 310.

Art Silverman
McKees Rocks, Pa.

Cessna 340

As a relatively easy step up to the high-flying comfort of pressurization, the 340 has proved itself a popular personal transport and corporate runabout.

If sheer numbers are any indication, the 340 actually is the second most popular pressurized twin. There are nearly 1,000 registered in this country (out of about 1,200 built), placing the 340 a close second to its big brother, the 421 (with 1,300 registered). In third place is another one of Cessna's medium twins, the 414, with just shy of 800 on the registry.

Though the service ceiling nearly reaches 30,000 feet, most owners operate between 16,000 and 24,000 feet.

The 340 and 414 are very similar, sharing the same wing, flaps, ailerons, landing gear and engines. (The 421 has geared engines.) Because it's lighter and has a smaller cabin, the 340 cruises about seven to 12 knots faster than the 414 on the same fuel. But for the speed, the 340 sacrifices payload; and even the most ardent aficionado (and most 340s owners seem to really like their airplanes) will admit that if you fill all the seats, you won't be able to carry enough fuel to go very far at all. One owner quipped that the six seats in his airplane are little more than an illusion.

However, most 340 owners seem to have little use for all six seats; they typically fly with only two or three people aboard and enough fuel for a good three or four hours, with reserves. Owners say their airplanes are pleasurable and easy to fly, though they do give rightful nods to the airplane's labyrinthine fuel system and its tendency to sink readily when dirty and slow.

If the prospect of flying above most weather and traffic snarls, free of the constraints of nosebags, appeals to you, the price for admission varies from about $65,000 for an early model to over $300,000 for one of the last off the line. After that, to stay in the game, figure on shelling out anywhere from $160 to $260 for each hour you fly the airplane.

Smaller Step

Cessna Aircraft Co. introduced the 340 in 1972 as "the step-up airplane for light twin owners." The company had said pretty much the same thing two years earlier when it unveiled the 414, but that airplane really was a lower-cost option for those considering purchase of a pressurized medium twin, such as a Beech Duke, Piper P-Navajo or 421. The 340 was intended to be a step up from unpressurized light twins, such as the 310, Aztec and Baron. Though a 300-series twin, the 340 has the aura of a heavier airplane. It sits tall on its 400-series gear and has an air-stair door behind the left wing.

Engines installed on 340s from 1972 through 1975 were Continental TSIO-520Ks, which produce 285 horsepower at 33 inches manifold pressure from sea level to 16,000 feet. However, most of the K engines in early 340s have been converted to Js (by Riley and Western Skyways) or Ns (by RAM). The TSIO-520J engine, used on early 414s, produces 310 hp at 36 inches manifold pressure. The N engine, installed on later 414s and 340s, produces 310 hp at 38 inches. The major difference between the K engine and the J and N variants is that the latter are equipped with intercoolers (which reduce temperature of induction air as it moves from turbocharger compressors into induction manifolds).

Changes

Although the airplane incurred a host of minor tweaks during its production run, there were very few significant changes. The most significant of these occurred in 1976, when Cessna began installing TSIO-520N engines on the airplane. This change was accompanied by an expansion of the model designation to 340A.

The N engines produce their rated 310 hp up to 20,000 feet and provide higher cruise speeds and better climb and single-engine performance. Three-blade McCauley propellers, formerly an option, also became standard equipment in 1976; earlier 340s came with two-blade McCauleys.

Certification for flight into known icing conditions, when properly equipped, came in 1977. The next year, a maximum ramp weight of 6,025 pounds was approved, and max weight for takeoff and landing was set at 5,990 pounds for the 340A (compared with 5,975 pounds for the 340).

The last notable change occurred in 1979, with the switch to TSIO-520NB engines (the B denotes use of a heavier crankshaft). Subsequent modification of cylinders, valve lifters and piston pins by Continental increased TBO of the NB engines from 1,400 to 1,600 hours in 1983. But Cessna didn't build any 340As (or much of anything else) that year; and after putting together a scant 17 of the airplanes in 1984, production was terminated.

Performance

Though service ceiling nearly touches 30,000 feet, most owners operate between 16,000 and 24,000 feet, where they get 190 to 205 knots on about 30 gallons per hour at 65 percent power and 200 to 217 knots on 32 to 34 gph using 75 percent power.

Rate of climb at sea level is a rather sprightly 1,650 fpm, but climb performance tapers rapidly above 20,000 feet to a dawdling 300 to 400 fpm in the mid-20s. The 340's single-engine ROC is 315 fpm, better than the 414 (290 fpm), Beech P58 Baron (270) and the Piper 601P (240) and 602P (302) Aerostars. In its class, the 340 is outshined only by its much lighter, centerline-thrust stablemate, the Pressurized Skymaster, which climbs 375 fpm on one engine. Single-engine minimum control speed is 82 knots. Stall speeds are 79 knots, clean, and 71 knots in landing configuration.

To its credit, Cessna provided information on accelerate-stop and accelerate-go performance in 340 POHs. The book indicates that, under standard conditions, a

340 that loses an engine at lift-off speed (91 knots) can be brought to a full stop within 3,000 feet of brake release. The book also indicates that should a pilot decide to go after losing one on lift-off, the airplane will clear a 50-foot obstacle after traveling less than 4,000 feet over the ground after brake release.

The performance figures above are for 340s with 310-hp engines. Those that still have 285-hp K engines (if any) are nearly 20 knots slower in cruise, use roughly 200 feet more runway for takeoff and climb 1,500 fpm on both engines, 250 fpm on one.

Handling and Comfort

"No bad habits" is how most owners characterize the handling characteristics of their 340s, and most claim to have had very little difficulty transitioning to the heavier twin from lighter and less complicated aircraft.

The airplane does present a double whammy of sorts, being rather clean and therefore difficult to slow down on one hand, and having relatively low gear and flap operating speeds on the other. For example, flaps can be extended 15 degrees at 160 knots (the limit is 156 knots in the first 300 airplanes built) to help slow the airplane down to max gear-extension speed, a pitiable 140 knots. But slowing the airplane to 160 knots without shock-cooling the engines can be a problem (especially in the keep-em-high and drop-em-like-anchors ATC environment). Owners say descents and approaches require careful planning.

Once the airplane is slowed down with gear and flaps deployed, however, it tends to sink like a rock, according to owners, and some power must be maintained right into the flare.

The heavy-iron ambience of the air-stair door wears off quite quickly when occupants must squeeze through a very narrow (seven-inch) aisle to their seats. Once seated, though, the cabin is quite comfortable. The 340's cabin is 46.5 inches wide and 49 inches high, about the same size as an Aerostar's and 4.5 inches wider than a P-Baron's.

Systems

The pressurization system is the same as those found in Cessna's 400-series twins. Maximum differential is 4.2 psi, providing an 8,000-foot cabin up to 20,000 feet; above that, the cabin "climbs" with the airplane. Most buyers passed on the standard automatic-control set-up, which activates and deactivates while climbing or descending through 8,000 feet, and equipped their 340s with the optional variable-control system, which allows the pilot to program cabin altitude and rate of climb. The variable system maintains a sea level cabin up to 9,000 feet, then maintains the pilot-selected cabin altitude until a 4.2-psi differential is reached.

Managing the pressurization system actually is a piece of cake, requiring only a few seconds each flight. The pilot merely dials in field elevation plus 500 feet before takeoff and landing, and cruise cabin altitude on initial climb. (Of course, saying that you don't have to fuss much with the system doesn't mean you don't have to monitor it carefully during flight.)

Fuel Fun

It's the fuel system that keeps a 340 pilot on his toes. Start with the tip tanks, the mains, which hold 100 usable gallons. Add up to four auxiliary wing tanks, two holding 40 gallons, the other two holding 23 gallons. Throw in locker tanks, which add another 40 gallons. That's up to 203 gallons in containers strewn throughout the length of the wings. Remember to use the mains, alone, for takeoff and landing. The engines will feed directly from the auxiliary tanks, but fuel in the lockers has to be transferred to the mains. Of course, you have to make room in the mains, first. And if you have only one locker tank (which many 340s do have), remember to use crossfeed; dump all 120 pounds from a locker into one tip tank, and the imbalance will be enough to upset even your autopilot.

Unfortunately, Cessna never got around to simplifying the fuel systems in its 300-series twins (Crusader excepted) as it did in most of the 400s.

Empty Seats

Probably the biggest drawback to the 340 is its load-carrying ability. Most are very well equipped and can accommodate only around 1,600 to 1,700 pounds of fuel and payload. (The useful loads shown in the accompanying specifications table are maximums and valid only for unequipped airplanes.) Load enough gas for a 4.5-hour flight with reserves, and you can take along only two passengers and their bags. Fill the seats with 170-pound FAA clones and pack away their regulation 30 pounds of baggage each, and you can carry enough fuel for a 1.5-hour jaunt.

Considering the severe payload limitations, the baggage space in the 340 seems a cruel joke. Among the cabin, nose and locker compartments, there's a cavernous 53 cubic feet of space in which a maximum of 930 pounds can be crammed. That is, however, the maximum. Most 340s have at least one fuel tank occupying a locker, and nose baggage compartment space typically is compromised by avionics gear.

Clamshell airstair door spells cabin class. C-340 was appropriately promoted as a "step-up" airplane for light twin owners.

Modifications

More than a quarter of the 340 fleet has had engine modifications performed by RAM Aircraft Corp. in Waco, Tex. (817-752-8381). RAM, which enjoys an excellent reputation among owners of 300- and 400-series Cessnas, has offered a variety of mods under different names. Currently on deck are the Series II and Series IV packages, which feature new camshafts manufactured by Crane, brand-new steel cylinders, and Hartzell Q-tip props, among other things. Both packages include a seventh stud on crankcase cylinder pads, which reduces the stresses in these areas that often cause cracks.

According to RAM's specs, the Series II mod improves climb performance by 500 fpm, single-engine climb by 30 fpm and cruise speeds by five knots. Also, it provides a 150-pound boost in useful load for the 340A, 165 pounds for the 340.

Series II engines are rated at 310 hp, but the Series IV mod increases the rating to 325 hp (at 41 inches manifold pressure and 2,700 rpm). RAM's figures include 600 fpm and 60 fpm improvements, respectively, in two-engine and single-engine climb performance, and 10 knots more cruise speed. Useful load is increased 300 pounds in the 340A, 315 pounds in the 340.

Cessna 340 Resale Value

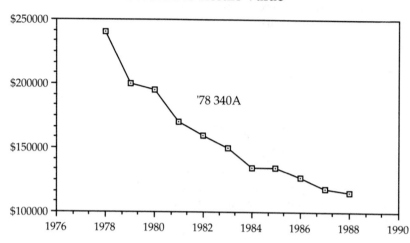

Improved intercooling systems now are available from American Aviation of Spokane, Wash. (509-838-5354). The installation includes ram-air inlet ducts below the engine nacelles and more efficient (American says 28 to 70 percent more efficient) heat exchanger cores. The company says its system cuts the temperature of air entering the engine from about 170 degrees to 80 degrees, improving rate of climb by up to 300 fpm and adding up to 15 knots in cruise.

A STOL mod for 340s is offered by Sierra Industries in Uvalde, Tex. (512-278-4381). It includes installation of Robertson-designed Fowler flaps and a trim spring that precludes the need to retrim the elevators when the flaps are raised or lowered. Sierra says the mod decreases accelerate-stop distances by 40 percent and improves short-field performance about 15 percent.

Precise Flight, Inc. in Bend, Ore. makes speed brakes for the C-340. They're of novel design, and come projecting in the airstream from a snug enclosure at the aft end of the engine nacelles. Price of a 340 kit is $5,995, with 40-60 hours required for installation, according to the company. Their address is 63120 Powell Butte Rd., Bend, Ore. 97701, (800) 547-2558.

Maintenance

Like any other high-performance airplane, a 340 is not one to tolerate skimpy maintenance. If overhaul prices in the $14,000 range (times two), annual inspections costing at least $1,500 to $1,750 and operating expenses above $200 an hour are enough to curl your toes (as they do ours), don't expect to have a good time owning a 340.

Those with the wherewithal to have a good time, though, should be aware of a few items gleaned from recent service difficulty reports that might conspire to ruin their day. First, there are the TSIO-520 crankcases, which have a history of cracking. In mid-1976, Continental switched to heavier cases, which helped a bit but certainly were no panacea.

A couple of knowledgeable sources estimated that about two-thirds of the engines flying in 340s right now probably are cracked in one place or another. But not all cracks are critical, and the same sources said they've been seeing far fewer catastrophic engine failures caused by crankcase cracks. The reports also showed cracked cylinders and cylinder heads to be a rather frequent problem. Cracked and blown-out cockpit windows were the subject of several reports, as were cracked Bendix mag housings and distributor blocks, loose horizontal and vertical stabilizer attach bolts and cracked waste gate couplings. Also among the reports was a smattering of leaking and chafed fuel system fittings, cracks and loose bearings in wheels, broken and frayed airstair door support cables, broken turbocharger oil scavenger pump gears and cracked and corroded exhaust system components.

Of course, any prepurchase inspection will include a check for compliance with all ADs, and there have been quite a few—including five in the past two and a half years. The most recent AD (at this writing, anyway) requires removal of certain oil filters, which were found prone to leak. Another recent AD (88-03-07) requires inspection of fuel crossfeed lines for chafing and modification of firewall stiffener flanges and fuel lines. AD 87-23-08 calls for ultrasonic inspection of the crankshafts in TSIO-520J, K and N engines for cracks during the next overhaul or teardown.

AD 87-21-02 requires installation of restrictors in fuel filler ports to prevent misfueling (and several 340s have been mistaken for turboprops by line personnel). AD 86-13-04 requires cylinder pressure checks for leaks. One very important directive to check for is 82-26-05, which requires visual checks for cracks in the rudder balance weight rib every 100 hours until a new rib is installed. Such cracks have been the subject of numerous service difficulty reports.

The cabin holds six in pressurized comfort, but don't expect more than minimal range with full seats. The 4.2 psi pressurization (in a '78 model) gives a cabin altitude of 10,000 feet when the aircraft is at 23,500 feet.

Safety Record

Several owners told us their 340s are easy to fly. Stout fellows, these; but truth be told, we'd be hard-pressed to think of any other type of civilian airplane that extracts higher premiums on a pilot's discipline and good headwork than a pressurized (ergo, turbocharged) piston twin. We're talking high work load in an airplane with enough systems and assorted gizmos to trick any pilot into illusions of all-weather capability.

Among recent accident reports (1984 through 1986) are several involving 340 pilots who tangled unsuccessfully with Mother Nature on an off day. Three airplanes bearing loads of ice stalled when their pilots attempted to land them. One pilot lost control after radioing that he had flown into "a cell"; another hit a mountain while trying to pick his way VFR through a line of thunderstorms. Three airplanes were damaged when they slid off icy runways during landing attempts.

One 340 pilot hit trees after spotting the runway environment during a localizer approach on a dark, foggy night; another collapsed his landing gear after completing an ILS approach to minimums. One 340 settled back onto the runway, gear-up, after losing an engine during takeoff; another, with its fuel selectors improperly positioned, was damaged in a forced landing after losing an engine on initial climb.

Wing lockers are great for extra loading, but some nacelles may have aux. fuel tanks, adding to the complexity of a by no means stone simple system.

Both engines in yet another 340, with fuel selectors positioned on empty tanks, lost power at the start of a VOR approach. Two airplanes crashed when their pilots unsuccessfully attempted to transition from single-engine approaches to two-engine go-arounds during training flights. One pilot lost control after losing both vacuum pumps during an IFR flight. Another pilot aborted takeoff when the left nose baggage door popped open and locked upright, and the 340 rolled off the runway and down an embankment.

It was determined that a support channel for the baggage door was bent and would allow the door to be closed and apparently locked without actually being locked.

In another case, a pilot radioed that he was returning to the airport shortly after takeoff because of a "serious problem." The 340 crashed in a heavily wooded area, killing all four people aboard. Investigators found it had been refueled with Jet-A.

Back in 1980 the fatal crash of a C-340A into the sea near Ketchikan, Alaska triggered an AD that grounded the fleet briefly, and beefed-up tails were eventually fitted to all 340s. That crash was apparently caused by structural failure of the aircraft's horizontal stabilizer. The pilot had reported a tail vibration, and then radioed that the tail had fallen off and the plane was going down.

Summing Up

If it's a light pressurized twin you're looking for, there aren't that many choices. Besides the 340, there are the Aerostar 601P and 602P, and the Pressurized Baron. The Aerostars are the "pilots' airplanes" of the group; they're fast (about 20 knots faster) and demand no less than sharp, heads-up flying. However, payload capacity is even worse than the 340's, and though the cabin is the same size, the Cessna twin's feels more roomy and comfortable. The Baron is slightly faster than the 340 and has a greater useful load; but it is a bit more expensive.

More than the Aerostar and even the Baron, the 340 exudes cabin class, thanks to its airstair door and tall stance. And it can outclimb the other airplanes. (If you really want a cabin-class twin, check out a 414. It isn't that much more expensive, and the 414A has a much simpler fuel system.)

Of course, we can't overlook (or can we?) the 340's little half-brother, the Pressurized Skymaster, which is much lighter (4,700 pounds gross) and push-pull powered by a pair of 225-hp Continental TSIO-360s. As detailed elsewhere in this volume, the Skymaster has fallen woefully short of living up to its intended role as a "safe" twin. And, though one of the airplanes can be picked up for a fraction of what the other pressurized twins cost, it won't be an inexpensive airplane to own, thanks to design and production flaws.

Owner Comments

We operate our 1975 Cessna 340 an average of 150 to 175 hours per year. All operations are Part 91, and we file IFR on all trips. It is our first pressurized aircraft, and it has been a good choice for our normal trip length. Typically, we carry two to four people 500 to 600 nm. It is a very comfortable airplane and, except for the extremely narrow aisle, provides plenty of room for the passengers.

Performance and handling also are good. Our 340 usually is flown between 16,000 and 24,000 feet, where 205 knots at 65 percent power and just over 30 gph are normal; with 75 percent power giving 215 knots at closer to 35 gph. Traffic is rarely a problem at these altitudes, and the 4.2 psi cabin pressure differential allows us to get over most weather and take advantage of winds.

Care must be taken in balancing cabin payload and fuel. We carry 163 gallons of fuel, but some 340s can hold as much as 203 gallons. This, coupled with a full avionics package, deicing equipment, radar and air conditioning, will drastically cut available cabin payload. However, I appreciate the loading flexibility; if I need to fill the cabin, I can still make most trips with one fuel stop.

At first, maintenance was horrible. The aircraft had been flown only 50 hours in the three years before we bought it, and the inactivity and lack of care took a toll. Once the problems were solved, the upkeep became reasonable. Annual inspections run $1,600 to $2,000, if there are no major surprises. Among our surprises were cracked crankcases at 900 hours and ensuing overhauls that ran about $12,000, each.

Total operating cost, including insurance, reserve for overhaul and avionics, ranges from $160 to $165 per hour. Parts seem to be readily available, but they don't come cheap. Two or three days is an average wait for parts.

Cost/Performance/Specifications

Model	Year Built	Average Retail Price	Cruise Speed (kts)	Useful Load (lbs)	Fuel Std/Opt (gals)	Engine	TBO (hrs)	Overhaul Costs
340	1972	$65,000	226	2,278	100/180	285-hp Cont. TSIO-520-K	1,400	$14,000
340	1973	$69,000	226	2,252	100/203	285-hp Cont. TSIO-520-K	1,400	$14,000
340	1974	$75,000	226	2,219	100/203	285-hp Cont. TSIO-520-K	1,400	$14,000
340	1975	$83,000	226	2,219	100/203	285-hp Cont. TSIO-520-K	1,400	$14,000
340A	1976	$91,000	244	2,122	102/203	310-hp Cont. TSIO-520-N	1,400	$16,300
340A	1977	$102,000	244	2,112	102/203	310-hp Cont. TSIO-520-N	1,400	$16,300
340A	1978	$115,000	244	2,126	102/203	310-hp Cont. TSIO-520-N	1,400	$16,300
340A	1979	$130,000	244	2,116	102/203	310-hp Cont. TSIO-520-NB	1,400	$16,300
340A	1980	$140,000	244	2,114	102/203	310-hp Cont. TSIO-520-NB	1,400	$16,300
340A	1981	$163,000	244	2,104	102/203	310-hp Cont. TSIO-520-NB	1,400	$16,300
340A	1982	$185,000	244	2,077	102/203	310-hp Cont. TSIO-520-NB	1,400	$16,300
340A	1983	$300,000	244	2,077	102/203	310-hp Cont. TSIO-520-NB	1,400	$16,300

Overall, we have found the Cessna 340 to be an excellent step into the owner-flown, pressurized twin market. The average owner/pilot will find that, despite sometimes high cabin workloads and a complex fuel system, the 340 is a comfortable and easy plane to fly.

Eric E. Maurer
Cleveland, Tenn.

I own a 1982 Cessna 340 with approximately 700 hours total time. The aircraft had been stored for about two and a half years before being put into operation in the fall of 1985. It now is on a lease-back for charter operations.

A 100-hour check runs about $1,800. Expense for other routine maintenance averages about $10 per hour. Thus far, major maintenance items have included: prop overhaul for $2,200; repair of corrosion in numerous wing areas, $2,000; cylinder work because of low compression, $1,500; and repair of cracks in the supercharger turbine for about $2,000.

I suspect some of the wing corrosion began during the storage period. The engine and turbosupercharger work probably was necessitated by a number of different pilots flying the aircraft in charter work and giving less than the tender loving care these engines require.

One other significant, but not terribly expensive structural repair was required on the aft mount of the left tip tank. The doubler was cracked and the fasteners were loose.

Stop-start distance with an engine loss at liftoff is a fairly tidy 3,000 feet.

As an owner, I would be happier with less exposure to major maintenance costs. As a pilot, I am delighted with the aircraft. It is fast, comfortable and a joy to fly. Below 10,000 feet, it is much like many other light twins; but, with the comfort of an excellent pressurization system at 15,000 to 18,000 feet, the airplane really comes alive with both speed and fuel efficiency. True airspeed of 220 knots is realistic.

There is one characteristic a pilot should be aware of. Limiting speeds for 15 degrees of flap and gear-down are 160 and 140 knots, respectively. So, some planning for an ILS or even a VFR landing is required to avoid significant power excursions and concomitant pain to the superchargers.

When clean, the airplane wants to fly and doesn't want to slow down. Once dirty, however, without substantial power, the 340 is a rock. Flap extension does require trim change; and, whether by accident or design (Cessna, take a bow) electric trim switch activation during the full period of flap movement results in a perfect and smooth transition.

With a careful check on current condition and previous maintenance, a well-priced C-340 is the best pressurized twin in its class on the market.

Frederick J. Lind
La Mesa, Calif.

Our cloud-seeding company owns five Cessna 340s, four of them RAM or Riley 310-hp conversions, the other a 340A. We also maintain a couple more for outside customers. Our 340s mostly are flown at altitudes between 17,000 and 26,000 feet, and are loaded near gross. At 65 percent power (without external seeding equipment), they cruise around 190 knots true and burn 16 to 17 gph per engine. We lean conservatively, on the theory that gas is cheaper than cylinders. Though the airplanes are flown by several different pilots, cylinders have not been a major problem.

Most operational flights are conducted in icing conditions. The 340 handles ice fairly well, though you can count on losing airspeed. The inboard boots are a help, and a yaw damper is nice in turbulence.

Engine-out characteristics are good at lighter weights, but the tail loses authority at higher loads. It is an easy airplane to land smoothly, even in bad crosswinds; the airplane stays put once on the runway. The fuel system keeps you on your toes, but it isn't unmanageable. The worst feature is that, if you lose an engine-driven fuel pump, you are restricted to using only the main tank on that side, neither the aux tank nor crossfeed is available. A recent AD (87-23-11) requires inspection of the crossfeed lines behind the firewall, which is time-consuming and expensive if new lines are needed.

Most parts are readily available, though overpriced. But, for some reason, fuel selectors and their parts are hard to come by. Watch out for the ARC radios, of course; the 400 series avionics are junk. Make sure the main gear side brace links aren't loose; they serve as downlocks and are easily rebushed.

A leading cause of early engine overhauls is cracking cases, even the latest "heavy" cases. Look out for exhaust cracks in the wye and elbow beneath the turbos (even the newer Inconel "AD-proof" ones) and in the older turbo housings. The new AD requiring ultrasonic inspections of crankshafts needs to be done only when an engine is apart; it should be done during overhauls, anyway, since the original service bulletin came out in 1981. To avoid this, however, you can change to -B engines from TCM.

An excellent source of advice, parts and modifications is RAM in Waco, Tex. They know these aircraft and their engines inside and out.

Hans Ahlness
Weather Modification, Inc.
Bismarck, N.D.

My love affair with my Cessna 340A began in November 1977, when I found her in a Cessna dealer's hangar in Atlanta. She was one of those very rare and very desirable Cessnas without any factory-installed avionics. I was, therefore, able to outfit her with a complete complement of King avionics, including a KFC 200 autopilot/flight director, and two loran receivers, an Arnav 40 and a Northstar.

The airplane has been a true joy to own and fly, although, as in any relationship, there have been a few testy moments. The worst occurred several years ago, when an AD note required an inspection of the horizontal tail after every 10 hours of flight. Ultimately, Cessna solved the problem by replacing all of them, at no expense to the owners.

Since the gear lowering speed is rather low, a useful mod is Precise Flight's speedbrake system. The brakes are stowed in the aft engine nacelle, and deploy in the airstream laterally, then dropping additional blades underneath for drag.

The 340A is a good performer but not a true "scorcher." This is the small price paid for more room and comfort. One can plan on 195 knots, true, at 10,000 feet and 215 to 220 knots at FL 230 while burning 50 gph in climb and 32 gph in cruise. Speeds 10 knots or so faster are possible, but the expenditure for fuel is not worthwhile.

Climbing to FL 230 in 20 minutes at maximum gross weight while indicating 120 knots is about average. Range is excellent (with 182 gallons of fuel). I routinely return to Georgia from the West Coast IFR with only one stop enroute.

Handling is excellent and the airplane has no bad habits. It is a good instrument platform. Though comfortable, it is not designed for really tall or large people. It is, I believe, a little small for cabin-class charter work.

Maintenance is routine for any turbocharged piston twin, and pressurization has added virtually nothing to the cost of maintenance. Parts availability and backup are excellent, especially when dealing with RAM Aircraft, Inc. in Waco, Tex., or Yingling Aircraft, Inc. in Wichita.

No pressurized twin is really economical to operate, but the 340 is probably one of the least expensive. I average about $300 per hour, including fuel, annuals (which usually run about $7,000), routine maintenance and insurance, while flying about 125 hours per year. Being able to fly at the higher altitudes in complete comfort is well worth the price.

Anyone owning a Cessna 340 should early-on become acquainted with the people at RAM Aircraft. They are the finest source of useful modifications and expertise. My airplane has their brake, Q-tip prop and electronic synchrophaser mods. It soon will have their Series IV engines installed, and I look forward to the attendant increases in climb performance, single-engine performance and speed, as well as the 300-pound increase in useful load. These will no doubt make a fine airplane even finer.

For me, the Cessna 340A is the ultimate personal airplane. The love affair goes on, and the relationship grows even stronger with each flight.

William D. Lowery, Jr.
Albany, Ga.

We've owned our 1981 340A about a year. We had a Seneca but wanted pressurization and the capability of flying a little higher. I love to fly the airplane. It's a pretty nice, comfortable small twin. Transitioning was no problem. The airplane is pretty straightforward, but you really do have to take care in fuel management.

The 340's big downfall is payload; if you fill it up with fuel, you don't have much left. One of the reasons I bought the plane with high-time engines is that I hope next year to have the RAM conversion done, which adds 300 pounds to the gross weight.

Elwood Scaggs
Ellicott City, Md.

I am the pilot/mechanic for a gentleman who used to operate his 340A, a 1978 model, about 300 hours a year in corporate transportation. He has sold the company but still uses the airplane for personal flying.

We recently had an American Aviation intercooling system installed and have found better climb performance and better cruise speeds, along with slightly more fuel usage. At gross weight, here at Farmington, elevation 5,000 feet, it will hold 800 fpm at 130 knots indicated all the way up to 23,000 feet.

Performance up there before was so poor, we hardly ever operated above 18,000 or 19,000 feet; the rate of climb would drop off to 400 fpm, and it would take 40 minutes sometimes to get to 23,000. Now we do it in 25 minutes.

Before the new intercoolers, it would get book; at 19,000 feet, running at 62 percent power, it was doing about 203 knots. Now it does 217. Fuel consumption has increased about a gallon an hour per side.

The 340 has a limited useful load. By the time you get four or five people in there, you just have a couple hours endurance. If we put in a full 160 gallons of gas, there's room left for two adults and baggage. Any 340 driver will agree that those six seats are an illusion. That's why RAM's modification is so popular; it adds about 300 pounds to payload. And they have the reputation of doing awfully good work.

I can't think of anything that sticks out as being unusual, in terms of maintenance. The only big problem was that we had to pull the engines 100 hours early for cracked crankcases. And those were the heavy cases, factory-new in 1978.

We've also had some problems with the auxiliary fuel pumps; I think I've gone through four or five of those in 1,000 hours.

Overall, the 340 is a very pleasant airplane to fly. It has no bad habits. Anyone who has flown a lighter twin should have no problem transitioning; it just has more systems and is a little heavier.

Stuart Ott
Farmington, N.M.

Champion Citabria & Decathlon

Champion Decathlon—out of production since 1980, but growing in demand and price today.

When a line of airplanes goes out of production, the models become outcasts and their value drops. Right? Wrong—if you're talking about those venerable aerobatic performers called Citabria and Decathlon.

There are few airplanes that are as much fun to fly as the aerobatic Champions. The creature comfort is good, yet not so lavish as to over-complicate what is basically a very simple design. Though aerobatically capable, they aren't limited to just that. The aircraft are great at short cross-country flights, where the visibility affords as good a view as you can get in a modern lightplane, without going the ultralight route.

History

Did we say "modern?" Tube-and-fabric tail-draggers, with wooden spars? Well, they are. But they are also about the highest refinement of old-fashion technology as you can come by in aviation. This was exactly the tone of the marketing copy issued by Bellanca Aircraft (the last real producer of Champion aircraft) in the late seventies. Archaic things like bungee landing gear had been replaced with spring steel. The cowling became a two-piece fiberglass affair with an attractive, streamlined shape. And toe brakes and gas tanks in the wings made the plane less different from what was being produced in Wichita.

Similarly, the aerobatic Champions, produced from 1964 to 1980, should not be lumped together with what most people think of as "tail-draggers." You know—Cubs, Stinsons, Taylorcrafts and so on, many of which have been out of production for decades. While it is heartening to see these airplanes still flying, many of them meticulously restored and maintained by owners, most of them suffer from outdated attributes: Things like generators instead of alternators, two-piece windshields, old-style gauges and coffee-grinder radios (or no radios at all). In contrast, the Champions are modernized in all respects, save the wood, fabric and landing gear configuration. And it is arguable that these are still the best designs for an airplane that does what the Citabria does.

In 1980 the Bellanca Aircraft Corp. filed for bankruptcy. The production line stopped, not only for the Champions, but the Vikings as well. The Champion assets of Bellanca were eventually sold to a company in Texas, which intended to restart production at their facility at Tomball Field. But after moving parts and tooling there from Osceola, Wis., they were able to finish only a couple airplanes before having to file for Chapter 11 themselves.

The bank that had security interest in the assets sold everything in turn to the present owner, Tetelestai, Inc., of Austin, Tex. These people have no interest in building Champions again. Rather, their goal is entirely speculative. The Champion type certificates, STCs, tooling and remaining inventory are presently for sale to the highest bidder. Parts are not being individually sold. We talked to Tetelestai, and they indicated that there was moderate interest in the Champion line, especially from some foreign countries.

Alphabet Soup

The first Citabria came off the production line at Champion Aircraft in Osceola, Wis. in 1964. When the factory was finally shut down in 1980, over 4,000 Citabrias, and other models of its ilk, had been produced. The first Citabria, a direct outgrowth of the old Aeronca 7AC Champ, was the 7ECA model, which stayed in production to the end. Originally powered by a 100-hp. Continental O-200, the 7ECA was soon converted to the 115-hp Lycoming O-235. All of the subsequent models of Citabrias, Decathlons and Scouts were derived from this airplane.

The Champion line is awash in a sea of alphanumerics. Though there must have been some rationale behind the resulting model designations like 7GCBC and 8KCAB, we shy from such an etymological treatise here. See the accompanying table of specifications for more details on the several Citabria (actually only four), and two Decathlon models.

The similarity in airframe appearance leads most pilots to infer that the various Champion models are just combinations and permutations of one fuselage design with different engines, wings, aerobatic oil systems, propellers and the like. In fact, there is much more to it than meets the eye. You can't just hang a 150-hp engine, Decathlon wings and Christen inverted oil system on a 7ECA, for example, and have it automatically become an 8KCAB. Among other things, the 8KCAB has a beefed-up fuselage, different angle of incidence of its tail, battery in the rear (a bigger one, too), and a separate fuel header tank in the cockpit just above the pilot's shins.

The Decathlon was introduced in 1971 as a higher-performance "big brother" to the Citabria. The primary difference between the Citabria and Decathlon is the wing. The Decathlon has a semi-symmetrical airfoil and a shorter span. There is only one degree of dihedral in the Decathlon's wing, and a thicker windshield with a brace help raise redline airspeed to 180 versus the Citabria's 160. Redesigned ailerons mean that Decathlons can complete a roll in three seconds, while a

Citabria takes nearly six. Designed to FAR Part 23 standards, (The Citabria was built to the older CAR 3 regs.) the Decathlon wing has more ribs and internal bracing than a Citabria, so it is certified for +6 and -5 g-loading.

A constant-speed propeller was an option on the 150-hp Decathlon. The empty weight of a Decathlon is over a hundred pounds more than a comparable Citabria (the 7KCAB). At sea level we have seen the little 115-horse "Standard" Citabria outclimb a Decathlon CS quite handily. As soon as you ask a Decathlon to go negative in a maneuver, however, the different wing shows its stuff. Slow rolls in a Decathlon aren't accompanied by the unnerving shaking and complaining that comes with the Citabria. A Decathlon is quite happy upside-down, but a Citabria wants desperately to right itself. We haven't checked the stall speed of a Citabria inverted, but it must be much higher than normal. That flat-bottomed wing really is designed to produce lift at positive, not negative, angles of attack.

The Decathlon is approved for all aerobatic maneuvers, except the lomcevak (which it can't do anyway) and tailslides. But we know of Pitts Special owners who don't allow tailslides in their airplanes (the forces are so tough on an airframe), so that isn't a real limitation. The Decathlon, therefore, can take a true aerobatic enthusiast well along in sanctioned competition, at least to the "Intermediate" and "Advanced" levels, but with some difficulty to the "Unlimited" category. Since it is more difficult to coax high-quality maneuvers out of a Citabria or Decathlon than a Pitts Special, there is talk in aerobatic circles about a handicapping scheme (like with sailboat racing) for the types of airplanes used in competition.

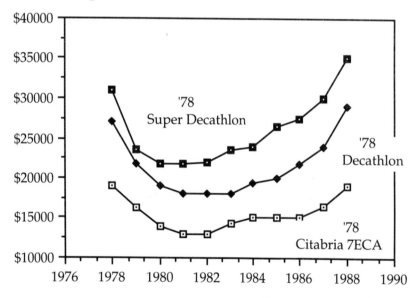

Champion Citabria/Decathlon Resale Value

Adding a bigger engine to the original Decathlon was inevitable, and in 1977 the Super Decathlon was born, fitted with a 180-hp engine. The extra 30 horsepower provided sufficient excess power to make the airplane what it should have been from the start. Recognizing this, the used aircraft market now places a premium on Supers, and a clean low-time one commands upwards of $30,000, getting close to the price it could have sold for new in 1980.

Performance

The best all-around medal goes to the 7GCBC ("C" Package), with its longer wing and flaps. Stall speed is a low 46 mph with flaps at their full 35-degree down position, and a landing ground roll of 310 feet is listed in the owner's manual. Takeoff ground roll is 289 feet. The extra foot and a half or so of span drops cruise speed by two mph, however, to 127 at 75 percent.

The 7GCBC is the most popular of the Citabria models, and many see service as bush planes on skis, or with over-sized tires, to say nothing of those enlisted to tow gliders and banners. Its simple carbureted engine burns between six and seven gph of 80/87 fuel. Tasked to doing prolonged full-power low-speed climbs, the cylinder head temperature can rise dramatically. An optional split door and window make the 7GCBC a good photo ship and general workhorse.

Nearly equal in numbers, the baby of the line 7ECA seems to have a very pleased following of owners indeed. The reliable O-235 gives it remarkably good cruise performance, just eight to 10 mph slower than its 150-hp brethren. Climb performance suffers, however, in comparison, particularly at a high density altitude. But still, there's a lot of wing out there for such a light bird, so performance is better than a Cessna 150's under similar conditions.

With 35 usable gallons of fuel the 7ECA "A" Package consumes less than five gph while still delivering 100 mph down at a 50-percent power setting. At 40 percent it can stay aloft fully 10 hours and cover a range of 880 miles, but unless you're a fish spotter, we can't imagine sitting in one of these that long. With an auto-fuel STC, you can cut the direct operating cost of a 7ECA to nearly pocket change, making the model that much more attractive. Because of its lighter engine up front, some think that the 7ECA is actually the best balanced of all the Citabrias when it comes to doing aerobatics.

Though derived from an ancient line, the Citabria (spelled "airbatic" backwards) has modern features like a starter and spring steel gear struts.

The 7KCAB was dropped from production after 1977, indicating that inverted work ought really to be done in a Decathlon. We concur wholeheartedly, for though the engine can certainly hack limited "outside" stuff, the flat-bottomed wing of the Citabria endures altogether too much stress for many hours of inverted aerobatics. Not to say that this plane doesn't have its market. Many were purchased by schools to cover both tailwheel transition and introductory aerobatic work, without having to purchase two airplanes to cover both bases.

The star performer is clearly the Decathlon, at least in the aerobatic realm. Cruise speed is a few mph faster than the Citabrias, but takeoff distance is twice that of a 7GCBC, owing to the different wing. Of course we're talking a whopping 575 feet here, which would still be STOL performance in comparison with other 150-hp airplanes. The performance difference with the constant-speed prop on the Decathlon appears minimal-to-none, according to the book, as well as our real-world experience. Unless you're concerned with accidentally over-revving the engine in aerobatics (something we don't think is a problem with this plane), the controllable prop only adds weight and expense at overhaul time.

On the 180-hp Super, however, it is nice, and all Supers have the constant-speed propeller. Cruise speed does go up another five or so mph with the Super, but the real advantage is in a better rate of climb, up to 1,230 fpm. The ability to gain speed quickly in a dive in order to then translate that energy back into altitude is helped by the bigger engine. Vertical performance is better, and really only Supers can perform vertical rolls with any degree of consistency for the competition pilot. Vertical performance is still meager when compared with the Pitts, though there are some Decathlon owners who would disagree on this point.

Handling

These airplanes are unstable on the ground. Simple physics says that when the center of gravity is behind the main wheels (which it is—the plane rests on its tail doesn't it?), you have an unstable situation. Left to its own devices when in motion, the tail wants to swap ends on you, leading to directional-control problems for those used to just following along behind a nosewheel.

So why conventional gear, when we said this plane was otherwise quite modern? It's lighter, less complicated, has less drag, and is better-suited to rough-field operation. The only exception we might make to this generalization is the design of the nose gear on Cessna's Caravan I, the single-engine turboprop, which appears to be a stout solution for tricycle geared rough-field operations.

Perhaps it is the added full-time attention to directional control on the ground in Champions, coupled with powerful rudder and pitch controls in the air that give pilots the feeling that they're really flying in these planes. There is no aileron-to-rudder interconnect. Tandem seating and control sticks keep the cockpit more of a cockpit and less of a living room environment. Overall, you feel more a part of the plane.

One clear problem, with the Citabrias at least, is the control force needed to work the ailerons at higher speeds. You can literally pull shoulder muscles doing rolls to the right. Some people even let go of the throttle and use two hands. Others turn their stick hand upside-down for better geometry. Most do rolls only to the left, where torque effects help a little, and human physiology allows pushing the stick more easily. Gap seals were an option on Citabrias, and they seem to help roll rate a bit. Other than some serious weight training at the club, the only solution to heavy aileron forces is to install a set of "spades." These dramatically reduce the pressures needed, and many Decathlons have them, even though forces are lower than in the Citabria to start with.

The only handling problem that pilots transitioning to the Champion taildraggers seem to have is one of a pilot-induced pitching oscillation (PIO) that starts after a botched landing. Wheel landings in these planes must happen with a near-zero sink rate. Otherwise the spring-steel gear bounces the plane back into the air before the pilot can reduce angle of attack to keep the plane on the ground. But, of course, with the stick now forward (too late) and the plane airborne again, it heads for the runway for another touchdown at too high a sink rate, followed by another bounce and more of the same. Until you add power, climb back up and try it again.

Or else you risk catching a prop tip on the pavement. There is no trick to it, and any pilots that live by the misconceived gouge that forward stick will save a hard touchdown are looking for trouble in a Citabria. The solution is practice and honing the skill of bringing airplanes to the runway at nice shallow angles. Glider pilots have to cultivate this, for their planes have very little shock absorption capability in the landing gear (usually just the tire itself). Once accomplished by the Citabria pilot, the skill has a noticeably beneficial effect on landing control in any airplane, and one often hears that "if you can land a Citabria, you can land anything."

Cabin Load and Comfort

Which Citabria can carry the most load? The one with the biggest engine and wing, right? Wrong. The little 115-horse 7ECA can, since it is the lightest of all the Champions, and all the models have the same maximum gross weight of 1,650 pounds. This means that with Citabrias, and Decathlons as well, if you put in full fuel, two 180-pound adults and parachutes, you are over-gross by a hundred or more pounds. The only thing you can do is to fly with reduced fuel. This is what most people do, though many feel that, since the airplane is strong enough for aerobatics, they can ignore the limitation. Not advisable.

The real problem isn't so much weight as it is center of gravity. The owner's manuals repeatedly caution not to exceed the aft limit when doing aerobatics. The problem is that spins can become unrecoverable. We experienced a touch of this first-hand when a spin took over one turn to recover. Citabrias and Decathlons are usually delightful to spin, and just releasing back pressure immediately breaks the stall. What was different about our spin was the presence of a 30-pound video recorder in the baggage area. Needless to say, aerobatics aren't to be taken for granted when it comes to weight and balance. This holds true for any airplane certificated for same.

Cabin noise is more than in a Cessna 150, and a good deal more than in a Bonanza. Headsets are a must in Champions, and most people use the intercom capability of the factory-installed radio system. Many, however, go one better and install one of the popular voice-activated intercoms, a pair of David Clark headsets and a "pickle" switch on the stick to transmit. Convenience and comfort are well worth this installation, especially because of the tandem seating.

Ventilation is good, and many an instructor has been grateful for it when an aerobatic student has become queasy. Cabin heat is controlled by a simple air valve at the firewall, and the pilot's legs get blasted with very hot air. It's like the person with one hand on the stove and one in the freezer. On the average he's

Spades on underside of Decathlon aileron decrease stick forces greatly. Flat plate of the spade bites into free-stream air when aileron is deflected. STC'd for Decathlons, but not Citabrias.

comfortable. You can open the vents to drop the heated air temperature for the pilot, but the rear-seat passenger won't get as much benefit. Citabria pilots get used to burning up in the front seat, in order to make things comfortable for their passenger in the back.

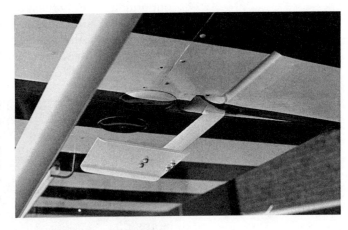

There is a rear-seat heater option that helps out, and it is probably worth trying to find one if you fly a lot in cold weather. Flying Champions in rain and snow requires dressing for it, for it is not unusual for water to drip from vents and the top edge of the windshield onto the pilot. There simply isn't any duct work in the airplane at all to trap moisture.

Citabria instrument panels, more often than not, don't have gyro systems, except for the required turn-and-bank. If you do much aerobatics, we advise putting a switch on it, so you can turn it off. Many don't even have a vertical-speed indicator. Further, the night-lighting of the panel may be nonexistent, or else consists of the old military-style bullet light mounted on the window frame. Since there are no courtesy lights whatsoever in the airplane, some owners have installed post lighting and a rheostat to control brightness. Night flying in Champions requires thinking ahead enough to plan some panel lighting and to bring along a flashlight. (You always have a flashlight for night flying anyway, don't you?)

Citabria seats are comfortable, and the controls are easily reachable for both occupants (except for the radio and mixture control, which you've got to get the guy in front to take care of). So-called "adjustable" seats became available in 1977. The adjustment range isn't that great, but it could be nicer for a very tall or short pilot. The seat belt system can be supplemented with a Pacific Scientific five-point harness system. With dual shoulder straps and a crotch-strap to prevent submarining in the event of a crash, this is without a doubt the best restraint system in any production (or ex-production) lightplane.

The proper way to handle all the belts, since the regular seat belt system stays in the plane along with the acro harness, is to buckle into the harness and then hook the seat belt over that as well. This means that with a parachute on, you definitely can feel uncomfortable, especially since you have to pull the straps quite tight to do inverted work. In the words of a veteran aerobatic pilot and parachute jumper, "If it isn't uncomfortable, you haven't got it on right." We frequently fly Citabrias with everything hooked up, even on cross-country flights.

Safety Record

Examining the Champion accident records reveals that the airplanes aren't used like most tricycle-geared ships. The Citabrias have an unusually high percentage of off-airport incidents; that is, arising out of operating from fields, wooded areas, lakes and snow—not from paved runways, in other words. These planes are subject to pilots who hit trees or swerve into ditches (or even cattle). There were also enough banner-towing accidents to make us wonder whether we'd ever allow ours to engage in such behavior.

Decathlons, on the other hand, are seldom so abused. They are simply offered the opportunity to defy the laws of nature by doing aerobatics at too low an altitude. The records showed lots of instances where show-offs were doing loops, rolls and spins down on the deck. There were only a handful of true stall-spin accidents, however, and these were mostly after takeoff from strips with obstacles, where

Wing spars are wood, but ribs are metal. Decathlon wing has shorter span with more ribs than the Citabria. Here's one being rebuilt at Air Repair in Santa Paula, Calif.

the pilot let airspeed decay.

All of the Champions are afflicted with loss of control on the ground, mostly on landing. The vast majority of accidents are "ground loops," or (more accurately) loss of directional control, but mixed with these are hard landings, prop strikes and outright nose-overs. These accidents aren't as damaging to bodies as they are to egos. But they can be expensive. Replacing a spar and recovering a wing damaged in a ground loop can cost over $4,000.

Maintenance Considerations

These airplanes don't cost diddly to maintain—if you've got a good one to start with, and can keep it in a hangar. There just isn't that much to go wrong. Most of the hardware is standard AN or MS stuff. A misconception about the "modern" Champions is that the fabric is the weak link, and mechanics who don't know these planes are fond of poking holes in your fabric with the old testers used with cotton. The covering is lifetime Dacron and there is little reason to expect it to deteriorate, if it is treated properly. If you must "test" fabric strength, do it in a hidden spot—under a fairing or access cover.

Gear leg of Champions is strong steel. Watch for cracking of attaching U-bolt (by brake line in photo) after rough-field operations or hard landings. Main gear leg can also lose its normal bowed shape after a hard landing.

Corrosion of the tubing is a far-more-serious thing to concern yourself with. Typically, the areas around the tailwheel and just aft of the baggage area are the ones to watch. Water collects here, and rust gets started. A competent dope and fabric man can fix this without unsightly silver dope patching. With a little forethought the fabric can be cut in a strategic place, peeled back and replaced so that it doesn't require a complete repaint of the plane. Wing struts and screws can be kept free from rust by most owners. The landing gear U-bolts are susceptible to cracking, and eventual failure, after hard landings, or rough-field operations. Make sure that you and your mechanic keep a good eye on these. Engine mounts wear through in only a couple-hundred hours, if you do a lot of aerobatics. An external indication that this hasn't been kept up is that the 150-horse engines will sit low enough to blister the fiberglass cowling near the exhaust system.

The fuel cap washers need to be replaced from time to time, or else siphoning can cause loss of fuel (look for stains on the wing). An early sign is that fuel will burn unevenly from the tanks. The removable door, with its emergency hinge-pin release, is also nice when you need to load some out-sized cargo through the door frame. If you haven't pulled the pin and taken the door off recently, do it. Corrosion and ridges can wear into the hinges. This is something frequently missed by mechanics on Champions, even though the FAA has issued bulletins that doors on all aerobatic airplanes be periodically checked.

One of the more dangerous things that can happen to these airplanes is that the back seat can flop forward and limit stick travel. There are restraint cables on the seats to prevent this, but we have seen Citabrias come out of annuals with the cables disconnected. Some people cut them so the seat back comes all the way down to aid in loading things into the baggage area. Not recommended. We're in the habit of looking for these on any Champions we fly, since it's something the pilot can check easily.

Mecca for Champions

The best support for the entire Champion line is at Air Repair in Santa Paula, Calif. Air Repair was the preeminent warranty repair station when the factory was still going. Next door is Screaming Eagle Aircraft Sales, which sells more Citabrias and Decathlons than anyone. They were also the largest dealers of new Champions before production stopped. Owners have flown across the country just to have their planes worked on at Santa Paula.

Some parts are hard to come by, but Harrison Bemis of Air Repair seems to always get his hands on whatever it takes to get your Citabria or Decathlon airborne. There are always wings being rebuilt and planes being recovered at his shop. Harrison is fond of showing people through his facility, pointing out the differences in all the models as he walks them through the dope-filled atmosphere of a spray room.

Parts, service and owner's manuals are available through Air Repair. They will even copy all the service bulletins since time immemorial for you, if you must have them, but be prepared to pay for the copying. Air Repair says that the following service bulletins are musts for all Citabrias and Decathlons: C-135, which covers the landing gear U-bolts; C-139A, on wing rib nails; C-141, regarding the fuel manifold in the aft fuselage; C-127, strut replacement; C-140, calling for belly fabric stringer supports.

Citabrias have an unusually high percentage of off-airport incidents, but even on paved runways they are prone to the classic groundloop, as is any taildragger.

Any airplane that has had its wing struck in any manner is covered by an FAA Airworthiness Alert (AC43-16). This is to detect possible spar damage. Airplanes that have been on their backs are highly suspect. Investigate closely the repairs to any Citabria or Decathlon that has flipped over. Air Repair is at P.O. Box 813, Santa Paula, Calif. 93060, (805) 525-5553. Screaming Eagle is at 825 E. Santa Maria St., Santa Paula, Calif. 93060, (805) 525-7121.

Modifications

There is a plethora of STC'd modifications to the Citabrias, most of them involving the installation of various bush gear—floats, tundra tires and the like. The unleaded auto-fuel STCs are available from the EAA and Petersen Aviation for the carbureted models. And the Decathlon can be fitted with spades from either Marion Cole, 8906 Countryaire Drive, Shreveport, La. 71107, (318)929-2618, cost is $500; or Don Jackman, P.O. Box 3160, Riverside, Calif. 92519 (714)781-3121, $450. Air Repair says it takes two and a half mechanic-hours to install the spades, including a flight test. Performance of the two spade kits is said to be identical.

The Christen Inverted Oil System can be retrofitted to the pre-1974 models of the 7KCAB, and we'd consider this mandatory. You also avoid complying with a required inspection every 400 hours on the old system from Lycoming. The STC for the conversion to the Christen system is held by Lloyd Land, Star Route Box

65A, Hudson, Colo. 80642.

Resale Value

As we said earlier, the entire Champion line is holding its value very well. Because of the expense involved in recovering and repainting an airplane, clean ones are especially sought-after. As a rule, the year of a particular model isn't as important as its condition. A mint 1977 Decathlon, with all the service bulletins complied with, is easily worth more than a 1980 that has been neglected or abused.

The premium is on the Super Decathlon. But the spry little 7ECA is becoming hard to find. The low cost of ownership and pleasant flying qualities must be endearing them to their present owners. One of our editors owns one, and values it highly. Of course, he'd like to see one of our more well-heeled readers buy the Champion line and keep it from going to Libya.

Owner Comments

I am the owner of a 1968 8GCAA, 150-hp, fixed-pitch Citabria—as in no flaps. As a 22-year USAF fighter pilot and eight-year FBO owner, I use the Champ as my outlet for earthbound frustrations. Fifteen or 20 minutes of aerobatics is still the best therapy for the mind.

A few years ago my bird went through a complete rebuild, including new ceconite, interior, new cables, electrics, etc. The 150-horse Lycoming is without doubt the best engine on the market and has performed flawlessly. With a thousand hours on an overhaul, it still burns only a quart or so every 12-15 hours. In fact, the only problem I have with the bird is keeping the Escort 110 working—my "avionics" package.

Cost/Performance/Specifications

Model	Year	Average Retail Price	Cruise Speed (kt)	Useful Load (lb)	Std/Opt Fuel (gal)	Engines	Remarks	TBO (hr)	Overhaul Cost
7ECA	1964-65	$9,100	95	590	36	100-hp Cont. O-200-A	No flaps	1,800	$7,000
7ECA	1966-69	$10,300	104	590	36	115-hp Lyc. O-235-C1	No flaps	2,000	$7,500
7ECA	1970-73	$11,800	104	590	36	115-hp Lyc. O-235-C1	No flaps	2,000	$7,500
7ECA	1974-77	$15,500	104	590	36	115-hp Lyc. O-235-C1	No flaps	2,000	$7,500
7ECA	1978-84	$21,500	104	590	36	115-hp Lyc. O-235-K2C	No flaps	2,000	$7,500
7GCAA	1968-71	$11,500	112	510	36	150-hp Lyc. O-320-A2D	No flaps	2,000	$7,800
7GCAA	1972-75	$15,000	112	510	36	150-hp Lyc. O-320-A2D	No flaps	2,000	$7,800
7GCAA	1976-78	$19,000	112	510	36	150-hp Lyc. O-320-A2D	No flaps	2,000	$7,800
7GCAA	1979-84	$26,500	112	510	36	150-hp Lyc. O-320-A2D	No flaps	2,000	$7,800
7KCAB	1967-70	$14,000	112	510	36	150-hp Lyc. IO-320-E2A	Inverted	2,000	$8,500
7KCAB	1971-74	$16,300	112	510	36	150-hp Lyc. IO-320-E2A	Inverted	2,000	$8,500
7KCAB	1975-77	$20,000	112	510	36	150-hp Lyc. IO-320-E2A	Inverted	2,000	$8,500
7GCBC	1967-70	$12,700	110	500	36	150-hp Lyc. O-320-A2B	Inverted	2,000	$8,500
7GCBC	1971-74	$16,000	110	500	36	150-hp Lyc. O-320-A2B	Flaps	2,000	$7,800
7KCAB	1975-78	$19,000	110	500	36	150-hp Lyc. O-320-A2B	Flaps	2,000	$7,800
7KCAB	1979-84	$27,500	110	500	36	150-hp Lyc. O-320-A2B	Flaps	2,000	$7,800
8KCAB-150	1971-75	$20,000	121	530	40	150-hp Lyc. IO-320-E1A	Inverted	1,600	$9,000
8KCAB-150	1976-78	$27,000	121	530	40	150-hp Lyc. AEIO-320-E1,2B	Inverted	2,000	$9,000
8KCAB-150	1979-84	$37,500	121	530	40	150-hp Lyc. AEIO-320-E1,2B	Inverted	2,000	$9,000
8KCAB-180	1977-79	$37,000	131	530	40	180-hp Lyc. AEIO-360-H1A	Inverted	1,400	$9,500
8KCAB-180	1980-84	$42,800	131	530	40	180-hp Lyc. AEIO-360-H1A	Inverted	1,400	$9,500

Ground handling is a bit tricky due to the heel brakes—a true test of one's patience. There are techniques, such as keeping it rolling and using a little power on tight turns. Once rolling, it taxis smoothly, and forward visibility is actually pretty good.

The little bird is a dream to fly, trims up quite well and is a fine performer. Climb rate is about 1,000 fpm—it's hard to tell exactly since my Spartan panel doesn't include a VSI. On the rare X-C I've flown (It is not a great bird to fly all day) I've gotten true airspeeds of 135-140 mph. One must recall this is the same engine the Warrior 151 has, at 500 pounds less weight.

Aerobatics are nice, a genuine treat. She goes over the top with the best of 'em and the various rolls, while requiring good technique to avoid "dishing out," are okay. Much better than anything else I've flown. As usual, landings are fun—taildraggers do make it interesting. I have found three-point, stall landings to be consistently a piece of cake. To taxi a taildragger is to learn never to get cocky until it's shut down and tied down!

I burn 9-10 gph doing aerobatics and 8.5 gph on trips (70-75%). Tires and brakes will last forever once you learn how to use them. Oh, there are a few minor glitches: the fuel gauges are hard to read, I think questionable in accuracy and, well, sort of a guide. I tend to keep it full, y'know? The heel brakes, well, what can you say about them? Once you get the hang of it, they're sort of okay, honest.

Why does the FAA insist on chutes in an aerobatic airplane? First of all, there's never enough time to get out, if indeed you could. Uncomfortable and unnecessary—also hot!

Maintenance cost is a good point. Just isn't much to break—or fix. Brakes occasionally, tires even less often, some plugs once in a while, and the usual 50-hour oil changes. Annuals will run $350-400. The radio, however, is a problem. I've tried Genave and Escort with poor reliability. Insurance isn't bad, particularly if you've got 10,000 hours, fighter experience and a couple of lunar landings. It helps if you can hangar the machine.

All in all, it's not really a very practical machine, but the thrill of looking back over your head through the greenhouse at the earth makes it all worthwhile. A fun airplane that every pilot should spend 5-10 hours in. It'll teach you more about flying than all the simulator/hood time in the world. I love it!

• • •

For some reason (possibly because it wasn't built in Wichita) the Champion line has received little, if any, press—and that's a shame, because I've enjoyed no other aircraft quite as much as my own Super Decathlon. I've owned two of the last Supers built, the first having been destroyed when another plane ran into mine on the ground. The second has 550 hours since new in 1980, and most of that was aerobatic training, tailwheel checkouts, chase flying for a friend's jet and an occasional cross-country for business or pleasure.

I truly love the wide range of activities that can be performed with the plane, and I wouldn't trade it for the world.

I've added a few things to make it a bit nicer, foremost of which was a pair of Marion Cole's spades for the ailerons. I figure these alone reduce full-deflection stick force by about 30%, and greatly reduce fatigue during a lesson. The factory hot mike intercom is adequate, but I added David Clark military headsets (lighter than the green ones), and a volume control. I also added the Holmsley smoke system, but have not been pleased with its construction, nor the mess it makes on the exterior of my plane, so I rarely use it.

The engine has been wonderful for aerobatics, and it's never even coughed in any attitude. The Scott tailwheel went back, because of a broken part, but they replaced it free. The factory-installed Edo radio is adequate, but has been in the shop more than once for various reasons. Several Decathlon owners I've met have gone to a King package, and at least three owners I know have full loran and IFR panels installed.

My Super is a beauty in the air. I can roll rings around almost anything, shy of a Pitts. Inverted flying is a breeze, although the one-degree angle of incidence necessitates a two degree pitch change going negative. Aileron response is good and well-balanced. The elevator is very effective, and rudder is extremely authoritative. Flat turns are easily possible with rudder and outside aileron alone. The restraint system is very good and features a crotch strap. Too many people I knew were killed (in other airplanes) when they submarined underneath their harnesses in an otherwise minor crash landing.

Super Decathlon has a 180-hp engine and constant-speed propeller, which give it better vertical performance than the others.

Normal aerobatic power setting for me is 23/24, and I can usually count on 135 mph indicated. The handbook tends to be a bit optimistic on the speeds, but not way off. I have the factory "speed" kit on mine and haven't noticed a bit of difference over my first Super, which wasn't so equipped. It does look much nicer, however. My fuel burn is normally right at 10 gph, but I can better that, if I'm not in a big hurry. The Decathlon is a very good cross-country airplane, with lots of visibility, leg room and fuel, but mediocre baggage space.

As an aerobatic trainer it can't be beaten. But beware of the weight and balance envelope. When I first got my plane, and discovered that two adults and full fuel put us 145 pounds over gross, I was shocked. I called the FAA, Bellanca and a few well known Super drivers, and they all said the same thing—"just load it up, fill it up, and keep your mouth shut! It won't hurt anything."

After finding out that this is typical with all aerobatic aircraft, I went to the trouble of getting a waiver on the VFR fuel minimums. This way I don't jeopardize my insurance by flying outside the FARs, since I never fly with full tanks for aerobatics.

Insurance costs are high, and are getting higher, especially if you instruct in aerobatics. I keep my plane in a hangar, as outside storage will rapidly fade the finish and age the plane before its time and drop its value significantly. The present value of my plane is equal to or better than when I bought it. I've had several offers for it, but won't part with it. It's simply the best of all the worlds I need, and very few compromises have to be made.

Marion Cole puts the Champ through its paces at an air show. Only the Decathlons are able to manage sustained inverted flight.

Dan Stroud
Oklahoma City, Okla.

I would like to put in my two cents regarding the Bellanca aircraft. I cannot offer much in the way of specifics as far as operation of the aircraft, but I can tell you that they are as much fun as you can have.

I have owned both a 7ECA and a 180-hp 8KCAB. These aircraft have been flown by my wife and myself and they are delightful both in the aerobatic mode, as well as the short-to-moderate length cross-country mode.

Both aircraft have been extremely economical, with annuals running from $100 to $200. There have been a few minor problems with windshield molding screws backing out as well as fatigue cracks in the wheel pant mounting plates. Keeping them hangared is important in maintaining the paint and fabric.

William Steen
Shreveport, LA

I bought a 1967 Citabria 7ECA and liked it so much that I bought my present one in 1974 new. Like most taildraggers, it is a good short-field and rough-terrain airplane. The airport where I keep it in Massachusetts is not plowed in the winter, so I bought snow skis and find this very enjoyable. I marvel at the consistently smooth landings you get with skis; the disadvantage is that it doesn't have brakes.

I was checked out in aerobatics and found that you need a longer stick to make it easier to do some of the maneuvers. Of course, for serious stuff you're better off with a Decathlon.

Except for a couple ADs, it has been inexpensive to own. It burns about 6-7 gph, and with the Petersen auto-gas STC it costs only about $5-$6 per hour for fuel. Annuals cost about $150.

It is comfortable and roomy and I have flown it twice to Florida (without skis), and it has plenty of baggage space. If I were to order the plane over again, I would get the model with flaps—but then it might take the challenge out of flying a taildragger.

Raymond Sansoucy
Worcester, Mass.